Mexico Reading the United States

MEXICO READING

THE UNITED STATES

Edited by
Linda Egan and Mary K. Long

Vanderbilt University Press • Nashville

© 2009 by Vanderbilt University Press
Nashville, Tennessee 37235
All rights reserved

13 12 11 10 09   1 2 3 4 5

This book is printed on acid-free paper made from
30% post-consumer recycled content.
Manufactured in the United States of America
Text design by Dariel Mayer

Library of Congress Cataloging-in-Publication Data
Mexico reading the United States / edited by Linda
Egan and Mary K. Long.
p. cm.
Includes bibliographical references and index.
ISBN 978-0-8265-1639-8 (pbk. : alk. paper)
ISBN 978-0-8265-1638-1 (cloth : alk. paper)
1. United States—Foreign public opinion, Mexican.
2. United States—Civilization—Public opinion.
3. Public opinion—Mexico. 4. Mexican-American
Border Region—Social conditions. 5. Mexico—Intellectual life. 6. United States—In literature. 7. Mexican
literature—History and criticism. I. Egan, Linda.
II. Long, Mary K.
E183.8.M6M477 2009
303.3'80972—dc22
2008031748

Contents

Acknowledgments

The editors first wish to express their sincere gratitude to the scholars who contributed their time and work to this volume. Their dedication and creativity exemplify the best of our profession. Warm thanks also to our editor Michael Ames at Vanderbilt University Press for his enthusiastic reception of our project and his always insightful and incisive advice as well as to our managing editor, Jessie Hunnicutt, for guiding us through the process, and our copyeditor, Bobbe Needham, who found so many ways to improve our work.

Linda Egan is immensely grateful for the opportunity to work with Mary K. Long on a project that often required her tranquil spirit, her tact, and her wisdom. Mary possesses an awesome ability to switch many hats at work, attend lovingly to diverse family activities, cheerfully dialogue with her coeditor and the contributors, and put in long, long hours *after* hours to write, translate, edit, proofread, format, and perform many additional tasks that cannot be named here. Linda freely confesses she could not have survived this project without Mary's much friendlier relations with computer technology.

Mary K. Long would like to thank Linda Egan for agreeing to coedit this anthology. Her vast knowledge, quick pen, and amazing capacity to work under pressure are as inspiring as her friendship is heartwarming. In addition Mary would like to thank her colleagues in the Department of Spanish and Portuguese for their encouragement, in particular Isolde Jordan, Ellen Haynes, Nina Molinaro, Susan Hallstead, and Anne Becher, as well as Leila Gómez and Juan Pablo Dabove, who read parts of the manuscript and provided valuable input, and Ricardo Landeira, chair, mentor, and friend, for his practical and moral support. During the first summer of this project, undergraduate Sean Kenney provided invaluable research support through the Summer Undergraduate Research Experience (SURE) program. Finally, many thanks for their love and patience are due her family, Rafael Moreno-Sánchez, Angela Moreno-Long, Elaine Long, and all the extended family in Mexico, in particular her late mother-in-law, Nohemi Sánchez, whose reflections on U.S.-Mexican cultural interactions stimulated many of the questions that led to this project.

Research and travel expenses as well as costs for reproduction rights for the cartoons in Chapter 11 were covered in part with funds provided by the Department of Spanish and Portuguese, the University of Colorado–Boulder, the Center for International Business Education Research (CIBER) at the University of Colorado–Denver, and Hilda Chacón. Indexing costs were covered by grants from the office of the Vice Chancellor for Research and the Division of Humanities, Arts and Cultural Studies at UC Davis. Many thanks also go to our indexer, Sherri S. Dietrich.

Mexico Reading the United States

Introduction

Linda Egan and Mary K. Long

> An ability to understand the hybrid nature of culture develops from an experience of dealing with a dominant culture from the outside.
>
> —Guillermo Gómez Peña,
> *The New World Border*

> Naming our others means understanding them and accepting them in the multiplicity of their differences. . . . But more importantly, there is something radically democratic in admitting that many times we do not know how to name our others.
>
> —Néstor García Canclini,
> *La globalización imaginada*

From the perspective of today's global village, change arrives with the speed of the Internet, and news of altered realities arrives even faster. Writings on the Mexican-U.S.-Chicano relationships that came to the forefront of international and domestic consciousness in the 1960s and 1970s constitute a well-aged literary and ideological tradition, much of which has now come under the umbrella term "borderland studies." Texts such as Miguel Méndez's *Peregrinos de Aztlán* (1974), Ernesto Galarza's *Barrio Boy* (1971), *The Collected Stories of Amado Muro* (1979), Tino Villanueva's anthology *Chicanos* (1980), and Gloria Anzaldúa's groundbreaking *Borderlands/La Frontera: The New Mestiza* (1987) were strikingly original and controversial discourses that shocked us all into a new awareness of the importance of the shaky line that had historically done such a questionable job of dividing North from South, first world from third, the United States from Mexico, rendering the two countries neighbors in little but the word. As collections such as *Aztlán: Essays on the Chicano Homeland* began to come out in the late 1980s and 1990s, their authors were already looking back on the time when Mexican immigrants and subsequent-generation Mexican Americans were institutionalizing the myths that would underlie much of today's writing about the new world border. And even then, that terrain was an intermediate space experiencing radical economic, political, cultural, and conceptual expansions. Affirmative action was already in place throughout public and private institutions in North America. Bilingual education was a fixture in public schools. Some were already debating the official language of California. Congress was grappling with immigration control at the permeable Mexican-U.S. border. Hispanic population as a percentage of the total North American census was climbing fast. Entrepreneurs were beginning to publish Spanish-language newspapers and business magazines from coast to coast. Californians visiting Massachusetts missed their salsa. At the border itself, the maquiladoras—the factories owned and operated by Americans and Mexicans employing cheap Mexican labor—were turning El Paso/Juárez and San Diego/Tijuana into bilateral megacities that shared shabby barrios on both sides of the ephemeral line demarcating their sovereign separation. These changes suggest that in many ways the border can no longer be "located at any fixed geopolitical site" (Gómez-Peña 750).

The thirteen essays included in this volume, published here for the first time, insert themselves into the multilayered discourse of this lived and transcribed tradition of bilateral realities. They read various aspects of the U.S. experience from the Mexican side of the metaphorically disputed border, finding their texts in literature and other cultural artifacts such as film, but in every instance holding a Mexican point of view. Often that is not an easy distinction to make or maintain, particularly in relation to the blended societies presented in some of the most recent works analyzed here.

Comprehensive examinations of the Mexican perspective on the United States are underrepresented in the scholarship; we speak of studies in which Mexico is seen to generate meanings about North America rather than viewed as an object of analysis in relation to the United States. The vast majority of borderland studies and literary production originates from a North American perspective. These can be generated in universities or government think tanks. They can also emerge from artistic works identified with the Chicano aesthetic and ideology, despite Mexican art critic Gabriel Trujillo Muñoz's observation, regarding the relationship of Mexican, U.S., and Chicano art, that "one of the most common errors of judgment into which many critics have fallen [is] that of considering border art as a Chicano aesthetic produced on this side of the line" ("Art and the Border" 30).[1] In a similar vein, U.S. university critics have long engaged in the hunt for evidence of North American and European influences in Mexican literary works, implicitly hinting that without John Dos Passos, William Faulkner, or Kafka, Mexico's most preeminent fiction icons—such as Carlos Fuentes, Juan José Arreola, or even Juan Rulfo—might not have risen to the meteoric heights they have reached. More recent scholarship has proposed that "discussion of the United States by Mexican intellectuals is rarely intended as an end in itself, but rather as a discursive means to explain and create a narrative on Mexico" (Morris 160).[2] Alan Riding offers another angle on the apparent lack of Mexican analysis of the United States in a recent edition of his classic portrait of the Mexicans: "While Mexico has vainly demanded to be understood by the United States, . . . it has made little attempt of its own to understand its neighbor." To elaborate, Riding quotes Mexican historian Daniel Cosío: "One of the Mexican's most disconcerting traits is his Olympian intellectual disdain for the United States, which he secretly envies, while blaming it for all his ills and which he has never tried to understand" (327).[3] Put another way: "Thanks to massive migrations, the one that remains and the one that leaves, [both rural and urban realities in Mexico] discover their promised land, that which they left behind and that which they will never reach. Through the intervention of millions of Mexican individuals living on the outside, the Mexico still living within can verify the velocity of the changes it experiences" (Monsiváis, "De los otros aportes de los migrantes" [Of Other Migrant Benefits] 18).[4] This collection of essays thus chooses the road less traveled in the borderlands, one that will lead our readers to see the United States through the eyes of creative Mexicans who ponder the centuries-old conundrums of our binational conflicts from their point of view—who hold a mirror to our face and invite us to see ourselves as they do, and not as we think they might or ought to be thinking of us.

Their opinions—running the gamut from hostile to comical, neutral, inspiring, clichéd, profound, or surprising—come at a crucial juncture in the history of bilateral relations, as Mexican political commentator Enrique Krauze reminded us during a PBS television interview a few years ago: "You have Mexico within the United States. It's not just a neighbor. . . . It's also a partner. A very important commercial partner . . . [and] you have 20 million Mexicans within the borders of the United States, and that is changing American culture, and it's bound to change it both ways. It's changing Mexican culture, and American culture" (1). Yet, despite the transcendent import of shared interests involving human border traffic, poverty, nutrition, health, water, air pollution, hazardous waste disposal, economic development, distribution of wealth, and countless other vital concerns, "there is little if any cross-border communication." Overwhelming statistical evidence "suggests that most border problems are resolved on an ad hoc basis," if at all (Herzog 254): "The enormous political-economic polarization between the United States and Mexico has impeded the evolution of any sustained form of transboundary cooperation in the management of . . . problems. . . . The two nations cling to their sovereignty and, at this time, seem reluctant to trade off control over national territorial destiny for the recognition of a transboundary 'community of interests' " (256–57).

At the same time, Mexican news coverage of the border region is rigorous because it represents one of the nation's key economic resources (Herzog 10)—directly, because of the enormous number of its citizens employed there, and, indirectly, because of the even greater number of its citizens who cross from that jumping-off point over to the other side, thus relieving Mexico of the burden of providing jobs and social services for them (Grayson 2, 4, 7–8).[5] Celebrated Mexican journalist and author Elena Poniatowska, speaking in November 2007 on a U.S. university campus, chided her government for failing to provide jobs and opportunities for Mexicans forced to migrate to the United States. According to Martín Martínez's description of the event, Poniatowska said that remittances from her compatriots living in the United States are keeping Mexico afloat economically, something that no domestic leader should brag about, as did former president Vicente Fox, who left office in 2006: "It's not possible that Fox is saying he's proud of the fact that remittances are the second-largest source of income (for Mexico), instead of creating jobs. If those people had jobs, they wouldn't feel the need to abandon their country." She described a gardener she had met years earlier in California who lived in fear of the U.S. Border Patrol: "Every time the Border Patrol would drive by he would jump into the bushes. I asked him how he could live like that—always fearful and in danger. He said he would rather live with fear than live in Mexico because at least here if he died his body wouldn't be left to rot and be eaten by the buzzards." Poniatowska cited Zacatecas as an example of a state in which the local government relies "on remittances rather than internal economic growth, where 90 percent of families receive assistance from relatives living and working in the United States" (Martínez).

Poverty is not the only factor that pushes millions of Mexicans illegally to the United States. There are other, complex circumstances that cause them to want to leave their country (García y Griego 86–87), but economic need (and the availability of jobs in the North, which depends on their presence to "remain competitive, keep inflation in check, enjoy the fruits of cheap labor, etc." [Payan 84]), is nonetheless the overriding cause.[6] Of course, immigrants do not always or even usually leave poverty behind when they manage to find a niche in the land of opportunity: Hispanics tend to have some of the lowest socioeconomic indicators in the country. "Hispanics are projected to comprise about 25% of the total population of the United States by the year 2050; in a hundred years, Hispanics will outnumber non-Hispanic whites in this country" (Ramos xvii). "As the country becomes more Hispanic, the poverty factor does not bode well for the border states—or for the nation as a whole" (Payan 137). Payan points with his statistics to the need to unite the Mexican and U.S. societies more closely through more effective bilateral cooperation at the government level, including U.S. help with the Mexican external debt and Mexican development of civil and economic opportunities for domestic advancement: a sustained joint effort, in short, to relieve suffering and the psychic pressures that feed xenophobic racism and class consciousness.

Six of the essays in this collection address the issues of immigration, Mexican identity, and the phenomenon of transculturation directly, while in others the subject of the Americanization of Mexico is a more or less implicit thread in a discourse explicitly focused on different concerns. In a way, immigration has become a dual metaphor for cultural contact and sociopolitical influence, if not outright control, themes which course through this anthology as leitmotifs fraught with ironic contradiction.

The irony, of course, is implicit in the fact that Mexico invited U.S. colonists into Texas in the early 1800s and then could not stop the flow—and soon after lost that territory and much more as a result of the war of 1847, which Andrés Reséndez and José Emilio Pacheco rightly call the unjust war (9–31) in their beautifully written and illustrated *Crónica de 47*. The corollary irony, also implicit, is that the United States invited Mexican guest workers into the country during World War II to help resolve a labor shortage and—no surprise—could not then, nor can it now, stop the flow. In a very real way, it is in the process of "losing" Texas, New Mexico, Arizona, and California—as well as other unforeseen chunks of North America—right back to Mexico: "Texas is now 38 percent Hispanic; New Mexico is 43 percent Hispanic; Arizona is 30 percent Hispanic; and California is 35 percent Hispanic. Nevada and Colorado now have large Hispanic populations as well" (Payan 137).

The contradictions—also amply illustrated in this anthology—enter into discourse when "fear and anxiety" brought about by such a rapid transformation in the assumed cultural identity of a society cause disorientation and resentment (Suárez-Orozco and Páez 42–43). Speaking either of Americanized Mexico or Latinized America, the reaction is perhaps merely a schizophrenic love-hate attitude that we have identified as another leitmotif strongly present throughout this volume. It's the tone of voice that one former Mexican citizen uses, for example, when he announces in a poem he calls "Naturalization":

Now I am officially American.
So what?
. . .
I wish the judge would hurry up,
give the room full of Vietnamese and Mexicans
and a few French, Koreans, Italians and Chinese
their paper awards
that allow them to claim
a history of slavery and murderous imperialism
as their own.
Now we can profit from the inequality of this country,
we can exploit our own race more freely,
we can celebrate the fourth of july . . .
. . .
I have nothing to celebrate. (García 110–11)

We recognize it especially in the dichotomy "spirit-material," cited in a majority of these essays by Mexicans discomfited by their attraction to things American or just to the United States itself. They are drawn to a better economic life and perhaps even to the freedoms so much promised in this land, but then they feel compelled to qualify their impulse to transmigrate as something like a betrayal of national origin. They condemn U.S. materialist consumerism in high contrast to their culture's historical emphasis on spiritual values, a dualism detailed elsewhere by Alan Riding; he concludes a long characterization of the Mexican as a being governed by "the predominance of the spiritual over the material," as well as by a profound connection to the past, which tends to dictate perspectives on the present and future (5, 14–15). Students of Carlos Fuentes know that his entire work dramatizes the eternal presence of the pre-Hispanic past in contemporary Mexican life. Similarly, well-known culture theorist Néstor García Canclini is struck by the apparent paradox in Octavio Paz's promotion of modernity in Mexican literature while pursuing at the same time a constant return to the premodern roots of his society (cited in Saldívar 31).

Understanding this aspect of the Mexican character helps explain the psychic paradox implicit in many essays of this volume, as well as elsewhere in Mexican writings about the United States, for it is the very material well-being that the United States possesses that compels Mexicans to leave their country, often at risk to their lives, and that most do not abandon once they too possess some of it, even in small measure. They return to visit family and friends in Mexico, but seldom to live there again permanently. This angst—what Herzog calls a "friction-fusion" relationship (249)—leads to the related discourse of cultural identity (either the loss of it or the need to protect it), another dominant theme of this collection.

Carlos Monsiváis, for one, places the question in a dryly pragmatic context. For him, any notion of purity—or even superiority—of culture merely "emphasizes the idea that culture is being protected by a people who, at the middle-class level, want nothing more than to be like their American models, and who, at the mass level, have no material resources or cultural organizations with which to achieve such a desirable ethnicity" ("Culture of the Frontier" 53). To Mexicans who criticize barrio gang members for wearing American blue jeans or an indigenous girl for trekking off to the jungle with a U.S. boombox on her shoulder, thus destroying national efforts to preserve the native Mexican culture, Monsiváis offers a more compassionate—and historically realistic—viewpoint: "How can we condemn . . . the youth of the lower classes who, as they Americanize themselves on diverse levels, believe that they are thus exorcizing their thunderous lack of a future?" ("Duración de la eternidad" 42).[7] Do not, in short, worry that buying American products is going to drain Mexico of its cultural spirit (whatever that is), says Monsiváis: "Resistance to 'Americanization' is only weak because the seduction is not, in principle, ideological but technological: How can anyone say no to comfort?" ("Para un cuadro" 94).[8]

The argument about cultural purity and superiority in Mexico festered as far back as 1847, albeit among a very small, informed minority. Mexico had been virtually committing slow suicide since Independence, with constant civil war; economic bankruptcy; an isolated, uneducated, poverty-stricken and therefore apathetic citizenry; and, in short, a national being that was close to anarchy, with almost all its resources centered in the capital. After years of futilely fending off American encroachment in Texas, New Mexico, and others of its underpopulated and undefended northern territories, and in the midst of a poorly managed and devastatingly unequal war, during which the common citizen often cheered the Yankees more than the Mexican army (see *Crónica de 47*), some Mexican government officials and intellectuals held secret talks about turning Mexico over to the United States: Let's just let Americans run the country and be done with on-again, off-again dictators and *vendepatrias* (sell-outs) like Santa Anna, the thinking went, and maybe they can save us from ourselves. Among those who seriously considered such a plan were some of Mexico's most illustrious thinkers and writers: Guillermo Prieto, Mariano Otero, Manuel Payno (Reséndez and Pacheco 23).[9]

Some of these men had traveled to the United States. Common threads run through the reports they pen on their return: The worst that America has to offer is better than the best that Mexico can produce (Prieto 1:32–35); would that Mexico's education system, like America's, were actually about learning rather than inculcation of ideology (Prieto 1:149; Cuéllar 22–25); why can't we have a postal system in Mexico that in fact delivers letters, or even allows businesses to prosper by sending products through the mail? (Prieto 1:235–38; Cuéllar 89). Viewing the Mexican collection of the Bancroft Library, Prieto was sadly awestruck (1:207). Gutiérrez Nájera, who is otherwise hostile toward the predatory North American giant, observes how the unemployed workers of Coxey's Army marched, unmolested, on the government in Washington, D.C., in 1894, "like a caravan of pilgrims to Mecca . . . vaguely conscious of their right to do so" (192);[10] the poet exclaims with admiration over the Americans' evident trust in the law and sees the march as a symbol of a democracy Mexico had not yet grasped in concept or in fact.

What Gutiérrez Nájera was seeing was a piece of the "whole package" that the United States offered—and still offers—immigrants from the world over, as "the first modern nation to free itself deliberately from the fetters of colonialism and to repudiate feudal notions of privilege, . . . that guaranteed its inhabitants 'certain inalienable rights,' . . . including freedom of religion, the press, and assembly" (Wills 7). To be clear on this point: It is not that U.S. citizens are nicer than people elsewhere; we share the global human propensity to practice racism, sexism, classism, homophobia, xenophobia, and all other evil that people can do unto each other. What underlies the ugly top layer of shameful behavior, however, is a tried and still-true system of law based on civil and human rights that somehow persistently makes desire for justice, change for the better, and patient upward mobility the bedrock characteristics of our culture. Specific or inchoate knowledge of that promise is what ultimately pulls immigrants toward what Wills calls "desti-nation America" from virtually every corner of the world, knowing that hard times await them, yet believing that better times will come. In this context, several of our contributors have selected themes that explore the historical anxiety that Mexico, among other newly formed Latin American nations, faced as its inhabitants com-pared themselves to those of the United States and Europe in their struggle to forge viable national projects and world-class, yet independent, aesthetic expressions to embody the spirit of those new societies.

Perhaps the overriding theme of this collection recalls the tension between two economic structures in transition: the more traditional culture of the less industri-alized, less consumer-oriented economy of Mexico versus the assumed superiority (from both the Mexican and U.S. points of view) of the comforts of materialism and modernization of North America. Closely related to this first theme is the subcategory of an intermittent interest in the political and personal freedoms pro-posed by the democratic model followed in the United States. These ultimately are the central debates today about globalization in which critics see the impera-tives of consumer society overwhelming traditional societies and the capitalist eco-nomic model overpowering the democratic political model. Can democracy reap the benefits of capitalism, but also check its excesses? This is the question many Mexican intellectuals have asked since at least the early 1990s. The arrangement of this collection highlights the historical evolution of these and related tensions over time and shows Mexico as it evolves into a skilled critic and modifier of the meth-ods prescribed by the United States for those who wish to achieve fuller freedom. Each part responds to the example that the United States has historically presented for its southern neighbor. Mexico's readings exemplify strategies to define material comfort and freedoms according to the needs of its own cultural imperatives.

Separate and Unequal: Mexico Struggles for Autonomy, 1920–1960

The essays in Part I, encompassing chapters one through four and covering the his-torical period from the end of the Mexican Revolution to 1960 set the stage for the evolution of the cultural and political tensions just described by offering new criti-cal angles on texts from the period. These essays will broaden the reader's under-standing of familiar debates that assume two principal stances: the first, the well-known rejection of North American utilitarianism in defense of Hispanic culture's spiritualist base, a reflection of José Enrique Rodó's arielist notions; the second, a willingness on Mexico's part to experiment with the practical benefits of material well-being and personal liberties offered by the more individualistic U.S. society.[11] The adaptation of North American models represented in the first four chapters is pragmatic, not yet taking the shape of a political movement; the two states are still perceived as spaces that one can enter and exit, in spite of the increasing move-ment of products and media between them.

Inseparable Differences:
Mexico Adapts U.S. Models, 1960–1990s

The next four chapters, Part II, cover the period from 1960 through the 1990s and have as common themes how Mexicans deal with the ever-present anguish of deciding whether or how to live with the temptations and tribulations of the "superior" and always influential United States from within a clearly defined Mexican state. This angst develops around such issues as civil rights, literary trends, and questions of identity. As Stephen Morris has noted in *Gringolandia*, often the United States is mainly a backdrop against which Mexico struggles to define itself while inevitably being unable to entirely reject ready-made U.S. models. At the same time, the essays here highlight more direct responses to the United States as an exemplary object. They all depart from a U.S. model traditionally held as exemplary and assume a disobedient stance in their interpretation of it, reading it from inside "that second skin we Latinos all live with, although we know very well how to hide it when we need to," as contributor Oswaldo Estrada wrote in a personal communication to the editors.[12]

Chapters 5 and 6 reveal how Mexico adapts politically liberating principles that do not follow the methodological rules as they apply the U.S. model (i.e., the shifted priorities of social/economic/ethnic liberation in Monsiváis; the rejection of coming out as an obligatory step in the Mexican gay movement). Chapters 7 and 8 express still more scathing criticism of the U.S. model, because rather than modify political exempla for an internal, non-U.S. end, they reject outright what the United States would consider the best it has to offer: generosity and the charitable spirit, wealth and a more hygienic, organized, and convenient lifestyle. These are redefined in multiple (and almost joyfully) negative ways in spite of the fascination they provoke. In these chapters, the two countries are still represented as separate spaces, in spite of evidence in the texts of more frequent dual national existences.

At Home with the Other: Mexico Deals
with Virtual Nationhood into the Twenty-first Century

The last five chapters bring us to the twenty-first century, fraught with its themes of consumerism, neoliberalism, globalization, transculturation, the virtual realities of cyberspace—and the consequences of these issues carried to the extreme. Chapters 9 and 10 analyze fictional representations of the human effects of transnationality and the creative (liberating) but also anguished suffering of individuals in a (U.S.-model) society driven by consumer norms. Chapters 12 and 13 explore nonfiction modes that propose different normative stances for understanding the increasing complexity of our ever more borderless countries, for which the concept and lived reality of nationality is problematical at best. Mediating between these is the linking Chapter 11, in which the spatial issues of online consumption allow a reader to experience the freedom—and the anxiety—of a landless virtual community that places the "citizen" mentally in Mexico but physically in no-man's-land, anywhere on the planet. This "empty space" echoes the ways in which the characters in Hind's binational novels and Chapter 9's bilingual *Diablo Guardián* occupy diverse mental and physical spaces simultaneously. This is not to say, however, that Chapter 11 does not also express strong, independently critical Mexican perspectives, as aggressive (and at times as prejudiced) as the U.S. conservative critic of Hispanic immigration in Chapter 12. Mexican perspectives on the United States in these chapters propose new visions of Mexican autonomy, such as the Latino world within the United States that Ramos describes in Chapter 13. In all these essays, the issue of separate spaces and separate cultures of, within, and between the United States and Mexico becomes permanently problematic.

The thirteen essays cover a broad and rich range of topics. Still, we are moved to return to Gutiérrez Nájera's observation of Coxey's Army as the incarnation of civil society at work in North America; it could be one more contribution to the varied arguments in this volume, a definition of "pure" Mexican culture as (so often in this volume) contrasted to U.S. culture—and it would be submitted by Carlos Monsiváis. It is the one argument missing here, the one definition of U.S. culture not offered—at least explicitly—from the readings of the United States from south of the border that we include in this anthology. We describe it in inverted fashion now—by way of a Mexican yearning to see it in Mexico—to suggest possible future readings by Mexicans taking a close look at their neighbor to the north. Nearly thirty years ago, in a two-part retrospective on the 1970s with the disheartening title "Los de atrás se quedarán" (Those Left Behind Will Remain There), Monsiváis examined his country's failure to make noticeable progress toward social democracy—job creation; upward mobility; racial, gender, economic, and political equality; criminal justice—all that makes a civil society civil, and named cultural chaos as the raw material of democracy that was wanting: the untamed, unmonitored, free practice of human creative activity (22). Then he defined culture itself as "the forging of a civil society that permits alternatives susceptible to maturation in direct relation to their right to public expression" (42), which we may take as an anachronistic definition of Coxey's march on Washington.[13] Against all evidence of success in his teachings, Monsiváis has continued to lecture his society on this singular cultural point from that 1980 chronicle until today.

However, in another retrospective piece, this time a masterful survey of Mexican society from 1985 to 2005, Monsiváis documents his eternal optimism: He enumerates what he now observes as progress his country has made toward the beginnings of a true civil society—toward a stable Mexican culture—since the devastating 1985 earthquake shook the citizenry out of its apathy and galvanized it into the untamed, unmonitored, free practice of altruistic love of fellow human beings. In the chronicle he wrote at that time, he observed how collective selfless action taught anonymous Mexican citizens the value of a single life extracted from the ruins (*Entrada libre* 19–21). In the uplifting title of his recent retrospective examination of postearthquake Mexico, *"No sin nosotros"* (Never Again without Us, the motto of the EZLN, or Zapatista Movement of Chiapas), Monsiváis finds the metaphor for the civil society he can now perceive rising above the rubble of the natural disaster and the successive political, economic, and social collapses that followed.[14] Among other proofs he cites of substantive forward movement toward civil democracy in Mexico, the list he provides includes the fall of the PRI (Partido Revolucionario Institucional) in 2000, which cracked open a long-awaited door to plurality (52); the gay liberation and feminist movements that broke down crippling barriers to social community (24–29); a change in the meaning of the word "history" from permanent, indelible truth to something merely memorable (52); a beginning, through globalization, of respect for human rights—although high officials and drug traffickers still remain beyond justice's reach, in small ways there have been Mexican versions of Coxey's Army getting away with public marches for farmers' and other human rights (33–35).

Monsiváis is prone to making lists, and this eye-opening chronicle is full of them. The items they contain do not always make the news—they are too diffuse to constitute a story that can be published on a given day, representing the author's own years of observation and synthesis. Yet the events and phenomena he itemizes bear the hallmarks of those verifiable realities that all of Mexico and the world that reads Monsiváis trust him for. And what they describe are markers of a genuine Mexican culture that is becoming ingrained within the national spirit—not subject to colonization, contamination, or contraband. If "cultural battles for diversity constitute one of the major advances toward civil society" (Monsiváis, *"No sin nosotros,"* 43), then major progress toward civil society constitutes a victory for the defense of Mexican culture, both as an active agent responding to invasive U.S. prerogatives and as a sender, rather than a receiver, of autonomous meanings.[15] From a position of widespread inner societal strength, Mexico would no longer need to view the United States as a threat to its cultural authenticity, its political hegemony, or its economic viability, but could confidently criticize and adapt elements the United States has to offer, choosing at will what to accept or reject.

The Mexico that has read the United States through this volume has most harshly criticized a materialistic consumer society gone wild. And, while the tensions and contradictions inherent in the simultaneous desire and scorn for material wealth can be called hypocrisy, that is too easy a label to append, for these readings also point out how object fetishism in a consumer society consistently separates individuals from other uses of their talents and resources—and deprives all of society of more humane and productive benefit of that collective human treasure. This criticism, as Maarten Van Delden notes, comes not merely from Mexico, but from within the United States as well. If we view this reading of the United States from such an angle, these Mexican observers are not ungrateful or disloyal users of U.S. space and resources but, rather, modern subjects appraising U.S. practices against a broader—let us say transglobal—set of values and goals. The material-versus-spirit argument, which so easily offers itself as a weak defense or justification for bolting from third to first world, becomes instead a truly cross-border, cross-cultural, bilateral search for a more fully rounded human existence in which the United States + Mexico = one much better space for living.

NOTES

1. In his 1991 work, Trujillo Muñoz emphasized a radical divide between Mexican border art and that produced by Chicanos: "The visual artists from the North of Mexico have little to do with Chicano iconography and even less with the mythologies that sustain it. It is certain that there are personal contacts among Chicano artists and Mexican border artists, but while Chicano artists have made of the barrio and the celebration of brotherhood an epic where the old nationalist ideals and the public art emanating from Mexican muralism are resuscitated, for border artists, in contrast, the recovery of Mexican muralism is less important, and they pay more attention to the obscure figures . . . of the Mexican visual tradition: they prefer to closely follow new, demystified tendencies of international and national visual arts. In each case they want to cast down idols instead of putting up altars" ("Art and the Border" 30). It is worth noting here that recent works in Chicano studies have begun to expand dialogues across the border, although still from the North American side of the line. See, for example, Debra A. Castillo's *Redreaming America: Toward a Bilingual American Culture* and her exploration of the dual questions, "What would U.S. literature look like if we included literature from the United States in languages other than English?" and "What would Latin American literature look like if we understood the United States to be a Latin American country?" (14) Tom Miller, in his 2003 *Writing on the Edge: A Borderlands Reader*, brings together many predominantly Spanish-speaking voices from south and north of the border to consider what gives border writing its unusual scope and texture.

2. Political scientist Stephen Morris in his *Gringolandia: Mexican Identity and Perceptions of the United States* makes a recent and valuable contribution to the rich scholarship in the fields of political science and history about the U.S.-Mexican relationship. Other key texts in this vast tradition include works by Jorge Castañedas, Robert Pastor, David Lorey, and Andrew Selee, as well as others cited in the body of the introduction. Morris's work was published in 2005, just as this critical anthology was taking shape, after a number of the contributors had presented papers on the topic at the Mid-America Conference on Hispanic Literature (MACHL) in Colorado in 2003 and the Latin American Studies Association conference in Puerto Rico in 2005. Many of our essayists subsequently read his study and have included references to it. Morris's book complements and differs from *Mexico Reading the United States* both in point of view (he examines primarily how the representation of the United States is used to define Mexican identity) and discourses analyzed (he depicts the United States through several media: political speeches, school textbooks, political cartoons, intellectual writings, national cinema, consumption and marketing, and opinion surveys.)

3. Just as there can be no "free Mexican culture . . . without economic independence" (Monsiváis, "Culture of the Frontier" 54), there can be no economic independence so long as Mexico continues to fail "to find a social space for its very poorest"

(Guillermoprieto 55). Throughout its history and at least until the end of the PRI's one-party rule, Mexico's government displayed "a scavenger's genius for wasting nothing and no one, and a truly pre-Hispanic vocation for building pyramidal social organizations" that left a tiny clutch of the very rich at the top and a vast mass of disenfranchised poor at the bottom (55). Cultural identity or security and economic safety go hand in hand.

4. "Gracias a las migraciones masivas, el que se queda y el que se va [las realidades rurales y urbanas de México] descubren su tierra prometida, aquella que se dejó y aquella que no se alcanzará. Por intercesión de los millones de personas del México de fuera, el México de dentro verifica la velocidad de sus cambios."

5. As the United States clusters most of its now heavily militarized resources at the major metropolitan border crossings, Mexican and OTM (Other Than Mexican) immigrants planning their run across the line have established gathering places in isolated points along the two-thousand-mile stretch from Tijuana to Juárez, such as James Johnson's farm outside Columbus, New Mexico, or the dusty little town of Palomas, which has an inordinate number of hotels for a spot no tourist would be interested in (Payan 53–54).

6. A recently published Pew Hispanic Center poll found that "a full 43 percent of Mexicans would leave Mexico today for the United States if they could" (Payan 61). Although Poniatowska cites remittances from Mexican immigrants in the United States as the second-largest source of income for her country, a 2008 source states that money sent home from workers in North America had reached 128 percent of petroleum earnings by 2005 (Ganster and Lorey 140–41). A statistic like that suggests there is little on the Mexican side of the border, officially or humanly, with the will or the means to slow the tide of Mexican job seekers heading to the United States. These figures may change in the future, of course. For example, a May 2008 *New York Times* article reports that the recent economic downturn experienced in the United States is having an effect on the confidence of large numbers of immigrants in their ability to find and keep jobs that will allow them to send money home and indicates that these levels may be dropping, though at present it would seem that, as of this year, remittances are holding steady and even growing, but only in comparison to most recent years (Preston). The news demonstrates, as ever, the codependent linkages between Mexico and the United States, at every level, beginning with the economic and moving, as this volume indicates, up into the sociopolitical and cultural.

7. "¿De qué modo condenar . . . a los jóvenes de las clases populares, que al americanizarse en diversos niveles creen así exorcizar su estruendosa falta de porvenir?"

8. "La resistencia a 'la americanización' resulta débil porque la seducción no es, en principio, ideológica sino tecnológica: ¿cómo decirle que no al confort?"

9. Historian Justo Sierra, whose *México, su evolución social* was in the mid-twentieth century still must reading for Mexican schoolchildren (Reyes 249), is among those who believed Mexico was incapable of governing itself (Sierra 208–9) and said the War of '47 was a good kick in the pants for the country and that Mexico should just give Texas and the entire northern Mexico desert to the United States (212), although he much admired Santa Anna's "benevolent" dictatorship (224–25); held Mexico's principle problem to be the alcoholic mestizo and Indians' vagrant nature inherited from the Aztecs (35–36, 96); and, in short, advised his people that they were better off without Texas and California (245). Sierra was secretary of public education under Porfirio Díaz from 1905–1911.

10. "como caravana de peregrinos que va a la Meca . . . [con] conciencia vaga, nublada, de un derecho."

11. José Enrique Rodó (1871–1917), is the Uruguayan essayist who is held to have infused modernism with its cultural spiritualism, and whose seminal work *Ariel* (1900) may be, more than any other, the source of the now-axiomatic conviction that Anglo-Saxon America is synonymous with materialism while Latin America is synonymous with spirit. Rodó, allied with Spain's Leopoldo Alas (Clarín) and famed Nicaraguan modernist Rubén Darío, encouraged Latin America's youth to reject Anglo-Saxon materialism at a time when the Industrial Revolution was instituting mass production. For Rodó, the values of modern, mechanized capitalism were exemplified in the opposing characters of Shakespeare's *The Tempest*—Ariel representing Latin America and Caliban representing North America; he called on Hispanic society to embrace the ancient classical values of cultural autonomy and spiritual enrichment in the face of the specialization (repetitive work) that a modernized industrial society required. It is important to note that twenty years before Rodó's landmark essay, José Martí had begun grappling with these tensions, which he explored in a number of chronicles written in New York in the 1880s and published in newspapers all over Latin America. See, for example, "Coney Island," Martí's magnificent portrait of America in miniature (published in 1881 in Bogota, Colombia), in which he articulates the materialism/spirit dichotomy with melancholy elegance: "Other peoples—ourselves among them—live in prey to a sublime inner demon that drives us to relentless pursuit of an ideal of love or glory. . . . Not so these tranquil [American] spirits, disturbed only by their eagerness to possess wealth. The eyes travel across these reverberating beaches; the traveler goes in and out of these dining rooms, vast as the pampas, and climbs to the tops of these colossal buildings, high as mountains; seated in a comfortable chair by the sea, the passerby fills his lungs with that powerful and salubrious air, and yet it is well known that a sad melancholy steals over the men of our Hispanoamerican peoples who live here. . . . Nostalgia for a superior spiritual world invades and afflicts them . . . , and though their eyes may be dry, the frightened spirit breaks into a torrent of the bitterest tears because this great land is devoid of spirit" (92).

12. "esa segunda piel con la que todos los latinos vivimos, aunque sepamos muy bien cómo ocultarla en determinadas situaciones."

13. "la forja de una sociedad civil que permita otras alternativas susceptibles de madurar en razón directa de su capacidad de expresión pública."

14. " 'No sin nosotros' podría ser la consigna generalizada, en la nación que, en lo relativo a la equidad, siempre se ha caracterizado por incluir a casi todos en la exclusión" ["Not without us" could be the overall slogan for the nation which, with respect to equality, has always characterized itself by including almost everyone by excluding them] (Monsiváis, *"No sin nosotros"* 50).

15. "las batallas culturales por la diversidad constituyen uno de los mayores avances de la sociedad civil."

WORKS CITED

Aguilar Melantzón, Ricardo. *A barlovento*. Torreón, Cohuila, Mexico: Editorial de Norte Mexicano/Universidad Iberoamericana Laguna, 1999.

Agustín, José. *Ciudades desiertas*. Mexico City: Alfaguara, 1995.

Anzaldúa, Gloria. *Borderlands/La Frontera: The New Mestiza*. San Francisco: Aunt Lute Books, 1987.

Castañeda, Jorge G. *The Estados Unidos Affair: cinco ensayos sobre un "amor" oblicuo.* Mexico City: Aguilar, Nuevo Siglo, 1996.

———. *Ex Mex: From Migrants to Immigrants.* New York: New Press (W. W. Norton), 2007.

Castillo, Debra A. *Redreaming America: Toward a Bilingual American Culture.* Albany: State University of New York Press, 2005.

Cuéllar, José Tomás de. *La linterna mágica.* 2a época. *Artículos ligeros sobre asuntos trascendentales por Facundo (1882).* Vol. 9. Santander: Blanchard y Compañía, 1890.

Fuentes, Carlos. *La frontera de cristal: una novela en nueve cuentos.* Mexico City: Alfaguara, 1995.

Galarza, Ernesto. *Barrio Boy.* Notre Dame and London: University of Notre Dame Press, 1971.

Ganster, Paul, and David E. Lorey. *The U.S.-Mexican Border into the Twenty-first Century.* 2d ed. Lanham, Md.: Rowman and Littlefield, 2008.

García, Ramón. "Naturalization." *The Flight of the Eagle: Poetry on the U.S.-Mexico Border. El vuelo del águila: poesía en la frontera México-Estados Unidos.* Ed. Harry Polkinhorn, Rogelio Reyes, and Gabriel Trujillo Muñoz. Calexico: Binational Press/Editorial Binacional, 1993. 109–11.

García Canclini, Néstor. *La globalización imaginada.* Buenos Aires: Paidós Estado y Sociedad, 2000.

García y Griego, Manuel. "A Bilateral Approach to Migration Control?" *Mexico in Transition: Implications for U.S. Policy. Essays from Both Sides of the Border.* Ed. Susan Kaufman Purcell. New York: Council on Foreign Relations, 1988. 81–91.

Gómez Peña, Guillermo. "The New World Border." *The Mexico Reader: History, Culture, Politics.* Ed. Gilbert M. Joseph and Timothy J. Henderson. Durham and London: Duke University Press, 2002. 750–55.

Grayson, George W. "Mexican Officials Feather Their Nests While Decrying U.S. Immigration Policy." *Backgrounder.* Washington, D.C.: Center for Immigration Studies, 2006. 1–11. *www.cis.org.*

Guillermoprieto, Alma. *The Heart That Bleeds: Latin America Now.* New York: Vintage Books, 1995.

Gutiérrez Nájera, Manuel. *Divagaciones y fantasías: crónicas de Manuel Gutiérrez Nájera.* Ed. G. Boyd Carter. Mexico: Secretaría de Educación Pública, 1974.

Herzog, Lawrence A. *Where North Meets South: Cities, Space, and Politics on the U.S.-Mexico Border.* Austin: Center for Mexican American Studies, University of Texas at Austin, 1990.

Krauze, Enrique. Interview with Kaljit Dhaliwal. "Wide Angle." 5 September 2002: 1–4. *www.pbx.org/wnet/wideangle/shows/mexico/transcript.html.*

Lorey, David E. *The U.S.-Mexican Border in the Twentieth Century.* Wilmington, Del.: SR Books, 1999.

Martí, José. "Coney Island." *Selected Writings.* Ed. and trans. Esther Allen. New York: Penguin Books, 2002. 89–94.

Martínez, Martín. "Elena Poniatowska on Immigration: Why Mexicans Would Rather Live in Fear Than in Mexico." *New America Media: Expanding the News Lens through Ethnic Media.* 27 November 2007: 1–2. *news.ncmonline.com/news/view_article.html?article_id=4lcl.*

Méndez, Miguel. *Peregrinos de Aztlán.* Tempe: Bilingual Press/Editorial Bilingüe, 1974.

Miller, Tom, ed. *Writing on the Edge: A Borderlands Reader.* Tucson: University of Arizona Press, 2003.

Monsiváis, Carlos. *Amor perdido.* Mexico: Era, 1977.

————. "The Culture of the Frontier: The Mexican Side." *Views across the Border: The United States and Mexico*. Ed. Stanley R. Ross. Albuquerque: University of New Mexico Press, 1978. 50–65.

————. "De los otros aportes de los migrantes." *La compañía de los libros* 2 (2002): 18–19.

————. "Duración de la eternidad." *Nexos* 172 (1992): 37–45.

————. *Entrada libre: crónicas de la sociedad que se organiza*. Mexico: Era, 1987.

————. "Los de atrás se quedarán II: cultura y sociedad en los 70." *Nexos* 3.28 (1980): 11–23.

————. *"No sin nosotros": los días del terremoto, 1985–2005*. Mexico: Era; Santiago de Chile: LOM Ediciones; Montevideo: Ediciones Trilce; País Vasco, España: Editorial Txalaparta, 2005.

————. "Para un cuadro de costumbres: de cultura y vida cotidiana en los ochentas." *Cuadernos Políticos* 57 (1989): 84–100.

Morris, Stephen D. *Gringolandia: Mexican Identity and Perceptions of the United States*. Lanham, Md.: Rowman and Littlefield, 2005.

Muro, Amado. *The Collected Stories of Amado Muro*. Austin: Thorp Springs Press, 1979.

Nigro, Kirsten F. "Looking Back to Aztlán from the 1990s." *Bilingual Review/La Revista Bilingüe* 18 (1993): 75–78.

————. Review of *Aztlán: Essays on the Chicano Homeland*, ed. Rudolfo A. Anaya and Francisco A. Lomelí. Albuquerque: Academia/El Norte Publications, 1989.

Pastor, Robert A., and Jorge G. Castañeda. *Limits to Friendship: The United States and Mexico*. New York: Knopf, 1988.

Payan, Tony. *The Three U.S.-Mexico Border Wars: Drugs, Immigration, and Homeland Security*. Westport, Conn., and London: Praeger Security International, 2006.

Preston, Julia. "Fewer Latino Immigrants Sending Money Home." *New York Times*, 1 May 2008. *www.nytimes.com/2008/05/01/us/01immigration.html*.

Prieto, Guillermo. *Viaje a los Estado-Unidos por Fidel (Guillermo Prieto)*. Mexico: Imprenta del Comercio, de Dublan y Chávez, 1877. 2 vols.

Ramos, Jorge. *The Latino Wave: How Hispanics Will Elect the Next American President*. Trans. Ezra E. Fitz. New York: HarperCollins, 2004.

Reséndez, Andrés, and José Emilio Pacheco. *Crónica de 47*. With special collaboration of José Manuel Villalpando César. Mexico: Clío, 1997.

Reyes, Alfonso. "Justo Sierra y la historia patria." *Obras completas de Alfonso Reyes*. Vol. 12. Mexico: Fondo de Cultura Económica, 1960. 242–55.

Riding, Alan. *Distant Neighbors: A Portrait of the Mexicans*. New York: Vintage Books, 2000.

Rodó, José Enrique. *Ariel*. Mexico: Factoría Ediciones, 2000.

Saldívar, José David. *Border Matters: Remapping American Cultural Studies*. Berkeley: University of California Press, 1997.

Selee, Andrew, ed. *Perceptions and Misconceptions in U.S.-Mexico Relations*. Washington, D.C.: Woodrow Wilson International Center for Scholars, 2005.

Serna, Enrique. "El desvalido Roger." *Amores de segunda mano*. Xalapa: Universidad Veracruzana, 1991. 17–38.

Sierra, Justo. *Evolución política del pueblo mexicano: obras completas del maestro Justo Sierra*. Ed. Edmundo O'Gorman. Vol. 12. 1890–1902. Mexico: Universidad Nacional Autónoma de México, 1948.

Suárez-Orozco, Marcelo M., and Mariela M. Páez, eds. "Histories, Migrations, and Communities." *Latinos Remaking America*. Berkeley: University of California Press, 2002. 41–43.

Trujillo Muñoz, Gabriel. "Art and the Border: A Preliminary Sketch." *Visual Arts on the*

U.S./Mexican Border: Artes plásticas en la frontera México/Estados Unidos. Ed. Harry Polkinhorn, Rogelio Reyes, Gabriel Trujillo Muñoz, and Tomás Di Bella. Calexico: Binational Press/Editorial Binacional, 1991. 25–34.

Velasco, Xavier. *Diablo Guardián.* Mexico City: Alfaguara, 2003.

Villanueva, Tino, ed. *Chicanos: antología histórica y literaria.* Mexico: Fondo de Cultura Económica, 1980.

Wills, Chuck. *Destination America: The People and Cultures That Created a Nation.* London, New York: DK Publishing, 2005.

Wolfe, Tom. *Radical Chic and Mau-Mauing the Flak Catchers.* New York: Farrar, Straus and Giroux, 1965.

PART I

Separate and Unequal

Mexico Struggles for Autonomy, 1920–1960

CHAPTER 1

Writing Home

The United States through the Eyes of Traveling
Mexican Artists and Writers, 1920–1940

Mary K. Long

The two decades between 1920 and 1940 mark a unique period in cultural relations between the United States and Mexico. Prior to 1920, "frequent tensions and mutual disdain" (Delpar 7) had prevented either country from learning much about the culture, art, music, and literature produced in the creative spheres of its neighbor. But various general world changes during the first two decades of the twentieth century, in addition to the broader international significance of both Mexico and the United States after World War I and the Mexican Revolution, would lay the groundwork for "a flowering of cultural relations" (7) between Mexico and the United States.[1] The central catalyst to this new relationship was the Mexican arts (as expressed both in popular and high culture) and pre-Columbian culture and artifacts, which enjoyed dramatic popularity and influence in the United States and beyond. In addition, in both countries it was an exhilarating time for the arts and letters, lauded by idealistic artists and utopian thinkers for what the president of Columbia University called (in his speech dedicating the new Academy of the Arts building in New York City in 1930) their power to help "maintain the primacy and the influence on life of the human spirit" in an "age of materialism" ("Academy").[2] Furthermore, the arts and letters were funded from a more pragmatic and imperialistic angle (both privately and by each of the governments, though from different power bases, of course) as vehicles of diplomacy that could promote beneficial political and economic interactions beyond the sphere of the arts by counteracting negative stereotypes.[3] Increased travel between the two countries is a significant aspect of this period of cultural relations, and the list of travelers from both countries constitutes a who's who of the cultural (as well as other public) leaders of the era.[4] This increase in travel, along with the combined public and private efforts of utopians and pragmatists alike, generated multiple new meanings for Mexico and the United States during these years.[5]

Since the 1960s there has been a growing body of scholarship (in a variety of disciplines) dedicated to documenting and understanding the significance of this period and to defining these new meanings.[6] However, in much of the scholarship published so far the tendency has been to focus either on the understanding of Mexico developed by visitors from the United States and how this influenced their own work and through it the creative sphere of the United States, as well as the status and meaning assigned to Mexican culture in North America, or on how interest from the United States influenced Mexico's understanding of itself. Less work has focused on how this period of intense exchange influenced Mexico's articulation of meanings about its northern neighbor, and, consequently, "scholars still lack a comprehensive perspective that addresses not only politics, art, and social ideas but also the international dimension of the phenomenon, including its equally important United States and Mexican components" (Tenorio-Trillo 226).

This essay aims to add to the "comprehensive perspective" on this period by comparing and contrasting the visions of the United States presented in chronicles, letters, autobiographies, and travel texts by a cross section of the foundational twentieth-century Mexican artists and writers who traveled to or lived in the United States during these years. All these texts were subsequently circulated and published in Mexico; the visions of the United States that emerge in them represent a significant contribution to Mexican institutionalized knowledge of U.S. high and popular cultures in the first half of the twentieth century. They are: by famed muralist José Clemente Orozco (1883–1949), sections from his autobiography, which recount visits to the United States (1917–1920, 1928–1936) and letters written from New York between 1927 and 1928 to the French artist Jean Charlot (1898–1979), who spent much of his career in Mexico; letters to painter Manuel Rodríguez de Lozano (1895–1971) written from New York between 1929 and 1930 by Antonieta Rivas Mercado (1900–1931)—writer, influential patron of the arts, and legendary lover of José Vasconcelos (1882–1959); sections from the travel narratives *Return Ticket* (1928) and *Continente vacío* (Empty Continent; 1935) by *Contemporáneo* Salvador Novo (1904–1974), one of the country's most talented poets and literary journalists in the first half of the century, who was highly controversial because of his publicly proclaimed homosexuality in an intensely homophobic era; letters to Novo written from Yale between 1935 and 1936 by *Contemporáneo* Xavier Villaurrutia (1903–1950), an equally influential poet and essayist who was also attacked for his more privately expressed homosexuality; and, finally, a select few chronicles from the late 1920s and 1930s of the over seven hundred written by the poet, art critic, and diplomat José Juan Tablada (1871–1945) about New York and life in the United States in general between 1921 and 1940, which were published in numerous Mexican periodicals and finally compiled in 1996 under the title *Babilonia de hierro* (Iron Babylon).[7]

Before entering into a detailed analysis of these personal texts, here it is useful to reflect a moment on the nature of travel writing in general and to underline some of the particularities about the contact between the United States and Mexico in the years I am examining. In a recent article, Leila Gómez reminds us that the concepts of power, knowledge, and identity are integral to the travel narrative as a genre (1). These three concepts are also central to any consideration of interactions between the United States and Mexico, as well as to the texts I study here. For though I have introduced this topic with emphasis on the idealistic hopes placed on the arts to improve relations between the countries, it is important to remember that in both nations powerful negative stereotypes of the other existed: Mexican elites regarded North Americans as "vulgar materialists" incapable of distinguishing themselves in "artistic creation or appreciation," while North Americans in general saw Mexicans through a haze of "racism, ethnocentrism, and antipathy toward Catholicism" and by the end of the Revolution were hard put to conceive of Mexicans as anything but bandits (Delpar 5). During the years studied here, however, the flow of products and information between the two countries increased dramatically, and this expanded the body of cultural details available for the formation of impressions and definitions between the two countries, albeit in a somewhat unbalanced way. For example, the dominance of Hollywood films in the Mexican market during these years meant that Mexicans in general had a better sense of everyday life (or at least the film version of everyday life) in the United States than U.S. nationals did of life in Mexico.[8] This dominance also meant that Mexicans were more aware of the stereotypes of Mexicans in the United States than vice versa, and the frequent negative portrayal of Mexicans in U.S. films was a source of extreme tension between the two countries.[9] From a more positive angle, the improved flow of news across the border also meant that travelers could stay in touch with events at home.

The texts analyzed in this study present both positive and negative aspects of the United States, as well as evidence of the increased flow of film and news; the visions of the United States that emerge in these Mexican discourses provide valuable insights into the new meanings for the country that would emerge in the Mexican imagination during the first half of the twentieth century. A central feature of these new understandings is a more nuanced and flexible concept of the relationship between the two societies that provides a counterpoint to the line of thought (influenced by partial adaptations of the ideas expressed by Jose Enrique Rodó in his essay *Ariel*) which would have Latin America reject all influence from the United States. For example, these letters and chronicles coincide and contrast in significant ways with José Vasconcelos's more widely read accounts of travel to and residence in the United States during this same time period, in which he recognizes economic advantages to be found in the United States but is nevertheless gravely concerned by the threat of spiritual conquest and ultimately rejects the idea of any advantages to be gained from cooperation between the two countries; he emphasizes instead the need for Mexico, and Latin America in general, to develop their unique Latin societies and economies independently of the United States.[10] In addition, the confidence and independence of thought with which these travelers explore the United States problematize theories developed by Samuel Ramos in his landmark psychological and historical analysis of Mexican identity, *El perfil del hombre y la cultura en México* (Profile of Man and Culture in Mexico; 1934) about a Mexican inferiority complex in relation to metropolitan culture and the limits this complex places on Mexican destiny.[11]

It is not my intention to reject Ramos's entire line of thought, but rather to nuance the curiously closed-ended nature of the possibilities he defines for the Mexican future. For example he states:

> The Mexican never takes into account the reality of his life: that is to say the limitations that history, race, biological conditions impose on his future. The Mexican plans his life as if he were free to choose any of the possibilities that occur to his mind as the most interesting or valuable. He doesn't know that the horizon of life's possibilities is very limited for each people or each man. Historical heredity, the ethnic mental structure, the atmospheric peculiarities predetermine the line of life development with a rigidity that individual will cannot alter. We call this destiny. (95)[12]

Ultimately, I see that the letters and chronicles examined here disrupt simplistic binary oppositions between spirit and industrialized society while also providing concrete examples of Mexican interaction with metropolitan culture: They can serve as "case studies" through which to reconsider any proposal about a Mexican inferiority complex, as well as limits to self and national realization created by destiny. Finally, these texts represent significant contributions to the larger artistic, philosophical, and existential discussions in the first half of the twentieth century about the threats posed by metropolitan modernization, mechanization, and market, and the power of spirit (as expressed through the arts) to defend civilization, culture, and, ultimately, humanity from these forces. An exploration of the nuances of this earlier era can perhaps also facilitate a departure from contemporary views of binary oppositions between globalization (often considered to be synonymous with Americanization) and cultural identity.

The travelers considered here made the trip north for a variety of reasons. Orozco left Mexico in 1917 and 1927 because of what he describes as an unfavorable atmosphere for art (*Autobiografía* 59, 119), resolving to make a new financial and artistic beginning each time. He covered the initial costs of the first trip himself and for the second received a stipend to cover travel and three months' expenses from Genaro Estrada, who was then Mexican secretary of foreign relations. During both stays he generated further income through art-related endeavors. Rivas Mercado fled alone to New York in 1929 after the violent end (marked by the deaths of three young supporters) of José Vasconcelos's failed presidential campaign to which she had contributed countless hours of labor and undisclosed amounts of money. Once there, she began a whirlwind lifestyle marked by intense exploration of cultural events, determined networking within the art world to promote non-muralist Mexican painters like Rodríguez Lozano and Abraham Ángel, multiple social events where she crossed paths with nearly every notable artist or diplomat from the Spanish-speaking world who was in New York at the time (including García Lorca, with whom she found a mutual and intense, if brief, affinity), manic periods of writing, and eventual hospitalization for emotional and mental exhaustion (Rivas Mercado 91–137). Novo made both his trips as an official representative of the Mexican government, traveling by train and ship from Mexico, through San Francisco, to Hawaii in 1928 to an international education conference and stopping for a few weeks in New York both on his way to and upon his return from the 1933 Pan-American conference in Uruguay. Villaurrutia's year studying theater at Yale University was funded by a Guggenheim scholarship. Tablada, after going into exile because of his support for the Huerta regime (which he later withdrew), ended up settling in New York City from 1920 to 1937 and also spent the last year of his life there (1944–1945). He was paid during these years by several Mexican administrations to promote Mexican art in particular and Mexican interests in general in a variety of venues, and he also opened the Fifth Avenue Spanish-language bookstore, La Latina, which became the creative center for Latinos in the city (Williams 14).[13]

Whatever their reasons for travel, these wanderers occupied a similar place among the Mexican intellectual and artistic elites of their time: They were all firmly established as influential leaders in nationalist artistic and government projects and yet also on occasion attacked as outsiders for their artistic visions, political values, and/or personal lifestyles.[14] In addition to (or perhaps because of) this shared status as both insiders and outsiders, a common energy emerges in the narratives examined here: These writers and artists travel with an optimistic sense of curiosity, purpose, autonomy, and self-confidence; they are open to the new, relieved to be free for a time of the political and social tensions of the home setting, yet also completely confident that they will return home. While the texts, of course, reflect the individual personalities and values of each author, some significant similarities emerge in their overall vision of the United States.[15]

Certainly, descriptions of physical settings vary according to place. San Francisco appears as a vibrant, colorful city embraced by the beauty of its natural setting, and is made picturesque and even somewhat exotic by the presence of so many sailors (Orozco, Novo, and Villaurrutia);[16] New Haven is cold and gray, both because of the weather and because of the architecture (Villaurrutia); New York is alternately dehumanizing and richly diverse, ultimately valued more for its repositories of high culture (the library, theaters, art museums) and culturally diverse neighborhoods like Harlem and Little Italy than for its skyscrapers and the economic power of Wall Street (everyone).[17] But underlying these place-specific differences, the descriptions all define certain characteristics as typical of physical space in the United States: Order, uniformity, and technological efficiency, which at times inspire admiration, are occasionally overwhelming but ultimately do not need in-depth analysis because they are known to all, an assumed given. For example, when describing Coney Island, Orozco states: "Up and down the beach the typical big American fair is set up with its endless attractions, which *don't need to be described since they are so familiar to both young and old*" (*Autobiografía* 70, emphasis mine).[18] Villaurrutia, on his first trip to the United States, describes Yale in one of his first letters as "the gothic university surrounded by the *standard American city*" (32, emphasis mine).[19]

The sense of a bland, boring, and familiar uniformity as the defining backdrop to everything also characterizes the descriptions of North Americans themselves in group settings. On the train from El Paso to San Francisco, Novo observes: "The people who populate the [cars] are all the same and cover their crystallized faces with the same sort of magazines" (627).[20] And later when shopping in a used-book store in San Francisco, he states: "North American books, like North Americans themselves, become old and common as they age. They are beautiful and uniform when they are young and new . . . but they soon go out of style" (633).[21] Tablada's description of the weekend influx of city folk to the country takes advantage of a literary reference to convey what he sees a bit more harshly:

> We arrived at the panoramic valley of Woodstock . . . that was about to be invaded by the lobster cloud of the bourgeoisie. Thousands of *Babbitts* arrive from New York wanting to invade the picturesque oasis and flatten it into a total *Main Street*, populated by automatons, unanimous in their vanity, alcohol, sex, and the five percent of their lives that is the only goal. (*Babilonia de hierro* 281)[22]

Initially it might seem that there is not anything particularly different about these descriptions in relation to Rodó's vision of the North American nation as admirably efficient when achieving practical, concrete, short-term goals (39) but ultimately lacking any passion for the ideals of truth and beauty (44). In fact, they seem even to confirm the negative visions of the United States as a country made up of metropolitan, modern spaces, which, though efficiently shaped by the uniformity of industrialization, are nevertheless populated by spiritless clods. Yet there is a significant difference in tone, for these travelers are less concerned about deploring the lack of spiritual or moral sensitivity of their hosts and more interested in exploring the practical aspects (in a utilitarian sense) of this world. Though these Mexican travelers may find little new in terms of ideas or content, they do find new techniques, experiences, and individual freedoms, and they are eager to discover the possible uses they can make of these unique elements to further their personal, artistic, or national cause.

For example, Villaurrutia complains to Novo about the boring classes at Yale, where he spends the mornings "listening to all the things I already know, that we already know, inflated to the point of exhaustion," finally concluding: "I have already squeezed all the juice out of the Yale University Theatre Department. I have sat in on all the courses, as well as registering officially for others. The day that I return to Mexico and we are in your library you will be convinced that you have the books that these people use to inform themselves" (41, 47).[23] Yet he does find something of value for his theatrical goals: "The directing workshops at least have a little human value: the presence of students of both sexes, or of no sex, who compose silent scenes in order to demonstrate where the emphasis should lie, how to create a sequence, how to achieve balance" (41).[24] He concludes that "there is only one thing that I feel, inside myself, to have been worthwhile: I have lost my fear of stage directing; I think that I could, when necessary, direct a play scientifically, technically. I have learned to analyze a play from the point of view of the director and to objectify the results. That is all" (47).[25]

This influence of lived experiences and a willingness to adapt new techniques from the United States becomes even more apparent when we focus on the way the narrators discover personal freedoms as they move within America's modern space. For though the overall project has been introduced from the angle of attempting to define and articulate Mexico's understanding of the otherness of the United States as object, upon an initial reading of these texts, one is reminded of the highly self-reflexive nature of travel writing in which "home" serves, as Gómez states, both as a point of physical and emotional reference and as an epistemological starting point (1). For these authors, coming to the United States certainly provides the opportunity to consider issues about Mexico with the clear-minded reflection that distance often affords, as well as to take a rest from intense social and political pressures.[26] But even more significant are the descriptions of how the entrance into the United States leads each of these authors to reexamine his or her sense of self. The strategies each uses for self-understanding in the new setting are emblematic of the strategies they use for understanding the United States.

For Novo, entrance into the "neighbor to the north" implies a change of costume: A few hours in El Paso between trains are enough for him to "confirm that my walking cane would be too distinguished" and he is quick to resolve the problem: "I leave it at the consulate, in the same way as I abandon my straw hat and a suit in the station where I put on the new suit that I just bought, thus, like an illusionist, transforming myself" (627).[27]

For Rivas Mercado, travel to the United States, at least initially, offers freedom from national duty and time to begin a process of self-realization: "This morning when I was crossing Central Park, I clearly felt my Mexican wrapping detach. . . . I feel like I have canceled my debt with my country, that I no longer have it, that I am outside countries and beginning to live a universal truth" (94).[28]

For Villaurrutia, time in the Unites States brings a change in custom: "When one lives abroad and far away from one's habits (my only vices) one loses any sense of time, or to be more exact, one acquires a true sense of time. The rigid linear time that I lived in Mexico has been replaced by an elastic time" (17).[29] He goes on to elaborate how this new sense of time has freed him. The process of liberation does not come without culture shock. He states early in his stay: "I am afraid that I will never be able to breathe naturally in this country where everyone goes straight for their goal, where the only attention paid to others is full of superficial, empty smiles" (41).[30] But by the end of the trip he sees benefits for personal independence in this more individualistic way of life.

In Los Angeles, Villaurrutia runs into a mutual friend, Pérez Gavilán, and comments to Novo that this friend "lives here just as he pleases without any of those complexes that were making him unhappy in Mexico" (74).[31] And Villaurrutia himself is able to live just as he pleases also: "I went to spend the weekend in Los Angeles. If by day the city is ugly, by night it is marvelous. Not even in New York does desire and the satisfaction of desire flow the way they do here. I scarcely slept on Friday and Saturday" (75).[32] Such freedom from social restraints leads to a transformational experience in San Francisco that he describes ecstatically to Novo as he sits "completely naked" and "exhausted" in his hotel room:

> I don't allow myself time to think about my destiny; I simply live it, without daring to contradict it, without pretending to anticipate it in my thoughts. I have lived these last few days at an extraordinary level of pressure and speed. I scare myself sometimes but how to resist temptation without making it stronger? I prefer to fall into it. . . . Here . . . life does not stop for one second to be analyzed. . . . Yesterday's Xavier, as well as tomorrow's, admire, applaud, envy, all at the same time today's Xavier. You understand what I mean. There is not the least shadow of vanity in what I say: I have felt completely alive, young, intelligent here as never before. (77)[33]

This new completeness of identity will be significant to Villaurrutia's self-understanding and artistic production as well as to the expression and acceptance of homosexual desire in Mexico, since one of his most significant poems, "Nocturno de los ángeles," results from this experience and adds a significant representation of the United States to the Mexican literary canon.

It is important to note from these examples that, in spite of the economic and political power imbalances, and in spite of homesickness for Mexico that each writer expresses at one point or another, time spent in the United States is not an abject experience for these travelers. They are resilient and quite capable of embracing new possibilities (Rivas de Mercado, Villaurrutia) while also maintaining a sense of self in this new setting: After the exhilaration of a new suit and a new haircut, Novo loses his equanimity but soon recovers it after a long afternoon visit to a bookstore in San Francisco, confiding: "I have found myself again. I no longer feel inferior to all these robust people going quickly along the street newly wet [with rain]" (633).[34] Thus they prove to themselves that they are capable of surviving and prospering in the supposedly more advanced U.S. context and also find the freedom to explore their individual impulses in a more anonymous way that allows them to experience a sense of inner completeness. In addition to such private discoveries, these travelers also reveal their strength when confronting false public versions of Mexican identity in the United States.

Orozco's writing reveals much about the strategies used in relation to questions about identity. During his time in the United States, this traveler is frequently frustrated by misinterpretations about identity. These include those imposed by, first, unassailable authorities: His first border crossing in 1917 brought the destruction of seventy of his paintings by customs officials who labeled his artworks "immoral." although, according to Orozco, "the paintings were far from immoral, there was nothing insolent, not even any nudes" (*Autobiografía*, 60).[35] Second, misinterpretations that are the result of ignorant marketing: In San Francisco he visits a number of "saloons" that recreate the boom atmosphere of the 1840s and are "decorated with photographs of the most famous Mexican 'bandits' from that era and who were actually people whose land had been taken from them" (64).[36] And third, misinterpretations due to irresponsible journalism: When his visit to Niagara Falls is cut short by a Canadian police officer who, upon learning he is Mexican, urgently deposits him back over the border into the United States lest the Prince of Wales's visit be disrupted, Orozco notes: "That day the muckraking newspapers had published the news of a train robbery by the *villistas* in Sonora during which all the women had been raped. Mexican and bandit were synonymous" (66).[37] Orozco is not, however, defeated by these official misinterpretations that impose an "incorrect" meaning. He sets out to learn the ropes of his new setting and develops strategies for furthering the interpretations that he deems to be correct.

The issue of U.S. interpretations and the always present implication of Mexican inferiority are central to all the texts considered here, appearing over and over, even in the most positive settings and interactions with supportive American friends who have a great interest in and knowledge about Mexico and who are eager to be hospitable and gracious. For example, Novo is given a tour of the Mexican section of the Berkeley library by a history professor. The library houses an impressive collection of Mexican poetry and manuscripts. But curiously, before the professor shows these books to Novo, he takes him first to see "the books in English; the pro and the con: *Is México Worth Saving? The Land of the Sleeping Burro, The Land of Mañana, The People Next-Door*" (635).[38] Novo deflects the negativity of these titles with his trademark irony: "It's my opinion that it's a case of some very unilateral bookshelves" (635).[39] But this episode is emblematic of a broader issue: that even the best-intentioned Americans who seek to celebrate Mexico create interpretations that for Mexicans seem to somehow miss the point.

This is particularly clear in the New York art scene, where both Orozco and Rivas Mercado (who worked diligently during her time in New York to promote the work of nonmural artists) are frustrated by the way high and popular art are lumped together indiscriminately and angered when work by artists that they consider to be inferior is privileged over the work they wish to promote. Orozco was extremely upset by the February 1928 exhibition at the Art Center: "The only things that anyone could see were the pictures by Pacheco, Ruiz, and the large number of *aficionados*, or amateurs who are regarded as 'great artists' . . . the people laughed and howled . . . there were also many of Hidalgo's little wax monkeys and dressed fleas" (*Artist* 34). This leads them not only to criticize the projects but also to occasionally doubt the sincerity of promoters of Mexican arts like Anita Brenner, Alma Reed, and Frances Flynn Payne, who are at times portrayed, at best, as too naïve to truly understand and, at worst, as motivated by greed or self-interest (Orozco, *Artist* 34; Rivas Mercado 101).

Orozco, in particular, becomes frustrated and discouraged, but he does not accept defeat. Rather, he decides that he must learn the rules of the marketing game himself if he is to maintain control of his message. He writes to friend Jean Charlot: "I know this little game quite well now. I haven't had anything to do with caricatures, /magazines/, or other lesser absurdities, instead I have proceeded directly to formal painting, galleries, dealers, painters etc.; . . . I'm telling you all this so you will see clearly that only the *painters themselves, personally*, can handle their affairs and know and see everything, and all that the middlemen can do is ruin one" (*Artist* 49–50).

The desire to create true and "correct" understanding through art, and the need to learn the nuances of the marketing game to do so, present some interesting contradictions for the individual artist, as well as for those involved in the diplomatic projects that seek to create positive cross-cultural perceptions through art and for those who have faith in the ability of the arts to counter the dehumanizing effects of modern mechanized society. In these writings we see Mexican artists and thinkers grappling with dilemmas similar to those that shortly would be theorized in the work of Walter Benjamin, namely that, in order to communicate the "spiritual" message, it is essential to connect with an audience, and in order to reach the audience, it is necessary to take advantage of techniques developed by "dehumanized" modern society. But in doing the latter, there is the risk of turning the work of art into a simple consumer product in which its market value (i.e., appeal to the buyer) is the main measure of success, thus fossilizing and in essence deactivating any spiritual truth or aura the work might contain. Both Orozco and Rivas de Mercado are intensely sincere in their attempt to make these contradictory forces work together. Orozco, at least, feels he has some success; he leaves the United States satisfied with the exposure he has been able to achieve for his messages and is not so troubled by the corresponding lack of economic profit. Alma Reed's biographer describes a significant conversation held when Orozco was returning to Mexico after six years: "Alma voiced her extreme frustration at not having translated Orozco's genius into a comparable financial success. But he was quick to remind her that their goal had been walls, not wealth. This they had achieved—in New York, in California, and in the heart of conservative New England. Surely in these places his name would be forever identified with the beginnings of truly American continental art" (May, 242).

Jose Juan Tablada takes a different view of the relationship between art, consumer society, and wealth in a chronicle written in January 1928. In it he reviews the history of economic exploitation of Mexico as a source of raw materials to underline the positive importance of then-current interest in Mexican arts as a revindication of the value of Mexicans who had, according to him, previously been seen as "the only obstacle between . . . dizzying wealth and the greed of those who coveted it" (*Babilonia de hierro* 252).[40] He considers it the duty of every Mexican to take advantage of the current interest:

> We on the one hand, are a people with abundant manifestations of beauty and pure aesthetic products, but without a market to consume them . . . and [the United States] on the other hand is abundantly wealthy, able to satisfy their smallest whim and pay for our artistic products in all possible forms, from the largest architectural project to the most trivial object. . . . The law of supply and demand has never before presented us with such a propitious occasion on which to affirm our spiritual capability and to . . . get rich. (261)[41]

In this chronicle, Tablada turns the tension between spirit and the modern world into an issue of supply and demand. And while in this text he essentially confirms and reinforces the binary opposition between North American and Mexican identity, he changes the balance of power in the relationship by showing his compatriots to be, if not on the same level in terms of economic power, certainly on the same level as far as marketing guile, while North Americans, still shown as lacking spiritual capability, are at least also evidently interested in spiritual themes. In other texts, North Americans are portrayed not only as eager consumers of the spirituality in Mexican art, but also as active seekers of higher truth. In several columns, Tablada explores aspects of this spiritual quest and related themes that are presented as worthy of his readers' serious consideration and that he followed in his personal life.[42]

> Spiritualist studies, which have intensified throughout the world ever since that great moral and economic catastrophe called the Great War, are gaining new followers every day in the United States. Every week the book review journals study new books with clear spiritualist tendencies. . . . Faced with the skeptic's smile I can only point to the huge volume of these facts, which demonstrate a universal orientation toward the theory of immortality and spiritual progress. Such a movement is serious, almost solemn, as it indicates the religious reaction of mankind deceived by materialism. (*Babilonia de hierro* 141)[43]

While still acknowledging a past that was defined by inequality and conflict between the countries, as well as noting the dangers of excessive materialism, in these chronicles Tablada creates a more nuanced vision of the United States as a metropolitan arena full of opportunity, open and accessible to all, in which both Mexicans and Americans partake of the possibilities, confront the challenges, and pursue spiritual as well as material goals. This opens a sphere in which creativity and spirit are not erased by money and market but supported by the structures that accompany them.

The positive energy that characterizes Tablada's chronicles is generated by all the texts considered here. The understanding of the United States present in these works is significant, not only for a view at least partly accepting of the United States at a time when other Mexicans were articulating a defensive one, but also for the playful approach to understanding the methods that offer freedom for continued growth, exploration, and creativity, and thus development and preservation of individual spirit and confidence in their cultural identity. The travelers who wrote these letters and reports are free to negotiate and create their own meanings—meanings they will allow to evolve over time.

It is not so much that the authors propose radically different articulations of the issues of their time, but rather that through the strategies they use to enter the northern metropolis, learn its tools, and use them to impose their will, these artists and writers negotiate the spaces between binary oppositions in ways that allow for a much more hopeful and autonomous identity than Ramos's vision. These Mexicans do indeed behave as if they "were free to choose any of the possibilities that occur to [their] mind as the most interesting or valuable" (Ramos 95).[44] Not, however, because they are ignoring their history, as Ramos proposes. They remain connected to Mexico but are not paralyzed by those ties. This self-confidence, in turn, allows for a more humorous, resilient positioning in relation to the cultural, political, and economic power of the United States.[45] From this stance, being an efficient user of technology, the modern market, et cetera, is not the equivalent of being Americanized, nor are these travelers simply imitators or promoters of what Rodó called "Nordomanía" (35). Rather, they seem to have heeded a less often cited part of Rodó's vision (or discovered the same possibility on their own), namely that "the fruits of North American positivism will serve the cause of Ariel" (49).[46] And from this shifted point of view it is possible to consider the stresses and benefits that modernization, mechanization, and market represent for both countries from a more continental perspective in which the United States is no longer a threat to cultural identity but rather an extension of Mexico's own possibilities, a repository of information, techniques, and experiences to be used or rejected at will.[47]

NOTES

1. On the one hand, Mexico "represented a season of revolutionary fascination, primitivism, and social hope to modernist and radical activists, artists, and writers . . . and constituted for many foreigners . . . an essence of summer that could rejuvenate the self and recover peace, permanence, and intellectual concord" (Tenorio-Trillo 224). On the other, "the United States had emerged as a major economic and military power . . . [and] American economic ascendancy was accompanied by the export of American values, . . . faith in private free enterprise, [and] support for the free flow of goods, information, and culture, . . . which war-weary Europe willingly accepted . . . as an inevitable consequence of the economic and technological superiority of the United States" (Delpar 7).

2. There are numerous examples of this utopian faith in the arts in both Mexico and the United States. In Mexico, for example, Secretary of Education José Vasconcelos's faith in the spiritual powers of art and literature (which grew in large part from his early involvement with the Ateneo de la Juventud, and which he expressed in his writing and his speeches from the 1920s and 1930s) was central to the renovation of education in Mexico. The muralist movement is perhaps one of the most internationally famous results of his efforts, but equally important was his emphasis on the reading of classical and world literature (*Obras*). The muralists themselves, in addition to playing a central role in the renovation of Mexican national identity, articulated an even more utopian political vision for the role of the arts through the communist Artists and Sculptors Union and its weekly newspaper *El Machete*, which strove to create support from intellectuals for working-class issues (Orozco, *Autobiografía* 110–11). In the United States, in addition to many publicly funded museums and grants for artistic production and study (see Delpar), there were private artistic patrons like the Delphic Society (headquartered in Greece but with a "colony" in New York, 1928–1935) that brought together international artists and humanitarians for cultural evenings in a Manhattan apartment called the Ashram in honor of Mahatma Gandhi. The brainchild of Eva (Palmer) Sikelianos, wife of Greek poet Angelo Sikelianos, the Delphic Society was described as a "cultural movement with a philosophic base" (May 212). In New York, Eva was aided in her efforts by Alma Reed, a journalist and promoter of world arts, who had strong ties to Mexico, first through her engagement to the governor of Yucatan, Felipe Carrillo Puerto (executed by de la Huerta forces in 1924), and later, during the years studied here, through her intense patronage and promotion of Mexican arts in general and of the work of Jose Clemente Orozco in particular. The goal of both women was through these gatherings to ultimately "reestablish ancient Delphi . . . as a center of universality and the source of a peaceful new world." In practical terms, the society and later the Delphic studios, which Reed ran, provided a forum through which the work of Orozco and numerous other foreign authors and artists was presented to the New York cultural community (May 212).

3. In Mexico, government patronage of the arts was a significant element of the post-revolutionary project of nation building. This was not limited to the national scene. The Mexican government also recognized the power of the arts to promote national interests abroad and funded travel for both artistic and educational purposes as well as sponsoring cultural events, art shows, concerts, and so on, and paying authors (like Juan José Tablada) to publish articles promoting Mexican arts in the U.S. press. Delpar explores thoroughly the overall vision of the arts in government projects and provides numerous specific examples of efforts made by both the Mexican and U.S. governments. Others have studied the U.S. government's involvement in the

area of film, in particular the State Department's cooperation with and control over Hollywood to produce films that would promote both a positive view of the United States and the "American way of life" outside the United States, and a more positive reception of Mexico among the middle class of the United States in order to strengthen support of the Good Neighbor policies for hemispheric relations. See Fein, for example. Ricardo D. Salvatore has examined the U.S. business community's incorporation of both high and low culture into the capitalist project to create receptive consumer markets for U.S. products and services in Latin America.

4. A partial list includes, from Mexico: Carlos Chávez, Miguel Covarrubias, Genaro Estrada, Manuel Gamio, Frida Kahlo, Ramón Navarro, Salvador Novo, Gilberto Owen, José Clemente Orozco, Antonieta Rivas Mercado, Diego Rivera, Dolores del Río, Moisés Sáenz, José Juan Tablada, Rufino Tamayo, José Vasconcelos, Lupe Vélez, Xavier Villaurrutia; and from the United States: Carleton Beals, Anita Brenner, Stuart Chase, Aaron Copland, John Dewey, John Dos Passos, Waldo Frank, Joseph Freeman, Francise Flynn Paine, Ernest Gruening, Langston Hughes, Charles Lindberg, Tina Modotti, Ambassador Dwight Morrow (and his wife, Elizabeth, and daughter, Anne), Walter Pach, Katherine Anne Porter, Alma Reed, Nelson Rockefeller, William Sprattling, Frank Tannenbaum, Frances Toor, Edward Weston, Bertram and Ella Wolfe.

5. My thoughts on the mutual creation of meaning between the United States and Mexico during these years have been enriched by Mary Louise Pratt's discussion of "imperial meaning-making" in her landmark study, *Imperial Eyes: Travel Writing and Transculturation.*

6. See Delpar, González, May, Morris, and Lozano Herrera. In addition, the article by Tenorio-Trillo gives an overview of eight significant titles.

7. These works were chosen as representative of travel writing and chronicles from this time period after extensive bibliographical searches for primary texts by Mexican writers and artists who were involved in the cultural exchange boom between the United States and Mexico during these years. These were the most extensive writings initially found. Other famous Mexican travelers did not write as explicitly about the United States (for example, Frida Kahlo's journal entries from the period corresponding to her stays in the United States focus much more on internal thoughts, personal challenges, and artistic projects). This is the first step in a broader project that will most certainly include more testimony of artists and writers as well as that of other travelers. For example, I did not examine travel narratives and testimonials by Mexican working-class or businessmen and -women for this study since I considered that those groups would represent different historical and cultural issues. In the case of Tablada's chronicles, while one could argue that New York City is a separate reality from the general United States, Tablada states several times throughout that he considers New York representative of the United States. Finally, any one of the authors included here would merit a longer individual in-depth study. However, the intention of this essay is to provide a broader overview and to highlight common themes. The reader who desires more can look to works by Guillermo Sheridan, Mary Long, and Salvador Oropesa (in list of Works Cited) as starting points.

8. Delpar states that, "besides popular music, the motion picture was the dominant form of American culture to penetrate Mexico after 1920 . . . [and] by the mid-1920s over ninety-five percent of the offerings of Mexico's theatres were American films" (187).

9. See Delpar (5) for a brief discussion and the article by Aurelio de los Reyes for an extended explanation of this conflict.

10. Lozano Herrera summarizes well the views that Vasconcelos develops throughout the four volumes of his memoirs (203–4). The article by Robert Conn in this volume also examines Vasconcelos's views of the United States in more depth.

11. Ramos is not the first to posit the idea of a national inferiority complex. He states: "Others have already spoken before about the inferiority of our race, but no one, to my knowledge, has developed this idea systematically as a way to explain our character" [Ya otros han hablado antes del sentido de inferioridad de nuestra raza, pero nadie, que sepamos, se ha valido sistemáticamente de esta idea para explicar nuestro character] (67). Ramos's essay covers a broad period of history and uses a combination of analytical frameworks, in particular the psychological theories of Austrian Alfred Adler (1870–1930), to explain Mexican history and the nature of the Mexican character. Ramos published this essay in 1934 at a time when a rigid postrevolutionary nationalist movement sought to reject all outside influence and aggressively labeled those who were open to such influence as *europeizantes* (Europeanizers) and/or *extrangerizantes* (foreignizers). Neither the authors/artists studied here nor Ramos agreed with this closed vision. Ramos in fact saw it as the primary proof of Mexico's inferiority complex: "It should be assumed that an inferiority complex exists in all individuals who manifest an exaggerated preoccupation with affirming his own personality" [Debe suponerse la existencia de un complejo de inferioridad en todos los individuos que manifiestan una exagerada preocupación por afirmar su personalidad] (67). This and all subsequent translations are mine, except those from Orozco's *The Artist in New York*, which was published in English.

12. "Nunca toma en cuenta el mexicano la realidad de su vida, es decir, las limitaciones que la historia, la raza, las condiciones biológicas imponen a su porvenir. El mexicano planea su vida como si fuera libre de elegir cualquiera de las posibilidades que a su mente se presentan como más interesantes o valiosas. No sabe que el horizonte de las posibilidades vitales es sumamente estrecho para cada pueblo o cada hombre. La herencia histórica, la estructura mental étnica, las peculiaridades del ambiente, prefijan la línea del desarrollo vital con una rigideza que la voluntad de los individuos no puede alterarar. A esta fatalidad le llamamos destino."

13. For a thorough account of these years and an extensive study of the chronicles, see Lozano Herrera.

14. Orozco was, of course, one of the big three muralists, but during these years was often in conflict with Diego Rivera and Rivera's supporters for artistic reasons as well as over the direction of left-wing politics; Novo and Villaurrutia, like the other *Contemporáneos*, were extremely influential because of their skill as poets and because of their position in key government institutions, but their more cosmopolitan view of art and nation increasingly distanced them from the nationalist vision. In addition, as mentioned earlier, they were frequently attacked for their sexual orientation. Well before her support of Vasconcelos's political mission, Rivas Mercado's vision and money backed numerous individual writers and artists as well as such groundbreaking and diverse cultural enterprises as the Ulises Theatre, the Mexican Symphonic Orchestra, and El Pirata, a "respectable" dancehall where upper-class couples could gather to dance tango, danzón, fox, and shimmy in the newly cosmopolitan Mexico City of the 1920s (Bradu 127). Her status as a partial outsider stems in large part from the fact that she was a woman seeking to be independent, struggling with her role and the societal pressures that came with being divorced, worrying over the well-being of her son, facing family rejection, and balancing the need for romantic love that often is blended in her writing with the need to commit herself to utopian causes. Tablada weathered two periods of influence and scorn: He enjoyed dramatic early influence

through his poetry, which introduced the Japanese haiku form to Mexico, but also faced scandal because of the bohemian values promoted in his poem "Misa negra." During the revolution, because he had supported Huerta, he was forced into exile, but from there he again became influential because of his ability to represent Mexico abroad and to open doors for young artists in the international New York art world; for example, he was a key figure in facilitating Miguel Covarrubia's dramatic and long-lasting success (Williams).

15. In recent years there has been a growing body of scholarship about Latin American travelers during the nineteenth and twentieth centuries (for example, the anthologies edited by Fey and Racine or Fernández Bravo et al.) that recognizes the confidence of these travelers and "aspire[s] to decolonize these voices, to recognize that Latin Americans made their own choices and, far from being the passive recipients of others' ideas and products, considered carefully what they saw abroad and even dared to offer comments to their hosts" (Fey and Racine xi). In general these studies focus on the way the travel experience prompted Latin Americans "to explore . . . the secret of themselves" (xi). While certainly much can be learned about individual and "national identity formation" (xi) from these travel texts, my study proposes that another step in the "decolonization" process is to also explore the definitions of the other generated in these texts.

16. For example Villaurrutia says of the drive up the California coast from Los Angeles to San Francisco: "I doubt that there are many, if any, places in the world where Nature thinks, and stimulates thought in such a definitive and profound way" [Dudo que haya muchos, qué digo muchos, algunos lugares en el mundo en los que la Naturaleza piense y haga pensar de modo tan definitivo y profundo] (77).

17. The anecdotes and observations about New York City present in these texts, in addition to vividly registering the flappers, dance halls, and booming art scene of the 1920s and the somber struggles of the 1930s depression era, also provide insights into the beginning of the "museums, cultural centers, and galleries" that "throughout the entire twentieth century . . . have consolidated the image of New York as a platform for the introduction and launching of Spanish and Latin American artists in the cultural marketplace" (Valdés and Kadir 683).

18. "A lo largo de la playa está instalada la gran feria típica Americana, con un sin fín de atracciones que no hay necesidad de describir, por ser tan conocidas de chicos y grandes."

19. "La Universidad gótica está rodeada por la ciudad Americana standard."

20. "Las gentes que pueblan los [carros] son todas iguales y cubren sus caras cristalizadas con la misma clase de revistas."

21. "Los libros norteamericanos, como las personas, vuélvense feos e innobles al envejecer. Son hermosos e iguales cuando son jóvenes y nuevos . . . pero pasan pronto de moda."

22. "Llegamos al panorámico valle de Woodstock, . . . a punto de ser invadido por la nube de langosta de la burguesía. Millares de *Babbitts* llegan de Nueva York queriendo invadir el pintoresco oasis y aplanarlo en una total *Main Street* poblada por autómatas unánimes en la vanidad, el alcohol, el sexo y el cinco por ciento que de sus vidas es el fin único."

23. "oyendo, infladas hasta el cansancio, todas las cosas que ya sé, que ya sabemos"; ". . . ya exprimí al Departamento de Teatro de la Universidad de Yale todo el jugo. Me he asomado a todos los cursos, además de llevar, regularmente, otros. El día que vuelva a México y que estemos en tu biblioteca te convencerás de que tienes los libros en que esta gente se informa."

24. "Apenas si las prácticas de dirección tienen, siquiera, algo de humanidad: la presencia de los estudiantes de ambos sexos, o de ningún sexo, que componen escenas mudas para demostrar dónde reside el énfasis, cómo se hace una secuencia, cómo se logra un equilibrio."

25. "Una sola cosa de provecho siento dentro de mí: le he perdido el miedo a la dirección escénica; creo que llegado el caso, podría dirigir científicamente, técnicamente, una obra de teatro. He aprendido a analizar un play desde el punto de vista del director y a objetivar prácticamente al resultado de este análisis. Eso es todo."

26. They were often reluctant to return to these social and political issues. For example, near the end of his stay, and in spite of his earlier expressions of intense homesickness in the letters, Villaurrutia comments: "When I go into the Mexican Consulate I see death, inescapably" [Cuando entro en un Consulado de México veo la muerte. Irremisiblemente] (*Obras* 74).

27. "comprobar que mi bastón sería demasiado notorio"; "lo dejo en el consulado, como abandono mi sombrero de paja y un traje, en la estación, donde me pongo el que acabo de comprar como un transformista."

28. "Esta mañana cuando recorría yo el Central Park, sentí claramente un desprendimiento de mi envoltura Mexicana. . . . Siento que he saldado con mi país, que ya no lo tengo, que estoy fuera de los países y comenzando a vivir una verdad universal." Due to her fragile psychological state and the stresses of both public and private tensions in Mexico, Rivas Mercado would not be able to take full advantage of the freedom she found in her first days in New York. But in spite of suffering a nervous breakdown during the second month of her visit, she participated actively in the Mexican art scene as well as general nightlife in New York City and made many pertinent observations about the United States in her letters.

29. "Cuando se vive fuera y lejos de las costumbres: mis únicos vicios, se pierde la noción del tiempo o para ser más exacto, se adquiere la verdadera. El tiempo lineal y rígido que vivía en México ha sido substituido por un tiempo elástico."

30. "Temo que nunca lograré respirar naturalmente en este país donde cada quien va directamente a su objeto, donde no se presta a los demás sino una atención llena de sonrisas pero superficial y vacía."

31. "vive aquí como le da la gana, sin aquellos complejos que lo estaban haciendo desdichado en México."

32. "Fui a pasar *el week end* a Los Angeles. Si la ciudad es fea de día, es maravillosa de noche. Ni en Nueva York fluye, como aquí, el deseo y la satisfacción del deseo. El viernes y el sábado los pasé sin dormir casi."

33. "Yo no me doy tiempo para pensar en mi destino; lo vivo, simplemente, sin atreverme a contradecirlo, sin pretender anticiparlo en el pensamiento. Todos estos últimos días he vivido a una presión y a un tiempo extraordinarios. Me doy miedo a veces pero ¿cómo resistir a una tentación sin hacerla más fuerte? Prefiero caer en ella . . . aquí . . . la vida no se detiene un momento en su curso para analizarse. . . . El Xavier de ayer y el de mañana admiran, aplauden, envidian, todo al mismo tiempo, al Xavier de hoy. Tú me entiendes. No hay ni sombra de vanidad en lo que digo: me he sentido plenamente vivo, joven inteligente, aquí, como nunca antes."

34. "Me he recuperado a mi mismo. Ya no me siento inferior a todas estas gentes robustas que van de prisa por la calle recién mojada."

35. "las pinturas estaban muy lejos de serlo, no había nada procaz, ni siquiera desnudos."

36. "decorados con fotografías de los 'bandidos' mexicanos más celebres de aquella época y que no eran otra cosa que los desposeídos de sus tierras."

37. "Ese dia publicaban los periódicos . . . la noticia amarillista de un asalto a un tren por los villistas en Sonora, en el cual habían sido violadas todas las mujeres. Mexicano y bandido eran sinónimos."

38. "los libros en inglés; el pro y el contra: *Is México Worth Saving? The Land of the Sleeping Burro, The Land of Mañana, The People Next-Door.*"

39. "Opino que se trata de unos estantes muy unilaterales."

40. "el único obstáculo interpuesto entre . . . vertiginosas riquezas y la avidez de quienes las codiciaban."

41. "Por una parte estamos nosotros, un pueblo abundante en manifestaciones de belleza, en puros productos estéticos, pero sin mercado que los consuma . . . y por otra parte está esta nación colmada de riquezas para satisfacer el más leve de sus caprichos y retribuir nuestros productos de arte en todas las formas posibles, desde el máximo proyecto arquitectónico hasta el más trivial objeto . . . Jamás la ley de oferta y demanda nos presentó ocasión más propicia para afirmar nuestra capacidad espiritual y para . . . enriquecernos."

42. By 1921 when the following text was written, Tablada had spent five years studying theosophy and had moved from being "first curious, then interested, and today a believer" [curioso primero, luego interesado y hoy identificado] (Lozano Herrera 14).

43. "Los estudios espiritualistas que en todo el mundo se han intensificado después de esa terrible catástrofe, moral y económica, que se llama la Guerra Mundial, tienen cada vez mayor número de adeptos en Estados Unidos. Cada semana las revistas bibliográficas estudian nuevos libros de tendencias francamente espiritualistas . . . Ante la sonrisa del escéptico opongo sólo el enorme volumen de estos hechos, que demuestran una orientación universal hacia la teoría de la inmortalidad y el progreso del espíritu. Tal movimiento es serio, casi solemne, como que significa la reacción religiosa del hombre defraudado por el materialismo."

44. "como si fuera libre de elegir cualquiera de las posibilidades que a su mente se presentan como más interesantes o valiosas." (See more extensive quotation and discussion earlier in the text.)

45. For further discussion of Novo's confident approach to North American culture in this era, see Long, "Salvador Novo: 1920–1940," 217, and "Writing the City," 196. Salvador Oropesa in this collection addresses the manifestation of this confidence in Novo's public persona during a later period.

46. "La obra del positivismo norteamericano servirá a la causa de Ariel, en último término." For an excellent discussion of this less often remembered aspect of *Ariel*, see Terán.

47. For an extensive discussion of a similar approach to the United States as "training ground" for the lower-class Mexican migrant worker in the work of Manuel Gamio during these years, see the article by Schmidt.

WORKS CITED

"Academy of Arts Dedicates Building." *New York Times*, 14 November 1930.

Benjamin, Walter. "The Work of Art in the Age of Mechanical Reproduction." *Illuminations*. Ed. Hannah Arendt. New York: Schocken Books, 1968. 217–51.

Bradu, Fabienne. *Antonieta*. Mexico: Fondo de Cultura económica. 1991.

Delpar, Helen. *The Enormous Vogue of Things Mexican: Cultural Relations between the United States and Mexico, 1920–1935*. Tuscaloosa: University of Alabama Press, 1992.

Durán, Ignacio, Ivan Trujillo, and Monica Verea, eds. *México-Estados Unidos: encuentros y desencuentros en el cine*. Mexico: Instituto Mexicano de Cinematografía, 1996.

Fein, Seth. "La imagen de México: la segunda guerra mundial y la propaganda fílmica de Estados Unidos." Durán, Trujillo, and Verea. 41–59.

Fernández Bravo, Álvaro, Florencia Garramuño, and Saúl Sosnowski, eds. *Sujetos en tránsito: (in)migración, exilio y diáspora en la cultura latinoamericana*. Buenos Aires: Alianza Editorial, 2003.

Fey, Ingrid, and Karen Racine, eds. *Strange Pilgrimages: Exile, Travel, and National Identity in Latin America, 1800–1990s*. Wilmington, Del.: Scholarly Resources, 2000.

Gómez, Leila. "Presentación." *Travel Narratives: From Columbus to the New Age*. Special issue, *Colorado Review of Hispanic Studies* 3 (2005): 1–13.

González, Gilbert G. *Culture of Empire: American Writers, Mexico, and Mexican Immigrants, 1880–1930*. Austin: University of Texas Press, 2004.

Joseph, Gilbert M., Catherine C. LeGrand, and Ricardo D. Salvatore, eds. *Close Encounters of Empire: Writing Cultural History of U.S.-Latin American Relations*. Durham: Duke University Press, 1998.

Kahlo, Frida. *The Diary of Frida Kahlo: An Intimate Self-Portrait*. New York: H. N. Abrams; Mexico: La Vaca Independiente S.A. de C.V., 1995.

Long, Mary K. "Consumer Society and National Identity in the Work of Salvador Novo and Guadalupe Loaeza." *CHASQUI* 30.2 (2001): 116–26.

———. "Nota introductoria." *Salvador Novo: viajes y ensayos II: crónicas y periodismo*. Ed. and comp. Sergio González Rodríguez and Lligany Lomelí. México: Fondo de Cultura Económica, 1999. 9–17.

———. "Novo y la fragmentación del yo." *Biblioteca de México* 22 (1994): 36–40.

———. "Salvador Novo: 1920–1940: Between the Avant-garde and the Nation." Ph.D. diss., Princeton University, 1995.

———. "Salvador Novo's *Continente vacío*." *Latin American Literary Review* 24.47 (1996): 91–114.

———. "Writing the City: The Chronicles of Salvador Novo." *The Contemporary Mexican Chronicle: Theoretical Perspectives on the Liminal Genre*. Ed. Ignacio Corona and Beth Jorgensen. New York: State University of New York Press, 2002. 181–201.

Lozano Herrera, Rubén. *José Juan Tablada en Nueva York: búsqueda y hallazgos en la crónica*. México: Universidad Iberoamericana, 2000.

May, Antoinette. *Passionate Pilgrim: The Extraordinary Life of Alma Reed*. New York: Paragon House, 1993.

Morris, Stephen D. *Gringolandia: Mexican Identity and Perceptions of the United States*. Lanham, Md.: Rowman and Littlefield, 2005.

Murrieta Saldívar, Manuel. "Visión sobre Estados Unidos de América en la crónica mexicana: un análisis ideológico." Ph.D. diss., Arizona State University, 1998.

Novo, Salvador. *Viajes y ensayos, I*. Mexico: Fondo de Cultura Económica, 1996.

Oropesa, Salvadro A. *The Contemporáneos Group*. Austin: University of Texas Press, 2003.

Orozco, José Clemente. *The Artist in New York: Letters to Jean Charlot and Unpublished Writings, 1925–1929*. Trans. Ruth L. C. Simms. Austin: University of Texas Press, 1974.

———. *Autobiografía*. Mexico: Ediciones Occidente, 1945.

Pratt, Mary Louise. *Imperial Eyes: Travel Writing and Transculturation*. London: Routledge, 1992.

Ramos, Samuel. *El perfil del hombre y la cultura en México*. Mexico: Imprenta Mundial, 1934.

Reyes, Aurelio de los. "El gobierno mexicano y las películas denigrantes, 1920–1930." Durán, Trujillo, and Verea 23–37.

Rivas Mercado, Antonieta. *Cartas a Manuel Rodríguez Lozano.* Mexico: Secretaría de Educación Pública, 1975.

Rodó, José Enrique. *Ariel.* (1900) Mexico: Editorial Porrúa, 1991.

Said, Edward W. *Orientalism.* New York: Vintage Books, 1979.

Salvatore, Ricardo, ed. *Culturas imperiales: experiencia y representación en América, Asia y Africa.* Rosario, Arg.: Beatriz Viterbo Editora, 2005.

———. "Panamericanismo práctico: acerca de la mecánica de la penetración comercial norteamericana." Salvatore 271–300.

Schmidt, Arthur. "Mexicans, Migrants, and Indigenous Peoples: The Work of Manuel Gamio in the United States, 1925–1927." Fey and Racine 163–78.

Sheridan, Guillermo. *Los contemporaneous ayer.* Mexico: Fondo de Cultura Económica, 1985.

Tablada, José Juan. *La Babilonia de hierro: crónicas neoyorquinas 1920–1936.* *www.tablada.unam.mx/poesia/publica/babilo.html.*

———. "México se revela." *La Babilonia de hierro: crónicas neoyorquinas.* Ed. Esther Hernández Palacios. Mexico: Biblioteca UV/UNAM, 2000. 251–62.

———. *Obras IV: diario 1900–1944.* Mexico: Universidad Nacional Autónoma Mexicana, 1992.

Tenorio-Trillo, Mauricio. "The Cosmopolitan Mexican Summer, 1920–1949." *Latin American Research Review* 32.3 (1997): 224–42.

Terán, Oscar. "El espiritualismo y la creación del anti-imperialismo latinoamericano." Salvatore 303–13.

Valdés, Mario J., and Djelal Kadir, eds. "New York City Center and Transit Point for Hispanic Cultural Nomadism." *Literary Culture of Latin America: A Comparative History.* New York: Oxford University Press, 2004. 679–702.

Vasconcelos, José. *Memorias I: Ulises criollo; la tormenta.* (1936). Mexico: Fondo de Cultural Económica, 1983.

———. *Memorias II: el desastre; el proconsulado.* (1936). Mexico: Fondo de Cultural Económica, 1983.

———. *Obras completas.* 4 vols. Mexico: Libreros Mexicanos Unidos, 1957.

Villaurrutia, Xavier. *Cartas de Villaurrutia a Novo (1935–1936).* Mexico: Instituto Nacional de Bellas Artes, 1966.

———. "Nocturno de los ángeles/L.A. Nocturne: The Angels." *Nostalgia de la muerte/Nostalgia for Death.* Port Townsend, Wash.: Copper Canyon Press, 1992. 44–49.

Williams, Adriana. *Covarrubias.* Austin: University of Texas Press, 1994.

CHAPTER 2

Vasconcelos as Screenwriter

Bolívar Remembered

Robert Conn

In this essay I discuss a little-known, never-produced screenplay, *Simón Bolívar (Interpretación)*, as well as an equally little-known prologue, both written by José Vasconcelos in 1939 at the time of his expulsion from the United States and short stint as rector of the Universidad del Noroeste in Hermosillo, Mexico, and published together in 1939 and 1940 at *Ediciones Botas* in Mexico City. In the prologue, which had the force of a manifesto, Vasconcelos, at the time one of Latin America's most well-known critics of U.S. military and economic incursions into Latin America, explained why he had decided to write in a genre in which he had never written before and never would again, as well as why he had decided to write about the liberator of northern South America. Part of that explanation centered on the U.S.-based movement known as Pan-Americanism, which in the 1920s and 1930s harnessed the figure of Bolívar to unite "north" and "south" economically and culturally and which Vasconcelos had already critiqued in an essay published in Santiago, Chile, in 1934, *Bolivarismo y Monroísmo (Temas Iberoamericanos)* (Iberoamerican Themes). Another part of it concerned the U.S. film industry and its Mexican affiliates, which with his signature vehemence Vasconcelos accused of indoctrinating Mexicans with the ideas of "our dominators." To illustrate this, he drew his readers' attention to one film in particular, Warner Bros.' *Juarez* (1939), with its U.S. and Mexican versions. Vasconcelos was not incorrect to characterize *Juarez* as ideological, although to present it as a reflection of an entire industry was hyperbolic, to say the least. Still, what is interesting is that this intellectual, who was primarily an essayist and cultural critic, should have responded to Hollywood by trying his hand at something he had attempted only sporadically in his long and turbulent career: art.

When talking about Mexico in the first half of the twentieth century, it would be difficult if not impossible not to mention Vasconcelos. He was secretary to Francisco Madero in Washington, D.C. (1911), founder of the Ateneo (1909–1913), rector of the National University (1921–1924), founder and secretary of the Department of Education (1921–1924), promoter of literacy and hygiene programs (1921–1924), patron of the muralists (1920–1924), candidate for the presidency

(1929), director of the National Library (1940–1958), and founder of literary journals. Vasconcelos was also a distinguished if not controversial exile, residing now in the United States (1930, 1935–1938), now in Spain (1931–1933), and now in Argentina (1933–1935). At the level of his intellectual production, with the exception of his famous memoirs, he is known primarily as an essayist whose visions of Mexican culture and history were defined by his understanding of his nation and the rest of Latin America as culturally different from the United States and as economically and racially subjugated to an "Anglo/U.S." order. Much has been said about the Vasconcelos of the 1925 *Raza cósmica* (Cosmic Race), with his messianic conception of a Latin America that would embody socialist principles and be home to a new hybrid race mixing over time "superior" and "inferior" breeds, an essay that obtained a wide readership throughout Latin America. Far less has been said about the later Vasconcelos who in the 1930s, with works such as *Bolivarismo y Monroísmo*, turned away from the concept of racial hybridity to embrace what would become the basis of his right-wing populist vision, white-bread Spanish Catholicism.

But the screenplay and prologue are not simply a curiosity in the life of a figure who would sympathize with the Axis powers, renouncing Mussolini and Hitler only after the discovery of the Holocaust but then expressing his support for Franco; they provide, as I demonstrate, an interesting window onto Vasconcelos's relationship to cultural developments in the United States, his Catholic politics in relation to reformist or liberal ideology in Mexico, as well as his understanding of the ideology of culture. In the pages that follow I examine first the film *Juarez*, then the prologue—a text from which the Bolívar screenplay, I argue, cannot be separated—and finally the screenplay itself. It perhaps could be said that no one in Mexican letters in the twentieth century has attached more significance to the power of myth and historical narrative than Vasconcelos. Previously, in his *Raza cósmica*, Plato's lost Atlantis had furnished him with a distinguished mythical origin from which to reimagine Latin America; now in his war against Pan-Americanism it was Bolívar, along with other Latin American emancipators, who provided him with so many objects through which to relate to his readers the "true" history of Latin America. But first, a word or two about the film Vasconcelos targeted in the prologue and that motivated him to put the Liberator on the big screen before, as he seemed to fear, his Pan-Americanist rivals in the United States and Mexico did.

Juarez, according to Paul J. Vanderwood, was conceived in a pact of sorts between Warner Bros. and the U.S. government.[1] The year was 1938. Warner Bros. had just completed a script for a new antifascist film based on the heroic figure of Benito Juárez, the leader who liberated Mexico from Maximilian, the Hapsburg prince imposed by the French and Mexican conservatives from 1864 to 1867, while the Roosevelt administration had just arrived at the decision that it would use Pan-American doctrine to oppose the German presence in the Americas. Throughout the mid to late 1930s, as Michael E. Birdwell tells us in *Celluloid Soldiers: The War-ner Bros. Campaign against Nazism*, Jack and Harry Warner, Polish Jews, had been making films to alert the public to the danger of fascism and to argue for U.S. intervention. To do so, they had to contend with the State Department and the Pacific Coast Anti-Communist Federation, which, on account of U.S. neutrality, "discouraged movie-makers from the production of films dealing with conflicts abroad" (Birdwell 35). The Warner brothers resorted, then, to plot lines that could not be seen as directly anti-German, although the topic of fascism at home was not off limits. The story of Benito Juárez fit their program, providing them with an allegory about national resistance, just as the figure of Robin Hood had for a film they brought out in 1938, a year earlier (66–68).

The United States, learning of the Warner Bros. project, asked the studio to present the struggle between Juárez and the French from the point of view of U.S. Pan-Americanism, the policy in the name of which it had been seeking to dominate and create markets in Latin America in the 1920s and 1930s. The studio complied, desirous, as Vanderwood explains, of pleasing FDR, with whom it had intimate connections, of currying favor to stop an antimonopoly suit against the movie industry, and of protecting itself from accusations of communist sympathiz-ing by Congress and action groups. The result was a new script that not only put forth a heroic vision of resistance to an illegitimate imperial power but also stated clearly U.S. Pan-American claims over the "democratic" hemisphere in the face of Nazi attempts at strengthening trade relations and cultural ties with Latin Ameri-can nations. As Vanderwood tells us, Juárez would now be portrayed not as he originally had been by the screenwriter Aeneas MacKenzie, that is, as an obtuse Zapotec Indian resisting an outside power, but rather as a hero of resistance less identifiable by his "ethnicity" than by his passionate admiration for Lincoln ("La imagen de los héroes" [The Image of Heroes] 68–69). Juárez, as a Mexican incarna-tion of Lincoln, would stand for a "democratic" Mexico and a democratic Latin America opposed to European expansionist desires.

The subject of Juárez had special significance for Vasconcelos. In *Bolivarismo y Monroísmo*, he attacked the leader, holding him responsible for creating the condi-tions that allowed the influx of foreign capital and Protestantism. Juárez had ousted the French and separated church and state, but for Vasconcelos—with his Catholic politics and his new racism influenced primarily by his certainty that Mexican politics was being driven by U.S. capitalist interests—weakening the Church was tantamount to weakening the nation. In fact, for the Mexican intellectual in ex-ile, who presented himself now as a defender of laborers not only in Mexico but throughout Latin America, Juárez was nothing but "an incarnation of panameri-canism even before this movement made its objectives clear in congresses" (1309).[2] Proof of this for Vasconcelos was the fact that Juárez's bust, together with those of other Latin American emancipators, stood in the Pan-American, now OAS, building in Washington D.C. Proof of this for him was also, more importantly, the Juárez-sponsored disentailment of Church lands, which, Vasconcelos passionately argued, led to the arrival of new landlords, U.S. and Anglo corporations, and new religious leaders, Protestants. In an interesting formulation in which the United States is presented not only as the place of refuge that we know it to have been for embattled Mexican leaders but also as a cultural space so seductive as to test their will to remain true to their "heritage," Vasconcelos describes Juárez's anti-Church politics as having been born not of his own lights or convictions as a lawyer or judge but of the supposed transformation he experienced during his residence in New Orleans. The list of Mexican intellectuals and politicians for whom the United States served as a place from which to organize is a long one, among them: Juárez and Melchor Ocampo in the 1850s, exiled by Santa Anna; the Flores Magón brothers in the first decade of the twentieth century, anarchist critics of the Porfirian regime; and Vasconcelos in the 1930s, exiled by Calles. In his revisionist conceptualization of Mexican history, if not Juárez, the hero of the modern nation, whom, then, was Vasconcelos asking Mexicans to celebrate? Whom were they supposed to idealize if the world depression now provided irrefutable evidence that this Mexican Pan-Americanist *avant la lettre*, falsely hailed as a hero for five generations, was, in fact, a traitor, having delivered Mexico to the world economy? There were two figures: one, the little known Lucas Alamán, who in the 1830s organized the Tacabuya Congress, to the disapproval of the United States, to establish a commercial pact between the Hispano-American nations; the other, Francisco Madero, who, assassinated with the assistance of the United States, was to be praised as a statesman for his alleged plan to restore to the Church the lands taken from it first by Juárez and later by Porfirio Díaz.

Arguably, then, any creative piece, whether Mexican or U.S., praising Benito Juárez would have disturbed Vasconcelos. Still, a film that had the potential to reach a large audience, that was made in the United States (as most were at the time), that was produced by Warner Bros., which advocated U.S. intervention in the European conflict, and that supported the United States' Pan-American agenda would have outraged this critic of Pan-Americanism who, during the 1930s, in his attempt to find a model of modernization to oppose to the United States, recuperated the Spanish colonial enterprise, celebrating it for the "technology" it brought to the manual laborers of Latin America.

That Vasconcelos would write a screenplay in reaction to the film industry and, more particularly, Warner Bros.' *Juarez*, was hardly the response one would have expected. This was not only because Vasconcelos was not an artist, although in the prologue, to make his "debut" comprehensible to the Mexican public, he claimed to be a playwright manqué, forced by historical circumstance throughout his life to write philosophical and historical essays. This was also because Vasconcelos was certain, as he also states in the prologue, that his foray into cinema would never go any further than the written word. First, as we know, Vasconcelos at this time enjoyed little influence in Mexico, having just returned from a long exile in the United States that had resulted from his call for civil revolt to protest the 1929 presidential elections stolen from him by Plutarco Calles's political machine with the help of the U.S. ambassador to Mexico Dwight Morrow, an injustice of which he constantly reminds readers until the end of his life. Second, even if he had had influence, in the prologue he tells us that he could expect no cooperation from the "nascent" Mexican film industry, the puppet, in his mind, of a Hollywood dominated by U.S. political and economic concerns, be they liberal or, as charged by U.S. representative Martin Dies Jr., creator of the House Committee Investigating Un-American Activities, and affirmed by Vasconcelos, Bolshevik. Whether this was paranoia or not, Vasconcelos was no doubt visible on the radar of the U.S. government not only for the reason that he had refused to walk away quietly from the 1929 elections but also because of the many public speeches he gave throughout Latin America in the aftermath in which he criticized U.S. economic and political incursions. Vasconcelos had, then, good reason to understand the U.S. Labor Department's denial of his visa renewal request in 1938 as retaliation for his political positions (see Taracena 121).

So why go to the trouble of composing a screenplay? One explanation is so that he could write a prologue, that is, so that he could have a stage on which to give expression explicitly to his conspiracy-based vision of politics. That vision was rooted in the betrayal of the democratically elected Francisco Madero at the hands of the U.S. ambassador Henry Lane Wilson and the Mexican general Victoriano Huerta, as well as in the betrayal he himself suffered in the 1929 presidential elections. Now, it had taken on a life of its own in his project to construct a Latin American consciousness, serving as the matrix for his famously Manichean, totalizing, racially based ideas pitting Catholicism against Protestantism and Judaism. A second explanation is that with U.S. cinema having become a mass-media industry and with the Mexican film industry in ascendancy, Vasconcelos, who more than any intellectual of his time envisioned for himself a large mass public, would have wanted to comment on this industry that threatened to eclipse his logocentric world and that, in the case of Warner Bros., sought to demonize fascism. A third explanation, related to the second, is that he wanted to propose a model or a form for a future Latin American cinema. What better way to go about proposing that model than to use as a foil the celluloid soldiering associated with Warner Bros.! As he told his readers in a formulation that naturalized the function of film as essentially ideological, this new medium that he saw as combining entertainment, learning, and indoctrination had the potential to be extraordinary, provided that the aesthetic were given a proper place. This had not occurred, he maintained, in the films of the era, particularly in Warner Bros.' *Juarez*, which he regarded as vulgarly nationalistic and, as it in fact was, costly. Nor had this occurred, one could think, in the films of liberal nationalist Miguel Contreras Torres, director of the 1933 *Juárez y Maximiliano* and of the documentary-like 1941, pro-Ally, "Mexican-made" *Simón Bolívar, El Libertador*, screened in New York City in 1943 with copious English subtitles (see Crowther). The Latin American cinema he imagined would represent a new era.

A fourth explanation concerns the historic prerogative of the "ciudad letrada" [lettered city]. Vasconcelos wrote the screenplay and prologue to declare the priority of the written word—el Verbo (the Word), as he called it, with his familiar embrace of Christian symbolism—over cinematic image. In a statement revealing his concern about the diminishing authority of the print intellectual, he tells his readers that the contribution of the script is more significant than that of the cameramen, the director, or the actors. A fifth explanation, which addresses the simultaneity of the writing of the prologue, is that Vasconcelos from the beginning planned on publishing the screenplay. To the Mexican public he needed to justify the idea that as a print form the screenplay had value in itself, independent of its function in a filmic production. Put differently, he needed to make the screenplay culturally intelligible as published text. Curiously, to this end, he uses the authority of the U.S. literary market, reporting that publishing "*filmodramas*" such as his "for general dissemination" (*Simón Bolívar* 1722) has become increasingly common in the United States, where movie scripts are valued as texts in their own right just as theatrical plays are. A final explanation is that Vasconcelos, positivist that he was, needed to announce his vision of the future, of future generations and glory. One day, as he promised his readers in the *Raza cósmica*, poverty, colonialism, physical ugliness, and injustice would be transcended by a new aesthetic order. Similarly, he now promised that one day the mediocrity of Hollywood would be superseded by a Latin American cinema which, while similarly mass produced, respected not only national interests but also quality, as constituted by such high culture activities as ballet and orchestral music. Perhaps then, his Bolívar would find its way on to the screen to take the place of that of filmmakers like Contreras Torres. Perhaps, at this time, too, the Mexican leaders he praised so, Alamán and Madero, would also be immortalized in film. For this admirer of Hegel, the positivists, and Christian theology, of all things structured around a trinity, Bolívar, Alamán, and Madero would assume their proper place in the Mexico and Latin America that he imagined, anchored in the Spanish-Catholic tradition and forming part of a new world order free of U.S. hegemony.

Faith in the redemptive power of the written word: No Latin American intellectual embodied this principle more than Vasconcelos. Yet the Bolívar whom Vasconcelos constructs is not the student of the famous educator Simón Rodríguez or the legendary writer and legislator for the ages. In fact, we never see Bolívar writing, as we do, for instance, in García Marquez's *El general en su laberinto* (The General in His Labyrinth). Nor do we ever see him, for that matter, on the battlefield. Rather, the Bolívar that we have before us is a ceremonial one wrapped in the monumentalism of Latin American Catholicism and in the medium of filmic representation.

To produce this iteration of the figure, Vasconcelos differentiates Bolívar culturally from the United States, portraying his social, ceremonial, and political life as transpiring gloriously in a Hispanic Catholic world. That world consists of monumental spaces in which the masses welcome the mythical hero as he enters the liberated city. In one scene, we see Bolívar depicted triumphantly entering the plaza of Caracas in 1813 (any plaza in the Spanish American Colonial style will do, Vasconcelos indicates in his scene directions). In another we see Bolívar being blessed in a Quito cathedral by the archbishop following the Pichincha victory. We also view the leader in a seat of honor at a Caracas dance hall watching couples move to Sevillian, Spanish rhythms. We are told in the scene directions that this style of dance is to be understood by the audience as distinctly Hispanic or Latin American: The dancers are to use their legs and hips, not their arms and shoulders, as Anglos do.

Furthermore, it is not simply that Vasconcelos presents Bolívar as part of a ritualized public world different from that of the North. It is also that he creates a figure who will convert to the Hispanic Catholic tradition, rejecting the English and U.S. liberal tradition he in fact admired. There is much that Vasconcelos does to prepare the way for Bolívar's epiphany. Throughout the text we see figures close to Bolívar warning him about the Anglo world. For instance, the German Alexander Humboldt, whom Bolívar met in Paris in 1804, is portrayed telling the young future leader that he must beware of England's commercial designs on Latin America. In this scene he also tells Bolívar that the person who liberates Latin America will need to be like Caesar, not Napoleon, although Bolívar was in fact compared with the latter during his lifetime and has been since. One can imagine several reasons Vasconcelos insists upon the Roman instead of the French imperial model. First, sympathizing as he did at the time with the Axis powers, he could not deploy the comparison of Bolívar to Napoleon since he did not want to be seen as supporting the French. Second, the Caesarian model of imperial power was being evoked by Mussolini; the construction of Bolívar as Caesarian, then, was a clear way of making the Venezuelan leader resonate with the "powers" of the moment. Finally, Vasconcelos, with his long-standing Hispanic-based cultural politics, saw the Gallic as a model of empire and culture that had already failed in the Americas. In the *Raza cósmica*, Napoleon is presented as a myopic, somewhat historically sinister figure to whom is attributed the rise of the United States in the Americas on account of his decision in 1803 to sell it the Louisiana Territory. As far as Vasconcelos was concerned, had Napoleon possessed the appropriate ethnic consciousness of solidarity with Latin-based cultures, he would never have made a deal that years later would pave the way for the United States to take or acquire the northern provinces of Mexico.

The issue of empire was central to Vasconcelos's reflection, then. In the screenplay, to make way for the Spanish Catholic Bolívar he imagined, he has the leader enter into a discussion with a fictional French abbot he is supposed to have met in Haiti in 1816 about the role of the Spanish as economic colonizers of the Americas.

As we know, Bolívar railed against the Spanish empire in his famous 1815 *Carta de Jamaica* (Letter from Jamaica). In order to "correct" this, Vasconcelos has the abbot Gerard address the matter of economic development. Characterizing the Spanish as capable economic administrators, the abbot cites Humboldt's findings that they successfully placed European crops in the New World, a formulation that directly refutes Bolívar's portrayal of the colonial administration in the *Carta de Jamaica* as obstructing Latin America's development. With this, we see Vasconcelos defending the notion he puts forth in *Bolivarismo y Monroísmo*, that is, the notion of Spain as possessing technologies accessible to laborers at large and as an alternative, therefore, to corporate and industrial modernity.

At the same time, racist that he was, Vasconcelos could not allow Bolívar's identity as emancipator of the Afro-Latin Americans to stand. To this end, he in fact dedicates an entire scene to Bolívar's visit to Haiti and to his relationship with Alexandre Pétion, who came to the aid of the Independence movement not once but twice. In a clear departure from his earlier, futuristic celebration of the tropics in the *Raza cósmica*, Vasconcelos portrays Haiti as the primitive bucolic location of an inferior race and Pétion not as an individual but as a representative of "his race," as the so-called black president. Not that Vasconcelos was concerned with being historically accurate, but we should note that Pétion was mulatto and that the politics in the Haiti of his time pitted "blacks" against "mulattos." Still, why would Vasconcelos have insisted on constructing a scene in Haiti when he easily could have avoided mention of Bolívar's extraordinary debt, just as so many others have? The reason is that Vasconcelos wants to explain how Bolívar could have come to take up the cause of liberating the enslaved blacks, and furthermore, how he could be regarded by later generations as an emancipator. Bolívar, as we are supposed to learn from the screenplay, was a realist who understood that in the moment he needed Pétion's assistance he had no choice but to acquiesce to the Haitian president's demand and proclaim that he would liberate the slaves. Vasconcelos, let us say, is "contextualizing" Bolívar's words. Haiti, we are told, at this time represented a historical axis, a strategic place to which Bolívar had to go for military assistance. With this in mind, we are to see Bolívar's proclamations to liberate the slaves, then, as a concession to the political project of the individual funding him and not a reflection of the true content of his thought.

Reconstructed in this manner, the new Bolívar disassociated from his commitment to liberating the slaves will stand not only for the union of church and state, opposing Juárez in this way, but also for the post-1824 dream of federation. Readers and viewers, particularly those among Latin America's youth, will now be able to find in Independence the lessons that will guide them in the future.

But how could Vasconcelos portray the liberal Anglophile, Francophile, anticlerical, anti-Spanish Bolívar in such a way? How could Bolívar, who never uttered a single significant public word of criticism against the United States or England, who in fact admired the civic and political traditions of the United States and also admired the English parliamentary system, who contemplated in the mid-1820s inviting the English to act as guardian of the new republics, be seen as an enemy of the United States and the Anglo world?[3] Furthermore, how could this figure, who in essence stood against the Catholic clergy, except in his final dictatorship when he sought out their political support, be reconciled not only to Catholicism but also to its pomp?

Vasconcelos could do this because of his relativistic understanding of the relationship between power, tradition, and interpretation. Addressing this relationship in the prologue, he speaks of his right to fashion his own Bolívar, one who was not only *castizo* (pure) and culturally Latin American in the way he imagined this but also one whose story of development and final spiritual redemption hinged on the critical knowledge Latin Americans had gained since the emergence of the United States as hemispheric power. Indeed, the figure he was presenting, he avowed, is no less an interpretation, as he underlines with his inclusion of the word in the title, than the Bolívars of the French and of the United States. This is significant. For in justifying his right to produce a Bolívar for the times, in explaining the grounds that authorized him to mine the Bolivarian archive for the religious statements that he would include in his drama, he says nothing of the multiple if not myriad appropriations of Bolívar in Latin America. Ricardo Palma, José Martí, José Enrique Rodó, to name just a few of the intellectuals and writers who positioned themselves through Bolívar, are neatly elided so that the story of Vasconcelos's relationship to the "Liberator" can be seen as that of a Latin American rescuing a foundational figure from foreign hands. Vasconcelos's Bolívar is to be an eminently useable one for Latin Americans confronted by the specter of the new antifascist Pan-Americanism, a figure in whose heroic story may be found all the evidence of Latin America's spiritual unity as well as all the evidence of the cause of its continued political fragmentation: the United Kingdom and the United States.

Most narratives about Bolívar, whether friendly or hostile, focus on the legitimacy of his desire to impose his Bolivian constitution together with his idea of an Andean Federation on the Gran Colombia of which he was president. In Vasconcelos's narrative, although there is a scene that deals with his response to the so-called calumnies directed at him during his dictatorship in 1828 and 1829, the failure of Bolívar to realize his dream of a federation is not presented as the result, as it in fact was, of irreconcilable differences between himself and the Granadan Francisco de Paula Santander, the Venezuelan José Antonio Páez, and other representatives of so-called local interests. Rather, it is seen as the result of British and U.S. economic and political interests. Bolívar is portrayed saying the following to one of his secretaries on the subject of the United Kingdom: "You are wrong, Martel. Behind Páez is England. . . . England does not want us to be strong. A collection of disorganized nations is easier to manage for its own interests than a great State like the one I had imagined" (*Simón Bolívar* 1760).[4]

The United Kingdom was, of course, interested in establishing trade relations with the new independent nations and did. But its experience with the Gran Colombia, which defaulted on a loan extended to it in 1824, discouraged investment in the following decades. As for the United States, in a scene based upon historical fact but greatly embellished, we hear Bolívar speaking to his aide-de-camp Florencio O'Leary about the U.S. thwarting of efforts by Mexico and the Gran Colombia to liberate Cuba: "Let us speak clearly, O'Leary; what is getting in my way is the ambition of foreigners. . . . In these moments the failure of Cuba hurts me most. The expedition that should have freed it was ready; Colombia offered the largest contingent; Mexico was also quick to assist. And who impeded us? The United States! Why is this country opposed to the liberation of Cuba?" (1752).[5]

Henry Clay did make a statement in 1825 expressing the United States' opposition to the Mexican-Colombian alliance for Cuban liberation. Still, as Hugh Thomas writes in his history of Cuba, had Bolívar truly desired to take the liberation process to Cuba under the command of Páez in collaboration with Cuban exiles in Mexico, supported by that country's president, as he threatened to do after the battle of Ayacucho in order to compel a complete surrender by the Spanish, Clay's statement would not have deterred him. At the same time, nor was it likely, Thomas adds, that the U.S. public would have supported a military effort against Bolívar's army (Thomas 104–5).

In Vasconcelos's revised version of the Bolivarian epic, the internal differences between Bolívar, Santander, and Páez are presented as being merely contingent. The "Liberator" explains to O'Leary that those who believe themselves to be his rivals will bow their heads to him if he is able to establish a federation of "pueblos americanos" [American peoples] including all of Latin America, not just Venezuela, New Granada (present-day Colombia), Ecuador, Peru, and Bolivia. Yet if the importance of the conflict with Santander and Páez is downplayed in this way, the ethnic identities of Anglo/Irish and Hispanic are described as being transcendent. In a scene in Quito in 1822, O'Leary, who collected and organized Bolívar's correspondence and who in his biography defended him against his detractors and enemies as a liberal, Enlightenment figure, is portrayed exchanging disparaging remarks about the "criollo" [Creole] Bolívar with an agent of the British Secret Service. O'Leary, referred to in the stage directions of this scene alone as the Irishman, attributes the success of the Independence movement to the participation of English and Irish recruits and mercenaries who like him joined the movement in 1817 and 1818. For his part, the agent tells him not to worry about defending British commercial interests, for Chile's hero of Independence, Bernardo O'Higgins, "another one of ours, has the command of the Chilean fleet. England will not relinquish the pursuit of its quarry. Ha, Ha, Ha" (*Simón Bolívar* 1744).[6] It is true, of course, that O'Leary would serve as British consul general in Venezuela and Colombia after Bolívar's death and the break-up of the Gran Colombia, just as another Bolívar aide-de-camp, the British Belford Hinton Wilson, would in Peru. Following this scene, indeed neatly juxtaposed to it, is that of the famous unrecorded meeting in Guayaquil in 1822 between Bolivar and the Argentine Liberator San Martín, after which San Martín ceded authority to Bolívar over the liberation of Peru and then left South America to retire in France. Here, in a portrayal of trust, agreement, and unity—rather than, possibly, as many conjecture, of power politics—San Martín is represented as willingly agreeing to withdraw from the campaign and, subsequently, as accompanying Bolívar, as he is said to have done, together with their respective staffs, for drinks and dancing. With this, Vasconcelos seems to resolve the enigma of San Martín's surprising removal of himself from the Independence movement, shunting aside the contention of Argentines that Bolívar threatened to withhold his forces from the conflict in Peru if San Martín did not cede his command to him. Vasconcelos may also be seen in this same gesture to shunt aside the matter of the political future of Guayaquil, which Bolívar declared to be part of the Gran Colombia but which many in the local elites wanted either to be part of Peru or to be independent. As for Vasconcelos's conception of history, the following, then, can be said: By supplying an "updated" version of O'Leary and O'Higgins, by "revealing" them to be part of a vast conspiracy of British capitalist interests, a providential, positivist Vasconcelos furnishes readers of his screenplay, if not perhaps one day viewers of his film, with a new mythical vision of cooperation among Latin America's liberators based on the fictions of racial coherence and difference.

The screenplay *Juarez* was based on Franz Werfel's 1924 play *Juarez und Maximilian*, translated into English in 1926 and performed that same year at the Theater Guild in New York City. In the play, Werfel, himself Austrian, portrays the Austrian Hapsburg prince Maximilian as an enlightened aristocrat who, combating the demagogue of democracy that is Juárez, defends till the end of his life his vision of a radical constitutional monarchy. As Vanderwood points out, Aeneas MacKenzie, in the first Warner Bros. adaptation, brought about two important changes. He presents Juárez as a Zapotec Indian who is intellectually inferior on account of his "race"; also, to meet the interpretive needs of Warner Bros., he replaces the climax of the original play, in which Maximilian lashes out against the new tyranny represented by Juárez, with a different climactic moment, the evacuation of French troops under threat of U.S. intervention, the significance of which the primitive Juárez does not entirely grasp. In the second adaptation, prompted by the agreement between Roosevelt and Warner Bros., MacKenzie, now in collaboration with John Huston, rewrites the role of Juárez in order to define him as a bearer of Pan-American values. To this end, Juárez is presented as a Lincolnphile, and a personal relationship that never existed between the two is invented. Thus there is a portrait of Lincoln hanging behind Juárez's desk in the moments of the film in which Juárez appears presiding over his government-in-exile; a scene in which Juárez is presented receiving a letter of support from Lincoln; and a scene where we witness the Mexican president-in-exile receiving with great sorrow news of the U.S. president's death. In the second script, Juárez is thus transformed from racialized Indian to a New Deal Lincolnesque figure representing liberalism and a democratic hemisphere. No doubt Vasconcelos, who vilified Juárez as being unable to assimilate to Hispanic culture on account of his "Indianness," would have preferred the racialized portrayal of his historical nemesis. But the second and final script would have also appealed to him, for therein could be found the "truth" of which he sought to convince his compatriots—Juárez's identification with the United States.

The Monroe Doctrine is also emphasized in the final screenplay. Louis Napoleon and his ministers are portrayed speaking of the need to show the United States that France is not in violation of it. At the beginning of the film we see them plotting to protect themselves from accusations by staging a referendum for the Mexican people on whether they want to have the Austrian Hapsburg Maximilian as their king. Equally significant is the scene toward the end of the film that Warner Bros. deleted from the Mexican version after reaction from Latin American viewers at the opening in New York.[7] Here we are shown a U.S. envoy who is sent, subsequent to the Union's defeat of the Confederates, to visit Louis Napoleon to inform him that the United States takes the Monroe Doctrine very seriously and is poised to support Juárez. As the English historian Jasper Ridley tells us, with the end of the Civil War, the United States no longer needed to tolerate the occupation since it had done so principally to secure from France assurances that it would not sell naval vessels to the Confederacy. But, as Ridley also tells us, the United States, which was supplying Juárez's army and was concerned about violence on the border, did not put pressure on Napoleon, who already wanted to evacuate his troops from France and was desperate to save face before his own public, outraged by the expense of the occupation. A meeting did, indeed, take place between Napoleon and a U.S. envoy, but this envoy was James Watson Webb, a friend whom Napoleon called upon to advise him. The meeting had nothing to do with the Monroe Doctrine, then. To the contrary, Napoleon asked Webb if the United States would help him politically by recognizing Maximilian. To which the envoy responded that public opinion prevented President Johnson from doing so and that such was the sentiment of the American people that in the event of a continued occupation there could be thousands going to Mexico to fight for Juárez. He "suggested that Napoleon might consider withdrawing his troops from Mexico in stages over eighteen months, for this would make it clear to the world that he was withdrawing in his own good time and not under duress" (Ridley 239).

Non-Hispanic U.S. viewers of the film, we can surmise, would have lacked the critical knowledge to question a version of Mexican history in which the United States was presented as the linchpin of independence from the French. Furthermore, Pan-Americanists or cultural hegemonists that they were, whether consciously or unconsciously, they would have perceived the U.S. prerogative over Mexico and the rest of Latin America, as embodied by the Monroe Doctrine, as correct and natural. On the other hand, viewers in Mexico, as Vanderwood tells us, saw in the film the same old story of U.S. paternalism and interventionism in Latin America.[8] For Vasconcelos, who considered launching a military assault from U.S. territory on the socialist president Lázaro Cárdenas in the years before his expulsion, that story of interference would have included the fraudulent elections of 1929 to which he saw Cárdenas as heir.

When we consider the meaning of Vasconcelos's intervention in the world of celluloid soldiering, it is important to keep in mind the larger context of this intellectual's life and political concerns. His desire to celebrate the continental figure of Símón Bolívar along with national figures such as Francisco Madero, assassinated at the hands of Huerta in collaboration with the United States, was no less valid than that of the Warner brothers, who searched for useable histories to get around the political imperatives and restrictions of the 1930s. What was indefensible, indeed, what was to be condemned, was not only the position he would take up as a supporter of the Axis powers but along with this his continued identification with racist hierarchies and binaries, based now in the 1930s not on *mestizaje* (racial mixing) and eugenics but rather on pure Caucasian Spanish Catholicism. In this, his last attempt at immortality and salvation of the nation and the continent, the racist ideology he embraced from the 1920s forward would make him a bedfellow of the century's most notorious and repugnant figures. But such are the vagaries of memory and the politics of culture that the Vasconcelos of the 1930s and 1940s would not be the one remembered. Instead, the one remembered would be the perhaps less odious though no less racist Vasconcelos of the *Raza cósmica*, celebrated by later generations for his clear statement of opposition to U.S. racial political hegemony and at the same time domesticated on both sides of the border, whether by the likes of Alfonso Reyes, the Chicano movement, or U.S. and Mexican textbook writers, as a voice attesting to the successful and exemplary racial mixing of indigenous and Spanish white.

This exclusive focus on the figure of the 1920s is significant because it leaves out earlier and later moments in the story of this major figure's engagement with ideology and culture, in particular the important transitional moment examined here from a ten-year exile that saw Vasconcelos go from Mexico to the United States, then to Spain and Argentina, later back to the United States, and finally back to Mexico. Curiously, both his departure from Mexico in 1929 and his departure from the United States in 1938 were expulsions. Some critics have posited that Vasconcelos in the 1920s, with his clearly articulated view of superior and inferior races, bore already the signs of the right-wing populist who would be a fascist sympathizer. Still others, like the Vasconcelos critic Luis Marentes, urge us to distinguish among the different embodiments of his political project. Marentes, for instance, differentiates Vasconcelos's vision of race in the 1920s from the one he elaborates and defends in the 1930s and 1940s. No doubt, such historical nuancing is important, especially when one considers the complexity of this intellectual's ideological war against liberalism and communism both inside and outside of Mexico.

Vasconcelos fought on many political and cultural fronts, including, as we have seen here, the celluloid front of the late 1930s, while using the very border that he and other Mexican intellectuals and politicians crossed so often to distinguish what was Mexican or Latin American from what was (U.S.) American. The Latin American cinema he imagined has still not come into being and, ironically, at the time he was writing, Mexico was entering its cinematic Golden Age. But in the end, no text or texts of Vasconcelos speak more eloquently than do *Simón Bolívar (Interpretación)* together with its prologue to what was of most importance to Vasconcelos throughout his long and embattled career: the creation of a political and cultural consciousness capable of resisting the assaults of the "powerful." In his response to *Juarez*, a motion picture in the service of the U.S. state, we see a vision that is self-consciously propagandistic, presented in the universalistic language of high culture, the same language in which he inscribed all his distinct projects rallying both the elites and the masses. We also see an intellectual who was both a realist and an idealist, waging his celluloid war in the print medium to which he had access but hopeful that his words and images would one day become something more.

NOTES

1. I will be referring primarily to Vanderwood's Spanish-language essay, "La imagen de los héroes mexicanos en las películas americanas" (The Image of Mexican Heroes in American Movies), based on the author's brilliant introduction to his edition of the screenplay *Juarez*, 9–41. In contrast to his original study, Vanderwood in the later essay attributes the last revision of the screenplay to the beginning of FDR's movement away from passive isolationism (64–65).

2. "una encarnación del panamericanismo aun antes de que éste precisara sus objetivos en congresos." All translations are mine unless otherwise indicated.

3. As is known, Bolívar in a private letter to the British chargé d'affaires to Colombia, Patrick Campbell, dated 5 August 1829, wrote: "Can you imagine the opposition that would come from the new American states, and from the United States, which seems destined by Providence to plague America with torments in the name of liberty?" [Cuánto no se opondrían todos los nuevos Estados americanos, y los Estados Unidos que parecen destinados por la providencia para plagar América de miserias en nombre de la libertad]. There is an important debate about the significance of the second part of the sentence, which has often been excerpted, particularly in Latin America since the 1960s, to show Bolívar to have been a critic *avant la lettre* of U.S. imperialism. But as the Bolívar scholar David Bushnell has explained, Bolívar penned these words to curry favor with the United Kingdom, with which he desired to foster political and economic relations rather than with the United States. Bushnell writes: "Those who make much of that quotation seldom mention, if they are even aware, the context in which it was uttered. Instead, they commonly imply that Bolívar was foresightedly warning against the later machination of the Central Intelligence Agency in Chile or the not-so-covert struggle of the Reagan administration against revolutionary Nicaragua. In reality, Bolivar's statement is contained in a letter to the British chargé in Bogotá—Harrison's counterpart and diplomatic rival—whose favor Bolívar at the time was ardently seeking, and the principal "torment" involved was nothing

but the conventional republicanism that U.S. agents throughout Latin America were then promoting in opposition both to the diplomatic and ideological influence of Great Britain and to the protomonarchist schemes associated with Bolívar and his supporters (These agents' methods often entailed blunt and brazen meddling in Latin American affairs, but their immediate objectives were essentially innocuous)."

4. "Te equivocas, Martel. Detrás de Páez está Inglaterra. . . . No quiere Inglaterra que seamos fuertes. Una colección de pueblos desorganizados es más fácil de manejar para sus propios intereses que un gran Estado como el que había soñado."

5. "Hablemos claro, O'Leary; quien me estorba es la ambición de los extraños. . . . En estos instantes lo que más me duele es el fracaso de Cuba. Estaba lista la expedición que debía libertarla; Colombia ofrecía el mayor contingente; México también estaba pronto a ayudar. Y ¿quién nos lo impidió? ¡Los Estados Unidos! ¿Por qué se oponen a la liberación de Cuba?"

6. "otro de los nuestros, tiene el mando de la escuadra chilena. Inglaterra no abandona su presa. Ja, Ja, Ja."

7. See Vanderwood's discussion of the reception of Juárez in New York and Latin America between 1939 and the early 1940s (*Juárez*).

8. For another view of the film in relation to Mexican cultural developments in the 1940s, see Seth Fein 171–72, who speaks of the negative response to *Juárez* in Mexico among both the elites and the masses as an early instance of the U.S.-Mexican pact that he sees developing at the time and that will strengthen, he argues, through the war and the postwar. If *Juarez*, with its "failure" in Mexico, stands for an ideological pact in formation, later films of the war period and of the cinematic Golden Age successfully perform the ideological work of the state linking Mexico to the United States.

WORKS CITED

Birdwell, Michael E. *Celluloid Soldiers: The Warner Bros. Campaign against Nazism.* New York and London: New York University Press, 1999.

Bushnell, David. "Simón Bolívar and the United States: A Study in Ambivalence." *Air University Review* 37.5 (July–August 1986): 106–12.

Crowther, Bosley. " 'The Life of Simon Bolivar,' a Mexican-Made Film, Opens at the Belmont—'Sarong Girl' at Palace." *New York Times*, 18 June 1943.

Fein, Seth. "Myths of Cultural Imperialism and Nationalism in Golden Age Mexican Cinema." *Fragments of a Golden Age: The Politics of Culture in Mexico Since 1940.* Durham: Duke University Press, 2001. 159–98.

Marentes, Luis A. *José Vasconcelos and the Writing of the Mexican Revolution.* New York: Twayne, 2000.

Ridley, Jasper. *Maximilian and Juárez.* London: Phoenix Press, 1992.

Taracena, Alfonso. *José Vasconcelos.* Mexico: Editorial Porrúa, 1982.

Thomas, Hugh. *Cuba: The Pursuit of Freedom.* New York: Harper and Row, 1971.

Vanderwood, Paul. "La imagen de los héroes mexicanos en las películas americanas." *México/Estados Unidos: encuentros y desencuentros en el cine.* Ed. Ignacio Durán, Iván Trujillo, and Mónica Verea. Mexico: Instituto Mexicano de Cinematografía, 1996. 59–83.

———, ed. *Juárez.* Madison: University of Wisconsin Press, 1983.

Vasconcelos, José. *"Bolivarismo y Monroísmo (Temas Iberoamericanos)."* *Obras completas.* Vol. 2. Mexico: Libreros Mexicanos Unidos, 1957. 1305–1494.

———. "*Simón Bolívar (Interpretación).*" *Obras completas.* Vol. 2. Mexico: Libreros Mexicanos Unidos, 1957. 1721–66.

Werfel, Franz. *Juarez and Maximilian: A Dramatic History in Three Phases and Thirteen Pictures.* Trans. Ruth Langner. New York: Simon and Schuster, 1926.

CHAPTER 3

Salvador Novo

The American Friend, the American Critic

Salvador A. Oropesa

In 1946, Miguel Alemán Valdez became the first civilian president in Mexico since the Revolution, and his administration falls within the period known as the "Mexican Miracle" (1940–1968), defined in part by the post–World War II expansion of the middle class—which by the beginning of the Alemán administration had reached 17 percent of the population (Smith, "Mexico since 1946" 330)—and the universal acceptance of its values as representative of true Mexicanness. These were also key years in which, as Peter H. Smith has observed, a relationship developed between Mexico and the United States "through movies, television, language and the marketplace" (332). In his first address to Congress in 1947, Alemán announced that this was the time in which the relationship between the United States and Mexico was at its peak. It was the "Era of Good Feeling" (Cline 316). Because of this, as Smith further observes, "Mexico underwent a steady and accelerated process of 'Americanization'—a trend which gave added urgency to the protection of national identity" ("Mexico since 1946" 332).

Salvador Novo, well known by this time in intellectual circles as a significant poet and essayist, as well as for his work in earlier administrations, was also well known by the Mexican middle class from his frequent chronicles in the popular press. He was named the director of the Department of Theatrical Productions of the National Institute of Fine Arts (Instituto Nacional de Bellas Artes, or INBA) during the Alemán administration. Novo accepted this position because he felt he had the right ideas to change Mexican culture for the better, and the position of director of theatrical production at INBA could allow him to reach his goal and also serve as a model for other cultural policymakers and even for future generations at the art institute. At the core of his confidence in his ability to better Mexican culture was his deep knowledge of the vibrant and dynamic U.S. culture. He felt with all his might that importing the right elements from the North could do wonders for Mexico. Thus, his selective reading and adaptation of certain elements of North American life are a central part of his influential efforts to simultaneously enrich and preserve Mexican culture during these key transition years. His chronicles from this period (which were subsequently collected in the volume *La vida en México en el periodo presidencial de Miguel Alemán* [Life in Mexico during the Presidency of Miguel Aleman]) provide valuable insights into Novo's efforts to transform Mexican culture.

After first contextualizing Novo's importance as the chronicler of and role model for middle-class self-definition, this essay examines how Salvador Novo used principles learned from Broadway theater; Earl Sennett, an independent U.S. actor and stage director; Seki Sano's production of Tennessee Williams's *A Streetcar Named Desire*; and José Limón, a Mexican American dancer and choreographer— all to improve Mexican theater. Thanks to these influences he changed the dynamics of staging plays at the national art institute. I also examine Novo's key role in making regional dances one of the staples of modern Mexican nationalism as a means to challenging certain parochial holdovers, such as the compulsory and narrow-minded nationalism of the Revolution. (Even as he was implementing his pro-American cultural agenda, however, he was critical of U.S. political policies toward braceros. Novo was very receptive to the corrective artistic tendencies from the North but rejected politics that hurt Mexico in socioeconomic spheres. The reader will also notice a queer subtext in most of Novo's narratives that serves to challenge the status quo.)[1]

Novo was typical of the members of the Alemán administration: educated, without military experience, and a child during the Revolution. He had turned forty-two by the time the new head of state named him director of the Department of Theatrical Productions of the National Institute of Fine Arts. The INBA was under the direction of the nationalist musician Carlos Chávez, who was known for incorporating aboriginal percussive instrumentation in his symphonies. Chávez, in addition to being Novo's new boss, was also his close friend. They had studied together at the Mexico City National Preparatory School, where they majored in law, although Novo ended up getting a degree in literature. Both were fluent in English. Raúl López Sánchez, the new governor of Coahuila (1948–1951), was Novo's childhood friend and another alumnus of the National Preparatory School. The secretary of foreign relations was yet another buddy of his, Jaime Torres Bodet of the avant-garde *Contemporáneos* literary group. Alemán's cabinet averaged forty-four years of age, and all members had college degrees (Smith, "Mexico since 1946" 341; Camp 25, 411, 505).

Novo's job at INBA cost him time and money but gave him prestige and the opportunity to influence the cultural life of the nation. At the peak of his career, with money, talent, and influence, he was ready to fight in the trenches of the cultural wars. Novo was not a stranger to the perils of Mexican politics. He had served in the government during the 1920s and early 1930s, enjoying power and suffering vicious public censure.[2] He had also written frequently about Mexican politics—he had fiercely criticized Lázaro Cárdenas and his socialism. Thus he was perfectly conscious of the rules of the game and, despite past negative experiences, decided to take the risk of entering politics again, partly because this was the first nonmilitary administration, and partly because he had enough connections in the government to be protected from the fierce attacks that sooner or later were going to come, as always happens with any political position. His acceptance of a post that was political and artistic at the same time meant that he wanted to be an active part in the transformations the country was experiencing; he was ready to endure both sets of challenges.

The story of this cultural transformation is also the chronicle of the development of the middle class. Salvador Novo, with his writing in the press and his appearances on radio and as a regular debater in the recently born television, was the perfect man to chronicle this period of gentrification. The rhetoric of the Revolution had been about peasants and the proletariat, but Novo's bourgeois upbringing and his admiration for the good things capitalism was bringing to the United States convinced him the authentic revolution was to be found in the expansion of the middle class; he was ready to be one of its voices in diverse media.

The admiration was mutual. The new middle class enjoyed reading Novo's articles and diaries because its members felt he was one of them. Novo's common sense, centrism, and humor, his ease of movement from popular to high culture, his understanding of nationalism and cosmopolitism, and the straightforward quality of his writing made him obligatory reading for professionals, store owners, small business owners, and "decent" people in general. We know the professions of his readers because he comments on them, and sometimes they become narratees of the articles. Even with his superior position and access to all kinds of social, cultural, and political events, as well as contact with the elite, Novo could communicate to his readers that he was an ordinary man merely observing, analyzing, and making the powerful and famous accessible to the Mexico of the economic miracle. One literary device Novo uses often is to describe an important social occasion and at the height of it leave, take his car, and drive alone through a city. Then he explains how cozy it is to be home and gives the reader a glimpse of his intimate surroundings.

Novo's articles were opinionated and full of social, cultural, and political insights. He told the people of the Republic how life was in the historical, cultural, and financial center of Mexico City, what books to read, which plays to watch if visiting the capital, what highballs to drink, and what to comment about. Although Novo was officially a member of the administration, his opinion pieces, his job as a publicist, and his income as a real estate speculator provided him with the means to be independent. But he inexplicably belonged to the Partido Popular, the opposition party of Vicente Lombardo Toledano, whose most notable member was Diego Rivera.[3] Novo's membership in this party, his homosexuality, and his private businesses allowed the chronicler to be an insider and an outsider at the same time.

The growth of the middle class is significant from another angle also. The mesocracy reflected the image that Mexico had of itself politically and economically, a success linked to the elites' fear of losing power. Another important element to understanding Mexican politics of this time was thus the Red Scare, by which "the Alemán government denigrated its critics by accusing them of being communists and agents of the Soviet Union" (Meyer 165).

Finally, nationalism is a fundamental element to complete this picture, because the PRI (the Institutional Revolutionary Party) administration saw its purpose as protecting Mexico from foreign ideologies like communism and imperialism.[4] Communism and the Soviet Union were real threats in the eyes of the statist government, and the police watched socialist movements carefully. A communist like Diego Rivera had to channel his political weight through Partido Popular because of the many problems of acting publicly as a Soviet follower.

The second function of nationalism was to check the influence of the United States. It is impossible to understand Mexico without taking account of the omnipresence of the United States and the attempt by Mexican governments to buffer that influence by stressing the importance of Mexican national pride. However, the side effects of nationalism were parochialism and shortsighted cultural policies. This is where Novo intervened, because he was convinced that the right dose of Americanization in Mexico was vital for the survival of Mexican culture.

Salvador Novo's task in this process was double: first, to distinguish which elements of U.S. culture in particular and foreign culture in general should become part of *alemanista* Mexico, and, second, to open holes in the Mexican nationalist wall so that these carefully chosen elements could gain entrance. As a gatekeeper of Mexican culture he thought the country needed more foreign cultural influence to balance the insular tendencies on the part of the government and the cultural elite.

Novo in New York

The new president commissioned Novo to travel to the United States and Europe to learn more about the new mass medium—television—and advise him on the model Mexico should follow: public like BBC or private like CBS and NBC. Besides the official report Novo produced for the president, he informed his readers through the press.[5] This extraordinary travel narrative is a reflection on the role of Mexican culture on the international scene, its deficiencies and virtues. Novo's purpose was multiple. He intended to view as much theater as possible to get ready for his new job at INBA because he wanted to adapt some of Broadway culture for Mexican production. He also wanted to make New York accessible to those of the middle class who could afford the trip. He becomes a Mexican Fodor guide with information about where to stay, where to eat, how to fly, and what to watch.

On 9 October 1947, Novo departed from Mexico City and arrived in Houston at three in the afternoon, his only comment being, "la comida horrible" [awful food] (*Miguel Alemán* 20). At four he boarded a Constellation that had mechanical problems and arrived at La Guardia at two in the morning, three and a half hours after the scheduled arrival time. In the city, he encountered yet another problem: The reservations made by Carlos Chávez at the Savoy Plaza had been cancelled, so they were transferred to the Barbizon Plaza (today, Trump Parc) at 106 Central Park South. The mention of the malfunctioning airplane and other inefficiencies is important because these problems occurred in the United States, the supposed model of technology and efficiency, and not in Mexico.

Novo spent six days in New York before his departure to London on the *Queen Elizabeth*. His agenda during those days was exhausting. The first day he met biographer Herbert Weinstock of the Knopf publishing house, which was interested in publishing a translation of Novo's *México y la cultura* (Mexico and Culture), a project that never materialized. They ate at Sardi's. That night, Carlos Chávez and Novo attended the 1943 musical *Oklahoma!* by Richard Rogers and Oscar Hammerstein II. The second day they had lunch at the Plaza and watched an Italian movie; they could not go to the theater because it was Saturday and they could not get tickets. Sunday they ate again at the Plaza and attended Stokowski's concert at Carnegie Hall. Later Novo visited his aunt Virginia in Riverside, New York. Monday he went to Macy's to buy a typewriter but did not like the place, so full of "tumultuous and awful old women."[6] He ate at Longchamps, another famous restaurant in the theater district, had dinner at Sardi's again, and saw Irving Berlin's 1946 classic *Annie Get Your Gun*. Tuesday he visited CBS, where he was given a VIP tour of the facilities, went to Nicholas Acquavella's gallery, and at 5:30 visited Nelson Rockefeller (the future governor of New York and vice-president of the United States), who during the war had been coordinator of Inter-American Affairs, an anti-Nazi alliance for Latin America. Novo admired Rockefeller's Matisse chimney and the quality of the old-fashioneds served for cocktails. He had dinner at the Astor and watched the play *Harvey* by Mary Chase, which had won the Pulitzer Prize for drama in 1945. Wednesday he finally bought his typewriter at Rockefeller Center, visited NBC and went to the Central Station studios of CBS for a second time, and had dinner at the French restaurant Lafayette with Herbert Weinstock. Novo, famed in Mexico for his culinary prowess, for the first time praises a meal, canard à l'orange: "It was as if I had made it."[7] That night he attended *The Heiress*, performed by Basil Rathbone (the famous Sherlock Holmes of the 1930s), who won a Tony Award in 1946 for his performance in this play.

Thursday Novo visited Dolores del Río's friend Carmen López Figueroa, who with her sister Bicha appear on a regular basis in Novo's articles as neighbors in Coyoacán and people who are obligatory guests at cocktail parties in Mexico City. Novo describes her apartment ironically, for even if López Figueroa is Mexican her apartment is quintessentially nouveau riche American.[8] His description establishes a clear distinction between a tradition of Western culture and class that Mexico has enjoyed for more than four centuries and the new money so obvious in New York and among the Mexican arrivistes—the mirrors, the candelabra, and the shelves have to look old to legitimize the new money of their owners. The only decor that is genuinely old is worthless—old dictionaries chosen to match the color of the shelves. López Figueroa's is not a library accumulated by generations of readers in the household. Her living room is a stage on which Carmen and Salvador are acting while sharing a drink at the core of New York's café society, and this was not the only performance of the day. That night Carmen took Novo to a gay party hosted by the hat maker John Fredericks "y su amigo" [and his male friend] (26). Novo does not hide the fact of the hosts' homosexuality, referring openly to their bedroom.[9] The room is the epitome of camp queerness in the late 1940s; it featured an eight-hundred-dollar macaw (26).[10] On Friday the seventeenth, he packed his bags and then read *Time* magazine.

In London Novo saw an American comedy, *Born Yesterday* by Garson Kanin, with Laurence Olivier in the main role; he found the casting superb (41). He also attended two productions of classics, Euripides' *Medea* and Shakespeare's *Anthony and Cleopatra*. Two months later, after further travels throughout Europe, he was on the *Queen Mary* on his way back to New York. The trip was uneventful except for a conversation with Loretta Young about her sister, the actress Sally Blaine, also Novo's neighbor in Coyoacán.

Novo's best new friend on the ship was a poet whom he refers to as Margaret Stranger, "the widow of Barrymore" [la viudad de Barrymore] (95). It is probable that he is referring to Blanche Oelrich, also known as Michael Strange—it was common at the beginning of the twentieth century for female writers to use masculine pen names—the widow of the famous Shakespearean actor John Barrymore. It is not clear why Novo refers to her as Margaret Stranger, but the biographical details he provides in relation to Margaret Stranger correspond to those of Blanche Oelrich. They became "amigos de confianza" [intimate friends] (95).[11] Novo was strongly attracted to queer individuals, gay or straight people who crossed gender lines, such as strong female artists like Frida Kahlo, Guadalupe Marín, or Dolores del Río, or gay men who challenged the sexual and artistic status quo of two conservative societies like the United States and Mexico.

When Novo invited "Margaret Stranger" (a.k.a Blanche Oelrich/Michael Strange) for lunch a few days later, she invited him to the Colony Club, "the city's most exclusive and prestigious private women's social club" (Horsly), where she told him how terribly she missed her life in London. They decided to exchange books. Novo's most outstanding and controversial volume of verse, *Nuevo amor* (New Love), had been translated into English, and it is probable that this is the volume he gave to her.[12] After these adventures, Novo flew to Mexico City aboard the Constellation; his seatmate was a student of psychoanalysis from Topeka.

The purpose of the queer references during the trip was to open the minds of his middle-class readers who had to move from a Catholic, conservative, and Victorian (Porfirian) concept of decency to the postwar concept of democratic coexistence based on individual freedom and dignity. Novo wanted to adopt from the United States a concept of individual freedom that was more developed than in Mexico. After the war the American middle class was experiencing a stunning increase in personal freedom that Novo could detect by reading *Time* and *Life*, and he wanted as much as possible of that for Mexico.[13]

Novo was successful on his trip. He had been able to conduct himself as a businessman, a statesman, an intellectual, and a celebrity. He had moved among roles with ease and discretion. He had demonstrated to the *alemanista* middle class that a Mexican born and raised in that middle class could achieve cosmopolitism. At the same time, he promoted his role as a celebrity. He turned his life into a spectacle, with the politicians and businessmen whom he visited as supporting characters in the show.

The texts also reveal to us, as contemporary readers, how Novo was gathering information about not only television but also theater in order to prepare for his new job as director of theatrical productions of the art institute. He knew that the best theater in the world at that moment was in New York and London, and he wanted to see as much as possible and learn as much as he could. What all the plays he saw in New York and London have in common is that they were produced for the enlightenment and entertainment of the middle class, were technically perfect, and featured highly professional actors. Novo wanted all these virtues reproduced in INBA.

He was not as impressed by the theater he saw in other world capitals during the trip. Madrid was in crisis because of its dictatorship, and his visit there terrified Novo, who was surprised by the extent of the repression. However, his brief stay in Madrid did bring him closer to the Spanish exiles in Mexico. The theater of García Lorca and Valle-Inclán had been replaced by mannered and reactionary plays. A liberal playwright like Carlos Arniches was having problems adapting to the asphyxiating censorship. The proof that Novo was paying attention in Madrid is that as soon as he learned about *Historia de una escalera* (Story of a Stairway; 1949) by Antonio Buero Vallejo, he brought it to Mexico.

Novo also gave Paris a chance, but he was not optimistic. France was in a deep crisis too: political, social, economic, and moral. Vicente Lombardo Toledano, who happened to be in Paris at the time, told Novo that civil war was unavoidable. Novo saw a *Hamlet* translated by André Gide that he found effeminate, and in Brussels a *Joan of Arc* by Charles Péguy with Madame Ozeray. The only play he watched in Rome was also French, *I piu begli occhi del mondo* (The Most Beautiful Eyes in the World) by Jean Seruent with Renzo Ricci and Eva Magni. Novo thought that in Italian it had to be better than in French.

It is clear that Novo most enjoyed what he saw in the United States. Broadway offered everything: comedy, drama, melodrama, classical (Greek and Elizabethan), musical. The technical aspect of the plays was impeccable—lighting, makeup, music, props, sets. The actors knew their lines (prompters did not exist), and the acting was natural, with neither mannerism nor affectation. Novo also liked the idea of a middlebrow theater with enough cultural redundancy to satisfy the intellectual elite and to entertain the more mundane middle class while still making it think. His *Culta dama* (Cultured Lady; 1951) is the perfect example of theater for and from the bourgeoisie that Novo sought.

Michael Alderson in his summary of Novo's work at INBA explains how Novo translated into plays what he learned in New York and London. Initially Novo produced three Mexican plays by Agustín Lazo, Xavier Villaurrutia, and Rodolfo Usigli, as well as four foreign plays. But in 1950 Novo felt more confident in his post as director of theatrical productions. "The season of 1950 must have made nationalists turn over in their graves," Alderson writes. "Five works by Mexican authors were staged . . . and fourteen foreign plays" (xl). Novo chose plays by Jean-Paul Sartre, Eugene O'Neill, Luigi Pirandello, Euripides (*Medea*, as seen in London), Prosper Mérimée, Alejandro Casona, Edmond Rostand, Emmanuel Roblès, Conrado Nalé Roxlo, Noel Coward, and Lillian Hellman (*The Little Foxes*)—"performed in the original English!" (xli). He also presented, in English, *Trespass* by Evelyn Williams (as seen in London) and T. S. Eliot's *The Cocktail Party*. Later he staged Jean Genet's *The Maids*. What Novo brilliantly achieved was to insert Mexican plays into the context of Western culture. At the same time, he vaccinated Mexican culture against autarky and indigenism. What he saw in Madrid frightened him, a cultural desert in the shadow of the caudillo; and what he saw in Rome and Paris lacked the sophistication he wanted for Mexico.

Novo used the limited resources of his budget extremely well to turn Bellas Artes (the home of INBA) into a Broadway theater. He took advantage of the classiness of Bellas Artes, one of the most extraordinary theaters in the world, to insert it into the core of Western civilization.[14] Bellas Artes and Novo deserved each other.

Americans in Mexico City

Once Novo was back in Mexico, he supported three Americans who had an impact on a Mexican stage that would also bear the stamp of Broadway: Earl Sennett, the Japanese American Seki Sano, and the Mexican American José Limón.

Earl Sennett was the director of the Mexico City Players, an independent group that performed mainly in English. Sennett was talented, leftist, and gay. He associated with a wide range of international figures in Mexico at the time, including the exiled American Communist Party member John Herrman and William Burroughs, one of the writers of the Beat generation.[15] James Grauerholz, Burroughs's biographer and editor, wrote about Sennett and Ted Robins of San Francisco that "neither Sennett nor Robins ever married" (21). "Single," "living together," and "San Francisco" were code words for "gay." Novo could see in Sennett his alter ego, a good professional who made others accept his homosexual condition.

Novo saw the Mexico City Players for the first time performing Jean Anouihl's *Antígona* in the Methodist church of Mexico City, without sets and in contemporary clothes such as the *frac*—a jacket with tails—and tuxedo. Novo commended the production, the acting, and the way the company made a virtue of lack of means (*Miguel Alemán* 127). We can appreciate his admiration in what he says after the Players performed Oscar Wilde's *Salomé* at the garden of the Banisters in San Ángel:

> This Earl Sennett is admirable. An example of tenacity and ingenuity for independent theater groups. Ours expect everything to fall in their laps from providence or the government, and while they wait for the miracle they do not do anything. Earl has put together a group of young Americans and Mexicans whom he trains and then stages their comedies and dramas wherever he can in the best way possible. Eustace Bourchier, Kay Millar and Francis Carnes are in charge of lighting. Luis de Unzueta is the director. The acting is done by fifteen individuals. The costumes and everything else were perfect and found in the beautiful garden the perfect frame. It broke my heart to think how the actors endured the freezing cold, half-naked on the wet grass and while Salomé was dancing barefoot. I myself was shivering because of the wind from the North. (206)[16]

There are some key ideas here. Independent groups have to be really independent. They have to work as if the government did not exist. They also have to aim for perfection, even if they do not act in professional venues. Very professional work can be done by Mexicans and Americans when they work together. All parts of the production have to be taken care of by the acting troupe: costumes, lighting, direction, and acting. They all are equally important. Novo avoids all references to imperialism, nationalism, or victimization. It is just a group of young people from two countries who work together without significant problems and with outstanding results. Novo stresses continuously their ability to work in all kinds of places (325). The message here is that Mexican artists and entrepreneurs of all kinds have to take the first step in whatever endeavor they pursue and forget about getting any public help. The fact that Mexico is not a developed country is not a valid excuse to stop following artistic impulses. It is also the job of the upper class to sponsor this kind of cultural event, as is done on a regular basis in the United States. It brings the upper class prestige and legitimacy.

On 9 June 1948, Novo characterizes Sennett's staging (*puestas de escena*) as "cuidadas, pulidas, perfectas" [careful, polished, perfect]. Novo asked Sennett to do *Little Foxes* in Bellas Artes, and he commented after the performance that it had been perfect (518). As Alderson had already noticed, it is commendable that Novo dared to stage plays in English in Bellas Artes, the epitome of Mexican pride. Such small steps can lead to permanent cultural change.

The other two Americans who arrived about the same time as Sennett were the producer of Tennessee Williams's *A Streetcar Named Desire*, Seki Sano, and the Mexican American choreographer José Limón. Novo had met Williams at the Covarrubiases' and was curious about the production of *Streetcar* by the Japanese American Seki Sano (*Miguel Alemán* 194).[17] One of the actors, Luis Manuel Pelayo, had worked for Novo in his theatrical adaptation for children of *Don Quijote*. Blanche was played by Mary Douglas (202). Novo was puzzled by the presence in the cast of the wrestler Wolf Rubinsky. It is interesting to note that *Streetcar* is quixotic, because it deals with the topic of reality and appearance in the context of a society in which gentlemen have disappeared. It is also about the transition between eras, homosexuality, and, in our case, the role of American culture in Mexico. *Streetcar* is a key text in the history of Western civilization in the twentieth century. It challenges the compulsory morality of the Victorian period and defends the new concept of personal dignity and freedom: In the play a false concept of decency hides homosexuality, incest, and domestic violence and does not let the characters be themselves.

At first, Tennessee Williams did not authorize this production, and Dorsey Fisher of the U.S. embassy, a close friend of Novo, had to intercede to get the necessary permits. Novo attended the premier and did not like the length of the play (more than three and a half hours) nor the fact that Sano did not censor the play as the movie did. Novo says that families were shocked when they saw Rubinsky take Mary Douglas to bed (*Miguel Alemán* 229). Nevertheless, as he did with Sennett, Novo invited this production to be performed at Bellas Artes (212). Novo had to defend the hiring of Seki Sano because the Union of Authors did not want foreign directors working in Bellas Artes (285–86). The press tried to create friction between the two men, but Novo stood firm about hiring Seki Sano. In 1949, Novo received an invitation from Dorsey Fisher, who was going to have a party to celebrate the one-hundredth production of *Streetcar* and the success of the play (320). By that time Novo had had many problems with Seki Sano and declined the invitation, but this does not detract from the influence that the success of the play had on Mexican theater and theatrical productions.[18]

The last direct influence of U.S. theater in Mexico that Novo notes in his articles is that of José Limón. Limón, born in Mexico, had lived most of his life in the United States. His father, like Novo's, was from Spain. At the end of the 1940s, Limón was a famous choreographer. He went on to a long and successful career and became director of the Lincoln Center's American Dance Theater from 1964 to 1965 ("José Limón").

Novo met Limón at a welcome reception for the choreographer at the Covarrubiases'. Limón's subsequent presentation at Bellas Artes began in March 1950 and continued during 1951; in 1952 Amalia Hernández founded the Ballet Folklórico de México. Novo's summary of Limón's choreography is informative and entertaining:

Dance is not yet an independent specialty in Mexico from the point of view of critics. The specialists in music, theater, society and generalists were present. They all enjoyed *The Moor's Pavana* very much, but there was a lot of disagreement regarding *Malinche* and *Llanto por Ignacio Sánchez Mejías*. The Spaniards did not like the last at all. Maybe they were expecting an *españolada* with an Andalusian sky. And then there were the Mexican painters with the same myopia who, regarding *Malinche*, did not understand that Limón did not intend to use realism or a precise tracing of history. They found the costumes inappropriate and by now quite biased did not perceive the perfect synthesis of symbols that Limón achieves in that ballet—for example the cross that becomes a sword, or plow, nor the Orozco influence that inspires many moments of the dance. (*Miguel Alemán* 418)[19]

Like many of Novo's paragraphs, this one is priceless. The public, Mexican and Spanish, liked the American part of the repertoire, *The Moor's Pavana* based on *Othello*. But they did not enjoy the Mexican and Spanish part of the ballet because they expected a more essentialist nationalism. Novo enjoyed everything—especially the use of Orozco to interpret the myth of Malinche, as he did in the fresco of San Ildefonso. The intellectual elite formed by Mexicans and Spaniards did not enjoy the middlebrow, Broadway-like vision of Mexican and Spanish culture.

On 14 April 1951, in a long article, Novo reminds readers that Limón had arrived in Mexico the year before. Limón was born in Sinaloa in 1908, he reports, but his parents took him to the United States as a child. Miguel Covarrubias brought Limón to Mexico when he was in charge of the dance department of the art institute. Once in Mexico, he became very interested in autochthonous dances such as the deer dance of Sonora or colonial dances like *morismas*. These dances, catalogued by Professor Efrén Orozco and Luis Felipe Obregón, Novo explains, are rich in color but poor and monotonous in their choreography. The dancers do not move their arms, and move their bodies only from the waist down. In Mexico City, a group like Los Concheros knows pre-Hispanic dance and transmits this knowledge from father to son, but they are repetitive. Novo explains that these dances are the equivalent of popular art, like *metates* or ceramics.[20]

By contrast Novo explains what Rivera, Orozco, and Siqueiros have meant for Mexican painting. They use popular elements, but they are excellent painters recognized worldwide. They transcend the naïve, perspectiveless form of the popular; add tragedy, landscape, and history; and as a result professionalize the commoners' art. According to Novo, Mexican dance had to follow a similar process to survive and improve, because as a popular art it was not successful. Cabarets and *revistas* (variety theater) adopted indigenous dances but they did not improve them. The *revistas* also adopted colonial dances, but they mixed up traditions without respect for them, such as using *chino* and *china poblano* costumes with the music of mariachis.[21]

Novo criticizes the Campobello sisters and Walden and Ana Sokolov because they put modern and indigenous dances together with barefoot performers, long skirts, hieratic and sexual gestures, sighs, and pushes that did not become organic dances.[22] Traditional Mexican dances did not need avant-garde choreographies. They did ballets like *La coronela* and *El renacuajo paseador* by Silvestre Revueltas, mixing traditional and avant-garde techniques, but what they needed, according to Novo, were choreographies closer to the Broadway musical. It was in 1947 that INBA created the Academia de Danza Mexicana with a department of research and creation. The administration understood that Mexican dance needed a new direction but did not know how to define it. One problem was that many women wanted to perform dance but very few men did. In addition, Ana Sokolov had her students and Ana Mérida hers; the same was true for Guillermina Bravo and Gloria Mestre. They were not able to integrate the parts. Then Carlos Chávez asked Miguel Covarrubias, who had seen Limón's work in New York, to head the dance department, and Covarrubias thought of Limón to bring the right influences.

Covarrubias and Limón worked well together because neither sought to promote a personal agenda, and they were able to bring order to chaos. Limón taught technique and discipline and adapted to work "a la mexicana" (Novo, *Miguel Alemán* 494) amid arguments, scarce resources, and little time. In one instance, the symphonic orchestra was not available during the less than three weeks the company had to rehearse a ballet. In another example of their creative teamwork, Covarrubias and Limón did *Tonanzintla* based on the extraordinary decoration of the Baroque church of Santa María Tonanzintla in Puebla. The dance illustrates the birthday of a mermaid with whom the other sculptures dance. Miguel Covarrubias's set included the arches of the church and baroque angels on pedestals. They also did *Los cuatro soles* by Carlos Chávez and *Diálogos* with Cortés and Cuauhtémoc and Maximiliano and Juarez. Novo contributed to part of the script of an *Antígona* (562–63).

Limón had arrived with a reception at the Covarrubias and left Mexico after a paella at Novo's house. Novo wrote on the Spanish dish "Viva José Limón" with red pepper; as sons of Spaniards they ate the Spanish national specialty, incorporating the colors of the flag. The influence of Limón had been outstanding. In 1951 the national institute of art put on four Mexican ballets, by Elena Noriega (music by Francisco Domínguez), Guillermo Arriaga (music by Blas Galindo), Rosa Reina (music by Mabarak) and Guillermo Keys (music by Bernal Jiménez). Keys's *El chueco* is "Mexicano en la forma, universal en el contenido" [Mexican in form, universal in content]. Novo saw it as putting together a painting by Orozco and a popular tableau: an "extraordinary ballet that the people received with delirious and justified ovations" (570).[23]

For Novo the explanation of this success is simple: "Artists have understood that neither inspiration nor genius is enough. It is indispensable to master technique" (571).[24] This goal, already achieved in painting, was now being realized for dance, thanks to a Mexican American and a pool of Mexican talent. Novo also observes how the "-isms" of Mexican art that refused to adopt technique were not having good results. He labels them "autoerotism" [mental masturbation], nothing more than tautologies that start and end up in themselves. Novel, poetry, theater: They all need technique. He mentions that he is at that moment reading plays for a contest, and he regrets that most of them are written without regard for technique. Broadway, instead of the avant-garde, was the answer to the ailments of Mexican dance. Broadway had color, happiness, queerness, and—as the song that Novo heard in one of the plays he watched in New York says, "There's no business like show business," that is, professionalism and a sense of entertainment, because a fossilized and anachronistic avant-garde could not renew Mexican dance. (This criticism is particularly significant coming from one of the best authors of the avant-garde in Spanish.)

Broadway, Sennett, *Streetcar*, and Limón are the influences Novo wanted for his national culture. The irony is that Mexican traditional dances that have become part of Mexican nationalism and are performed regularly in Bellas Artes reached this stage thanks to the influence of a Mexican American who studied and worked in New York.

Braceros and U.S. Politics

Novo enjoyed many aspects of the United States and its culture, as we have seen. He was bilingual, an avid reader of *Time* magazine, an admirer of U.S. literature and cinema; he had relatives in the United States and had even spent time up north during a brief exile during the Cárdenas administration. This did not add up, however, to an uncritical acceptance of the political and social policies of the United States.

Stephen B. Morris in *Gringolandia* dedicates one chapter to the vision of the United States held by what he calls "the intellectual elite" (159–87). One disturbing aspect of his findings is "the U.S. as a backdrop to define and describe Mexico": "Typical of this approach, analysts employ an incredibly wide range of oppositional or Manichaean categories to depict the U.S. and Mexico, prompting the notion that the U.S. represents the opposite of the Mexican, or as Castañeda contends, as 'radically, substantially and fiercely distinct from the U.S.' " (161). Among the intellectuals besides Castañeda who have taken this approach, we find Octavio Paz, Carlos Fuentes, Carlos Monsiváis, and José Vasconcelos. Once again, Salvador Novo stands out as different. He does not fall into phony epistemological traps. He adapts and makes Mexican what he enjoys, without an inferiority complex, and experiences firsthand with enthusiasm the cultural movements he admires.[25] (For example, he read the Harlem Renaissance poets while that artistic movement was in vogue.) At the same time, he demands dignity for his compatriots who do an honest job, even if they are poor.

At the time he was promoting North American theater art in Mexico City, Novo was also commenting on U.S. politics regarding Mexico, especially the contemporary bracero crisis. According to Lorenzo Meyer, more than three hundred thousand Mexicans were hired under the 1942 agreement between the two governments, and "an even larger number crossed illegally into the United States with the U.S. authorities' tolerance" (162). In March 1951 the *New York Times* estimated that "a million Mexicans entered the United States illegally in search of work," Meyer reports (167). August of 1951 and 1954 saw new bracero programs. What is important for Meyer from a cultural point of view is that two stereotypes were born with these programs, that of the "poor, dirty, uneducated Mexican of low social status" and that of the "discrimination and exploitation of Mexicans" by people in the United States (167). Analysts agree that the policies of the United States regarding Mexico are inconsistent, but the relationship between the two countries through immigration, vacation and retirement, family ties, mixed companies and trade, education, mass media, and drug trafficking is always developing, independently of the policies implemented by the two governments ("A Survey of Mexico").

On 30 January 1948, Novo reports on twenty-eight braceros who died while they were being deported back to Mexico in an airplane carrying thirty-one passengers that had a capacity for only twenty-one. Novo criticizes both governments for trying to make of this tragedy nothing more than a regrettable incident (*Miguel Alemán* 106). He also points out that during the war, when these men were badly needed, the paperwork was secondary; now that the war was over, suddenly papers were all-important.

In a 7 February chronicle Novo uses the word "imperialism" twice. It is not related to the bracero program but to foreign protectionism. His publicity company was in charge of the account of Aerolíneas Guest, which ran the Mexico–Madrid flight; the United States and Great Britain were boycotting the company. The United States allowed the company access only to border airports, where the travelers had to make connections with Pan-American and American Airlines. Great Britain tried to route the Mexico–Madrid flight through London.

In an additional note, Novo regrets that two young men had beaten up the consul of Mexico in San Antonio. He was not robbed, but—Novo quotes the official report—the authorities "rejected any political motive or revenge." Novo's comment is: "In other words, they may have confused the consul of Mexico with a Mexican—and they proceeded accordingly" (111).[26] What these three examples have in common is that they are substantiated happenings. This is not empty propaganda but commentary on the death of twenty-eight men because of the negligence of the U.S. government, economic protectionism that hurts Novo's client, and brutal racism against the consul of a foreign country. Adding insult to injury, in all the cases the authorities from both countries try to cover the incidents up. Novo's journalistic expertise also lends credence to his words.

It is important to stress how balanced Novo's reporting is. He denounces as equally bad the negligence of the government of the United States and the attempt of the Mexican government to hide the circumstances behind the attack on or minimize the death of twenty-eight Mexicans. On 3 April, he tells the story of Miguel from Guadalajara, who pawned his two horses to go to the United States. Like the rest of the braceros he went to Chapultepec Park to be hired. The authorities dispersed the workers because the press had complained about these invaders, who disturbed decent families drinking their Coca-Colas amid the beauty of the park. Miguel was not going to be defeated that easily. He wanted to return triumphantly to his town and recover his horses, Vencedor and Lucero. He bribed the corresponding authorities (132–33). Novo was always against *mordidas* (bribes) and saw them as a significant problem.

On 17 September, he returns to the topic when thousands of braceros crossed the border without a contract. The Mexican government wanted regulated contracts for the workers, and the American employers wanted to offer lower salaries. The logic of the market triumphed with the acquiescence of the U.S. government. Novo blames both governments (200–201).

Novo could have chosen to avoid controversial issues and concentrate on culture and gossip. Instead he decided to write about immigration, in which he dealt out harsh criticism to the governments of both the United States and Mexico while reminding his middle-class readers that human rights applied to everybody. The economic boom in the United States after the war was bringing a dignity to the working class that Mexico was not used to. For many Mexicans, *nacos* and *indios*— the indigenous and lower class—were not people.

On 13 January 1950, Novo reports that he usually receives more fan mail from the United States than from Mexico. That day he received two letters, one from Tujunga, California, in which a reader writes to him in Spanish that he finds him *antiyanki* (anti-American). Novo says that he does not know how to answer that. The other letter is from an inmate in the New Jersey State Prison in Trenton who writes in English with two questions about Spanish. It seems that he was studying Spanish by reading Novo (382–83).

On 25 October 1950 Novo asks himself about the people he knows who are having trouble getting visas to visit the United States. They are Fernando Wagner, director and professor of theater at the National Autonomous University (UNAM); the dancer Guillermo Arriaga; and the president of UNAM, Luis Garrido. Novo contrasts these arbitrary decisions with the number of U.S. tourists walking the streets of Mexico City in red hats (422–23). At the same time, Novo receives a letter from Emilio Carballido, who is in the United States on a scholarship, studying theater. Like Novo, Carballido describes what he enjoys and criticizes what he does not like. He liked the playwright "Seyril Schocham" (Seyril Schocken) and did not like Dallas: "odiosa ciudad, fea, chata y cursi" [hateful, ugly, narrow-minded, and tacky city] (424).

The Korean War rekindled the U.S. need for Mexican braceros, and Novo commented extensively on the matter on 17 February 1951. He first remarks on the discrimination they suffer in barbershops and restaurants and the fact that they will be expelled again once they are no longer needed. Novo makes the reader pay attention to a new phenomenon in mass media: that venues in various languages may offer information that a single media source is trying to conceal. The Mexican secretary of foreign relations fell into this trap. While the official position from Mexico City was that in new conversations scheduled to begin soon, the rights of Mexican workers were going to be the priority, Novo reveals that in Washington the conversations had already started. Senator Allen Ellender (D-Louisiana) had told the press that Mexico had already agreed to send fifty-five thousand workers to the United States and to leave in the United States thirty thousand who were already there, "arraigados" [rooted]. Mexico had also agreed not to request twenty-five dollars per worker from the U.S. employers and to allow police to apprehend in the United States workers who did not fulfill their contracts (Novo, *Miguel Alemán* 462–64).

Novo also denounces the way Mexican unions rubber-stamp decisions of the Alemán administration. Again, for Novo, as guilty as the United States might be, it is his own government he blames for failing to defend the rights of Mexican workers.

Meanwhile, more and more tourists are coming to Mexico from the United States: "The owners are coming in and the slaves are leaving" (464).[27] Novo is right: On 16 June there is news of airplanes landing in Guadalajara and San Luis Potosí, bringing back deported braceros, and two workers committed suicide in Monterrey when they were rejected as unfit to work in the United States (519).

Novo congratulates himself toward the end of July because the Rockefeller Foundation has given five young Mexican writers $1,500 scholarships: Juan José Arreola, Rubén Bonifaz Nuño, Emilio Carballido, Sergio Magaña, and Herminio Chávez Guerrero. Novo is happy because he knows four of them, and Magaña and Carballido were his "discoveries"—he invited these two to eat green tallarini. Novo regrets that similar scholarships do not exist in Mexico. During this same period, the Mexico City Writing Center invited him to give a lecture, although they were reluctant because of his fame as an *antiyanki*. Novo contends, "No lo soy sistemáticamente" [I am not systematically anti-Yankee] (529). He enjoyed the experience and was paid a symbolic fifty pesos.

In a 29 December article dedicated to the youth of Mexico, Novo enumerates many of the U.S. influences in Mexican society, neither condemning nor praising them: strapless dresses, Halloween parties, bridal and baby showers, and quick lunches of a sub and a Coca-Cola (580).

While other Mexican intellectuals have elaborated complex dichotomies about the differences between the United States and Mexico, Novo consumed and enjoyed American culture and adapted what he liked. At the same time, he criticized the abuses of the U.S. government and his own without using a rhetoric of victimhood. According to Novo, Mexicans had to learn how to use the tools of the trade, modern capitalism, and Western art, without forgetting their own roots. At the beginning of the new president's term, he decided to learn Náhuatl.

NOTES

1. I use the term "braceros" to refer to Mexican laborers, both documented and undocumented, who came to work in the United States after World War II, a term used both in Mexican and U.S. official and press texts to refer to these workers at this time. For extensive discussion of the power of queer elements in shaping Mexican culture during the 1930s and 1940s, see my book *The Contemporáneos Group: Rewriting Mexico in the Thirties and Forties*.

2. See Sheridan's *Los contemporáneous ayer* for a thorough history of the political and cultural influence and the public attacks suffered by Novo and the others writers and artists of the *Contemporáneos* group.

3. Founded by Vicente Lombardo Toledano in 1947, the Partido Popular was a leftist political party that brought together intellectuals like José Revueltas, David Alfaro Siqueiros, Diego Rivera, and Novo's protector during his youth, Narciso Bassols.

4. The Revolutionary National Party became the Institutional Revolutionary Party (with the acronym PRI in Spanish) in 1946. It governed Mexico as a state party for more than six decades.

5. He intended to publish this travel narrative as a book like his others travel volumes—*Return Ticket: viaje a Hawaii* (Return Ticket: Trip to Hawaii; 1928); *Jalisco–Michoacán: 12 días* (Jalisco–Michoacán: 12 Days; 1933); or his extraordinary *Continente vacío: viaje a Sudamérica* (Empty Continent: Trip to South America; 1933)—but he never did. The television mission—pages 19–97 of the 1994 edition of *La vida en México en el periodo presidencial de Miguel Alemán* (Life in Mexico during the Presidency of Miguel Aleman)—deserves to be published as an illustrated book with the official report as an appendix. (See also Mary Long's superb 1996 analysis of *Continente vacío*.) All Novo citations in the text and notes are from the 1994 edition, hereafter labeled *Miguel Alemán*.

6. "viejas tumultuosas y horrendas" (*Miguel Alemán* 22). All translations to English are mine.

7. "estaba como si yo lo hubiera hecho" (*Miguel Alemán* 24).

8. "Su departamento es muy grande y muy *chic*. Lo decoran estos espejos enormes, artificialmente oxidados, y estos candelabros con que los americanos pugnan denodadamente por asirse a una tradición que les falta; a un aire antiguo y respetable, distinguido y fino, que no logra ser más que costoso, y que aún así, enseña el cobre del artificio. La biblioteca, por ejemplo, es de estantes de madera apolilladas antes de construirlos, y está llena de volúmenes idénticos de diccionarios del XVIII, de un color uniforme que "va" muy bien con los estantes" [Her apartment is large and very chic. It is decorated with enormous mirrors that are artificially rusty, and by candelabra with which Americans strive tirelessly to claim a tradition that they lack; an old and respectable air, distinguished and refined, that only manages to be expensive and shows the true colors of affectation. The library, for instance, is made of shelves out of wood that is worm-eaten, before they make the shelves. It is full of identical volumes of dictionaries of the eighteenth century, of a uniform color that "goes" very well with the shelves] (*Miguel Alemán* 25).

9. "antes de marcharnos entramos en la recámara de los anfitriones" [before leaving we entered the bedroom of the hosts] (*Miguel Alemán* 26).

10. "El pajarraco nos miraba con desdén desde la jaula cubierta en que reposa sobre el ropero de terciopelo rojo capitonado frente a la cama de doble ancho que coronan dos rollizos cupidos, y que iluminan otros dos desde las mesillas laterales de espejos— naturalmente oxidados" [The big, ugly bird looked at us disdainfully from the cage in which it rests over the red and padded velvet armoire in front of the double bed crowned with two chubby cupids and illuminated by two more cupids from the mirrored nightstands, these being naturally rusty] (*Miguel Alemán* 26).

11. "Era encantador su desenfado, sus maneras bruscas y hombrunas, la rapidez con que soltaba barbaridades inteligentes a borbotones, la rudeza con que exponía sus opiniones literarias sobre, por ejemplo, Jean Cocteau, que fue en París su vecino de estudio y una vez se le apareció todo pintado y angustiadísimo porque se le estaba muriendo, intoxicado por el opio, un chico de los que ha improvisado literatos. '*Get the hell out of here*,' le gritó Margaret, '*I hate the guts of you, you dirty bitch!*' " [Her forwardness was charming, including her brusque and masculine manners and the way she gushed out witty remarks. She was rude when giving her literary opinions. For instance, Jean Cocteau was her neighbor in Paris. One day he showed up drugged and anguished because his young lover was dying of opium poisoning. Margaret yelled at him: "Get the hell out of here. I hate your guts, you dirty bitch!"] (*Miguel Alemán* 95).

12. *Nuevo Amor* was first published in Spanish in 1933, translated into English by Edna Worthly Underwood, and published in the United States in 1935. It is significant both as a masterpiece of avant-garde poetry and for its open exploration of homosexual love. As Carlos Monsivais has observed: "En *Nuevo amor* la piel es el territorio del ideal y el personaje poético es el ser ansioso de la plenitud que le niegan los prejuicios. . . . En sus sonetos 'secretos,' Novo elige un lenguaje suntuoso y el modelo por lo común es Sor Juana Inés de la Cruz, la cumbre canónica. Un idioma del Siglo de Oro y un impecable oído literario se ponen al servicio de las admisiones más terribles en el ámbito de la intimidad" [In *New Love*, skin is the territory of the ideal and the poetic figure is the being anxious to achieve the plenitude that prejudice denies him. . . . In his "secret" sonnets, Novo selects a sumptuous idiom and the model is most commonly that of Sor Juana Inés de la Cruz, that towering canonical giant. A language from the Golden Age and an impeccable literary ear put to the service of the most terrible admissions ever in intimacy's arena] (98, 101). For extensive discussion of the neo-baroque and the links between gay and baroque literatures also see Chapters 1 and 2 of my 2003 book, *The Contemporáneos Group*.

13. "A la vanguardia cultural le urge romper el aislamiento que ha caracterizado a México, estar al día de las experiencias de la modernidad" [The vanguard feels an urge to break the isolation that has characterized Mexico, to bring itself up to date with the experiences of modernity] (Monsiváis 88). "En *Novo*, a través de Novo, estos seres [homosexuales] valientes son presentados como emblemas de la modernidad a causa de su sexualidad: 'La precocidad va a la par de la compulsión sexual. Novo se considera triunfalmente moderno, y esto implica la eliminación del arrepentimiento y el afán de extremar el comportamiento ultrajante. Entonces, el amaneramiento depende no sólo de circunstancias biológicas, sino del estilo que convierte en placer psicólogico la "imposición de la fisiología." Aun para sí mismo, un homosexual no "afeminado" es una rareza y en Novo el "afeminamiento" es vigoroso, la aureola que es la más efectiva tarjeta de presentación' " [In *Novo*, through Novo, these courageous [homosexual] beings are presented as emblems of modernity precisely because of their sexuality: "Precociousness goes hand in hand with sexual compulsion. Novo considers

himself triumphantly modern, and this implies the elimination of repentance and an impulse to extremely aggravating behavior. Thus, his effeminate mannerisms depend not only on biological circumstances, but on a style that turns the 'imposition of physiology' into psychological pleasure. Even for himself, a non-effeminate gay is a rarity and in Novo, the effeminate character is very strong, the aura that is his most effective way to present himself"] (Monsiváis 43–44).

14. Bellas Artes is an extraordinary building, the jewel of the Porfiriato. It joins the center of the Ancien Régime, the Zócalo, and the most important space of the New Regime, the Paseo de la Reforma. Designed by architect Adamo Boari, it was the first art nouveau building in Mexico City and with its three vaults—the central and one on each side, according to the *Historia de arquitectura*, it had a "width, lighting and space very unusual at that time" (Chanfón Olmos 443).

15. "A photograph in the November 16, 1950, issue of M.C.C.'s [Mexico City College] student paper, the *Collegian*, shows Earl Sennett speaking to twelve students in his 'Studio Stages' drama group; among them . . . John Herrmann" (en.wikipedia.org/wiki/John_Herrmann, accessed 26 September 2006).

16. "Este Earl Sennett es admirable. Un ejemplo de tenacidad y de ingenio para los grupos libres de teatro, que entre nosotros todo lo esperan de la Providencia o del gobierno, y que mientras ocurre el milagro, no hacen nada. Earl ha reunido a un grupo de jóvenes americanos y mexicanos, los adiestra y ponen sus comedias o sus dramas donde pueden, pero lo mejor posible. La iluminación, a cargo de Eustace Bourchier, Kay Millar y Francis Carnes; la dirección por Luis de Unzueta; la actuación de los quince personajes, su vestuario, fue todo perfecto, y halló en el hermoso jardín el más adecuado marco. Partía el alma considerar el frío que tendrían los actores, semidesnudos en el pasto húmedo, y Salomé bailando descalza, cuando uno mismo estaba tiritando, gracias al 'norte.' "

17. The painter Miguel Covarrubias along with his wife, Rosa, a well-known dancer, were key figures in the Mexican cultural scene for several decades and also spent significant amounts of time living and working in New York. In her biography of Miguel, Adriana Williams describes the significance of their home in Mexico at this time: "At the time Tizapán was a quiet village twenty-five miles outside of Mexico City, a desert oasis of flowers and trees, open-air markets, and rambling colonial homes. Miguel and Rosa Covarrubias made their home here, at Number Five Calle Reforma. It became a well-known address in the 1930s and 1940s to both native and foreign artists of all disciplines. Many believed this period was Mexico's artistic Golden Age, and Number Five served Mexico City's intellectual and artistic membership as a gathering place much the way the Algonquin Hotel served New York's or Virginia Woolf's home served London's or Gertrude Stein's did Paris's" (xiii).

18. In the three volumes of *La vida en México en el periodo presidencial de Adolfo Ruiz Cortines* (Life in Mexico during the Presidency of Adolfo Ruiz Cortines), Sano is named frequently, and it seems that he and Novo were on good terms again.

19. "Como la danza en México no ha alcanzado a constituir una especialidad desde el punto de vista de la crítica, estuvieron los especialistas en la música, en el teatro, en la sociedad y en las generalidades. A todos les gustó mucho *La pavana del moro*, pero por cuanto a *Malinche* y al *Llanto por Ignacio Sánchez Mejías*, hubo sus discrepancias en los pasillos. Los españoles no estaban muy conformes con este último número. Seguramente se esperaban una 'españolada' con 'cielo andaluz.' Y hubo pintores mexicanos que con la misma miopía para entender que Limón no se propone la arqueología ni el realismo, hallaron inadecuado el vestuario de la Malinche, y ya prejuiciados, no percibieron la feliz síntesis de los símbolos que en ese ballet logra

Limón, por ejemplo con el juego de la cruz que se vuelve espada, o arado, ni la inspiración orozquiana que inspira muchos momentos de esa danza." Novo in this passage is referring to Orozco's fresco at San Ildefonso in Mexico City, in which he painted a strong Cortés, naked, protecting an equally strong Malinche, who is also naked and expressionless. A fallen body representing the defeated *mexicas* is in front of them.

20. A *metate* is a flat or partly hollowed stone on which corn is ground with a smaller stone called *mano* (hand). Tourists somehow have been interested in these "arts" but they have helped to degrade them by demanding very low-quality products. Novo's complaint is that tourists instead of purchasing good pieces made by local artisans just want the cheapest product, as long as it looks rustic and authentic. Artisans respond to the new demand for bad and inexpensive products and thus devalue their craft.

21. Mariachis are from Jalisco, and the *china poblana* costume is from Puebla. For Novo this is an unacceptable hybrid.

22. The Campobello sisters, Nellie and Gloria, were pioneers in the recuperation of autochthonous dances in Mexico. Nellie (1909–1986) is the famous author of *Cartucho* (1931).

23. "Ballet extraordinario que la gente recibió con delirantes y merecidas ovaciones."

24. "Los artistas han comprendido que no basta la inspiración ni el genio, sino que es indispensable la técnica y su dominio."

25. For discussions of Novo's confident approach to North American culture in an earlier era, see Long, "Salvador Novo" (217) and "Writing the City" (196), as well as her more in-depth discussion of a supposed Mexican inferiority complex in Chapter 1 of this collection.

26. "Descartaron todo motivo político o de venganza." "En otras palabras: deben de haber confundido el cónsul de México con un mexicano—y procedieron en consecuencia."

27. "Siguen entrando amos y siguen saliendo esclavos."

WORKS CITED

"A Survey of Mexico." *The Economist*, 18 November 2006, 1–16.

Alderson, Michael. "Introduction: About the Author." *The War of the Fatties and Other Stories from Aztec History*, by Salvador Novo. Trans. Michael Alderson. Austin: University of Texas Press, 1994. ix–lx.

Camp, Roderic Ai. *Mexican Political Biographies, 1935–1993*. Austin: University of Texas Press, 1995.

Campobello, Nellie. *Cartucho: relatos de la lucha en el norte de México*. (1931). Mexico, D.F.: Ediciones Era, 2000.

Chanfón Olmos, Carlos, ed. *Historia de la arquitectura y el urbanismo mexicanos*. Vol. 3. *El México independiente*. Vol. 2. *Afirmación del nacionalismo y la modernidad*. Mexico: Universidad Nacional Autonoma de México; Fondo de Cultura Económica, 1998.

Cline, Howard F. *The United States and Mexico*. Cambridge, Mass.: Harvard University Press, 1963.

Grauerholz, James W. "The Death of Joan Vollmer Burroughs: What Really Happened." Paper prepared for the Fifth Congress of the Americas at Universidad de las Americas, Puebla, 18 October 2001. *old.lawrence.com/burroughs/deathofjoan-full.pdf*. 7 January 2002.

Horsley, Carter B. "Colony Club." *www.thecityreview.com/ues/parkave/colonyc.html.* 26 September 2006.

———. "Trump Parc." *www.thecityreview.com/cps/cps106.html.* 21 September 2006.

"José Limón." Limon Dance Company Institute and Foundation. *www.limon.org/Heritage/Limon.html.* 2 October 2006.

Long, Mary K. "Salvador Novo: 1920–1940: Between the Avant-garde and the Nation." Ph.D. diss., Princeton University, 1995.

———. "Salvador Novo's *Continente vacío.*" *Latin American Literary Review* 24.47 (1996): 91–114.

———. "Writing the City: The Chronicles of Salvador Novo." *The Contemporary Mexican Chronicle: Theoretical Perspectives on the Liminal Genre.* Ed. Ignacio Corona and Beth E. Jörgensen. New York: State University of New York Press, 2002. 181–201.

Meyer, Lorenzo. "The Vicissitudes of Normality: 1941–1970." *The United States and Mexico.* Ed. Josefina Zoraida Vázquez and Lorenzo Meyer. Chicago and London: Chicago University Press, 1985.

Monsiváis, Carlos. *Salvador Novo: lo marginal en el centro.* México: Era, 2000.

Morris, Stephen D. *Gringolandia: Mexican Identity and Perceptions of the United States.* Lanham, Md.: Rowman and Littlefield, 2005.

Novo, Salvador. *La culta dama.* Mexico: Fondo de Cultura Económica, 1956.

———. *La vida en México en el periodo presidencial de Adolfo Ruiz Cortines.* Ed. José Emilio Pacheco. 3 vols. Mexico: Consejo Nacional para la Cultura y las Artes, 1994.

———. *La vida en México en el periodo presidencial de Miguel Alemán.* Ed. José Emilio Pacheco. Mexico: Consejo Nacional para la Cultura y las Artes, 1994.

———. *Nuevo amor.* México: Talleres de la Mundial, 1933.

———. *Nuevo amor.* Trans. Edna Worthly Underwood. Portland, Me.: Mosher Press, 1935.

Oropesa, Salvador A. *The Contemporáneos Group: Rewriting Mexico in the Thirties and Forties.* Austin: University of Texas Press, 2003.

Sheridan, Guillermo. *Los contemporaneous ayer.* Mexico: Fondo de Cultura Económica, 1985.

Smith, Peter H. *Labyrinths of Power: Political Recruitment in Twentieth-Century Mexico.* Princeton: Princeton University Press, 1979.

———. "Mexico since 1946: Dynamics of an Authoritarian Regime." *Mexico since Independence.* Ed. Leslie Bethell. Cambridge: Cambridge University Press, 1991. 321–425.

Williams, Adriana. *Covarrubias.* Austin: University of Texas Press, 1994.

CHAPTER 4

From the Silver Screen to the Countryside

Confronting the United States and Hollywood in "El Indio" Fernández's *The Pearl*

Fernando Fabio Sánchez

La perla (The Pearl), directed by Emilio "El Indio" Fernández, is based on the story of the same name by John Steinbeck.[1] Steinbeck himself collaborated on the screenplay with Jack Wagner and Fernández in Mexico in 1945, shortly after the story was published in the magazine *Women's Home Companion* under the title "The Pearl of the World" (Lisca 218).[2] This Mexican film is one in a series that El Indio made with Gabriel Figueroa, and was produced by Óscar Dancigers (in conjunction with Águila Films) and R.K.O. Radio Pictures. *La perla* was part of Fernández's broader cinematographic project, which included a second version in English, *Steinbeck's "The Pearl,"* launched in the United States at the beginning of 1948 as the first Mexican production with wide distribution in North American movie theaters (Corbett 122).[3] U.S. film scholars have taken the English interpretation as the only object of analysis, overlooking the Mexican one. The same in reverse has happened with scholarship produced in Mexico. Two examples are the work of Tuñón (who saw the Spanish-language film) and Millichap (who saw the English version). Yet there are significant differences between the two films. A comparison of the two to each other and to Steinbeck's novel, as well as a deeper analysis of the adaptation in Spanish, can reveal important details about Fernández's reading of Steinbeck's tale that also point to significant aspects of Mexican readings of the United States during these years.

In both cinematographic adaptations of the story, Fernández emphasizes Steinbeck's juxtaposition of nonspecified primitive and modern forces to stress the motifs of postrevolutionary Mexican identity. Also, he uses the cinematographic language he created in collaboration with Figueroa to allegorize Mexican specificity. Charles Ramírez-Berg has proposed that the principal purpose of this cinematic style, the Fernández-Figueroa approach, is to resist the hegemony of Hollywood, here a synecdoche for the United States. Thus, both *La perla* and *Steinbeck's "The Pearl"* openly construct a critical reading of Hollywood and the United States through visual elements; *La perla* adds dramatic elements to the visual, thus making explicit the implicit critical and aesthetic suggestions inherent in the cinematic project begun by these two Mexican filmmakers with *Flor Silvestre* (1943) and *María Candelaria* (1943).

It is important to emphasize that this criticism manifests more strongly in the version in Spanish; in the English film, the critical vision is somewhat diluted. For, in spite of the fact that the two adaptations are based on the same story and the casts are the same, there are important differences.[4] At first it would seem that the two films differ only in the language used, since visually it is hard to note any discrepancies. In the English-language screenplay the actors speak "pidgin English," as Joseph R. Millichap describes it, similar to the English spoken by Mexicans in North American films of the era.[5] But in addition, *Steinbeck's "The Pearl"* diverges radically from *La perla* both in details of the plot and in sequence development. For example, neither of two *La perla* scenes I discuss later appears in the English version: that in which the rich lady seeks an abortion and that in which the doctor drinks milk with a pearl in the cup.

Without a doubt the most important difference for our analysis is the influence of speech accents on the personification of the doctor and the moneylender. In the U.S. version the two brothers speak English with a "non-U.S. accent."[6] This creates the impression that these characters belong to the local coastal world of the film and might, as second- or third-generation foreigners, dominate a colonized land. In that way the movie is closer to the plot of Steinbeck's story, in which the doctor and the moneylender are white but not Anglo-Saxon (from Spain perhaps), as they are defined in the Spanish-language film as characters who speak Spanish with a strong North American accent. Similarly, the elimination of the abortion and cup of milk scenes in the English version softens the villainous character of the doctor. By contrast, the Spanish film form emphasizes the doctor's evil nature, a psychological dimension that is derived truculently from the nationality attributed to the doctor. In short, the disparities between the two versions create disparate critical, ideological, and political frameworks that guide their reception and interpretation.

The Spanish version, according to Julia Tuñón, contrasts "civilization and the primitive world," the "perverse and greedy foreigner with the kind, innocent, inoffensive indigenous native."[7] In the same way, the "exploitive North American" is contrasted with the "colonized Mexican" (Tuñón 113). This representation of the North American corresponds to one of the four stereotypes of U.S. subjects (the others are the tourist, the blond, and the racist) portrayed in Mexican films of the 1940s and 1950s (Wilt 166–384). In this way, through the brothers and their relationship with the protagonist Quino's family, Fernández stages the concepts—originating in Rodó's *Ariel* and Vasconcelos's *La raza cósmica* (The Cosmic Race), and later reinforced by Paz in *El laberinto de la soledad* (The Labyrinth of Solitude)—of Latin American (Mexican) spiritualism in contrast with a materialistic United States, which has "blocked" the South's access to progress and has made domination and expansion its primordial projects.

The Spanish film stages ideological tensions, as well as cultural and material

contrasts, between Mexico/Latin America and the United States, while the English
film creates similar contrasts between Mexico and a nonspecified metropolitan/
colonizing culture. Here I concentrate on understanding the specific characteristics
and implications that appear in the Spanish-language film. Also, I analyze the differences between this version, the novel, and the English-language film, which are
key to Fernandez's depiction in the Spanish film of the supposed materialism and
tyranny of a "civilized" North America.

The theme of the United States recurs frequently in Mexican cinematography
of the 1940s and 1950s.[8] These films emphasize themes "that are considered common in North American cinema and that are understood as part of the national
idiosyncrasy: beauty, capacity for action, simplicity, greater sexual freedom, indifference toward social problems, money, efficiency" (Tuñon 108).[9] I have already
mentioned the four stereotypes of Americans that Wilt identifies in Mexican cinematography, among which is the "exploiter."[10] In general the American exploiter
appears in Mexican films as a subject obsessed with money that leaves family and
love by the wayside. The exploiter is consumed by his search for greater power and
economic status, even though his actions lead him to moral misery, unhappiness,
poverty in some cases, and even death. The exploiter sees Mexico as a country rich
in natural resources not exploited to their potential. This condition exposes the
(supposedly) inferior (lazy) nature of the Mexican and Mexican culture (Morris
198; Wilt 298–303).[11]

In *La perla*, the doctor (Charles Rooner) and the moneylender (Fernando
Wagner) represent the American exploiter. The scene in which the doctor refuses
to treat Juanito (the son of the main characters, Quino and Juana) is one example
that illustrates this point. The doctor is about to eat breakfast. He is wearing silk
and linen and is lying on his bed as if it were a throne. His servant is preparing hot
chocolate. When he hears a knock at the door, the doctor gets angry. Whining, he
sends the servant to answer the door. Once alone, he pulls a box out from under a
pillow. The camera zooms in to show three pearls inside the box. While contemplating them, the doctor says in heavily accented Spanish: "Mis perlas, mis precio-
sas perlas" [My pearls, my precious pearls]. Next the doctor takes a pearl, puts it
in a cup of milk, and drinks the white liquid as if he were drinking the beauty and
value of the jewel. The inflections and actions of the doctor make the scene almost
satirical.

The maid returns and interrupts his moment of ecstasy. The doctor takes the
pearl from his mouth and shouts, making his accent apparent again. After a few
lines of dialogue, the maid shows in a veiled woman dressed in elegant clothes. In
contrast to the doctor, she does not have an accent and she looks Creole or even
mestiza. She wants the doctor to help her get an abortion. He says: "Surely you
must know that a *man in my position* cannot take on a case like yours. Besides
it is dangerous. Not only because of the law or religion, but also because I must
consider my professional ethics as the doctor that I am. Besides, those things are

very expensive" (my emphasis).[12] He pauses and then asks: "¿Tiene usted dinero?" [Do you have money?]. The woman gives him a roll of bills, and the doctor gives her the address of "someone" so that she can go there for the abortion. During this dialogue, Juanito's continuous cries of pain can be heard in the background.

There is a change of scene to Quino (Pedro Armendáriz), Juana (María Elena Marqués), the main characters, and their son, Juanito, the sick child. They are at the door asking for the doctor. Behind them is a burro tied to a pillar. These elements in conjunction with the white veil over Juana's head tie the image of the family to that of Jesus, Mary, and Joseph on their pilgrimage. The maid says the doctor is not in. At that moment the veiled woman is leaving and as she walks past the family, hears Juanito's screams. She asks what's wrong with the little boy, to which Juana responds: "It was a scorpion. He could die. Scorpions kill children."[13] The woman thinks for a moment. A change in the background music suggests that she has suddenly realized how deplorable are not only her own acts, but also those of the doctor. A long close-up of her face dramatizes the moment. She says painfully, "Es cierto, los matan" [It's true, they kill them]. In that instant she turns back toward the doctor's house and says to the servant: "The doctor is in and you know it."[14] In this scene, the film equates the doctor (who has aided in an abortion) with the scorpion that kills children. The American doctor is the serpent in this Mexican paradise.

These scenes do not appear in the film in English or in Steinbeck's story. In the Mexican version it is clear that the doctor refuses to see the family because they don't have money to pay him and also because they are indigenous. The doctor considers the blood that flows in their veins inferior. As the sequence continues (in both versions), the doctor adds—from the comfort of his bed and after hearing the family's problems: "All I needed was to be brought some animals. What do they think I am? A veterinarian? Who do I have to cure, the Indian or the scorpion?" Then he hammers his point home: "These Indians don't have any money. In their whole life they will never have a cent."[15] Seconds later the "Holy Family," denied entry to the house, sees the door close. The camera—from inside the house—focuses ironically on a cross hanging on the back of the door. Cut to the next scene. The camera focuses on Quino, who makes a fist and bangs on the door's wooden surface. His knuckles begin to bleed from the force of his blows. His face is filled with indignation. From this shot the film cuts to an image of wild ocean waves.

The representation of the doctor as an exploiter intensifies later in the film. When the fisherman (Quino) finds the pearl, the news spreads quickly through the village and the doctor is one of the first to find out, informed by his maid while he is having a drink in a hammock. Since the doctor's love of pearls has been exposed in earlier scenes, the viewer knows his ambition will have no bounds.

Almost at the same time, the moneylender, the doctor's brother, hears the news from two of his employees. From that point on his portrayal as an exploiter flourishes; his primary desire will be Quino's pearl. Later on we find out that the moneylender's employees get Quino drunk—on their boss's orders—and try to steal the pearl, though they fail. But the moneylender will have another opportunity: Quino and his wife come to his shop to sell the pearl. When the man sees the treasure, he lies and tells Quino that the pearl is like gold plate—it shines but is worth nothing. In this scene, the camera identifies with Quino. It is placed over his shoulder to distance the viewer from the moneylender. In contrast, when Quino appears, a low-angle shot from the front creates a sense of closeness. The moneylender mentions that, although the pearl isn't worth much, he will give them a "very generous" sum since he is their "friend." But the couple does not fall for this.

The moneylender tries to trick them with another tool. He has the couple look at the pearl through a magnifying glass. Of course, the pearl looks flawed. The husband and wife are surprised upon seeing the surface of their possession, but they get distracted when they see each other through the magnifying glass, and they laugh at their enlarged features. As the innocent couple forgets about the apparent defects of their pearl, the moneylender gets exasperated and, as a last try, tells Quino that he can prove to him that he is passing up a great opportunity by refusing to sell the pearl for the price the moneylender is offering. He sends for three jewelers, all in league with him. One by one they tell the fisherman that the pearl is an abomination. Quino is not convinced. He leaves with his pearl, frustrating the moneylender's efforts.

The way the doctor and moneylender interact emphasizes their portrayal as "evil exploiters." The moneylender, after failing to buy the pearl, practically sneaks into his brother's bedroom at night. The doctor is in bed and, as if awakening from a bad dream, discovers his brother standing in front of him. He pays tribute to his brother the moneylender by kissing his hand, which makes the doctor look ridiculous. It is clear the doctor fears him. The moneylender gives him a small black pearl and tells him he will have to be satisfied with that. He warns him, referring to Quino's pearl, that other pearls are dangerous.

In this scene the moneylender is established as a superior, ruthless character. During the conversation the camera views the doctor from a slightly low angle. He is sunk into his bed like an impotent invalid. In the English-language version, this scene establishes the moneylender as the only truly evil character (remember that the scenes about the abortion do not exist in this version and the audience has not seen so many elements proving the sinister nature of the doctor). In the Spanish-language version, this scene shows the doctor (already a primary villain) overshadowed by an even worse character. The scene is a battle between vicious rivals who evidence the decadence produced by materialism (two Americans whose fraternal values have been corroded by money). This scene—in both versions—foreshadows the moneylender's fratricide.

It is highly significant that the doctor and the moneylender are the only power figures in the village, and that they are related (in contrast to what happens in Steinbeck's story).[16] The appearance in the Spanish film of these two evil brothers, and the fact that they are explicitly identified by their accents as being from the United States, has several effects: The world is divided not only between good and evil, but also between corrupt (and corrupting) North Americans and good Mexicans, victimized and initiated into evil by the North Americans. This national dichotomy is not present in either the English-language version or in Steinbeck's story. The original story presents a world penetrated by evil after the pearl is found. The plot defines the conflict as one between men and the forces of nature. In contrast, in Fernández's *La perla*, the message is codified as a confrontation between American tyranny and ambition and the eternal ethical and spiritual values of the Mexicans (and as mentioned earlier, Mexican culture and a generic colonizing culture in *Steinbeck's "The Pearl"*). In the story, evil is an objective force that gradually possesses everyone: Quino, the doctor, the moneylender. In the films, evil defines only the last two, who threaten a community that is more than just a small coastal village and in fact represents the idea of Mexico.

Possibly, when writing the screenplay, Steinbeck and J. Wagner could have agreed to create the family tie between the antagonists to add plot tension. But they may not have foreseen the full significance that was to be tied to the brothers in the Spanish *La perla*, since this emerges more through the direction and production. Namely, Charles Rooner and Fernando Wagner are cast as the doctor and the moneylender, respectively, and they are allowed to speak Spanish with a gringo accent. (Why, for example, were not Spanish actors, who would have spoken Spanish with a Peninsular accent, chosen to play exploitive foreigners in representation of Mexico's colonial condition?) These factors, combined with the framing of the scenes and the final editing, which were the responsibility of Figueroa and Fernández, establish and reproduce the stereotype of American exploiter, which the Mexican audience—already knowledgeable about film culture—would identify on the screen.

In the sequence in both films of the popular festival, or Feria, Mexicanness is opposed to the colonizing evil of the doctor and the moneylender; but in the Spanish version, because of their accents, these characters represent a specific North American evil. Quino, Juana, and the boy are surrounded by a group of admirers and vendors in one of the huts. It is night. Simultaneous shots of faces and (very Mexican) scenes of the townspeople are intermingled with scenes of musical groups performing popular songs and villagers dancing. The celebration of finding the pearl has here become a folk celebration in which the Mexican viewer shares Quino's joy, recognizing on the screen the performance of nationalist rituals. The doctor appears at this festival as an invader who threatens the happiness of Quino and his family as well as that of the Mexican audience in the movie theater.

The doctor arrives asking in a loud voice for the sick child. The family's friends say that they no longer need his services. The child has recovered. Then the doctor tries to trick Quino by telling him that the boy is still very ill from the scorpion bite. His heartbeats are a symptom of his illness. The doctor puts the stethoscope to Quino's ears and to Juanito's chest. Quino is surprised to hear the rhythm of his son's heart. The camera emphasizes his innocence and surprise through the use of close-ups that allow the viewer to see the reactions on his face. This scene is similar to the one in which Quino and Juanita look at the pearl through the magnifying glass, making evident their ingenuousness and lack of scientific knowledge. In the end Quino catches on to the doctor's trick, but the doctor does not give up. He takes Quino by the arm to a corner of the hut, tells him that the people in the town want to steal the pearl, and suggests that it would be safer in his (the doctor's) hands. Quino doesn't believe him. The doctor then asks to at least see the pearl. When he has it in front of him, he is overwhelmed by greed. The sequence ends with an explosion of fireworks, celebrating the traditions of rural Mexico.

As I have proposed thus far, *La perla*, through the use of the stereotype of the American exploiter, presents an ideological content that is valid from the point of view of Mexican nationalism. From this point on I develop the other element of Fernández's double project. For if the Spanish film explicitly criticizes the image of the United States at the level of content, both films seek to construct a cinematographic language that will counteract the hegemony of Hollywood, here representing all of the United States.[17] In this way, *La perla* and *Steinbeck's "The Pearl"* create a space in which the oblique perspective and the motif of diagonal composition (a concept that I explain shortly) intertwine with the representation of Mexico/Latin America in contrast with external forces. The films thus dialogue with the artistic and intellectual tradition that criticizes the United States' apparent pragmatism while praising the supposed spirituality of Hispanic nations.

Beginning in the 1920s with the end of the silent film era, Hollywood became the leader in entertainment, popular consumption, and what some considered the "deformation" of a pure art form (Borge). The Hollywood film empire prospered in a way that was threatening for Latin American nations. Mexico (like other countries in the region) tried to resist Hollywood's advance by creating a local film industry (Usabel and Schnitman). Nevertheless, Mexico does not fully define this project until the end of the 1930s, when Hollywood has already achieved hegemony.[18] And at this time a paradox appears: The Mexican film industry, whose first objective had been to contain the expansion of Hollywood, becomes in the 1940s (just as in the case of Argentina) a replica of the ideological bases of the California enterprise.[19] This takes place through the assimilation of genres, dramatic formulas, and visual language, as well as through a dependence on materials and financial support from the United States.[20]

Films by El Indio Fernández appear to be a project aimed at breaking with the United States. In the movies *Flor Silvestre, María Candelaria, La perla / Steinbeck's "The Pearl," Enamorada* (1946), *Río Escondido* (1947), *Salón México* (1948), and *Pueblerina* (1948), Fernández emphasizes, almost to an extreme, key motifs of postrevolutionary Mexican identity: the Revolution as the point of origin, rural space as symbol of internal identity, and indigenous culture as the heart of eternal

Mexico. He constructs a cinematographic language that allegorizes Mexican specificity, using elements that diverge from the U.S. cinematic tradition.

This process defines the Fernández-Figueroa style, according to Ramírez-Berg. Fernández developed this style in collaboration with Figueroa, the cinematographer for the films just mentioned. The foundations for this style were Sergei Eisenstein's incomplete film *¡Que viva México!* (Long Live Mexico!; 1931), and *Redes* (Nets; 1934) by Paul Strand. In addition, Eisenstein's film shows the influence of José Guadalupe Posada, whose work was revived by postrevolutionary Mexican artists.

According to Ramírez-Berg, the Fernández-Figueroa Mexican style is characterized by: (1) the privileging of in-depth composition of cinematographic shots, with "crisply defined figures extending from the extreme foreground to the middle and background"; (2) complex staging that combines depth of focus with extended action on diverse plains; (3) privileging of low-angle shots, which lower the horizon (at times making it disappear); (4) "the framing of foreground figures placed on the left and/or right side of the frame"; (5) dialectical composition of elements: light/dark, close-up/long shots, plains/mountains, the coast/the sea, land/earth, clouds/sky, and so on; and (6) the predominance of an oblique perspective (19).

The Fernández-Figueroa style is also nourished by the work of the Mexican muralists (Rivera, Orozco, Siqueiros), as well as the artistic norms of Gerardo Murillo (Dr. Atl), whose landscapes reflect a curvilinear perspective and whose representational pattern emphasizes natural spherical figures, his object being to create a new interpretation of nature (Ramírez-Berg 16). Another goal of this form of representation is to complement the traditional or renaissance linear perspective predominant in the Western tradition (15). By basing his work on the curvilinear perspective of Dr. Atl and the films of Eisenstein and Strand, Fernández breaks with the main paradigms of Hollywood film.

According to David Bordwell, Hollywood shots privilege the human body, which appears in the middle, balanced in relation to other elements, placing the Hollywood style of representation in the renaissance tradition of frontal, linear perspectives.[21] The principal tool of the Fernández-Figueroa style is oblique perspective. This angle creates diagonal compositions in which the staging elements are organized in a line that is not parallel (as in the Hollywood renaissance tradition) but transversal. On some occasions the horizon itself defines this line. On others, it is the actors who are placed transversely. Ramírez-Berg states that this line marks divisions between social classes and races, divisions that must be overcome (as an order imposed by either a colonial or a foreign system opposed to Mexicanness). "Again the diagonal indicates an unbalanced ideology that Fernández-Figueroa's protagonists . . . battle against" (Ramírez-Berg 20). And the results of this struggle will almost always be the exaltation of the spirituality of *lo mexicano* (Mexicanness), particularly as found in all things rural and indigenous.

The diagonal perspective nationalizes *La perla* and *Steinbeck's "The Pearl,"* as we now see. The penultimate sequence of the film is this: Quino and his family are at the summit of a mountain. They are being chased from below. Quino tells his wife that they will have to attack the three men following them or they themselves, along with their son, will be killed. In this moment there is visual harmony between Quino and the landscape, which is, according to Dr. Atl and other muralists' norms, the receptacle of national identity. The geography of the region is visible behind Quino: the land, the cactuses, the Mexican grass. Before descending, Quino puts the pearl in his son's small hand. The audience, we assume, remembers that everything has happened with the aim of educating the boy.

As Quino starts down the mountainside, the two indigenous *tarahumara* trackers who accompany the moneylender appear on camera in a closed frame. Until now just a presence, bloodhounds serving a master, they become identifiable individuals. They have stopped tracking; they reflect on the meaning of their actions and the behavior of their boss. This is what the audience expects, since Quino cannot be betrayed by *his brothers*—in contrast to the doctor who dies by the hand of the moneylender. Quino cannot die at the hand of someone of his own race and nationality. The two trackers—not worthy of being shown in harmony with the land and so depicted with no landscape behind them—leave, abandoning the moneylender, thus morally condemning his attitude and physically endangering his body. Next, the image of the moneylender, a dark presence, appears framed against the cloudy sky.

But horror awaits Quino and Juana. The moneylender climbs a rocky peak and hears a noise. It is Juanito. The man kills the boy with a shot from his rifle. In an extreme close-up, the camera shows the little hand of the boy open and let go of the pearl—the inheritance his father had given him so that he could achieve his destiny. Quino at this moment leaps up and stabs the moneylender, who falls off the edge of the cliff, leaving behind his weapon. Quino picks up the rifle and shoots at his fallen body.

The moment of the stabbing is framed against a sky full of intense, dark gray clouds; below the frame, the dark stain of blurred fields marks the horizon line. And in the lower right part of the screen the rocky peak appears, almost black. The diagonal characteristic of the Fernández-Figueroa style is evident when the moneylender aims with his rifle at a point that is not parallel with the horizon—as it would be in a Hollywood film. This motif becomes even more apparent in the following scene, when Quino, in turn, shoots at the moneylender, whose wounded body lies at the bottom of the mountain. This high-angle shot is once again taken from behind Quino's left shoulder. The moneylender fills the upper left part of the frame. Quino fills the lower right. The diagonal is traced, then, by the rifle that Quino points at the moneylender as he wrests poetic justice from unbearable loss. Later, two wide-angle shots (one in which Juana cries with Juanito's body in her arms, and another of Quino on the peak, in pain and alone) confirm the tragic significance of the actions. Afterward, the broken, incomplete family goes back to the village and to the sea to return the pearl to the depths.

Resistance to the hegemony of North America and Hollywood has been a tradition for Latin American intellectuals since the end of the silent film era. Jason Borge proposes that some Latin American intellectuals attempted to counteract the threat of Hollywood and "the United States and the overall decline of Culture" through writing. According to Borge, Hollywood film displaces the man of letters—who had established his place in the public sphere through journalism—"to such a degree that the mere presence of the symbol of Hollywood through its formidable publicity system was able to radically reduce the *visibility* of the Latin American scholarly press" (10).[22] Through their critical texts then, intellectuals and artists pretend "to take control of the discourse and redefine," through their own Latin American norms, the world diffused by Hollywood and the United States (9).[23]

El Indio Fernández dialogues with this written tradition, borrowing and transforming themes as he pursues his own project of reclaiming and redefining Mexico through film.[24] As we have seen, the materialism of the doctor and the moneylender are challenged by the spirituality of Quino and his family. Yet this Arielesque trait is not opposed to progress, as evidenced in what motivates Quino to keep the pearl. When asked by friends how he will spend the money, he first talks of buying a rifle, clothes—things that reveal his dream, as an uneducated man, of emulating the powerful.

But what finally motivates him is something deeper: "My son will know how to read and he will know what a book is. Later he will learn to write and he will know what written words are. My son will learn to do his numbers and will know what numbers are. These things will make us free. He will learn to know and through him we will also learn to know."[25] He speaks as if in a dream. Quino sees the image of his son in a classroom with other children superimposed onto the pearl. But Quino sees not only a different future for Juanito. He prophesizes: "This is what the pearl will do. It will make us free."[26] From this point on when protecting the pearl, Quino will protect not only its material (monetary) value, but more importantly, its pragmatic potential to set the family spiritually and intellectually free. In both films this element diverges from the general condemnation of materialism and greed in Steinbeck's text, and it is explicit in the Spanish film that Quino (and thus Mexico and Latin America) "can and should adopt, without detriment to their character, North American pragmatism, not for themselves, or for their own ends, but rather as a means of realizing the idealistic potential that is the essence of spirit" (O'Gorman 68).[27]

The film ends with the loss of Quino's dream for his son. But this does not mean that the evil of the brothers has triumphed. On the contrary, the death of Juanito and the loss of the pearl highlight the triumph of Mexican/Latin American spirituality over a generalized materialism in the English version and over specific U.S. materialism in the Spanish film. And it is precisely this healthy space, this "subverted Eden" within the limits of the past, that will define the authentic national being (Bartra 32–33). The construction of this idealized rural image forms "part of a broad system of political legitimization, whose effectiveness is based not only, or even primarily, on the reproduction of deep psychological archetypes, but rather on its ability to reproduce (recreate) the deepest structures of social conflict" (33).[28] Roger Bartra points out that the rural hero "is a singular character, since he comes from a long-suffering and insulted line. He is an extremely sensitive, fearful, distrustful, touchy being. This rural hero has been shut in a dungeon of logic, sandwiched between a past of savage misery and a present of barbaric wealth" (34).[29] Bartra's description delineates precisely the characteristics of Quino and his family.

The dramatic scenes of the family's flight from the village construct this Mexican/Latin American essence. In the moment when Quino fights on the beach with the moneylender's henchmen, he realizes that if he really wants his son to read and write, he will have to leave the town. First they try to escape by sea, but the canoe can't make it. Next they try to escape through the swamp, where in the midst of the struggle the moneylender eliminates his brother and continues, now monster-like, along with his *tarahumara* trackers, to pursue the family through swamp, desert, and plains. It is during their flight that Quino and Juana confirm their values, their commitment to family, loyalty, and mutual love. This last aspect is emphasized in their quiet, slow dialogues. Eventually it becomes clear that even Quino's machismo and violence are one of the tools through which love is manifested. When Juana wants to give up in the middle of the countryside, Quino scolds her for her weakness and drags her along the ground, although when he realizes that her feet are bleeding, he says, "Or I stay with you or you come with me. But we can't ever be separated, Juana. You and I are like one person."[30] Then he makes her some rough shoes and they keep walking.

In the translation from the text to the scripts and the scripts to the screen, the presentation of the couple changes. In Steinbeck's novel, Quino tells Juana at the beginning of their flight: "This pearl has become my soul. . . . If I give it up I shall lose my soul" (87). In the films, the materialism the pearl may have engendered in Quino's heart has been eliminated, since the pearl is always associated with and valued only for the possibility of educating Juanito. And so in the films Quino speaks to Juana of the love between them. Their seemingly romantic gesture of returning the pearl to the sea thus underlines a significant moral point: No potential material improvement is worth the risk of allowing the corrupting forces of the brothers' pure materialism and greed to triumph.

In the final scene we see the couple dignified by suffering. Their final act confirms it. They throw the pearl back into the sea and thus, on the one hand, close the reflection about "foreign, western, North American evil" (which in its extreme promotes the love of material wealth as an end in itself) and on the other hand exalt the stoic and nonmaterialistic dimension of the Latin American/Mexican being as unwilling to accept material progress unless it is in the service of spirit. The couple rejects the pearl because they have something more valuable inside them now. This ennoblement is corroborated by the final scene, a close-up of Quino's and Juana's entwined hands. The two brothers have not been able to destroy the eternal bond between husband and wife.

The staging of spirituality achieved by *La perla* goes beyond the reaffirmation of Mexican national symbols and meanings. It contains a meaning that Fernández seems to propose could hold the key to regenerating the exhausted strength of the modern Western world, and consequently, the United States. In these films, spirituality is related to primitiveness, which is vindicated and rises up dignified in the face of modern civilization. The brothers, as the symbol of decadent modernity, are immersed in their pursuit of materialistic ideals. They are incompatible with the mythical, traditional, pure world that Quino represents. Instead of appreciating and understanding the original innocence in this space in order to find some redeeming knowledge, they dedicate themselves to destruction. *La perla* and *Steinbeck's "The Pearl"* are both, if to differing degrees, the tale of this fall.

One might say that this is simply a repetition of Steinbeck's original message, set in Mexico. But also, in these films, Fernández has created a piece that reactivates Antonin Artaud's premise that interaction with Indians in remote locations (like a Mexico still untouched by modernity) could awaken archaic natural pulsations that would reenergize a humanity exhausted by modernity. Steinbeck's original story does not emphasize this aspect in relation to indigenous culture. El Indio, in his films, builds a present instant that seeks its connection to a distant moment of origin. Using Paz's words, the spectator can be closer to the myth and the origin, "suspended between heaven and earth, oscillating between contradictory powers and forces, petrified eyes, devouring mouths" (18).[31] It is as if Fernández proposed that the Mexican countryside were the pathway to this connection and that listening to the message murmured there could restore potent flows that might reconcile humankind with the universe.

The pure, mythical image of family in *La perla* and *Steinbeck's "The Pearl"* is part of a system of foundational myths and tales that defines modern Mexico. Both films belong to the myth of "la inocencia rural" [rural innocence] (Monsiváis 118). This myth, created in film beginning in the mid-1930s, is based on the idea that postrevolutionary Mexico had progressed, that the agricultural reform project had been successfully completed, and that the country was ready for industrial and urban modernization. Thus the image of rural innocence presented in the films of this era is of an idealized countryside in which national problems, even the historical ones, are in the process of being resolved or have already been overcome.

This stable, closed image, emptied of any contemporary material conflicts, was filled with the idea that the state had achieved development thanks to the Revolution and the symbolic legitimacy that emanated from it. Thus through "rural" cinema and its ties to the Revolution, it was possible to consolidate one of the axes of the national narrative that unified the country into one historical period and one idea of Mexico. Paradoxically, the bases that authorized the state to aim the nation toward urbanization and industrialization apparently lay in the countryside; or rather, a constructed idea of the countryside.

But this is achieved not only through melancholy works that mourn the sacrifice of the peasant "on the altar of modernity and progress" (Bartra 43).[32] In the case of *La perla* and *Steinbeck's "The Pearl,"* it is also achieved through the cinematographic creation of dichotomies that organize the spectator's reality. And from among these dichotomies the oppositions between Mexico and the West/North America, between interior and exterior, spirituality and materialism, stand out most.

Returning to my earlier point about the mythical rural world in relation to the modern world, I would propose that the message of *La perla* and *Steinbeck's "The Pearl"* is dual. One part is directed to Mexico in the process of urbanization and industrialization. The country is obliged to maintain its spiritual essence in spite of an ongoing process of assimilation with the forms of production and development related to its northern neighbor. The second part of the message is aimed at the United States. That country should look into the heart of the primitive and spiritual (of which Mexico is the source), abandoning the values that tie it to materialism, civilization, and modernity. Thus, the dual production of *La perla* and *Steinbeck's "The Pearl"* holds knowledge that is equally important for Mexico and the United States. This story is not just a criticism but also a message that should lead to catharsis. Of course, Mexican film audiences would be able to decipher this message more easily because of the use of the stereotypical American exploiter. North American audiences may not have been able to extract this meaning as easily, since there is no specifically North American character for them to relate to in the English version. Still, the two American coauthors of the script, Steinbeck and J. Wagner, participated in the creation of this message. Together with El Indio Fernández they produced two films that represent a constant search for values higher than the price of a pearl, a search that the films propose both Mexico and the United States should begin.

NOTES

I dedicate this essay to Jennifer and Ana Rocío Sánchez. I would like to thank Mary K. Long, Linda Egan, and Elizabeth Goldberg for their help with this study. Mary K. Long translated the chapter from Spanish and provided much editing support, as did Linda Egan. Elizabeth Goldberg helped me to get a copy of the English version of *The Pearl*. And finally thank you to Karen Popp for her moral and intellectual support.

1. In 1937 Steinbeck set sail in the Western Flyer and navigated the Sea of Cortés. Sparky Enea comments: "In that area at the time there were lots of myths about boys finding pearls of great value and throwing them back into the sea. Maybe that's where Steinbeck got his idea for *The Pearl*" (34).

2. Steinbeck had begun work on the novel *The Pearl* shortly after finishing *Cannery Row* in 1945. The publication of the text in book form took two more years, since it was

scheduled to come out along with "El Indio" Fernández's cinematographic version (Lisca 218). Steinbeck wrote the screenplays for the following films: *The Forgotten Village* (1941), *The Red Pony* (1949), and *Viva Zapata!* (1952). In 1945 he wrote—along with J. Wagner, his collaborator on the screenplay for *La perla*—the story that would become the basis for the screenplay *A Medal for Benny*, written by Frank Butler. Other films based on Steinbeck's work are: *Of Mice and Men* (1939), *The Grapes of Wrath* (1940), *Tortilla Flat* (1942), *The Moon Is Down* (1943), *Lifeboat* (1944), *East of Eden* (1955), *The Wayward Bus* (1957), *Flight* (1961), and *Cannery Row* (1982).

3. *La perla* was released in México on 12 September 1947, and *Steinbeck's "The Pearl"* in the United States on 17 February 1948, in New York. References to *La perla* in Steinbeck's own work or in studies of his work are scarce. There is mention of it in E. Steinbeck and Wallsten and in Fensch. On the one hand, it seems that Steinbeck enjoyed participating in the making of the film (E. Steinbeck 262), but on the other, the author apparently declared in 1945 that he did not want to make any more films (Fensch 41). In this study I take license to make a few moderate speculations about Steinbeck's attitude, based on the fact that Steinbeck himself was a constant critic of certain social and ethical dimensions of the United States.

4. Initially, Olivia de Havilland was going to participate in the English version (Garcia Riera 85), but in the end María Elena Marqués acted in both films as the wife of Pedro Armendáriz.

5. Millichap says the following: "Neither of the leads proves very convincing; they do a lot of wide-eyed staring and speak in a kind of pidgin English which weakens Steinbeck's supple dialogue. Although this dialogue works on the page, on the sound track it takes on a pseudo-biblical quality that never lets the audience forget it is hearing 'movie Mexican' talk" (102).

6. Commercial concerns in the United States could be the reason for the difference in accent as well as the omission of the abortion scene and the one with the doctor drinking milk.

7. "la civilización al mundo primitivo," el "extranjero perverso y codicioso al indígena bondadoso, inocente, inerme." Mary K. Long translated all reference citations.

8. Some films from the 1940s and 1950s with marked North American presence are: *La devoradora* (The Devouring Woman; 1946) by Fernando de Fuentes, the saga of Ismael Rodríguez; *Los tres García* (The Three Garcias; 1947), *Vuelven los García* (The Return of the Garcias; 1947), and *Carne de presidio* (Prison Meat; 1951) by Emilio Gómez Muriel; *Una gringuita en México* (A Gringuita in Mexico; 1951) by Julián Soler; *Acá las tortas* (Get Your Sandwiches Here; 1951) by Juan Bustillo Oro; and *Campeón sin corona* (Champion without a Crown; 1945) by Alejandro Galindo. See John Mraz and Ricardo Pérez Monfort for studies of this theme.

9. "que se consideran comunes al cine norteamericano y que se entiende como parte de la idiosincrasia nacional: la belleza, la capacidad de acción, la simpleza, la mayor libertad sexual, la indiferencia hacia los problemas sociales, el dinero y la eficiencia." The United States also appears in "migration cinema"; a "cinema of exploitation" could be identified in a similar vein. For example, *La perla* could be grouped with *La Rosa Blanca* (The White Rose), set in the atmosphere of the oil expropriation of the 1930s and directed by Roberto Gavaldón in 1960 on the occasion of the fiftieth anniversary of the Mexican Revolution. Some of the migration films are: *Espaldas mojadas* (Wetbacks; 1955) by Alejandro Galindo, with a protagonist from the United States; *Adiós mi chaparrita* (Goodbye My Little Gal; 1943) by René Cardona; *El hijo desobediente* (The Disobedient Son; 1945) by Gómez Landero; and *Primero soy mexicano* (I'm a

Mexican First; 1950) by Joaquín Pardavé. In *Espaldas mojadas* the premises of *La perla* are also emphasized, since the Americans appear cold and oriented toward work and the Mexicans are oriented toward the social and spiritual realms. Similarly, in *Carne de presidio*, the character Mister Irving Lee values the treatment he receives in prison, which dignifies him and makes him feel like *something more* than just a number on the list of prisoners, as he had felt in the United States. Tuñón, in her article, comments extensively on the culture clash between the United States and Mexico. The cinematographic presence of the United States in Mexican film of this era does not only serve to criticize, however. These images on the screen represent an imaginary territory that the Mexican emigrants enter before crossing the border. The idea of the United States thus functioned as a warning and informed Mexicans about the world they were going to enter. Nevertheless, as we will see further on, these images create preconceived notions about the United States that cloud perceptions of reality, since the profiles that define U.S. reality (pragmatisms, tendency to be abusive, etc.) find their origins in nineteenth-century thinking. We could suggest that the emigrants enter a "gringolandia" (in the sense of simulacra emphasized by Stephen D. Morris) before entering the *concrete territory* of the country.

10. Perhaps because of his linguistic perspective, Wilt does not include *La perla* in his study of "North American exploiters."

11. An exception is John Smith (Clifford Carr) in *Los tres García*, who represents a good gringo since he does not make moral judgments or wish to achieve financial gains. He values "Mexicanness" (food and machismo) and is the father of a blond daughter (Lupita Smith, played by Marga López) who wants to stay in Mexico (Tuñón 113).

12. "Seguramente ha de saber que *un hombre con mi posición* no puede hacerse cargo de un caso como el suyo. Además, es peligroso. No solamente por la ley o por la religión, sino también hay que considerar mi ética profesional como médico que soy. Además, esas cosas resultan muy caras."

13. "Fue un alacrán. Se nos puede morir. Los alacranes matan a los niños."

14. "El doctor sí está y tú lo sabes muy bien."

15. "Ya nada más me falta que me traigan unos animales. ¿Qué se están creyendo, que soy veterinario? ¿A quién tengo que curar, al indio o al alacrán?"; "Estos indios no tienen dinero. Nunca en su vida van a tener un centavo."

16. For an earlier comparison of the film and the novel, see Millichap 96–107.

17. In this aspect, *La perla* and *Steinbeck's "The Pearl"* are similar to *La rosa blanca*, since Gavaldón's film—though it does reproduce some technical and editing aspects of the Hollywood aesthetic—shows the influence of Italian neorealism, especially the film *Arroz amargo* (Riso amaro; Bitter Rice; 1949) by Giuseppe De Santis.

18. For studies of the relationship between nationalism and film in Mexico, see Monsiváis and Bonfil, Doremus, Dever, Noble, Acevedo-Muñoz, and Mora.

19. See Fernández's opinions in Tuñón and Fernández, as well as in Taibo. See Fein, Vasey, and Agrasánchez about the relationship between the Mexican and U.S. film industries.

20. Along these lines, Ramírez-Berg proposes that the history of Mexican cinematography is defined by the tension between adherence to and rejection of the Hollywood paradigm, between the assimilation of U.S. values (transmitted in film) and the confirmation of Mexican values (13).

21. Based on the ideas of David Bordwell (1–84), Ramírez-Berg defines the three paradigms as: a logic centered on the cause and effect of narrative events with an adherence to an Aristotelian narrative poetic; the predominance of a cinematographic

system of time that controls all the elements of the film, from the length of takes to the order of final scene editing; and a spatial system that equates the filmic space with historical space (13).

22. "Estados Unidos y lo que se percibe como la vulgarización de la Cultura en general"; "hasta tal punto que la mera presencia del signo hollywoodense a través de su formidable sistema publicitario logra reducir drásticamente la *visibilidad* de la prensa letrada latinoamericana."

23. "anteponerse en el discurso y re-mitificar."

24. For an extended discussion of the nineteenth-century origins of the Latin American exploration of the dichotomy of pragmatism/spirituality as well as the relationship of Rodó, Vasconcelos, and Paz to this discussion, see Edmundo O'Gorman. Most pertinent for the discussion here is that during most of the nineteenth century, independent Latin America faced the dilemma of "continuing as it had been in keeping with its colonial heritage or becoming, through imitation, like the United States" [seguir siendo como ya se era por herencia del pasado colonial, o llegar a ser, por imitación, como Estados Unidos] (31). Ultimately, Latin America gave itself permission to aspire only to Anglo-Saxon prosperity and not a way of being (39).

25. "Mi hijo sabrá leer y sabrá lo que es un libro. Luego aprenderá a escribir y sabrá lo que son las palabras escritas. Mi hijo aprenderá a hacer números y sabrá lo que son los números. Estas cosas nos harán libres. Él aprenderá a saber y por él nosotros también aprenderemos a saber."

26. "Esto es lo que hará la perla. La perla nos hará libres."

27. "puede y debe, sin menoscabo de su índole, adoptar el pragmatismo pero se aclara que no por él mismo y para sus fines propios, sino como medio para actualizar la potencia del idealismo que es la esencia de su 'espíritu.'" This aspect reveals some of the contradictions and nuances of the dichotomy between Latin American spirit and U.S. materialism. For education is a pragmatic and, in many ways, nonspiritual objective. Its mention here could be seen to share some positive elements with U.S. views of education as a path toward upward social and material mobility; it might also bring to mind the importance placed on improved public education in rural areas by the campaigns begun by José Vasconcelos in the 1920s and carried out by many others during the postrevolutionary era. However, the film does not explore these contradictions.

28. "parte de un amplio sistema de legitimación política, cuya efectividad se basa no sólo—ni principalmente—en que reproduce los más profundos arquetipos psicológicos, sino que logra reproducir (re-crear) las estructuras más profundas de la conflictiva social."

29. "el héroe de esta epopeya es un personaje singular, pues pertenece a una estirpe de seres dolientes y agraviados. Es un ser extremadamente sensible, temeroso, receloso y susceptible. Este héroe campesino ha sido encerrado en un calabozo lógico, emparedado entre su pasado de salvaje miseria y un presente de bárbara riqueza."

30. "O yo me quedo contigo, o tú vienes conmigo. Pero no podemos separarnos nunca, Juana. Tú y yo somos como una única persona."

31. "suspendido entre el cielo y la tierra y oscila[ndo] entre poderes y fuerzas contrarias, ojos petrificados, bocas que devoran."

32. "en el altar de la modernidad y el progreso."

WORKS CITED

Acevedo-Muñoz, Ernesto R. *Buñuel and Mexico: The Crisis of National Cinema*. Berkeley: University of California Press, 2003.

Agrasánchez, Rogelio. *Mexican Movies in the United States: A History of the Films, Theaters, and Audiences, 1920–1960*. Jefferson, N.C.: McFarland, 2006.

Artaud, Antonin. *México y Viaje al país de los taraumaras*. Mexico: Fondo de Cultura Económica, 1984.

Bartra, Roger. *La jaula de la melancolía: identidad y metamorfosis del mexicano*. Mexico: Grijalbo, 1996.

Bordwell, David, Janet Staiger, and Kristin Thompson. *The Classical Hollywood Cinema: Film Style and Mode of Production to 1960*. New York: Columbia University Press, 1985.

Borge, Jason, ed. *Avances de Hollywood: crítica cinematográfica en Latinoamérica, 1915–1945*. Rosario, Arg.: Beatriz Viterbo, 2005.

Corbett, Davis Gary. "John Steinbeck in Films: An Analysis of Realism in the Novel and in the Film—A Nonteleological Approach." Ph.D. diss., University of Southern California, 1975.

Dever, Susan. *Celluloid Nationalism and Other Melodramas: From Post-Revolutionary Mexico to Fin de Siglo Mexamérica*. Albany: State University of New York Press, 2003.

Doremus, Anne T. *Culture, Politics, and National Identity in Mexican Literature and Film, 1929–1952*. New York: Peter Lang, 2001.

Durán, Ignacio, Iván Trujillo, and Mónica Verea, eds. *México-Estados Unidos: encuentros y desencuentros en el cine*. Mexico: Imcine, 1996.

Enea, Sparky, and Audry Lynch. *With Steinbeck in the Sea of Cortez: A Memoir of the Steinbeck/Ricketts Expedition*. Los Osos, Calif.: Sand River Press, 1991.

Fein, Seth. "La imagen de México: la Segunda Guerra Mundial y la propaganda fílmica de Estados Unidos." Durán, Trujillo, and Verea 41–58.

Fensch, Thomas, ed. *Conversations with John Steinbeck*. Jackson and London: University of Mississippi Press, 1988.

García Riera, Emilio. *Emilio Fernández, 1904–1986*. Guadalajara: Universidad de Guadalajara, 1987.

La perla. Emilio Fernández. 1945. DVD. Alterfilms, 2003.

Lisca, Peter. *The Wide World of John Steinbeck*. New Brunswick, N.J.: Rutgers University Press, 1958.

Millichap, Joseph R. *Steinbeck and Film*. New York: Ungar, 1983.

Monsiváis, Carlos. "Mythologies." Trans. Ana M. López. *Mexican Cinema*. Ed. Paulo Antonio Paranaguá. London: British Film Institute, 1995. 117–27.

Monsiváis, Carlos, and Carlos Bonfil. *A través del espejo: el cine mexicano y su público*. México: Instituto Mexicano de Cinematografía, 1994.

Mora, Carl J. *Mexican Cinema: Reflections of a Society, 1896–2004*. Jefferson, N.C.: McFarland, 2005.

Morris, Stephen D. *Gringolandia: Mexican Identity and Perceptions of the United States*. Lanham, Md.: Rowman and Littlefield, 2005.

Mraz, John. "Lo gringo en el cine mexicano y la ideología alemanista." Durán, Trujillo, and Verea 83–92.

Noble, Andrea. *Mexican National Cinema*. Abingdon, Eng.: Routledge, 2005.

O'Gorman, Edmundo. *México, el trauma de su historia*. Mexico: Consejo Nacional para la Cultura y las Artes, 1999.

Paz, Octavio. *El laberinto de la soledad.* (1950). Mexico: Fondo de Cultura Económica, 1990.

Pérez Monfort, Ricardo. "El contrapunto de la imagen nacionalista. El estereotipo norteamericano en el cine de charros 1920–1946." Durán, Trujillo, and Verea 93–104.

Ramírez-Berg, Charles. "The Cinematic Invention of México: The Poetics and Politics of the Fernández-Figueroa Style." *The Mexican Cinema Project.* Ed. Chon A. Noriega and Steven Ricci. Los Angeles: UCLA Film and Television Archive, 1994. 13–23.

Rodó, José Enrique. *Ariel.* (1900). Ed. Castro Belén. Madrid: Cátedra, 2000.

Schnitman, Jorge. *Film Industries in Latin America: Dependency and Development.* Norwood, N.J.: Ablex, 1984.

Steinbeck, Elaine, and Robert Wallsten, eds. *Steinbeck: A Life in Letters.* New York: Viking Press, 1975.

Steinbeck, John. *The Pearl.* (1947). New York: Viking Press, 1975.

Steinbeck's "The Pearl." Emilio Fernández. 1945. VHS. Mastervision, 1995.

Taibo, Paco Ignacio. *El Indio Fernández: el cine por mis pistolas.* Mexico: Mortiz, 1986.

Tuñón, Julia. "Una mirada al vecino: estadounidenses de celuloide en el cine mexicano de la edad de oro." Durán, Trujillo, and Verea 103–34.

Tuñón, Julia, and Emilio Fernández. *En su propio espejo: entrevista con Emilio "El Indio" Fernández.* Iztapalapa, Mex.: Universidad Autónoma Metropolitana, 1988.

Usabel, Gaizka S. de. *The High Noon of American Films in Latin America.* Ann Arbor: UMI Research Press, 1982.

Vasconcelos, José. *La raza cósmica.* (1925). Mexico: Porrúa, 2001.

Vasey, Ruth. *The World According to Hollywood, 1918–1939.* Madison: University of Wisconsin Press, 1997.

Wilt, David Edward. "Stereotyped Images of United States Citizens in Mexican Cinema, 1930–1990." Ph.D. diss., University of Maryland, College Park, 1991.

PART II

Inseparable Differences

Mexico Adapts U.S. Models, 1960–1990s

CHAPTER 5

Carlos Monsiváis
"Translates" Tom Wolfe

Linda Egan

As soon as his mother taught him to read, Carlos Monsiváis trained his eye on the world he could see outside Mexico from the window of a book's open pages (Menocal 17). Perhaps it was natural that he would develop a particular lifelong interest in North American culture, Mexico and the United States being such inescapably close neighbors. Monsiváis was spending a year as an exchange student at Harvard in 1965 when Tom Wolfe made his astounding publishing debut in what was being called the New Journalism with *The Kandy-Kolored Tangerine-Flake Streamline Baby*, an unnerving hymn to the newsworthy and artistic value of what Wolfe characterized as low-class "ratty people with ratty hair, . . . rancid people [who] are creating new styles . . . and changing the life of the whole country in ways that nobody even seems to bother to record, much less analyze" (Wolfe, "Introduction," *Kandy*).[1]

That is also when the young Mexican writer began his love affair with the kind of pandiscursive mix of reality and imagination that constituted a reborn chronicle in Mexico, resuscitated in the unsettling 1960s by supertalents like Monsiváis, Elena Poniatowska, and José Emilio Pacheco, who would recount rancid realities in their own (frequently ratty) neighborhoods. Carlos Monsiváis read deeply in New Journalism's ranks while cultivating an idiosyncratic style that intertwined something akin to Wolfe's "shotgun baroque" language (Shomette, citing Epstein xlv) and the muscle of journalistic truth to shoulder—like new journalists in North America—the weight of reporting vast complexities in postindustrial and postmodern society, and, as a bonus, to sometimes make people laugh as he did it.

True to his self-imposed job as an outsider who observes (mostly what's wrong with) his society, Monsiváis in fact employs humor—savage, black satire—as one of his most frequent weapons against those responsible for high levels of functional illiteracy, intractable poverty, domestic abuse, street crime, government by drug lords, surrender to neoliberal robbery, and what he calls, in short, "so many cretins in power" (Eltit and Monsiváis, "Un diálogo" 46).[2] Early on he was filled with such anger that, not being able to cure the economy or other social problems, he consoled himself with "the luxury of making fun, my very modest kind of activism, of the idiocy of the powerful" (47).[3] His journalism would always be marked by interest in political issues, themes and behaviors that encompass the life of the common people (popular culture), and a gift for taking several steps back in order to see the big picture—which is frequently at least a little bit funny, even when despair laces the laughter.

Elsewhere I have remarked on the seriocomic nature of the contemporary Mexican chronicle and of Monsiváis's vision in particular (Egan, *Carlos Monsiváis* 215–16, 230); U.S. New Journalism shares the trait, and Wolfe's pieces offer a particular hilarity that tickles the funny bone through incongruity of circumstance, pyrotechnical verbal hijinks, an antic sensibility that dares speak the unseemly, and a razor-strop streak of meanness that slices away hypocrisy to leave would-be gentility shivering bare nekked in the hog pen. Monsiváis isn't much nicer, although you sometimes think he might be because he can be subtler, or just more difficult to parse. In the remainder of this study I compare—and often contrast—the way Tom Wolfe and Carlos Monsiváis tattle on the pretensions to glory of the rich and famous, and how they spy on the way the poor and disenfranchised rattle government flunkies' cages to finally get themselves a piece of the pie. My focus is specifically on Monsiváis's reading of Wolfe's *Radical Chic and Mau-Mauing the Flak Catchers*, by way of my reading of his dialogue with that book in several *crónica*s of 1970 and 1977.

By 1970, Carlos Monsiváis had already made a name for himself in the field of poetry criticism, as well as with a narratively adventurous journalism and that trademark black humor that showed up like Jaws at the ballet. I refer to *Días de guardar*, whose thirty-three texts include a classic trilogy of *crónicas* on the doomed 1968 student movement that ended in blood on the wide expanse of Tlatelolco Square on 2 October 1968. Shortly after, from a visiting lectureship in England, during the salad days of British cultural studies, he was to write to his friend and colleague Elena Poniatowska and confide that, although he had received tempting job offers abroad, this was no time to be leaving Mexico, and that he was stuffing his head with everything he needed to pursue what he hoped could be a useful career as a journalist (Poniatowska 8).

His preparation included assiduous reading of U.S. literary nonfiction writers. Monsiváis once told me that he routinely divides his omnivorous reading about half and half between English and Spanish, and that among his favored genres are literary journalism and U.S. thrillers like *Silence of the Lambs*.[4] Although his opinion may have changed since 1991, at that time and in 1979 when he wrote a critical essay on the New Journalism, he admired Norman Mailer and Truman Capote enormously but favored Tom Wolfe in particular among those writing in the 1960s and 1970s. Among the *New Yorker*'s writers, he found Jane Kramer (*The Last Cowboy*) to be perfect. As the exemplary model of a literary journalist, Monsiváis cites Mailer in the prologues to the 1979 and 1980 editions of his anthology of Mexican chronicles (Monsiváis, *Antología* 8, *A ustedes* 13). (In the 2006 revised and expanded edition he eliminates his preliminary theoretical note on the generic nature of the chronicle and with it, all reference to non-Mexican authors.)

In the appendix he affixes to that first edition, he provides an excellent in-depth analysis of the New Journalism and many of its precursors and then-heaviest hitters: James Agee, Mailer, Capote, Wolfe. For his exaggerated, broadly gesturing style, which Monsiváis details through an analysis of *Kandy*, Wolfe became the decisive standard-bearer of the New Journalism, Monsiváis declares; the *cronista* sees this as a new movement both literary and informative that was born in the 1960s with a single purpose: to repudiate the naturalistic stance, refuse mere mechanical news reporting, and never turn a blind eye to the contemporary (Monsiváis, "Alabemos" 199). Based on his extensive reading of literary journalists in Mexico and the United States (see his appended bibliography 217–20), Monsiváis enumerates the characteristics of New Journalism (200, 215), which eerily echo what I was to see in 2001 as the defining elements of the contemporary chronicle of Mexico (Egan, *Carlos Monsiváis* 128–31). Chief among these is a visually dramatic style designed to "counteract the triumphal avidity of television" (Monsiváis, "Alabemos" 200), prose that Ronald Weber around the same time called "watchable" (21).[5]

What is most watchable about this text of Monsiváis's, however, is not his own compellingly baroque style but the steady gaze he casts on those in the United States who, like him, are connoisseurs of the art of truth telling. Monsiváis traces the history of aesthetic newswriting from *Insurgent Mexico*'s John Reed to *Let Us Now Praise Famous Men*'s James Agee and on through Truman Capote of *In Cold Blood*, Norman Mailer of *The Armies of the Night* and *A Fire on the Moon* (Mailer out-Hemingways Hemingway without having to shoot an elephant, Monsiváis says [211]), and Tom Wolfe, of the aforementioned *Kandy-Kolored* collection of essays on the youth culture and other underground themes, and of another much-mentioned early book, *The Electric Kool-Aid Acid Test*, about the LSD phase of Ken Kesey, author of *One Flew over the Cuckoo's Nest* (1962), a surreal take on the "loony bin" that Kesey claims he wrote while high on acid.[6]

Followers of Monsiváis in Mexico readily acknowledge his debt to or at least his admiration for the new journalists of North America. A reviewer of the chronicler's second collection, *Amor perdido* (1977), credits him with introducing New Journalism's virtuosity into Mexican newswriting (García, "México," "Monsiváis"). One noted critic, Christopher Domínguez Michael, goes so far as to suggest that, without predecessor Salvador Novo and contemporary American new journalists in his literary lineage, Monsiváis's own career is inexplicable (69). Adolfo Castañón says Monsiváis and Wolfe may share a sad fate, however: to burn brightly in a short arc that darkens before reaching truly literary status (20). The judgment is surely premature but, in the context of this study, it at least puts them at the same crash site, where they can compare notes.

I doubt that Wolfe has ever looked farther south than Mississippi, but Monsiváis, at least, was comparing notes with his northern colleagues from the beginning of his career. I invite you to listen in with me, so to speak, on two parts of the dialogue Monsiváis was conducting with New Journalism in the 1970s: one was theoretical and one was literary. Whereas other chroniclers contemporaneous with him did not delve into the theoretical side of their art as avidly as did Monsiváis, he was consciously pursuing guidelines to define what he and his fellow Mexican journalists were doing with the *crónica*; at that same time, U.S. academics, including Tom Wolfe, were tracking the generic specificity of New Journalism.[7]

First let us eavesdrop on an imagined round table discussion among Carlos Monsiváis, Ronald Weber, Dwight MacDonald, John Hellman, and Tom Wolfe.[8]

Weber proposes a 1974 "working definition" of the genre to start the dialogue: "It's what Tom Wolfe writes" (13), he says. Wolfe, wearing a tailored, white three-piece suit, does not object, but he does murmur, "Don't forget Mailer's *Armies of the Night*, and remember Hunter S. Thompson: 'He's developed into the greatest humorist in America' " (cited in Scura 65). Monsiváis offers his 1980 "definición de trabajo" [working definition] (*A ustedes* 13) as a literary reconstruction of real events or figures, a genre whose formal intent weighs more heavily than its informative duty. By this definition, he says, Mailer's *Armies* is less news report than art. Weber says that's the trouble with New Journalism: How can you domesticate a "slippery beast" that goes after two opposing goals, one aesthetic and one factual? (14); John Hellman interrupts to agree, speaking of a form that is at the same time "wholly fictional and wholly journalistic" (19). Monsiváis, wearing something wholly forgettable, growls that it is "inútil y bizantino" [useless and byzantine] to try bridging the generic abyss between chronicle and reportage (13). Dwight MacDonald, wearing a curmudgeonly frown, says there is nothing remotely journalistic about a book like *The Kandy-Kolored Tangerine-Flake Streamline Baby* (every offense probably intended), although it is fine as fluffy entertainment and presents some poignant urban dilemmas that "one recognizes as real" (225). You cannot have it both ways, guys, he says; this stuff you call New Journalism is too much of a "bastard form" to merit "the factual authority of journalism" (223). Monsiváis, emitting a curmudgeonly grunt, retorts, speaking also to his own society's disastrous news profession:

> From a formal point of view, a very renovating influence on the chronicle is, in some respects, North American New Journalism. The works of Norman Mailer, Tom Wolfe, Hunter Thompson, Truman Capote, Gay Talese, etc., have revived interest in the genre, adding to it a diversity of techniques: the powerful insertion of the "I" or of fashion, the cult of the "intimate history," an eagerness to narratively document new lifestyles, the pursuit of personalities and archetypal figures. If, as a dominant tendency, the New Journalism is displaced by Watergate-style investigation, as a style it has imposed permanent attitudes and procedures. (*A ustedes* 75)[9]

In this imagined scenario, MacDonald sulks silently as Hellman, Weber, Wolfe, and Monsiváis go on to hash over the details, dwelling at length on the way New

Journalists take over the novelist's third-person omniscience, invading at will the consciousness of the other, as Monsiváis puts it (*A ustedes* 13); "experiencing the world through his [the interview subject's] central nervous system," as Wolfe puts it ("New Journalism" 33); and with a deliberately unobjective, first-person point of view, while making free use of metaphor, irony, and humor.[10]

Now let us hear how Monsiváis continues his dialogue with U.S. New Journalism on the creative plane. A brief demonstration here focuses principally on one book by Tom Wolfe (consisting of two texts) and a handful of texts by Monsiváis that I think most clearly echo those of Wolfe.[11] I stress at the outset that they do not parrot Wolfe, but instead engage him in intertextual play and leave open gaps through which discerning listeners can hear the historical distances that separate the speakers. Monsiváis admires New Journalism and its practitioners, most especially Wolfe, but his is a *positional* view sharpened by that very historical space: Although Wolfe is but a few years older than Monsiváis, his society has been practicing pluralist democracy for two hundred years longer than has Mexico, whereas Monsiváis's society is still unburdening itself of an additional hundred years of colonial rule, a hundred years of near anarchy after independence, and almost a century of much resented one-party rule.

The first edition of Monsiváis's unprecedented anthology of modern Mexican chronicles was published in 1979 with an appended study of New Journalism that I have earlier mentioned. In this study, Monsiváis provides a thumbnail review of Wolfe's 1970 *Radical Chic and Mau-Mauing the Flak Catchers*, which he characterizes as a "viaje simbólico" [symbolic trip] that becomes a "caso arquetípico" [archetypal case] ("Alabemos" 214). The book contains two long chronicles, one a report on a New York cocktail party held by Felicia and Leonard Bernstein to raise money for a Black Panthers legal fund and the other an in-depth feature on the way ghetto gangs in San Francisco confront, or "mau-mau," low-level government functionaries (flak-catchers) to get poverty-program money. If these reports' shelf life depended solely on their subject matter, Adolfo Castañón might have a point, but they stay in print because of the way they are written.[12] As Ezra Pound once said: "Literature is news that *stays* news" (cited in Coy 93).

Monsiváis's response to these chronicles is hyperbatonic. He takes the concept of radical chic and scatters it among several texts that belong to a single syntactical unit in *Amor perdido* titled "The Very Best" and subtitled "Overall Project: High Society Ambiance."[13] This is already an editorial margin note for Wolfe: The subtext for your wonderfully entertaining report on a cocktail party and its aftermath is all of New York's—and by extension, America's—class system. Let's see how U.S.-style "radical chic" works in Mexico.

Indeed, he prefaces one of the latter pieces in this group on high society with the same brief summary of Wolfe's *Radical Chic* that I mentioned earlier and then begins the text itself with the rhetorical question: "Is there or can there be Radical Chic in Mexico?"[14] Like Wolfe, Monsiváis gives us a "symbolic reality," a thick description of a specific situation or a highly significant person, and lets us decide what the resonances stand for. In this instance, the example given us in "The Dissident (Radical Chic): The Bourgeoisie with a Low-Class Heart," we do not find ourselves in a tony uptown duplex filled with well-dressed jet-setters and some rather menacing-looking members of the underclass in provocatively vulgar clothing.[15] We are in an assembly hall at a private university, which means the room is filled with "young people of considerable means," luxury cars, summer houses, their futures already assured (*Amor* 180).[16] And this is precisely why they have come to this meeting "with doubts and a worried frown" (180).[17] It's a disgrace to be rich, they feel, and one way to become a responsible citizen is to speak out against the wealthy.

The radical chic facet is activated when Monsiváis, speaking from inside the consciousness of these poor little rich kids, just as Wolfe does in *Radical Chic*, adds that the politically correct posture they loudly assert does not of course mean they should give up what they already have, or endure any kind of inquisition about the origins of the fortunes they possess. I mean, one is above that kind of trivial insignificance:

> Damn it, one *is* radical, one detests the damned oligarchy and one must obliterate exploitation, otherwise, how is one to inherit the factory without problems, how can one go to Europe for three years to get one's doctorate, how can one install the new stereo in the cabin, how can one acquire the new sports car, how can one live through those trivial conversations on the weekend. (181)[18]

This is the tone perfected by Wolfe for the blatant hypocrisy of the radical chic of New York, which Monsiváis assumes with equal ease to castigate those of Mexico. He had been dripping sarcasm over the Establishment Mexicano, the Monstruos Sagrados (Sacred Monsters) and the Ancianos de la Tribu (Ancients of the Tribe) since *Días de guardar* (1970), and he has not run out of motives to do so in 1977's *Amor perdido*. As with Wolfe's relentlessly snide reporter in the corner, popping canapés in his mouth as he ruthlessly takes Felicia Bernstein's guests apart, Monsiváis lurks like an expectant undertaker as the revolutionary bourgeois teenagers read manifestos and shout insults at the system while failing to recognize either irony or the bottom line: that they mostly want to play at revolution "with neither the intervention of consequences nor the fear of consequences" (181)[19]—very much like the politicized socialites of New York whose favorite radicals were grape workers and Panthers in California and Indians in Arizona because "they weren't likely to become too much . . . *underfoot*, as it were. Exotic, Romantic, [and] Far Off" (Wolfe, *Radical* 42).

Both Monsiváis and Wolfe step back from the dramatized portions of their chronicles to layer in the impressive amounts of in-depth reportage they are careful to document. In the case of the radical chic, both writers provide stellar histories of the old and nouveau riche that underscore the fact that the old are always more nouveau than they would like to admit (Wolfe, *Radical* 33–38; Monsiváis, *Amor* 155–63). Both writers also stress emphatically the role that the press plays in defining, shaping, and sustaining a "high" social class. Image is all, and very often, that is all there is to class.

Monsiváis makes this laughable point most cruelly in a Charlie Chaplinesque take on Mexican high society at the ballet, in a piece perfectly titled, "Light(Weight) Deceptions: Nureyev in the Palace of Fine Arts."[20] Where Wolfe simply points out the recent immigrant status of many of contemporary New York's toniest power brokers, Monsiváis peels back a thick layer of history to expose an "aristocracia pulquera" [moonshine aristocracy] as "little Indians who, scarcely thirty years ago, could barely lay claim to a mule cart and now they drive Cadillacs" (*Amor perdido* 156, 159).[21] So when this bunch throws on its smoking jackets and files with "el tout Mexique" into the grand opera house for a special evening with the famous Russian ballet dancer, Monsiváis knows he will have pocketfuls of what in New Journalism parlance is known as "found fiction." He picks out his favored victim—engineer Edmundo Serna—and, with classic new journalistic privilege, crawls inside his mind: "this dance is for fags but his wife insisted and this Russian is famous and that's all there is to it" (169).[22] Shortly after, a few male dancers come out on stage and Edmundo observes that they move around "suspiciously" or simply incomprehensibly (170). Still, everyone loves everything about the evening, except that they had been told Nureyev floats and instead he displayed a lot of controlled technique and stayed low to the ground and made very tiny movements: "What? He couldn't fly even a little bit?" (170).[23] And after viewing a dozen scene and costume changes, Betty and Verónica and Martha and Patricia and Rossy and Lolita and Vicky and Paola and Doris and Silvia,

> each in her own way, as befits a plural society, expresses . . . a discreet feeling of betrayal. And throughout Bellas Artes there arises a collective spirit of deception, the league of the defrauded. Yes, he's sensational, but why did he refuse to dance for us? What, do you suppose he saw us as ignorant Indians? . . . The Happy Few . . . are very confused. Nureyev came and didn't feel like showing off his virtuosity. An unforgettable evening . . . but thanks to them and their elegance, not because of an egotistical Russian dancer, who failed to understand that in Mexico there is now a discerning society, that there now exists a religion of Culture and the Arts. (172)[24]

Where Monsiváis may be heard to sustain a more explicit conversation with *Radical Chic* is in a longer piece, "The Self-Made Man: With No Help from Anyone, He Made It on His Own."[25] The story is not about the rich wanting to call public attention to their politically correct support for leftist causes, but there is a splashy party in a rich man's home and a strong subtext about classism and hypocrisy, as well as the more symbolic psychological message, just as there is in *Radical Chic*, about the importance of personal myths to men of wealth and fame such as Leonard Bernstein and, here, the banker Rogelio de la Bada, "greatgrandson of *The* Rogelio de la Bada, forerunner of industrialism in Querétero and, like his descendents, a famous man of fame" (*Amor* 164).[26]

To be acclaimed, loved, and respected is hugely important to Bernstein, and the scandal that resulted from the fund-raiser at his house caused him literally to be booed at a concert. In a more subtle but perhaps just as poignant way, Rogelio also sees to the false bottom of the myth that has supported his proud rise in society as a self-made man: He has in fact risen on the fortunes of his father and grandfather before him, and on the backs of uncounted thousands of laborers about whom the mariachi he hired for the party has been singing all night, and is crooning still at six o'clock in the morning (168).

Wolfe is largely self-effaced at the Bernsteins' party, although we see him occasionally reach out a hand and grab a Roquefort ball rolled in crushed nuts. Monsiváis is as invisible as the flocking on the wallpaper, just a set of ears overhearing snatches of conversation as guests take themselves on tours through the pretentious pile of marble Rogelio has built to advertise his status. Like Wolfe in *Radical Chic*, the narrator of "Self-Made Man" steps away from the crowd at times to editorialize on what he is seeing and hearing and to place it in a sociohistorical context. Also as in Wolfe's piece, Monsiváis at others times shows up inside Rogelio's head, his thoughts presented in free indirect discourse on the "irremediablemente erótico" [irremediably erotic] allure of being thought of as a self-made man. We can almost feel sorry for Rogelio when he realizes at the end that he has no right to that erotic self-delusion. Almost.

Wolfe develops a leitmotif around the theme of the Bernsteins' and other chic radicals' servants, the notion being that, rather than do without servants altogether as a radically chic move—especially given that in this instance the guests are militant Black Panthers—they had switched from black or ethnic immigrants to combing the horizon for suitable *white* servants (*Radical* 5, 9–11, 42–41). This became such a difficulty at times that some high-society matrons were known to put on an apron and be a maid for themselves and each other. Anything at all to preserve the *principle* of the thing: You simply could not do without servants. In his party piece, Monsiváis suggests the same through a snippet of overheard conversation that hilariously adds the element of Mexico's high percentage of illiteracy. A woman complains to a friend that she cannot have a lover "because my maid is illiterate. Since she can't write messages down, she learns them by heart and repeats them to me in front of everybody" (*Amor* 165).[27] The leitmotif Monsiváis develops is similarly related to the topic of servants and the vast subjugated underclass, here represented in the plaintive song of the mariachi who throughout the narrative threads his laments of loss, poverty, and rural pathos among the voices describing the indescribable splendor of de la Bada's lifestyle (163, 165, 166, 167, 168). One of the conversations that Monsiváis pointedly highlights establishes an ironic contrast between this mansion with its exclusive guest list and "the problem of confronting the hordes of Ciudad Nezahualcóyotl," a sprawling slum community that mushroomed as the impoverished rural landscape continued to drive its poor by the millions toward the hope of jobs in the city.[28] These *paracaidistas*, or "parachutists," who appear overnight to squat on unoccupied land at the fringes of the cityscape will, Rogelio's guests fear, end up devouring everything: "What maws! They multiply like rabbits. Where there was one miserable shanty there's now a whole village" (164–65).[29]

Wolfe develops the theme of the two Americas, black and white, and Monsiváis develops the theme of the two Mexicos, rich and poor, or Indian and white. What is noticeably different, however, is that while Wolfe devotes seventeen pages of his chronicle to a heated argument—a spontaneous dialogue—between the Black Panthers and the white guests at the Bernsteins' and between some of those with differing opinions, Monsiváis's alienated social classes remain separated and silent, even as they brush shoulders with each other in the house and face each other across a short geographical space outside the mansion: There is no dialogue between any of the Mexicos. And while Monsiváis does not explicitly make that difference a focus of his series on Mexico's high society, it is a consistent element of the point he has made throughout his fifty-year career about the possibility of democratization in Mexico. That ungoverned dialogue at the grassroots level— that capacity for autonomous self-criticism—is one of the national character traits that Monsiváis and other Mexican intellectuals, such as Octavio Paz and Carlos Fuentes, always most admired about the U.S. people and wished to cultivate in Mexico.[30]

If the Panthers and, by extension, César Chávez's grape pickers and Arizona reservation Indians can be considered the victims of Felicia and Leonard Bernstein, civil servants drawing miserable salaries to administer government poverty programs in the 1960s can be considered quasi victims of the urban black, Chicano, and Indian gangs who learned the art of mau-mauing, or confrontational tactics to get large money grants funded by government poverty-programs after the civil rights movement. In Wolfe's version, machismo is a major issue, used as a weapon by the government to sucker minorities into thinking they had gained something when in fact the office confrontations—a self-parody of terrorism—boiled down to a kind of swaggering gamesmanship on both sides (Wolfe, *Radical* 117–19): The mau-mauers got the satisfaction of making the flak catchers look scared, and the flak catchers got the satisfaction of flushing gang leaders out of hiding so they could identify people to give money away to.

Wolfe entertains himself hugely in this hyperbolic reality with extravagant tropes that depict the mannered machismo of neighborhood toughs as, for example, the unbending secretary birds, who liked to run meetings with the flak catcher while sporting their hypercool pimp look:

But the pimp-style aristocrats had taken the manhood thing through so many numbers that it was beginning to come out through the other side. . . . It was like saying, . . . We're so confident of our manhood, we're so hip and so suave and wise in the ways of the street, that we can afford to be *refined* and not sit around here trying to look like a bunch of stud brawlers. So they would not only cross their legs, they'd cross them further than a woman would. They would cross them so far, it looked like one leg was wrapped around the other one three or four times. . . . They would look like one of those supercool secretary birds that stand around on one long A-1 racer leg with everything else drawn up into a beautiful supercool little bunch of fluffy feathers at the top. (134–35)

He also extends himself for pages on the flamboyant way that an African American and his theatrical flock of children armed with melting ice-cream cones (a ludic metaphor for filth) invade San Francisco's elegant City Hall to "mau-mau" the mayor himself out of his office for a meeting and a concession.

Monsiváis's version of the mau-mauing gimmick is much more subtle. He trails a bevy of young true-believers—survivors of the 1968 student movement—to the place where democratic reform is struggling to put down grass roots: the farthest outskirts of sprawling Mexico City, its so-called lost cities, the overnight slums where desperate rural migrants "parachute" onto the urban landscape to become squatters on undeveloped land. They hammer together tin and cardboard shacks, string together horrifically dangerous tangles of extension cords to plug into far-distant pole lines, dig shallow trenches down the middle of a row of hovels and call them a sanitary system, and brace themselves for travel that may take four or five hours each way into the city's center, where they will sell Kleenex or swallow fire or stand in a subway car to sing songs for a living. They live without water, without transportation, without nearby shopping, with no schooling for their children, with no medical service, and with no notice of the government.

But the Mexican equivalent of the civil rights movement—of those fire-eating, bus-riding, constitutional evangelizers of the 1960s who rode down South into the valley of the shadow of death to register the black vote—young graduates of Tlatelolco, took notice of the millions of Mexicans who decided that maybe not starving to death in the city was better than starving to death for sure in the countryside. Monsiváis picks out a woman as the symbol of change. She is the one, after all, who is home with the children while the man is away struggling to earn enough for dinner. She goes to a meeting convened by some of those student activists, where symbolic members of both Mexicos will finally begin speaking to each other. The diametrical opposite of Wolfe's secretary-bird gangster, this woman scurries to her first meeting with fast little steps, head down, mouth shut, terrified. Eventually, though, she puts her head up, acquires a name among the neighbor women, and begins to understand something about water, civil rights, and herself. One fine day, she raises her hand and says that she's had it up to here, all that huge distance she has to cover with the buckets, the guy with the water charges whatever he likes, there are creeps who throw the water at her, it's just not fair, she feels like crying but she really would rather say that she's not putting up with it any more, she's getting angrier and angrier and she screams that it's not right, she is a human being and her friends and acquaintances applaud her words with glances and hands. (Monsiváis, *Entrada* 240)[31]

She has discovered the strength of her voice, just when a government representative—a flak catcher—is sent to explain that it's not in their hands, that the city administrator . . . and here she dares to interrupt the man and demand that the administrator come and speak to them himself.

The underling has no answer ("I'm sorry that Mr. Johnson isn't here today," says Wolfe's flak catcher [*Radical* 109]), and while we're waiting to hear what comes next, Monsiváis takes over to explain how such colonies came to be organized, with the indispensable help of student activists, in ways that empowered them to deal effectively in confrontations with government agents. These are not gang members intent on winning money through fear; but all the same, the dominant emotion is fear, for Mexico's government had never until the late 1960s experienced an informed and organized civil society willing to confront power and insist on its rights and on the government's obligations to serve.

Now Monsiváis slips back inside the anxious mind of the government delegate facing these young people from the poor district. What in the world do they *want*, he wonders? I've given them some of what they demanded. This is a nightmare. They won't go away. They're full of facts, even the women, and we can't just beat them up the way we used to. And the worst is, there's never a shortage of people in this country, and they'll all come and stand in front of his desk with "esos semblantes estólidos" [those stolid faces] (244). (Wolfe's flak catcher, meanwhile, has tried to "shuck" a roomful of mau-mauers, to no avail; huge black and brown men, they begin beating on the floor until he promises to make a phone call. Later they chortle: "Did you see the look on his face? Did you see the sucker trembling? . . . He was *scared*, man!" [*Radical* 118].)

Back at the lost city where the migrant woman was demanding water, she is now asking for title to her plot of land. She's willing to sit for hours and hours and hours. She'll wear that delegate down. "The waiting rooms have spread out all over, and the use of their patience is now political" (245).[32]

Some time before Carlos Monsiváis was observing how disenfranchised Mexican women gently mau-maued public flak catchers, he had observed that, "like all movements at the service of triumphant topicality, the New Journalism exhausts its themes or begins to parody its own style. What [else] is it to do?" ("Alabemos" 202).[33] Perhaps a part of that observation is based on the fact that, unlike the Mexican chronicle from the 1960s onward, U.S. new journalism articles and books are much less likely to center on political themes. Politics may be a part of the overall message—Wolfe's *Radical Chic* touches on the political problems of white and black, poor and rich, and his *Mau-Mauing* is about the politics of poverty and the confrontation of government and citizen. Similarly, in "The Last American Hero," for example, as Wolfe mesmerizes us with a tale about Junior Johnson the Southern stock-car racer, he weaves politics into the background story about whiskey running and the way poor Appalachia folk are hounded, taxed, and jailed (*Kandy* 126–72). Still, Wolfe's concerns are almost never overtly political. He is interested in what makes the American people tick, especially in the vitality of the underbelly, of the life that swarms up when a rock is kicked over.

Mailer's extensive work—books about such seminal events as political conventions, rockets to the moon, executions of prisoners, antiwar protests, and so forth—might be considered much more substantive in a sociopolitical sense. But if we consider other magnificent writers—John McPhee, Joan Didion, Jane Kramer, Tracy Kidder, Hunter S. Thompson, Annie Dillard, Richard West, Studs Terkel, Michael Parfit, et al.—and the themes of their works, among them, Alaska, Georgia back roads, flying across America, Antarctica, famous restaurants, cowboy culture, blue-collar workers, woods and creeks, Las Vegas, public schools, the orange, Venice, California, et cetera, it is clear that, while the tag of frivolous would be unfair, neither would political be an accurate label for U.S. New Journalism as a whole. As a general rule, the Mexican chronicle tends to be more directly political.

The difference is nonjudgmental, however—in this respect: It is most likely a consequence of disparities in U.S. and Mexican social and political development, status, and perceived goals. On the surface of daily life, at least, the need for social, political, and economic reform in the United States does not appear to be as crushingly imminent as it does in almost any city, village, and neighborhood in Mexico, from almost any vantage. In the same way that Mexico routinely views North America as materialistic and itself as cultural and spiritual, U.S. new journalists feel a freedom Mexican chroniclers may not to select topics for in-depth reportage that can, from across the border, appear less than essential to the well-being of society, if not outright irresponsible: the pecking order for seating at a posh New York restaurant, blood sport in heartland America, strip-mining in Montana, a Vietnam vet returning home from the war. These are, in fact, deeply political realities, but they examine a mature democracy from sophisticated angles and from an admittedly privileged socioeconomic perch.

That being noted, it seems clear that one benefit not known to Tom Wolfe and other new journalists, in the heyday of New Journalism or now, of Carlos Monsiváis's literary dialogue with them—besides that he is, in fact, carrying on a dialogue with them—is the way his texts give the practice of novelized reportage and its followers fresh life. The insistent secretary bird in Wolfe's *Mau-Mauing* is perhaps already overly precious in 1970. But in both Wolfe's and Monsiváis's pieces, the plight of the flak catcher makes us laugh, and almost sympathize with the poor guy; however, the difference between the Mexican and the U.S. representation of mau-mauing is telling: The quiet escalation of the woman's political use of patience is not as splashy as the gangster's storklike contortions, but we sense that the ripples she stirs will spread farther.

NOTES

1. The title essay, about the custom-car culture in California, was first published in *Esquire* magazine in 1963 as "There Goes [Varoom! Varoom!] That Kandy-Kolored Tangerine-Flake Streamline Baby."
2. "tanto cretino con poder." All translations of the original Spanish are mine.
3. "el lujo de burlarme, en mi modestísimo grado de acción, de la estupidez del poderoso."
4. These comments were not included in the final version of an interview I conducted at his home in Mexico City in 1991 (see Egan, "Entrevista"). *Silence of the Lambs* is but the most widely recognized of Thomas Harris's chilling psychological thrillers, in part because of the popular movie based on it, starring Anthony Hopkins and Jodie Foster. His novels include *Red Dragon* and *Black Sunday*, which have also been made into movies, as were *Hannibal* and *Hannibal Rising*, sequels to *Silence*.
5. "contrarrestar la avidez triunfal de la televisión." Richard Kallan puts it similarly: "The stylistic components of Wolfe's symbolic expression coalesce to create an oral, 'televisionic' journalism" (54).
6. John Reed spent a year (1914) with Pancho Villa's army before writing *Insurgent Mexico*, at once a detailed reportorial look at the waning days of Villa's revolutionary strength and a lyrically symbolic overview of the underlying historical and collective psychological forces that for Reed explained the Mexican Revolution's failure, just a few years before he traveled to Russia to report on that country's massive popular insurrection. James A. Agee's *Let Us Now Praise Famous Men* (1940), a "poetic documentary" [documental poético] (Chillón 196) of poor Depression-era farmworkers during Roosevelt's New Deal, famously illustrated by Walker Evans's photographs, is perhaps the most laudable and well-known precursor of the New Journalism twenty years later. Truman Capote's *In Cold Blood* (1965) echoes some of the stark black-and-white realism of Agee's and Walker's documentary of hardscrabble life, for Capote's meticulous recreation in what he calls a nonfiction novel of the murders of all the members of a Kansas farm family by two drifters has something of the hopeless injustice depicted in Agee's account. Mailer's Pulitzer-Prize winning *The Armies of the Night* (1968), subtitled "History as a Novel, the Novel as History," is a fiction-styled chronicle of a march on the Pentagon to protest U.S. involvement in Vietnam and is, according to another Mexican student of U.S. New Journalism, "a singular work, at once journalistic and autobiographical, because Mailer not only covered the event as a reporter, but also as a most noticeable protagonist" [una obra singular, a un tiempo periodística y autobiográfica, puesto que Mailer no sólo cubrió el acontecimiento en calidad de reportero, sino también como protagonista destacado] (Chillón 276). In another literary chronicle, *Of a Fire on the Moon* (1969), Mailer confronts and demystifies the science of NASA, computer technology, and the quest to conquer space. Kesey "wrote several passages of the book under peyote and LSD. He even had someone give him a shock treatment, clandestinely, so he could write a passage in which Chief Broom comes back from 'the shock shop' " (Wolfe, *Electric Kool-Aid* 44).
7. New journalist chronicler José Joaquín Blanco is an exception in Mexico. Somewhat

younger than Monsiváis, Blanco has published numerous analyses on the *crónica* genre. See, for example, his "Otra prosa periodística" and *Crónica de la literatura reciente*.

8. The number of participants could be larger, including such well-known New Journalism theorists as John Hollowell (*Fact and Fiction: The New Journalism and the Nonfiction Novel*) and Mas'ud Zavarzadeh (*The Mythopoetic Reality*), but round tables with more than five or six members tend to drive off the audience.

9. "Desde un punto de vista formal, una influencia muy renovadora en la crónica es en algunos aspectos, el New Journalism, el nuevo periodismo norteamericano. Los trabajos de Norman Mailer, Tom Wolfe, Hunter Thompson, Truman Capote, Gay Talese, etcétera, han revivido el interés en un género, agregándole diversidad de técnicas, la feroz intromisión del Yo o de la moda, el culto por la 'pequeña historia,' el afán por documentar narrativamente los nuevos estilos de vida, la persecución de los personajes y las figuras arquetípicas. Si como tendencia dominante, el *New Journalism* es desplazado por el reportaje de investigación a-lo-Watergate, como tendencia impone perdurablemente actitudes y procedimientos."

10. Although Albert Chillón comes on the scene too late to join the imaginary round table, his excellent study *Literatura y periodismo: una tradición de relaciones promiscuas* (1999) adds another Spanish speaker's perspective on the New Journalism. Chillón calls it "reportaje novelado" [novelized reportage] (192) and says that "since it was born, besides suckling from the novel of fiction, novelized reportage was absorbing proprietary traits from diverse testimonial literary modalities, such as newspapers and account books, biographies, autobiographies and memoirs, travelogues, chronicles, descriptions of manners and customs and even epistolary literature. . . . And something else: In novelized reportage today one can detect traits of composition and style that are not exclusively literary: for example, traces of narrative techniques characteristic of cinematic art and of documentary TV—parallel montage and the taste for scenic representation, for example" [Desde que nació, además de mamar de la novela de ficción, el reportaje novelado fue absorbiendo rasgos propios de diversas modalidades literarias testimoniales, como los diarios y dietarios, las biografías, las autobiografías y memorias, las narraciones de viajes y de experiencias, las crónicas, la prosa costumbrista e incluso la literatura epistolar . . . Y aún más: en el reportaje novelado de nuestros días se detectan rasgos de composición y estilo no exclusivamente literarios: por ejemplo, la huella de técnicas narrativas características del arte cinematográfico y del documentalismo televisivo—el montaje paralelo o el gusto por la representación escénica, por ejemplo] (193).

11. One could perform an exhaustive stylistic study, for example, of the ways in which Wolfe's and other new journalists' tics of punctuation, diction, trope, use of white space, and so forth seem visibly reflected in Monsiváis's early work, particularly in *Días de guardar* (1970), *Amor perdido* (1977), and *Escenas de pudor y liviandad* (1988). More specifically, and just to name a single example, a chronicle such as the one in *Días* covering the presidential election campaign of Luis Echeverría ("Saluda al sol, araña" [Greet the sun, spider]) could be viewed in the light of Norman Mailer's 1968 chronicles on the Republican and Democratic campaigns, *Miami and the Siege of Chicago*.

12. Marshall McLuhan would call this a case of the medium becoming the message. Monsiváis is also a close reader of the North American McLuhan's messages; he frequently refers to the media guru's most famous dictum throughout his chronicles and conducts an intertextual dialog with McLuhan's "medium is the message" and "Global Village" themes in "México a través de McLuhan" (*Días de guardar*).

13. "La crema de la crema": Literally, from the French expression English has stolen: la crème de la crème, the cream that has risen to the top of the cream, or the richest and purest of the milk: the best of the best. The subtitle: "El proyecto general: atmósferas de alta sociedad."

14. "¿Hay o puede haber Radical Chic en México?"

15. "El 'disidente' (Radical Chic): los burgueses con corazón de masa."

16. "hijos de la abundancia."

17. "con inquietudes y ceño preocupado."

18. "Uno, qué diablos, es radical, detesta a la maldita oligarquía y hay que hacer añicos a la explotación, de otro modo cómo heredar sin problemas la fábrica, cómo irse a Europa tres años al doctorado, cómo fijar el nuevo estéreo en la cabaña, cómo adquirir el carro sport, cómo aceptar las conversaciones triviales del fin de semana."

19. "sin que intervengan ni las consecuencias ni el temor a las consecuencias."

20. "Las decepciones leves: Nureyev en Bellas Artes."

21. "Aristocracia pulquera" is virtually untranslatable to English, as *pulque* is the "lowest" or cheapest and most ubiquitous of three alcoholic drinks made from the *maguey* or century plant in Mexico, important in the culture from prehispanic times to the present. Throughout colonial and nineteenth-century nation formation, *pulque* was held to be responsible for the rampant alcoholism that came to characterize the indigenous population and, in general, the poor and disenfranchised, the pariahs of society. *Pulque* and the *pulquerías* (bars selling the drink) on every corner were an emblem of premodern, underdeveloped Mexico. With the phrase "*pulque* aristocracy," Monsiváis slams pop Mexico's wannabe radical chic with a vicious satirical hammer, "inditos que hace treinta años apenas podían con una carreta de mulas y ahora manejan cádillacs."

22. "la danza es para mujercitos pero su esposa insistió y el ruso éste tiene fama y no hay más que hablar."

23. "¿qué no podría volar un poquito?"

24. "cada una por su lado como corresponde a una sociedad plural, emiten . . . una discreta sensación de engaño. Y se eleva en Bellas Artes el espíritu coaligado de la decepción, la liga de los defraudados. Sí, es sensacional, pero ¿por qué no quiso bailar para nosotros? ¿Qué, nos habrá visto inditos? . . . Los happy few . . . están muy confundidos. Vino Nureyev y no le dio la gana exhibir su virtuosismo. Una velada inolvidable . . . pero gracias a ellos y su elegancia, no por un egoísta bailarín ruso, que no llegó a entender que en México ya hay sociedad exigente, ya hay religión de la Cultura y el Arte."

25. "El Self-Made Man: sin ayuda de nadie, se hizo a sí mismo."

26. "biznieto de *The* Rogelio de la Bada, precursor del industrialismo en Querétero y, como sus descendientes, famoso hombre de fama."

27. "porque mi criada es analfabeta. Como no sabe escribir recados, se los aprende de memoria y me los repite delante de la gente."

28. "el problema de enfrentarse a las hordas de Ciudad Nezahualcóyotl."

29. "¡Qué fauces! Se multiplican al mil por uno. Donde había un miserable ahora hay una colonia."

30. "The Mexican intelligentsia as a whole has not been able or has not known how to use their own intellectual weapons: critical thought, examination, judgment. . . . In Europe and the United States [for] the intellectual . . . his main mission is critical thought; in Mexico, political action" [La "inteligencia" mexicana, en su conjunto, no ha podido o no ha sabido utilizar las armas propias del intelectual: la crítica, el examen, el juicio . . . . En Europa y los Estados Unidos el intelectual . . . su misión

principal es la crítica; en México, la acción política] (Paz 171). Fuentes, while noting that "the United States has been successful at everything that we Mexicans have
failed at" (*New Time* 208), contrasts the classical Greek civilization that underlies U.S.
culture and the indigenous (Aztec) civilization that underlies contemporary Mexican
culture, finding that Greece was an open democracy and Aztec Mexico was a closed
theocracy, and that Greece, up against other nations, had to develop tolerance for
"criticism and . . . self-analysis" [la crítica y . . . la autocrítica], while "in Mexico there
was a complete absence of critical thought in the succession of the imperial war of the
world" [en México, hubo una completa ausencia de crítica en la sucesión guerrera,
imperial, del mundo] (*Tiempo* 27).

31. "que ya está hasta la madre, todo el tramo inmenso que debe recorrer con los baldes,
el pipero les cobra lo que se le antoja, hay maloras que le tiran el agua, y no es justo,
tiene ganas de llorar pero prefiere decir que ya no aguanta, se enoja todavía más y
grita que no es justo, ella es un ser humano y sus amigos y conocidos aprueban con
mirada y manos sus palabras."

32. "Han extendido por doquier las antesalas, y es ya político el uso de su paciencia."

33. "como toda corriente al servicio de la actualidad triunfante, el Nuevo Periodismo
agota temas o cae en fatigas estilísticas. [Y] ¿qué le va a hacer?"

WORKS CITED

Agee, James A., and Walker Evans. *Let Us Now Praise Famous Men: Three Tenant Families.*
Boston: Houghton Mifflin; Cambridge: Riverside Press, 1941.

Blanco, José Joaquín. *Crónica de la literatura reciente en México (1950–1980).* Mexico:
Instituto Nacional de Antropología e Historia, 1982.

————. "Otra prosa periodística." *Función de medianoche.* Mexico: Era, 1981. 19–24.

Capote, Truman. *In Cold Blood: A True Account of a Multiple Murder and Its Consequences.*
New York: Random House, 1965.

Castañón, Adolfo. "Un hombre llamado ciudad." *Vuelta* 163 (1990): 19–22.

Chillón, Albert. *Literatura y periodismo: una tradición de relaciones promiscuas.* Valencia:
Universitat Autónoma de Barcelona, Universitat de València, 1999.

Coy, Juan José. "De Norman Mailer a Vázquez Montalbán: a la sombra del Nuevo
Periodismo." *Letras en el espejo: ensayos de literatura americana comparada.* Ed. María
José Álvarez Maurín, Manuel Broncano, and José Luis Chamosa. Leon, Spain:
Universidad de León, 1997. 91–100.

Domínguez Michael, Christopher, ed. *Antología de la narrativa mexicana del siglo XX.* Vol.
2. México: Fondo de Cultura Económica, 1991.

Egan, Linda. *Carlos Monsiváis: Culture and Chronicle in Contemporary Mexico.* Tucson:
University of Arizona Press, 2001.

————. "Entrevista con Carlos Monsiváis." *La Jornada Semanal*, 26 January 1992, 16–22.

Eltit, Diamela, and Carlos Monsiváis. "Un diálogo (¿o dos monólogos?) sobre la censura.
Una plática con Diamela Eltit y Carlos Monsiváis sobre sus respectivas experiencias
con la censura en Chile y en México." *Debate Feminista* 9 (1994): 25–50.

Fuentes, Carlos. *A New Time for Mexico.* Trans. Marina Gutman Castañeda and the author. Berkeley and Los Angeles: University of California Press, 1997.

————. *Tiempo mexicano.* Mexico: Joaquín Mortiz, 1971.

García, Gustavo. "México bien vale una crónica." *Revista de la Universidad de México* 33.11
(1979): 41–42.

———. "Monsiváis: los rostros evanescentes y entrañables." *Revista de la Universidad de México* 32.6 (1978): 29.

Hellman, John. *Fables of Fact: The New Journalism as New Fiction.* Urbana: University of Illinois Press, 1981.

Hollowell, John. *Fact and Fiction: The New Journalism and the Nonfiction Novel.* Chapel Hill: University of North Carolina Press, 1977.

Kallan, Richard A. "Style and the New Journalism: A Rhetorical Analysis of Tom Wolfe." *Communication Monograph* 46.1 (1979): 52–62.

MacDonald, Dwight. "Parajournalism, or Tom Wolfe and His Magic Writing Machine." *The Reporter as Artist: A Look at the New Journalism Controversy.* Ed. Ronald Weber. New York: Hastings House, 1974. 223–33.

Mailer, Norman. *The Armies of the Night: History as a Novel, the Novel as History.* New York: Signet, 1968.

———. *Miami and the Siege of Chicago.* New York: Signet, 1968.

———. *Of a Fire on the Moon.* Boston, Toronto: Little, Brown, 1969.

Menocal, Nina. "Carlos Monsiváis." *México: visión de los ochenta.* Mexico: Editorial Diana, 1981. 11–26.

Monsiváis, Carlos. "Alabemos ahora a los hombres famosos (Sobre el Nuevo Periodismo norteamericano)." *Antología de la crónica en México.* 1st ed. Mexico: Textos de Humanidades; Universidad Nacional Autónoma de México, 1979. 199–220.

———. *Amor perdido.* Mexico: Era, 1977.

———, ed. *A ustedes les consta: antología de la crónica en México.* 2d ed. México: Era, 1980.

———. *Días de guardar.* Mexico: Era, 1970.

———. *Entrada libre: crónicas de la sociedad que se organiza.* Mexico: Era, 1987.

———. *Escenas de pudor y liviandad.* Mexico: Grijalbo, 1988.

Paz, Octavio. *El laberinto de la soledad. Postdata. Vuelta a El laberinto de la soledad.* Mexico: Fondo de Cultura Económica, 1981.

Poniatowska, Elena. "Las décadas en el espejo." *Nexos* 9.106 (1986): 7–10.

Reed, John. *Insurgent Mexico.* New York and London: D. Appleton, 1914.

Scura, Dorothy, ed. *Conversations with Tom Wolfe.* Jackson and London: University Press of Mississippi, 1990.

Shomette, Doug, ed. *The Critical Response to Tom Wolfe.* Westport, Conn., and London: Greenwood Press, 1992.

Weber, Ronald. "Some Sort of Artistic Excitement." *The Reporter as Artist: A Look at the New Journalism Controversy.* Ed. Ronald Weber. New York: Hastings House, 1974. 13–26.

Wolfe, Tom. *The Electric Kool-Aid Acid Test.* New York: Bantam Books, 1969.

———. *The Kandy-Kolored Tangerine-Flake Streamline Baby.* New York: Farrar, Straus and Giroux, 1987.

———. "The New Journalism." *The New Journalism.* Ed. Tom Wolfe and E. W. Johnson. London: Pan Books, 1975. 13–68.

———. *Radical Chic and Mau-Mauing the Flak Catchers.* New York: Farrar, Straus and Giroux, 1965.

Zavarzadeh, Mas'ud. *The Mythopoetic Reality: The Postwar American Nonfiction Novel.* Urbana: University of Illinois Press, 1976.

CHAPTER 6

From Fags to Gays

Political Adaptations and Cultural Translations in the Mexican Gay Liberation Movement

Héctor Domínguez-Ruvalcaba

In a text commemorating the fifteenth anniversary of Lesbian-Gay Culture Week (June 2001), Carlos Monsiváis offers a lexical distinction that seems useful for understanding the transformation that Mexican sexual culture has experienced since the introduction of the concept of "gayness" (*lo gay*) along with gay politics and lifestyle: "Gay is not a synonym of '*homosexual, maricón, puto, tortillera, invertido, sodomita*,' but rather a word which names attitudes, organizations, and behaviors that were unknown until recently. In the same way, *desclosetarse* or coming out of the closet used to be an action tied to shamelessness and the cynicism of those who had nothing to lose, but is now an act which proclaims the legitimacy of difference" (9).[1] Gayness marks a watershed in Mexican sexual culture. It is a concept that is not synonymous with *tortillera, maricón, puto o invertido*, although it refers to those very same concepts.[2] The semantic precision proposed by Monsiváis focuses on the politics of slander, which contrasts the pre-gay terminology (produced in the context of traditional homophobia) with the vindicating concept of gayness: tied to happiness, pride, community, and the declaration of legitimacy and difference. From this angle, the introduction of the word "gay" to the Mexican lexicon underlines the creation of a space of liberation, the designation of a legitimate social identity—in sum, the creation of a culture that would embrace subjects previously scorned because of their sexual preference. At the same time, the introduction of this word opens a new chapter in the ongoing debate over North American influence in Mexico, since some criticize the international gay rights movement as cultural colonization. In this chapter, I address the implications of the introduction of gay politics and culture in Mexico, emphasizing the contradictions in the Mexican gay movement, the politics of coming out of the closet and its socioeconomic and cultural effects, and the resignification of pre-gay categories in the era of globalization.

The Mexican gay liberation movement was founded in 1971 (two years after the Stonewall riots) on the liberating precepts produced in North American gay politics.[3] Nevertheless, civil inclusion and self-identification had already manifested in Mexico before that milestone. The history of antihomophobic resistance in Mexico should be traced back to the group of artists and writers gathered around the magazine *Los Contemporáneos* in the 1920s and 1930s, specifically in certain poetry by Salvador Novo and Xavier Villaurrutia and artwork by Abraham Ángel, Roberto Montenegro, Manuel Rodríguez Lozano, and Augustín Lazo. Attentive to the homophilic—that is to say, not homophobic—works produced in Europe during that era, these first attempts at dignifying the image of homosexuality and accompanying lifestyle inform us of the process that the politics of gender will follow in Mexico from that time on. Since these homophilic ideas were imported from imperialist nations (for example, Novo and Villaurrutia translated French homosexual authors such as André Gide), they had to carry the weight of a colonialist political label that threatened national identity. In 1925 and 1932, the newspapers of Mexico City published several vehemently critical articles that harshly equated the effeminacy of men of letters with the corruption of nationality. These arguments provoked a strong defense of the universalist culture represented by the *Los Contemporáneos* group in which criticism of nationalist virility suggests an antihomophobic politics. Nevertheless, this antihomophobic position was not completely free of pathological definitions of homosexuality. Robert M. Irwin notes there is a "freudianization" of the country in the beginning of the twentieth century (32). Psychoanalysis allows the homosexual subject to know himself as such, that is, to know himself through a pathological definition of self. If in the postrevolutionary period this affirmative homosexuality, although "unhealthy," awakened issues related to nationalism and cultural dependence, in the 1970s the specter of Stonewall as the founding saga of the international gay movement will inevitably also bear a colonialist hue that must be examined.

The appearance of gayness on the Mexican cultural horizon is part of a larger history of influences and translations of North American processes and as such is marked by a mixture of acceptance and resistance, as is the case with many of the ideas and fashions emanating from the United States. Among these, perhaps the gay rights movement faces the greatest obstacles to being admitted into Mexican culture, mainly because homosexuality is considered a threat to national identity by the most emphatic spokespersons of the postrevolutionary period.[4] Throughout Mexican history, homosexuality has been an other which through its exclusion defines national identity. Gay culture thus would be part of the Americanization that has threatened Mexicanness since the nineteenth century. This contradiction is essential to understanding the context of the terms Monsiváis contrasts: Gayness liberates us from Mexican homophobic culture, which has been especially scathing because of the need to define national profiles through exclusion. In this context, Mexican societal foundations were built upon slander, which now implies that the consolidation of gay culture will dismantle the bases of homophobia and force revision of nationalist discourses. Gender connotations are central to collective cultural definitions in the majority of genres that represent nationalist concepts (the novel of the Mexican Revolution, *ranchera* films, *corridos*, etc.). In these, the virile figure is privileged as the model of Mexicanness.

The confrontation of national homophobia with Americanizing liberation—that is, the beginning of the Mexican gay liberation movement—marks a profound shift in the political coordinates in which nationalist politics must give way to those of civil rights. Is it possible, then, to speak of a Mexican gay rights movement that differs from the North American movement? Is the gay liberation movement really more than a symptom of Americanization? Must it in fact necessarily be seen as an effect of globalizing politics, as various authors have suggested (Cruz-Malavé, Hawley, Altman)? Given the drastic cultural and historical differences between Mexico and the United States, how can we speak of similar conditions in the rise and development of the gay liberation movements in both countries? These questions help us to consider the Mexican gay rights movement as more than an emulation of its North American counterpart. It is a complex of adaptations and new meanings that tie the Mexican phenomenon to the international gay rights movement (which arose in the United States and was propagated as a necessity and a way of life throughout the planet), while at the same time it is responsible for the politics of the battle for sexual liberation in the face of Mexico's own unique problems. These adaptations and new meanings inscribe the Mexican gay liberation movement within the postcolonial processes of appropriation and redirection of metropolitan models.

North American and Mexican Gay Activism: Recurring Asymmetries

Since the struggles for independence at the beginning of the nineteenth century, lessons from North American history have been put to the test in Mexican political experiments. Beginning in that period, Mexican liberals closely followed the intellectual proposals of their northern neighbor, and they transplanted laws, protocols, and consignments that they judged necessary for the modernization of the country. Continuing this attentive reading of political proposals and movements in North America, the gay liberation movement arrives as part of an emancipating boom along with sexual freedom, pacifism, rock and roll, and fascination with psychotropic drugs.

Reading the North American gay movement is, then, a lesson of modernization involving politics and lifestyle. As we can find in different instances throughout this volume, a number of U.S. cultural elements incorporated into society teach Mexico about modernity. Antonio Marquet, a gay Mexican public intellectual and academic, when examining the lessons learned from the North American gay rights movement, underlines the act of coming out of the closet as a political phenomenon that has opened up spaces for gay society. Two questions Marquet poses in regard to Kenneth Paul Rosenberg's documentary *Why Am I Gay?* point us to this enlightening reading: "Why doesn't the equivalent of Eddie Rodríguez, the New York policeman who declares his preferences to the camera in the middle of his precinct, exist in Mexico? Why can't the Mexican policeman quit being the jackal that besets, bribes, and violates the rights of homosexuals?" (Marquet 145–46).[5] The questions formulated by Marquet introduce us to a comparative reading of the two judicial systems and activist practices. At the same time, they indicate the best way of reading the relevant events of North American gay politics as actions that exemplify civic participation. In this we encounter a reiteration of one of the ways of interpreting North America that has been legitimized by Mexican intellectuals: the exaltation of dissident subjects, the homage to North American civil society.

The admiration of dissidents also implies a criticism of the conservative aspect of the United States. In his note about the documentary *The Age of Harvey Milk*, Marquet alludes to the repudiated aspect of the image of North American society as puritanical and intolerant. An assassin of a gay politician from San Francisco is the pride of North American mothers in 1978 and represents the backward values of a dominant group characterized by fundamentalist ideology (140). Marquet concludes that this documentary shows how ethnic and sexual minorities, by joining together, can overcome the arbitrary rules of groups in power. This reading turns the U.S. gay rights sagas into instructional texts for the political practices of minorities.

But to what degree have these lessons about U.S. civil society prospered in Mexico? While North American gay activism has been remarkably effective in the area of legislation against discrimination and homophobia, Mexican activism faces setbacks in the area of human rights where, as in the case of women and indigenous peoples, the situation has become not only worse but even lethal——as is evident in the assassination of gay leaders in recent years, such as the cases of Jorge Armenta in 2003 and Octavio Acuña in 2005. These facts oblige us to delve into the systems, the organizational practices, and the contexts that influence the failure in one country of proposals that were successful in the other. The analysis of such differences will be a key task for conducting a gay politics that rearticulates the original U.S. agenda.

According to Margaret Cruikshank, the North American struggle for gay rights arose in the context of the hippie and civil rights peace movements. In her view, the antiauthoritarian climate that had fostered a method of protest against the prejudices of North American society is what made it possible for the gay rights movement to evolve (62). Let's take this context as a point of comparison with the Mexican phenomenon. The 1968 student movement is the epitome of Mexican-style political protest during the 1960s.[6] In Mexico, neither civil rights nor peace was the focus of the clashes between people and power. Rather, the student movement was defined by demands for democracy and a clearly socialist agenda, which identified Mexico more with the rest of Latin America than with the United States, where support for the socialist bloc did not enjoy the same popularity as civil rights and peace. Within this context, it is important to point out that Mexican resistance in the 1960s is not articulated in terms of minority groups but rather is more focused on protecting the nation and Latin American identity from North American domination: One is socialist because one is anti-United States.

The protest movements of the 1960s and 1970s in Mexico focused on correcting the Mexican Revolution within Marxist criteria as the only path to democratization, as can be read in greatly influential political works such as *Ensayo sobre un proletariado sin cabeza* (Essay about a Leaderless Proletariat) by José Revueltas (1982) and *La revolución interrumpida* (The Interrupted Revolution) by Adolfo Gilly (1978). This context influences the gay rights movement, for what could be considered the first public homosexual protest was really a contingent of the march on 2 October 1978 commemorating the tenth anniversary of the massacre of students in Tlatelolco by the Mexican army.[7] Rather than the antiauthoritarian profile of the civil rights politics that engendered the North American gay movement, Mexican sexual activism was embedded in the socialist agenda, which accounts for most of its inefficacy. Similar to what happened with leftist socialist and communist parties, the gay and lesbian activist groups in the 1970s (Movimiento de Liberación Homosexual de México, Sex-Pol, Lesbos, etc.) tended to fall apart because of disagreements over ideological position, dogmatism, and differences of opinion over organizational issues (Hernández Cabrera 290). The same criticism that José Revueltas expresses in his essays and novels with respect to the disorganization and dogmatism of the Mexican Communist Party applies to the errors that destroyed the first lesbian-gay organizations in Mexico. The transfer of gay politics from North American political culture into the Mexican context reveals the fissures of cold-war activism in Mexico. In this sense, the Mexican gay liberation movement is inscribed in the panorama of practices and vices of the Latin American left during the 1970s. Porfirio M. Hernández Cabrera lists the factors that contributed to the crisis of the Mexican Homosexual Liberation Movement, and they are very similar to those José Revueltas has pointed out with respect to the political left: "Internal struggles for power; disconnectedness from the base; the pretension by Mexico City groups that they were national representatives; the inefficient organization following partisan models; the *machismo* of some lesbians; the 'tearful' denunciations of persecution; the absence of an attractive sexual-political agenda which would generate cohesion; the lack of artistic and intellectual support which became a lack of 'theoretical support' " (291).[8]

North American gay activism was closely tied to forms of community democracy found in churches and, therefore was defined as a civil rights movement from the beginning. The North American historian John d'Emilio remembers, for example, that the Gay Activist Alliance met in a church in the Chelsea district of Manhattan (47). A large part of the civil rights movement was also based in churches, and therefore it can be said that the North American gay rights move-ment shares typical characteristics of the models of civil political action in U.S. society. Except for the Metropolitan Community Church, founded in Mexico City in 1981, the relationship between the Mexican gay rights movement and religious institutions has been primarily hostile. Another difference in the relationship of churches with the gay movements in the two countries is that in North America there is a plurality of religious institutions, which allows gay Americans to main-tain a certain continuity with the value system of their society, while gay Mexicans, because they are gay (if we understand gay to mean having gone through the ini-tiation process of coming out), must in general leave the Catholic church (one of the most aggressively homophobic religious institutions) and break with family—which can be understood as an extension of the Church in its role as creator and enforcer of moral codes. This circumstance leads us to consider how members of the Mexican gay population are more likely to lead a dual life than those of the North American gay population.[9]

Yet neither the shortcomings of activism nor the difficulty of breaking with the conservative framework of Mexican society has been able to destroy the politics of the Mexican gay rights movement. In spite of the crisis in leadership during the first era, diverse groups arose during the 1980s, in reaction in particular to the huge shock that the AIDS epidemic sent through the homosexual population. This revival in relation to the public health crisis reiterates the global nature of gay ac-tivism, a global nature that owes less to militancy and ideological propaganda and more to emerging situations in a community that has come together as the result of exclusions, threats, and multiple oppressions.

In their book *Empire* (2000), Michael Hardt and Antonio Negri observe that social movements in the era of globalization tend to be immediate and arise in re-sponse to emerging situations. Thus, what can be spoken of as a globalized move-ment does not owe as much to political projects as it does to contingencies that arise at the international level: It is not so much political discourse that is globalized but rather the phenomena that trigger the surge of spontaneous social movements (Hardt and Negri 52–56). The AIDS epidemic acts as one of the political triggers of global activism analyzed by Hardt and Negri. Another factor that stimulates the emergence of the global gay rights movement is the need for an international poli-tics that responds to growing conservatism. This political trend has become more and more firmly established in the arts, media, and academia; it is not, however, a projected political agenda, but rather a plural response to conservative pressure. Gloria Careaga points out that political proposals about sexuality have reached in-ternational academic and professional forums capable of making recommendations to governments about local legislation in favor of minority human rights. These recommendations have provoked aggressive responses from the Catholic Church and Muslim hierarchies, which have undertaken hostile erotophobic, antiabortion, and homophobic campaigns. The local movements have then articulated positions

in favor of the recommendations made in these global forums and against the attacks from conservative groups. In this way, gay regional politics would be oriented
toward bringing to fruition the implied promises the governments made through
the act of adopting these international recommendations (Careaga 311).

To Come Out of the Closet or Not

When speaking of the 1969 Stonewall riots in her essay "Gender in America,"
Drucilla Cornell offers us two terms that succinctly define the North American gay
rights movement: "The proclamation that one is gay and lesbian became as much
a matter of ethical and political significance as of personal self-definition" (49).
Thus the two concerns that define the gay rights movements are its ethical/politi-
cal component and the individual act of self-definition. The first is characterized
as antihomophobic politics, as well as the effort to assure civil rights for those of
sexual difference (which would be articulated with the creation and enforcement
of laws that would equally benefit the nonheterosexual population). The aspect of
self-definition can be understood as the creation of a space in the public sphere for
the expression of these sexualities. For the North American movement, coming
out of the closet is first and foremost a political act and therefore the organizing
axis for gay ideology. Coming out fundamentally implies "taking on or assuming
a condition . . . but it also demands a certain degree of integration into the homosexual community" (Marquet 37).[10]

The difficulty of publicly exposing one's sexual orientation and associating
with the homosexual community in Mexico necessarily creates scenarios in which
it is possible to come out whenever it might be necessary.[11] Many Mexican gays
live their everyday lives, one could say, in the closet, and come out only when they
return to the community of other homosexuals. Paradoxically, the open space implies being closeted, while the scenarios of the gay community (where one comes
out) exist in closed, exclusive, and often stigmatized environments. It can be said
that in Mexico one does not expose oneself definitively: One goes in and comes
out according to the precodified use of spaces. A large number of gays from rural
settings travel frequently to cities in order to liberate themselves temporarily. In his
ethnographic study of the homosexual population in western Mexico, Joseph Carrier tells how men from the countryside make special weekend trips to the city to
engage in sexual acts with other men (40–41). Within the immigrant population in
Colorado, we have found that one of the reasons for gay Mexicans to migrate was
being able to assume their homosexuality openly, which implies that when they
go home they go back into the closet. A few months ago, a gay activist in Mexico
City, about to visit his family in a mountain town in Puebla, was worried because
he had been interviewed by one of the newscasts with the widest national coverage
and he was afraid of facing the disapproval of his compatriots. Does this mean that
the Mexican gay rights movement is unsuccessful because it has not been able to

find a political solution for the problem of complete visibility that is considered fundamental to achieving social acceptance? Is coming out of the closet obligatory for defining oneself as "gay," or is it enough to take on an identity and live with the gay community intermittently, without overt demonstration?[12] Should the concept of gay identity be redefined, to the extent that cultural conditions in Mexico are neither favorable for—nor prone to—developing the North American form of gay politics?

Against the religious and civil rights backdrop of North American gay activism, coming out of the closet is first an act of public testimony—and then a political act—that is a sign both of membership in a community and of self-definition with all the accompanying social responsibilities and privileges. Many of my North American friends are perplexed when I describe the undefined nature of masculine sexuality in Mexico. For them one is or is not gay: Identity is an act and an effect of identification and is presented unequivocally. This reflects one of the foundations of North American politics which grew out of the civil rights movements: the construction of identity or what has been called the politics of identity—in other words, the politics grounded on the idea of developing a political agenda for communities that have been oppressed because of race, sexuality, nationality, et cetera. Yet it is precisely this politics of identity requiring self-definition that queer theory questions as it reconsiders the essentialist constitution of gender identity and proposes a more fluctuating definition of the subject.[13]

In one of the most representative novels of Mexican gay literature, *El vampiro de la Colonia Roma* (The Vampire of the Roma Neighborhood) by Luis Zapata (1979), we find an example of what in Mexican homoerotic culture could be considered queer. The protagonist, Adonis García, is a young prostitute whose relationships with clients lead him to experience all types of sexual contacts. As he learns about other pleasures through these contacts, this character continually redefines his identity until any stable definition is useless. Initially Adonis is characterized as a *chichifo*, a type of man who practices homoeroticism as a means of subsistence but who only penetrates during the homoerotic encounter and therefore does not lose his prestige as a male and is considered heterosexual both by society and by himself. Ethnographers like Annick Prieur, Patricia Ponce, and Marianella Miano Borruso locate this type (also called *mayate* or *chacal*) in the lower classes, in a field of sexual practices that are outside those characterized by gay culture. Adonis García (in his self-perception, if not in that of his clients) goes beyond the condition of *chichifo* and thus breaks out of the circle described by ethnography. Both the *chichifo* and the new character, not associated with any identity that Adonis assumes, escape gay politics. The *chichifo* does not take on any specific political or social identity nor, since he belongs to no community, does he participate in the political practices that characterize gay activism. There has never existed, to our knowledge, any self-named group of "*chichifos*" in the prodiversity marches in Mexico City.

The utopian proposal for sexuality expressed in *El vampiro de la Colonia Roma* suggests to us a contrast in relation to the orientation taken by North American gay concepts about the definition of identity as political performance and the Mexicans' stubborn resistance to categorizing, as well as their inclination to live in the margins of identities. In this novel, the public bathhouse, the most traditional and diverse space for homoerotic sexual encounters, is described as a community conceived and imagined on the basis of pleasure, that is to say, based on a consensus about the communal value (from communion: sacred communication) of hedonism. From this point of view the public bathhouse is a space of sexual democratization: "There you see everyone, from gentlemen that left the Galaxy outside and who just slipped in to get poked to bricklayers and carpenters and others who go to be distracted from their obligations eh but there in the equator something very curious happens that well there's a lot of cooperation between everyone, you see? As if everyone were equal there; sex wins out over social class, you know?— and everyone cooperates so that everyone enjoys" (201).[14] Just as in the bathhouse, with its social desire for equality, where everyone worries about everyone else having an orgasm without making distinctions of any kind, Adonis's body is a public good whose meaning derives from providing pleasure for others. This utopia of nondefined identities creates a paradise of sexuality where the ideological agency that organizes or gives meaning to Adonis's narrative can become transparent.

In contrast to this queer utopia, the direction followed by gay politics pursues a form of democracy that points toward the institutionalization of the gay couple: Building identity and building community are, in the end, ways of continuing to build the state. This is an institutionalization of the politics of identity, which is not possible without the political commitment that coming out of the closet implies. This perspective is reflected in the proposals presented to the legislative assembly in Mexico City, which significantly call such relationships "domestic partnerships," which includes any form of domestic association that needs to be legalized as a union in order to protect assets and access to benefits. While Adonis's utopia contemplates the universal right to pleasure—a proposal that would be difficult to express in parliamentary spaces—the formalizing and legitimizing benefits of gay politics are evident in the domestic partnership initiative. The right to pleasure and the right to civic inclusion seem to be the two contradictory ways in which gayness gains significance in Mexico. This does not mean that all North American gays want to get married and that all their Mexican counterparts prefer the bathhouse's deidentifying hedonism. What I am placing in opposition is not North America versus Mexico, but the contradictions that the presence of gayness produces in the Mexican culture, which is in many ways a result of a perception of U.S. gayness.

The preoccupation with pleasure and the construction of identity remind us of one of the most important texts in relation to the contrast between the United States and Mexico: the essay "La mesa y el lecho" (The Table and the Bed) by Octavio Paz, included in his 1979 volume *El ogro filantrópico* (The Philanthropic

Ogre). The exegesis that the Mexican intellectual makes of the table in order to explain the difference between the two countries can illuminate the distinction made here between the politics of pleasure and identity politics. Paz says: "North American cuisine is without mystery: simple ingredients, nutritional and lightly seasoned. No tricks: the carrot is the honorable carrot, the potato does not blush over its condition and beef steak is a bloody giant" (215).[15] While North American cuisine has its reservations about "camouflaging sauces and dressings," in Mexican food "the secret is in the collision of flavors: fresh and spicy, salty and sweet, warm and acidic, sour and delicate. Desire is the active agent, the secret producer of changes, whether it has to do with the transition from one flavor to another or the contrast between several" (217).[16] Without wishing to push the comparison too far, we find this culinary speculation useful for suggesting that the politics of coming out of the closet—that clear declaration that one belongs to a condition as honorable as the carrot and as shame free as the potato—are uncomfortable for a culture that conceives of itself in ambiguous and contrasting terms of desire. Thus the formative process of Mexican gay culture has fluctuated between the principles of identity (with the accompanying ethical demands of democratization) and the imperatives of pleasure, that hedonism so central to Paz's thought.

In his commentary on the theatrical production *Party* by David Dillon (1992), Antonio Marquet observes two characteristics of North American gay culture that are alien to a Mexican way of being, and therefore practiced very little by that society's gays: the obsession with health, and religious intervention. The difference noted by Marquet is reminiscent of the pages Octavio Paz dedicates to comparing Mexican and North American culture. For Marquet, the party represented in Dillon's work "refuses to blossom in the chaotic liberty of spontaneity and contingency" (111).[17] Marquet's observations echo Paz's comparison of the North American and Mexican parties in his essay "Todos santos, día de muertos" (All Saint's Day, Day of the Dead) in *El laberinto de la soledad* (The Labyrinth of Solitude), while also focusing on one of the formational nuclei for gay identity: leisure. While the North American party is governed by rules that protect the integrity of the event, the Mexican party risks excess.

Cultural Negotiations

Even more important than the incarnations of activism associated with gay culture are the social meanings and stratification this culture created in Mexico. The use of the term "gay" denotes a homosexual that belongs to the middle class, is educated, travels, and lives in the city. To live as a gay, then, contrasts with living as a *joto*, *marica*, *mayate*, or *chichifo*, all of whom belong to a culture of oppression in which effeminate men are the most frequent targets of homophobic violence.[18] Guillermo Núñez Noriega observes that the term "gay" in Mexico is used as a euphemism for *joto*, which undermines the original political meaning of the gay concept. While the term "*joto*" refers to the lower-class homosexual, which in turn implies a series of more risky erotic practices, a "gay" is a respectable person (Núñez, "Significados y política" 226–27). This anthropologist's observation suggests a cultural variation that distances itself from North American gay culture, assigning a meaning of acculturation and even privilege to gayness, in contrast with other homoerotic subjects constituted by the national tradition of homophobia. What this author is calling a euphemism consists of a translation of gayness by middle-class conformity, which from its privileged position no longer confronts homophobic violence because it no longer experiences it. Being gay, therefore, means maintaining an appearance and behavior that do not disturb dominant or mainstream society. This distancing from the victims of homophobia is evidence that being gay has taken on connotations of class prejudice and apathy that are contrary to its original activist concerns. We have witnessed, for example, how in the city of Guadalajara, a large number of self-proclaimed gay men feel no solidarity with the transvestites who have been victims of violent attacks in recent years. They explain their position by stating that the physical assaults are rooted not in homophobia but rather in the circumstance that dressing as a transvestite is in itself an act of aggression toward society.

Who is gay and who is not gay in Mexico is defined primarily by the fact of belonging or not belonging to a collection of cultural practices. In North America, the designation "gay" does not depend necessarily on the activism or the market that defines the term's dominant features: It is possible to consider someone gay who has homoerotic desires without this implying a definition of social class, and thus one can conceive of an indigent gay person. In Mexico, while being gay does not necessarily imply participation in incipient gay activism, it does imply a certain identification with the model propagated by the market specifically designed for gays: It is first and foremost a consumer citizenship that determines recreational activities, fashion, and ways of expressing sexuality, and that defines a certain literature, film industry, language, and specific uses of space. García Canclini states that the market is the device used to define identities beyond the ties established by entities like nation and race, around which human groups have traditionally organized themselves: "Men and women perceive that many of the questions asked by citizens—where do I belong and what rights does that give me, how can I inform myself, who represents my interests—can be answered more through the private consumption of goods and through mass media than by the abstract rules of democracy or by collective participation in public spaces" (29).[19] As an identity constituted by the market, gayness is an acculturated way of being that can be practiced all over the world and that therefore can be defined by its global nature; in other words, gay culture understood in terms of consumption can define a globally disseminated identity. Nevertheless, we must emphasize that this market effect on the creation/definition of gayness takes place among middle- to upper-class Mexican homosexuals, while the sectors excluded from the market end up being excluded also from the definition of homosexual identity. Because of this relationship with the market (which is for the most part dominated by the North American economy), being gay in Mexico has the connotation of being Americanized.

This then leads us to the question, Are "Americanization" and "globalization" interchangeable terms in relation to gay culture? At first glance, granting the gay movement a global nature avoids reducing it to North American culture. For Antonio Marquet, for example, the gay movement is oriented toward "the proclamation of a nation organized not by a social history, common language, religion or ideology but rather by something much more binding: by a sexual identity which defines the individual as being persecuted, a social pariah which leads him to organize and pursue an intense communal life" (22).[20] A nation that transcends its sovereign limits takes on the dimensions of a global community. But is this just a discursive tactic to avoid the much-feared judgment about Americanization? Globalization and Americanization in many cases are synonymous. Stephen D. Morris observes that the concepts of globalization and nationalism are particularly relevant in Mexico, where it is very difficult to distinguish transnational and North American phenomena (27–28).

The global nation that Marquet imagines contrasts with the fierce fragmentation observed by Mauricio List Reyes, who notes that Mexico's social stratification prevents gays from "bonding in spite of shared cultural traits. And therefore we must take into account the fact that identity based on sexual preference is not given so much importance among gay Mexican individuals as to make it stand out in their social interactions" (86).[21] List's observation forces us to turn our eyes to the population whose socioeconomic status prevented them from affiliating with gay culture. Ethnographic studies carried out in Mexico of homoerotic practices reveal nuances that displace, redefine, or reinvent proposals about gay identity by placing them in dialogue with traditional sexualities. Thus a series of lifestyles exists, which without taking on the definition of gay have been transformed by contact with what we could call "hegemonic" gay culture.

In her ethnographic study about the structuring of gender in the region of the isthmus of Tehuantepec in the state of Oaxaca, Marinella Miano Borruso describes the traditional homosexual in Zapotec culture, called the *muxe'*, as a privileged subject in relation to other Mexican homosexuals because in the isthmus society, the *muxe'* holds a place of respect in the community (149). The idea of liberation is unnecessary, since the *muxe'* is already liberated and the acquisition of gay culture is important only in distinguishing between the proud Zapotecs, who prefer their traditional dress and social structures, and the middle class that lives in accordance with the "modern" customs of urban mestizos (159). A *muxe'* is feminine to the extent of taking on the roles of Zapotec women; a gay is not necessarily identified as effeminate, and all classes of gender expression are possible. Often, Miano includes the *muxe'* as a subcategory of gayness, and in effect, these differences do not indicate any conflict between gay culture and traditional *muxe'* culture. Contemporary

Zapotec society, like indigenous communities before the conquest, is extremely flexible when incorporating foreign cultural elements. It is significant that the Vela (a traditional religious festival organized by neighborhoods or groups identified by their occupation) has incorporated a *muxe'* version since the 1970s as a result of the influence of gay culture: the "Vela of the Authentic, Intrepid Seekers of Danger."[22] It is thus a matter of the appropriation of gayness as a concept that inscribes the regional in the global, enriching the frame of legitimacy that it already enjoyed.

The closeness between gayness and *lo muxe'* simply reiterates the postcolonial nature of cultural interaction: hybridization. Local culture is not ignorant of the proposals that arrive from the metropolis; rather it adopts and transforms them, being careful not to renounce its communal values. By inscribing themselves in the global, the *muxe'* increased their prestige, no longer only a subject with "the mind of a man and the sensibility of a woman" (Miano 150), but a subject valued by gay ethnography. That is to say, the value of the *muxe'* within the frame of gay culture is defined by his representative capital: as a subject that places homosexual liberation in a time before memory, before the gay movement, proof of the Rousseauian utopian vision of the superior justice of non-Western societies. Because of this primitive nature, the *muxe'* functions as the foundational image of Mexican gayness.

The argument that before the gay movement a liberating homoerotic practice (that is to say, separate from the homophobic tradition of heterosexual hegemony) already existed in Mexico can also be inferred from the ethnographic work of Guillermo Núñez Noriega with respect to the sexuality of men from Sonora. Núñez reports that a large number of those he interviews about their relationships with other men refuse to identify themselves as gays, *jotos*, *mayates*, homosexuals, or bisexuals. They prefer to define themselves simply as men who like *el cotorreo* [to mess around or have a good time]. This term places "the homoerotic practice in the field of adventure, fun, shared pranks/jokes" (27); in this way, categories of identity that normalize sexuality can be avoided and eroticism is related to friendship and homo-society. According to this anthropologist, this lack of definition subverts the politics of identity (into which the gay movement inscribes itself) imposed by the patriarchal structure (understood as the homophobic and misogynist hierarchy). As with the character of Adonis in *El vampiro de la Colonia Roma*, we can see one of the main asymmetries between the concept of gayness as identity central to the understanding and practice of gay identity in the United States and the recurring lack of definition that defines Mexican homoeroticism.

It is appropriate to question whether the *muxe'* and the men from Sonora through their "liberated" practices are able to escape the homophobia endemic to Mexican society. According to Miano, since the 1970s and their contact with gay culture, the *muxe'* have become more dramatic in their practices as transvestites and have been rejected in some settings. In relation to those interviewed by Núñez, one could say that their reluctance to define or name homoerotic contact stems directly from homophobia. After all, a large number of these men are heads of families and live publicly as heterosexuals, a situation in no way nebulous or unnamed. So what at first appears to be a liberating utopia is on the contrary a strategy of hegemonic heterosexuality for maintaining its place as the only legitimate and normalized form of sexuality. In his 1994 book *Sexo entre varones* (Sex between Males), Núñez affirms that achieving "homosexual identity depends, in large part, on the structure of the sexual field, and on the fight to achieve legitimate representation of sexual existence" (167). With this statement, Núñez is implicitly recognizing that the undeclared homosexuality of his interviewees cannot be legitimized because it is not represented. Perhaps what is lacking from the proposal of nondefinition as a liberating practice is the political term: If nondefinition is aimed at delegitimizing heterosexual structures, then a truly liberating act has been achieved, but if not, we are observing only another of many forms of homophobia that keep homoerotic practices at risk in the shadows.

Another subject who engages in homoerotic behavior but remains outside gay identity, and whose role further problematizes the map of sexual identities, is the *mayate*. Just like the *muxe'* and the undefined man, the *mayate* is a pregay category that persists at the margins of gay culture, which we insist on calling hegemonic because of its central, legitimizing position. The *mayate* is another name for the active member of the traditional homoerotic relationship, where the *joto* is defined as the passive homosexual. The *mayate* does not identify himself as homosexual and therefore cannot be defined as gay. This subject has sexual relations with women and justifies his sexual relations with *jotos* by asking them for favors or money in exchange for sex. The *mayate* is, then, a sort of fortuitous prostitute. It is from this angle that the *mayate* maintains contact with gay culture.[23] Not many works have paid attention to the *mayate*. The ethnography by Annick Prieur and Joseph Carrier is the best known. But the documentary video *Amor chacal* (2001) by Juan Carlos Bautista and Victor Jaramillo is particularly valuable for indicating the status of the *mayate* in the globalized society. Here, we can observe how the *mayate* is redefined within the frame of contemporary gay culture. The documentary functions as a travelogue of a same-sex couple on the Veracruz coast. Repeatedly the *mayate* is presented as a tourist attraction of which the whole coastal society is aware. The locals justify the *mayate*'s activities as a traditional practice that forms part of the collection of local types. Just like the *muxe'*, the *mayate* are traditional homoerotic subjects who take on the value of ethnographic objects redefined by the tourist market. In this way, the *mayate*, like the *muxe'*, are part of the catalog of symbols and traditional practices of pregay culture. The *mayate* and the *muxe'* do not, then, remain separate from gay culture. Rather, they represent specific local phenomena that highlight and characterize Mexican homoerotic culture.

Yet the *muxe'* and the *mayate* do not rescue Mexico from the Americanization or globalization of gay culture. In their value as ethnographic subjects and tourist products, they are inscribed in the flow of signs that transnationalism puts into motion. Far from being expressions of resistance to gay culture, they serve as others to gay culture. Yet we cannot declare this otherness without also recognizing that these subaltern forms of sexuality have achieved their legitimacy in relation to their respective local settings, thanks in part to the attention paid them by the gay community. This process of legitimization brings us back to queer theory's criticism of the politics of identity.

Queerness is not so much a political movement as it is a broad range of practices and representations that extends beyond the proposals gay culture makes about identity. If globalization has had any consequences in the area of culture, it has been to diversify the sources of signs such that the gay community cannot be defined only by what is produced and propagated from the United States but must also include meanings circulated in networks of global contact. As Arnoldo Cruz-Malavé and Martin F. Manalansan, academic specialists in queer studies and globalization, propose, the transnationalization of capital has opened routes of "cross-cultural engagements that are more respectful of queer cultures and lives" (4). Even though the United States has been the principal site from which signs and lifestyles related to gay culture have been proposed, global markets have created exchange networks that decenter these cultural practices. Within this framework, the relationship between Mexican sexualities and North American gay culture can be understood as a give-and-take of interpretations, translations, and diverse forms of contact generated by contemporary mobility.

Nevertheless, this utopia of gay global culture does not imply liberation from oppression or, much less, the democratization of sexual minorities. The contradictions and diverse forms of power that accompany globalization and that Ianni and Hardt and Negri, among others, describe are particularly crucial in the area of homosexuality. The predominance of the market as an apparatus that legitimizes and merges social practices has also led to the violation of the human rights of children, who are not protected by the Mexican justice system, as illustrated in cases that the journalist Lydia Cacho denounces in her book *Los demonios del Edén* (The Devils of Eden). If global order gives preferential treatment to that which can enter the neoliberal market, then the prostitution of poor children and adolescents for international tourism in Cancún and Acapulco, inasmuch as it produces capital, is immune from the law. One could argue that this is a problem that belongs only to Mexico and has nothing to do with North American gay culture. But the businesses of prostitution and child pornography, like the drug trade, prosper because there persists a demand among the North American population. This form of consumerism does not in any way relate to gay practices, in the liberating sense, at least. These behaviors are a symptom of life in the closet, of the furtive behavior that homophobic society enforces. Thus we can affirm that not only the positive aspects of the gay liberation movement have arrived from the North, but also the effects of a homophobia that finds its escape valve in the exploitation of those who are the most vulnerable.

The appearance of gay culture in Mexico is a main focus of exchange with that country's neighbor to the north in recent decades. The analysis of this interaction allows us to draw at least these four conclusions: (1) The acquisition of the principles of North American gay politics in Mexico corresponds to a tradition of adapting proposals from North American civil society to Mexican reality; (2) there are strong cultural reasons that make it impossible in Mexico to follow the principles of the North American gay liberation movement exactly, and this creates a redefinition of Mexican gayness; (3) the functions of traditional Mexican forms of homoerotism have been changed but not eliminated by gay culture; and (4) Mexican homosexuality—including the category "gay"—has been fully introduced into the global market and communication systems (which are controlled in large part by North America), with accompanying consequences in the areas of acculturation and human rights.

NOTES

1. "gay no es sinónomio de 'homosexual, maricón, puto, tortillera, invertido, sodomita,' sino la palabra que nombra actitudes, organizaciones y comportamientos hasta hace poco desconocidos. De igual manera, *desclosetarse* o *salir del clóset*, ante acción ligada a la desvergüenza y el cinismo que nada tiene que perder, es ahora la proclamación de la legitimidad de la diferencia." This article, including all quotations from secondary texts, was translated by Mary K. Long.
2. *Tortillera* is a slang term, often pejorative, used in Mexico to refer to lesbians. *Maricón, puto*, and *invertido*, also pejorative, refer to homosexual males: *maricón* connotes effeminacy, *invertido* underlines the dissidence from heterosexuality, and the meaning of *puto* is associated with clandestine sexuality.
3. In June 1969, in Stonewall Bar on Christopher Street in New York, there was a confrontation between police and gay patrons protesting police abuse of homosexuals. This event marks the beginning of the worldwide gay liberation movement. In Mexico on 15 August 1971, Nancy Cárdenas called a meeting of gay and lesbian intellectuals to discuss and organize a movement based on sexual preference (Marquet 15).
4. Two of the most complete works about this nationalist homophobia are Victor Díaz Arciniegas's *Querella por la cultura nacional* (The Feud over National Culture) and Guillermo Sheridan's *México en 1932: la polémica nacionalista* (Mexico in 1932: The Nationalist Polemic).
5. "¿Por qué no existe en México el equivalente de Eddie Rodríguez, el sargento de la policía neoyorquina que declara sus preferencias frente a las cámaras en la misma delegación? ¿Por qué no es posible que la policía mexicana deje de ser el chacal que asedia, chantajea y viola los derechos del homosexual?"
6. According to Antonio Marquet, "Gay culture, as we know it currently, owes a lot to the 1968 student movement" [la cultura gay, tal y como la conocemos actualmente, debe mucho al movimiento del 68] (16).
7. Nevertheless, according to José María Covarrubias in 1972, the FLM (Frente de Liberación Homosexual Mexicana/Mexican homosexual liberation front) held a march protesting the Vietnam War, a fact which would support the idea that the Mexican gay liberation movement was in sync with the protests carried out by their North American counterparts (cited in Mogrovejo 64).

8.   "Las pugnas internas por el poder; la desvinculación con la base; la pretensión de rep-
     resentatividad nacional de los grupos chilangos; la ineficiente organización conforme
     al modelo partidista; el machismo de algunas lesbianas; la denuncia 'lacrimógena'
     de persecución; la carencia de una plataforma sexo-política atractiva que generara
     cohesión; la falta de apoyo de artistas e intelectuales que derivó en 'falta de sustento
     teórico.' "

9.   This doesn't mean that in the United States there are not cases of those who live a
     double life, as can be observed in the movie *Brokeback Mountain* (2005), set in one
     of the country's most traditional and conservative regions, and in the recent case of
     Pastor Ted Haggard of Colorado Springs, who resigned his post as president of the
     National Association of Evangelical Churches in November 2006 because he was
     discovered to have had a homosexual relationship—again a case associated with the
     most conservative of religious organizations in the United States.

10. "una condición asumida. . . pero exige también cierto grado de integración a la co-
     munidad homosexual."

11. Limitations to coming out also exist in the United States, for example, the "Don't
     ask, don't tell" policy of the military and some family interactions that demand that
     gay relationships be carried out discreetly. Mexico, however, offers considerably fewer
     open spaces of acceptance for homosexuals compared to those available in the United
     States.

12. Hernández Cabrera mentions that among the factors that broke up the center for
     Homosexual Liberation was the "inability to achieve support from the base when
     coming out of the closet was imposed as the only form of 'liberation' " [la incapaci-
     dad de lograr el apoyo de la base al imponer la salida del closet como única forma de
     "liberación"] (292).

13. For example, Michael Warner, based in the queer anti-identity view, throws out an
     interesting question: "What identity encompasses queer girls who fuck queer boys
     with strap-ons, or FTMs (female-to-male transsexuals) who think of themselves as
     straight, or FTMs for whom life is a project of transition and screw the categories
     anyway?" (cited in Cornell 50–51).

14. "Ahí ves desde señores que dejaron afuera el galaxie y que nomás van a que les den su
     piquete hasta albañiles y carpinteros y demás que se van a distraer de sus obligaciones
     je pero ahí en el ecuador pasa una cosa muy curiosa que es que . . . bueno . . . hay
     muchísima cooperación entre todos ¿ves? Como si todos fueran iguales . . . ahí . . .
     las clases sociales se la pelan al sexo ¿verdad?—y todos cooperando para que todos
     gocen."

15. "La cocina norteamericana tradicional es una cocina sin misterio: alimentos simples,
     nutritivos y poco condimentados. Nada de trampas: la zanahoria es la honrada zana-
     horia, la papa no se ruboriza de su condición y el bistec es un jayán sanguinolento."

16. "salsas encubridoras y aderezos, . . . el secreto es el choque de sabores: lo fresco y lo
     picante, lo salado y lo dulce, lo cálido y lo ácido, lo áspero y lo delicado. El deseo es
     el agente activo, el productor secreto de los cambios, trátese del tránsito de un sabor a
     otro o del contraste entre varios."

17. "se resiste a florecer en la libertad 'caótica' de la espontaneidad y la contingencia."

18. *Joto* is a pejorative word for homosexuals; its most probable origin is the word *chotear*,
     "to scorn." The terms *mayate* and *chichifo* define the person who takes the penetrator's
     role in a homosexual contact—in general they are prostitutes; however, they are not
     considered homosexuals in traditional Mexican culture.

19. "Hombres y mujeres perciben que muchas de las preguntas propias de los ciudada-
     nos—a dónde pertenezco y qué derechos me da, cómo puedo informarme, quién

representa mis intereses—se contestan más en el consumo privado de bienes y de los medios masivos que en las reglas abstractas de la democracia o en la participación colectiva en espacios públicos."

20. "la proclamación de una nación organizada no por una historia social, por una lengua común, por una religión o una ideología, sino por algo mucho más constituyente: a partir de una identidad sexual que coloca al individuo como un perseguido, como un paria social, lo cual lo obliga a organizarse y a llevar una intensa vida comunitaria."

21. "cohesionarse a pesar de compartir rasgos culturales. Por ello, es necesario tomar en cuenta que el elemento identitario establecido a partir de la preferencia sexual no está colocado en un nivel de importancia entre los individuos gays mexicanos, al punto de ponerla de relieve en sus relaciones sociales."

22. The appearance of this Vela *muxe'* was a strategy of the Institutional Revolutionary Party (PRI) in the face of the indigenous left-wing resistance group COCEI, which carried out significant protests against the authoritarianism of the PRI during these years. This use of the *muxe'* as a government-sponsored political spearhead shows how no single uniform political position can be defined in relation to the homosexual population.

23. *Chichifo* and *mayate* are in many cases interchangeable terms: they both fulfill the role of the penetrator in the homoerotic relationship, but they do not define themselves as homosexual; both belong to a subaltern social class, and both receive material benefits as payment for penetrating other men. Perhaps the only difference lies in that the *chichifo* is always considered a prostitute, whereas the *mayate* does not necessarily receive direct payment in exchange for sex.

WORKS CITED

Altman, Dennis. "Rupture or Continuity: The Internationalization of Gay Identities." Hawley 19–41.

Bautista, Juan Carlos, and Victor Jaramillo. *Amor chacal.* Video. Mexico: Producciones Pily y Mili, 2001.

Cacho, Lydia. *Los demonios del Edén: el poder que protege a la pornografía infantil.* Mexico: Grijalbo, 2005.

Careaga, Gloria. "Los acuerdos internacionales: un reto pendiente de la política nacional." *Memorias de la II Semana Cultural de la Diversidad Sexual.* Ed. Yesenia Peña Sánchez, Francisco Ortiz Pedraza, and Lilia Hernández Albarrán. México: Instituto nacional de Antropología, CONACULTA, 2005. 305–11.

Carrier, Joseph. *De los otros: intimidad y homosexualidad entre los hombres del occidente y el noroeste de México.* Mexico: Editorial Pandora, 2002.

Cornell, Drucilla. "Gender in America." *Keywords: Gender.* Ed. Nadia Tazi. New York: Other Press, 2004. 33–54.

Cruikshank, Margaret. *The Gay and Lesbian Liberation Movement.* New York: Routledge, 1992.

Cruz-Malavé, Arnoldo, and Martin F. Manalansan. *Queer Globalizations.* New York: New York University Press, 2002.

D'Emilio, John. *The World Turned: Essays on Gay History, Politics, and Culture.* Durham: Duke University Press, 2002.

Díaz Arciniega, Víctor. *Querella por la cultura "revolucionaria."* (1925). México: Fondo de Cultura Económica, 1989.

García Canclini, Néstor. *Consumidores y ciudadanos: conflictos multiculturales de la globalización*. Mexico: Grijalbo, 1995.

Gilly, Adolfo. *La revolución interrumpida*. Mexico: Ediciones el Caballito, 1978.

Hardt, Michael, and Antonio Negri. *Empire*. Cambridge, Mass.: Harvard University Press. 2000.

Hawley, John C. "Introduction." Hawley 1–18.

———, ed. *Postcolonial, Queer: Theoretical Intersections*. New York: State University of New York Press, 2001.

Hernández Cabrera, Porfiro Miguel. "El movimiento lésbico, gay, bisexual y transgenérico y la construcción social de la identidad gay en la Ciudad de México." Peña Sánchez, Ortiz Pedraza, and Hernández Albarrán 287–304.

Ianni, Octavio. *La sociedad global*. Mexico: Siglo XXI Editores, 1998.

Irwin, Robert M. *Mexican Masculinities*. Minneapolis: University of Minnesota Press, 2003.

List Reyes, Mauricio. *Jóvenes corazones gay en la Ciudad de México*. Puebla: Universidad Autónoma de Puebla, 2005.

Marquet, Antonio. *¡Que se quede el infinito sin estrellas!* Mexico: Universidad Autónoma Metropolitana, 2001.

Miano Borruso, Marinella. *Hombre, mujer y muxe' en el Istmo de Tehuantepec*. Mexico: CONACULTA; INAH; Plaza y Valdés, 2002.

Mogrovejo, Norma. *Un amor que se atrevió a decir su nombre: la lucha de las lesbianas y su relación con los movimientos homosexual y feminista en América Latina*. Mexico: Plaza y Valdés, 2000.

Monsiváis, Carlos. "Una exposición, varias exposiciones, un tiempo de inauguraciones." *Una exposición, varias exposiciones, un tiempo de inauguraciones*. Ed. Círculo Cultural Gay. Mexico: Difusión Cultural UNAM; Museo Universitario del Chopo, 2001. 9–11.

Morris, Stephen D. *Gringolandia: Mexican Identity and Perceptions of the United States*. New York: Rowman and Littlefield, 2005.

Núñez Noriega, Guillermo. "Reconociendo los placeres, deconstruyendo las identidades: antropología, patriarcado y homoerotismos en México." *Desacatos* 6 (2001): 15–34.

———. *Sexo entre varones: poder y resistencia en el campo sexual*. Mexico: Programa Universitario de Estudios de Género; Universidad Nacional Autónoma de México; Miguel Ángel Porrúa; El Colegio de Sonora, 1994.

———. "Significados y políticas de la 'diversidad sexual': ¿sanización de la otredad o reivindicaciones de lo polimorfo? Reflexiones teóricas para el activismo." Peña Sánchez, Ortiz Pedraza, and Hernádez Albarrán 225–38.

Paz, Octavio. *El ogro filantrópico: historia y politica, 1971–1978*. Barcelona, Caracas, and México: Seix Barral, 1979.

Peña Sánchez, Edith Yesenia, Francisco Ortiz Pedraza, and Lilia Hernández Albarrán, eds. *Memorias de la II semana cultural de la diversidad sexual*. Mexico: Instituto Nacional de Antropología e Historia, 2005.

Ponce, Patricia. "Sexualidades costeñas." *Desacatos: Revista de Antropología Social* 6 (2001): 111–36.

Prieur, Annick. *Mema's House, Mexico City: On Transvestites, Queens, and Machos*. Chicago: University of Chicago Press, 1998.

Revueltas, José. *Ensayo sobre un proletariado sin cabeza*. Mexico: Era, 1982.

Sheridan, Guillermo. *México en 1932: la polémica nacionalista*. Mexico: Fondo de Cultura Económica, 1999.

Zapata, Luis. *El vampiro de la Colonia Roma*. Mexico: Grijalbo, 1979.

CHAPTER 7

Misguided Idealism on a Mission of Mercy

Eleanore Wharton, U.S. Do-Gooder

Danny J. Anderson

ringos, yanquis, gabachos, norteamericanos, and *estadounidenses* are just a few of the labels used in Mexico to describe individuals from the United States. Even more numerous than the labels are the gringo characters in Mexican literary works who provide insight into the ways that individuals from the United States, with different cultural sensibilities and subjectivities, are imagined and understood in Mexico. Such characters embody certain national values, and they belong to what political scientist Stephen D. Morris calls the "imaginary 'United States' " (281). Echoing Benedict Anderson's concept of the nation as an "imagined community," in *Gringolandia: Mexican Identity and Perceptions of the United States*, Morris points out that the nation "is a psychological construct crafted through discourses about self and other" (281). Whereas Morris quickly moves his analysis to the dialectic of othering in this discursive field in order to explain what this "imaginary 'United States' " reveals about Mexico, in my analysis I linger in the space created by the construction of literary characters, a space that may be uncomfortable for readers from the United States.[1] I examine the cultural work performed within the Mexican literary imaginary by texts that portray the collective idiosyncrasy of behavior, values, feelings, and thought incarnated in characters from the United States. In particular, through an analysis of character in Enrique Serna's short story "El desvalido Roger" (Helpless Roger), I examine the Mexican cultural stereotype of the U.S. do-gooder and the task of cross-cultural reading produced by this text.

"Helpless Roger" appears in Enrique Serna's 1991 short story collection *Amores de segunda mano* (Secondhand Loves). Serna has described these stories as "character studies" (Carrera and Keizman 22), tales in which he explores "the transformation of a loving impulse into its opposite, into hatred, into contempt" (Hernández Cabrera). Many have applauded Serna for his crisp style, penchant for irony, and biting satire; critics consider him to be one of the most original of contemporary Mexican short-story writers (García Ramírez, Márquez, Pérez Gay, Torres,

Mosqueda). Because most of his works focus inward on Mexican social mores, critic and novelist José Joaquín Blanco describes him as a "savage moralist" or a Tartuffe who rails against "all the social classes and characters imaginable." "Helpless Roger" stands out among the texts in *Amores de segunda mano* because of its outward look at a subject from the United States: Eleanore Wharton emerges as the object of what Fernando Martínez Ramírez describes as Serna's "ethnographic gaze" into alterity (64), and the challenge for readers from the United States is to negotiate recognition and rejection when a figure like Eleanore Wharton is offered as a representative fellow citizen, an embodiment of certain aspects of a collective, national character.[2]

With this interest in literary characters foremost in my mind and hoping both to situate Eleanore within the wider population of gringos in Mexican literature and to clarify how I could analyze her characterization, I turned to the library shelves to consult an anthology that I believed would give me a broad panorama. I quickly located *Los ricos en la prosa mexicana* (The Rich in Mexican Prose; 1970), edited by John S. Brushwood, as well as *Los pobres en la prosa mexicana* (The Poor in Mexican Prose; 1978) and *La clase media en México* (The Middle Class in Mexico; 1972), both edited by Marcelo Pogolotti. Emmanuel Carballo led a group that created the anthology *¿Qué país es éste? Los Estados Unidos y los gringos vistos por los escritores mexicanos de los siglos XIX y XX* (What Country Is This? The United States and Gringos Seen by Mexican Writers in the Nineteenth and Twentieth Centuries; 1996). But I could never put my hands on the book I had in mind. I vaguely recalled its title: *Los norteamericanos en la prosa mexicana* (North Americans in Mexican Prose). Or was it simply *Los gringos en la literatura mexicana* (Gringos in Mexican Literature)? Unable to find this work that complemented the other character-based literary anthologies from the 1970s, I tried to recall how it was organized. I recollected a compilation divided into topical sections according to social types, recalling that soldiers, men of fortune, and maybe even the Saint Patrick's Battalion appeared in the historical section about the Mexican American War (known in Mexico as the North American Invasion); profiteers, investors, and city slickers were portrayed in a section about businessmen; artists, intellectuals, and bohemians mingled with the elite in "Writers and Artists"; all kinds of travelers wandered through the passages in "Tourists"; and with the long tradition of academic research in Mexico, surely there must have been a section devoted to professors.

This organizational scheme points toward the way that Mexican literature and its images of individuals from the United States have constructed an archive of stereotypes that reveal certain dynamics of nation-based identifications embodied in literary characters and inscribed by literary discourses. The stereotypes call upon readers to adopt positions vis-à-vis the differences between Mexico and the United States, or perhaps to observe as outsiders this dialectical othering. At the same time, the demographic distribution of literary characters points toward a heterogeneity of subjects within the United States, a multiplicity that impedes simplistic reductions to a single, shared national character. Collectively, these literary representations open discussion to the ways that images of individuals from the United States in Mexican literature invite a negotiation of identity among U.S. readers. Whether we read Mexican literary works in translation or in Spanish, when we see our image reflected in such texts, we are pushed to consider how we think and feel about our complex and often contradictory identities, to ponder to what degree we recognize ourselves or feel that we have been distorted.

As an academic who has worked in the United States and frequently traveled to Mexico for research, I was curious about the selections that I expected to find in the section about professors in a book titled *Los gringos en la literatura mexicana*. This category of stereotypes would include a fragment from Rodolfo Usigli's *Impostor: A Play for Demagogues* (written 1937; staged 1947), a work that examines the search for truth in identity as well as the vested professional interests of Harvard historian Oliver Bolton. The stage directions describe Bolton as speaking with the accent of Spain, having eliminated almost completely his U.S. accent. He is a thirty-year-old, sporty, sun-baked blond who first appears wearing a light summer suit. The professor bears all the visible privileges of class and leisure. How do I read his characterization? Do I read as a gringo myself, responding to the dynamics of identification or disidentification he may stir up for me? They dressed differently in the 1940s; I probably wouldn't go out on fieldwork in a light summer suit these days. But, beneath the clothes and the accent, are there ways in which Bolton is right on target? Perhaps more importantly, what does it mean for me to read as a gringo when other aspects of my identity also inform my academic work as a literary critic, scholar, and professional reader, not to mention my own leisurely reading for pleasure? Is my identity singular, or is it the privilege of a singular identity to presume its own pluralities, its identities?

If the question is one of identification between reader and character, I may need to deal with the professor in David Toscana's 2002 novel *Duelo por Miguel Pruneda* (Mourning for Miguel Pruneda), an individual who would have to be added to an updated edition of *Los gringos en la literatura mexicana*. The absurd and often oddly humorous enigmas of the present in this novel refer to a violent murder in the past when a U.S. academic was visiting Monterrey with a short-term study-abroad program. One of the characters reads from a newspaper article with the headline "Body in Obispado Identified": "It is that of Danny Anderson, from the United States, a forty-four-year-old professor from the University of Kansas, married with two children. He was in Monterrey accompanying a group of students who were visiting the Instituto Tecnológico for a week as part of its cultural exchange programs. The victim was murdered with a sharp cutting instrument of sufficient length to pass through the body" (72).[3] A few lines later, Miguel Pruneda reveals that Danny Anderson's murderer must be a local or perhaps even a national hero. Miguel bets that he was murdered "not for being a professor or for being

Danny Anderson or for being forty-four years old; it was because he was a god-damned gringo" (74).[4] This novel sets into play a curious game for me: Toscana's novel deals with a character, Miguel Pruneda, who wants to stage a simulacrum of his own death so he can read his obituary and thus explore the existential meanings of his life. Similar to the title character, Miguel Pruneda, who reads his obituary, as a reader myself—a U.S. professor from the University of Kansas who met David Toscana while accompanying a group of students to Monterrey—I am placed in the amusing position of reading the various reports and speculations about the possible meanings of the murder and death of my textual alter-image. How do I negotiate my reading position vis-à-vis the "goddamned gringo" named Danny Anderson? What kind of pressure does this novel exert through a proper name and attributes such as citizenship, profession, age, and family status that strive to impinge upon my response, thinking, and feeling? How do I explain my flattered laughter when responding to Toscana's literary joke based on the cultural connotations of national identities? What is the interplay between the gringo reader who may take himself too seriously and the more open-minded, border-crossing individual whom Toscana trusts to get the joke? Both *Impostor* and *Duelo por Miguel Pruneda* explore in part the dynamics of reading and identification that interest me here—the simultaneous mixture of attraction and repulsion in considering different subject positions possibly associated with my identity—but they do not get at the stereotype that captured my interest in the first place.

Rather than professors, the specific topic I wanted to consult in *Los gringos en la literatura mexicana* was the do-gooders. I was uncertain what works might have appeared in this section, or even if such a division about altruists existed in the edition from the 1970s. An up-to-date edition would undoubtedly include examples from the 1980s and 1990s. For example, two doctors stand out: Dr. Whitby Hull of Atlanta, Georgia, and Dr. John Brown of Eagle Pass, Texas. We get to know Dr. Hull in Carlos Fuentes's 1990 *nouvelle* "Constancia." In the experience of exploring the past of his enigmatic wife, Hull comes to a new understanding about borders, border crossings, and immigrants, and the novel concludes when he opens his home in Georgia to a family of refugees fleeing political strife in El Salvador. Dr. Brown lives at a geographical border, but his love is a bit ahead of his time when Tita, in Laura Esquivel's 1989 *Like Water for Chocolate*, declines his marriage proposal because of her enduring love for Pedro. Only in a later generation will descendants of these two families be united in marriage across national borders. Brown blends his Cherokee grandmother's knowledge of Native American medicine with modern, scientific practices to emerge as a proto–New Age healer in the early twentieth century. In Jorge Volpi's 2006 novel about globalization, *No será la Tierra* (Not the Earth), the sisters Jennifer and Allison Moore contrapuntally occupy altruist roles. Jennifer, as an economist for the International Monetary Fund, has her vision of contributing to global development and eliminating poverty. Allison, as a social activist in Greenpeace, the Susan B. Anthony Coven Number 1,

Earth First!, and eventually EMETIC (Evan Mechan Eco-Terrorist International Conspiracy), questions the vested interests of Jennifer's altruism and seeks other ways to do good, ranging from a struggle against economic, social, and gender borders (170) to participation in a plan to destroy the electric facilities in a nuclear power plant in Arizona (291–94).

There are other curious characters apt for updating this section of *Los gringos en la literatura mexicana*, but the one who fascinates me the most is Eleanore Wharton, a middle-aged legal secretary for the firm Fulbright and Robinson in Green Valley, Oklahoma. In 1985, upon seeing television coverage of the devastating Mexico City earthquake of 19 September, she is moved to sacrifice her vacation time to go on a mission to help an orphan in need. Serna's "Helpless Roger" provides a detailed character study of Eleanore Wharton. In contrast with the benevolence and unselfish love that guide Hull and Brown, or the Moore sisters' explicit ideological commitments, Wharton stands out for her contradictory spirit of self-sacrifice and self-indulgence. She embodies a darkly humorous, even grotesque version of U.S. altruism; because of her characterization as it relates to gender, age, body image, and a variety of other traits, every reader is bound to find at least one aspect of the short story troubling, if not offensive. In the so-called age of globalization, when border crossing and international contact are the currency of contemporary life, the construction of the altruist stereotype in Serna's disturbing tale allows perception of some possible understandings of good intentions abroad. By juxtaposing the construction of character in "Helpless Roger" with an earlier indictment of nondomestic U.S. idealism by priest, cultural critic, and social activist Ivan Illich, I examine here the cultural significance of Eleanore Wharton as a certain kind of do-gooder and the implications of her stereotype for the process of identification through reading.

Eleanore Wharton's Structure of Feeling

The central feature of "Helpless Roger" is the reader's constant access to the main character Eleanore Wharton's thoughts and feelings as she travels to Mexico on a mission of mercy. The narrative voice moves among (1) a distanced third-person objective position, (2) an internal indirect style that reports Eleanore's thinking process and internal dialogue, and (3) at times a direct quotation of her spoken words and internal thoughts. Recasting somewhat a key concept from Raymond Williams's *Marxism and Literature*, I propose that this story provides readers with a narrative analysis of Eleanore Wharton's "structure of feeling." Williams describes a structure of feeling as a dynamic way of conceptualizing ideology and experience as they are lived. Williams writes that with this term he is seeking to explore "meanings and values as they are actively lived and felt. . . . We are talking about characteristic elements of impulse, restraint, and tone; specifically affective elements of consciousness and relationships: not feeling against thought, but thought as felt and feeling as thought: practical consciousness of a present kind, in a living and interrelating continuity" (132).[5] Viewed through the lens of Williams's concept, "Helpless Roger" provides a portrait of Eleanore Wharton's "practical consciousness" as her actions blend feeling and thinking while she embodies the role of the do-gooder abroad. It is also in this way that "Helpless Roger" demonstrates Serna's affirmation that the short stories in *Amores de segunda mano* seek to move beyond the proposition that reality forms subjectivity, and to reveal the ways that subjectivity forms reality (Hernández Cabrera). Eleanore's "structure of feeling" does not merely represent a certain aspect of dominant North American character, but also demonstrates the effects that such a character has in the world.

The tale begins with a morning scene, a quick psychological profile of Eleanore Wharton, who is lying in bed feeling fat, old, decrepit, and simply not interested in reporting to work on time. She is forty-nine years old, soaks her dentures in Polident in a glass at her bedside, worries about her "drooping double-chin" but refuses "to make herself up." She was divorced at age thirty, has no children, avoids relationships with men, and only rarely agrees to get together with other women (Serna, "El desvalido Roger" 18). The narrator sums her up:

> Her individualism bordered on misanthropy. She took refuge from life beneath an impenetrable shell and rejected any show of affection that might chip away at it. She hated being like this, but how could she fix it? By taking a transcendental meditation class? She would run the risk of finding herself when what she most desired was to disappear from sight. No, meditation and psychoanalysis were hoaxes, make-up tricks to cover up wrinkles on the soul . . . and she needed a complete make-over, a change of skin. Eleanore Wharton was a bundle of phobias. (18–19)[6]

In her oppositional reaction against punctuality this morning, she checks the VCR to see if the timer caught the Bob Hope special she had programmed the night before. To her dismay, she discovers that the Panasonic caught NBC news coverage of the Mexico City earthquake and she is riveted by the image of a young boy crying beside the ruins of his apartment building. She rewinds the tape to watch the camera zoom in on the child's crying face. The reporter comments with a knot in his throat: "Children like this one are looking desperately for their parents . . . without suspecting that they may never find them again" (21).[7] With a jolt, Eleanore snaps out of her existential crisis. The narrator's indirect discourse captures Eleanore's own internal voice chiding her self-complacency: "What right did she have to stay in bed licking her wounds when there were so many unhappy children in the world so worthy of compassion. . . . She was touched. The young disaster victim had given back to her the desire to fight. . . . She leaped from the bed with her pride revitalized. That was what she needed to feel alive: a single pure emotion" (22).[8] This opening characterization evokes Eleanore's motivations as a potential do-gooder. She quickly discovers that a "pure emotion" has the power to dislodge her borderline misanthropy and give her the change of skin she needs to move forward in life. But as the narrator's word choice suggests, the events about to follow are less about others and more about her own ability to feel alive, about her pride, or as it is described in Spanish her "amor propio" [love of self].

The rest of the story follows Eleanore's vacation days in Mexico City searching for the orphan she saw on television with the hope of adopting him. In Mexico City she checks with the embassy regarding adoption procedures, speaks with the NBC television news team to see if they can identify the place shown in her videotape, and hires an interpreter-guide named Efraín Alcántara to help her visit various locations and orphanages. At each point individuals suggest that she help one of the many children in need of care, but she will not settle for anyone except the child on the television screen, the boy she has christened Roger. In these encounters it becomes clear that she has fallen in love with three images: the reproduction of a specific TV image that she can experience again and again by playing back the videotape; a reproduction of the reproduction, a blurry photograph of Roger that she carries with her ("product of the imperfect and deformed visual coitus between her Polaroid and the television screen" [28]); and the psychological image of herself as a generous, self-sacrificing individual, an image she supposedly embodies and brings to life in this mission to find and save Roger.[9] After enduring Eleanore's demeaning treatment and seeing her act up in an orphanage (she tries to take away a child, claiming that his own mother was a kidnapper), Efraín tries to bring her to her senses with a melodramatic slap and warns that she is going to end up in jail: "If you truly have such a good heart, adopt another child. Why does it have to be only this one?" (33).[10] When she refuses, he throws in the towel: "You know something? You're crazy. Go on. Go ahead. Make your little scene. I hope that once and for all they'll put you in a straightjacket" (33).[11] In these events, readers, like other characters in the text, see Eleanore's structure of feeling as an ability to persevere, often turning her feelings about the need to find Roger into thoughts that rationalize her obsession. At other times, we observe Eleanore's partially inchoate thoughts becoming feelings. For example, when she rationalizes about why she can help only Roger, these thoughts turn into feelings of mistrust and resentment about Mexicans, whom she believes to be prejudiced against "unipersonal and exclusive attachments" (35).[12]

Eventually, Eleanore decides that finding Roger and taking him back to Oklahoma is a question of self-esteem. The entire episode evokes the structure of feeling associated with Eleanore's misguided mission, feelings identified with Roger as a projection of her longings: "the child in whom she could see embodied the most noble and tender aspects of her neurosis" (34).[13] Reflecting on the situation, Eleanore has developed some level of self-awareness: "The whim of searching specifically for the child on the news could only take root in a sick mind. Normal persons who adopted children were moved by their generosity. Hers was a vile and

sordid matter. She didn't care about Roger, she had to admit. She simply liked herself in the role of adoptive mother. And naively believing that she would prolong
this idyllic moment with herself if she found the child, she had come to Mexico"
(34).[14]

More than the rescue of Roger, the mission has become one of demonstrating
what a person like her can accomplish once she sets her mind to it: "If anything
was motivating her to reach the goal of her philanthropic mission it was to show
the mindless herd in this country, this hive without individuals, that Eleanore
Wharton had her own ideas, that her wild ideas were very much her own, and that
if she had never before relinquished her independent thinking, she certainly would
not exchange Roger for just any little orphan" (35).[15] Without explicitly naming
her identification as a U.S. citizen, Eleanore understands her situation in terms of
nations, both what she seeks to represent in Mexico as well as her view of Mexican
society as an abstract, collective entity without individuals or personal agency.

On her last day and down to her last bottle of purified water brought from
Oklahoma, she decides to rent a car and go exploring, expecting chance to lead
her to Roger. She ends up in a neighborhood with homes made of tin and cardboard. She sees adolescents congregated in the streets with their spiked hair, "the
punkers of underdevelopment." She has been imagining how ungrateful Roger will
be when he grows up and abandons her once he turns eighteen. In this imagined
future, she will resent that he has put her through the experience of seeing so much
suffering and witnessing so many spectacles of what she considers poor hygiene
during her time in Mexico. He may become a good-for-nothing who will offer her
no love and she feels stupid for the desire "to adopt a pygmy who, on top of it all,
was a horrible cry-baby" (37).[16] She concludes that the problem in Mexico is one
not of economic development but of race. Exactly at the moment she articulates
this discriminatory thought, she hears a groan and the crunch of bones against
the fender of her car. She has run over a child and now worries that she will have
to make restitution to his mother "as if the child were a Swede" (37).[17] When she
sees a crowd approaching, she floors the accelerator and flees the scene of the accident. The narrator ends the short story by noting: "She had no regrets but she
had suffered a disappointment. That of not having run over the innocent, tender,
adorable, and helpless Roger" (38).[18] An epigraph, the fifth definition of the word
misericordia (mercy) from the *Diccionario de la Real Academia*, underscores the
irony of Eleanore's mercy: "Dagger with which knights were armed in the Middle
Ages in order to give the death blow to the enemy" (17).[19] In her effort to feel better about herself—to revitalize her pride, improve her self-esteem, and change her
skin—Eleanore has nurtured her own "new and more intense heartbeats of mercy"
(22), and in the end, as the epigraph suggests, mercy for Eleanore is about killing
the adoptive son she will never have and justifying her mercy on the grounds of
racial difference and ethnocentric superiority.[20]

Eleanore's Good Intentions

"Helpless Roger" is a masterful example of black humor taken to its extreme, a quality often found in Serna's writings. At the same time, it is a troubling indictment of U.S. altruism. In spite of the grotesque exaggeration, Eleanore Wharton belongs in the anthology of *Los gringos en la literatura mexicana* because as a do-gooder she illuminates awkward, unpleasant, and sometimes hard-to-recognize aspects of the United States. Whereas the story suggests that some do-gooders are motivated by generosity (34), Eleanore represents those who engage in love of neighbor for the pride that such service can generate, for the revitalization of love of self (*amor propio*). In shifting the examination of altruism from a philosophical value to a jumble of feeling, affect, experience, and practical consciousness, "Helpless Roger" evokes the kind of social analysis that Ivan Illich had aimed at U.S. do-gooders in Mexico a few decades earlier.

The radical philosopher, social critic, and one-time Catholic priest Ivan Illich (1926–2002) sought to deconstruct the misguided idealism that motivated do-gooders. A Viennese-born cosmopolitan wanderer, Illich established the Centro Intercultural de Documentación (Center for Intercultural Communication) in Cuernavaca, Mexico, in the 1960s, an experimental school for cross-cultural training, research, and language study where he worked with missionaries, volunteers, and social reformers seeking to "do good" in Mexico. In 1968 Illich was invited to address the Conference on Inter-American Student Projects (a volunteer organization for university students) at St. Mary's Lake of the Woods Seminary in Niles, Illinois.[21] In a speech today cited with the title "To Hell with Good Intentions," Illich questions the "unconscious hypocrisy" that sends young adults off on "mission-vacations among poor Mexicans" (315). Illich identifies a national stereotype that could probably serve as one of the cornerstones for the section about altruists in *Los gringos en la literatura mexicana*. He states:

> You cannot help being ultimately vacationing salesmen for the middle-class "American Way of Life," since that is really the only life you know. A group like this could not have developed unless a mood in the United States had supported it—the belief that any true American must share God's blessings with his poorer fellow men. The idea that every American has something to give, and at all times may, can and should give it, explains why it occurred to students that they could help Mexican peasants "develop" by spending a few months in their villages. (316)

Illich is categorical in identifying here the impulse to "do good" with the "American Way of Life" and middle-class values. He makes the national label of the do-gooder even clearer a few moments later when he notes: "Next to money and guns, the third largest North American export is the U.S. idealist, who turns up in every theater of the world: the teacher, the volunteer, the missionary, the community organizer, the economic developer, and the vacationing do-gooders" (316).

The contexts are different and the texts address vastly divergent audiences. Serna's short stories are written in Spanish; most of the works in *Amores de segunda mano* make humorous jabs at his own nation's character apt for the small, elite audience for "high literature" in Mexico. The success of Serna's works places him among writers with a distribution to a potentially international audience of Spanish-language readers, including the various groups of U.S. readers who keep up with Mexican literature in Spanish. Illich, in contrast, speaks in English, directly addressing a student audience he seeks to persuade not to make the mistakes he is describing.[22] In spite of these differences, I juxtapose Illich's comments with Serna's short story to help define the nation-based structure of feeling that is under examination in these two texts. In Serna's short story, Eleanore's Wharton's own middle-class frustration is evoked through numerous details; the neuroses and phobias created through her way of life will supposedly be eliminated by her mission to Mexico City to save an orphan. In Illich's text, students who know little about Mexico, who speak little or no Spanish but who want to do good, will spend their summers living in poor villages, motivated by their "own bad consciences" (318). In both cases, a gulf separates the do-gooder from those she or he would serve: Eleanore Wharton from the Mexicans whom she meets and the students from the underprivileged indigenous communities in which they will live.

The structure of Eleanore Wharton's personality can be grasped in outline through the ways it impinges upon choice and action. Eleanore acts on the basis of a dialectic between opposing character traits. On the one hand, she is driven by self-discipline, a sense of civic duty, and a belief in sacrifice. On the other hand, each trait is counterbalanced by egotism, oppositional attitudes, and a need to defend her own "sentimental territory" (Serna, "El desvalido Roger" 22). She frequently makes comparative value judgments involving racially constructed others, praising the Japanese for technological advances (17) yet deciding that one child could not be Roger because he looks too Japanese (32). She seeks help from the NBC news staff in Mexico City; however, upon hearing that she will have to talk with Abraham Goldberg, Eleanore reveals her anti-Semitism: "She didn't like at all that she would have to speak with a Jew" (24).[23] As noted earlier, she also employs a racial calculus to estimate human worth, cursing that she will probably have to pay restitution for the child she has run over as if he were Swedish and revealing her race-based appraisal of darker-skinned Mexican children compared with lighter-skinned Swedes.

In terms of cultural stereotypes, Eleanore is also a mixed bag of misinformation and commonplaces that circulate in the United States. From the beginning, she expresses uncertainty about Mexico's geographical location, but she feels more confident in identifying it as "that country where mariachi bands sing tangos" (21).[24] Upon arriving at ground zero of the collapsed buildings, she is indignant that she is not allowed to wander freely behind the roped-off area, resentful of having to give a bribe in order to do so, and impatient because the aftermath of the earthquake is slowing down her progress toward finding Roger (28). On the basis of articles in *Reader's Digest*, she is certain that the water in Mexico is poisonous and has brought along her own supply from Green Valley. In spite of the dramatic cataclysm that has just occurred, she also thinks about the cleanliness of home and the lack of hygiene she perceives in Mexico (29–30). Her sense of time and punctuality amplifies her impatience as she has to wait her turn in long lines with the families of earthquake victims. Her sexual alarms go off in reaction to her interpreter-guide Efraín: "He had his hair greased back, a gray moustache, and the mannerisms of an aged ladies' man" (26).[25] Although the short story is ambiguous about the reality of Efraín's actions and intentions, there is no doubt that Eleanore was rapidly growing weary of "his Latin-lover fawning and pawing. He knew perfectly well that she had come to Mexico in search of a lost child but he was treating her like a slut looking for a fling" (29).[26] In the end, however, it is her sense of pride, self-reliance, and competitiveness that take over. After a point, her choices and actions are driven by her decision to adopt a child and the embarrassment of returning home empty-handed.

Most importantly, Eleanore's structure of feeling is produced by a particular middle-class way of life that she wants to share with Roger. She struggles each day to conform to the clock and arrive at work on time, and she resents the decades of faithful service she has given as a legal secretary. Out of respect for her culture of origin, she ritually partakes of a Thanksgiving meal that in fact she doesn't like. As a member of the audience for the U.S. media, she obsessively worries about the effect of fat on blood circulation and why Michael Jackson isn't behind bars for child abuse. As a middle-aged secretary, she is angered by the injustice of sex-starved male lawyers who give better evaluations to the younger secretaries but withhold pay from her salary for her own late arrivals. As an example of middle-class taste, she sets her VCR to record the Bob Hope special, especially likes the Ray Conniff Singers performing the "Hymn to Joy," gets her important news from *Reader's Digest*, and dines on low-calorie frozen TV dinners. As a consumer, she admires and purchases products and brand names that make her life easier. She knows how to stand up for her consumer rights by arguing with the repair shop over their incompetence for failing to fix the recording timer on her VCR. She distrusts the media, which later makes her doubt the veracity of Roger's televised image: "NBC could lie about his being an orphan, or, in the absence of sensationalist images, they could have even shown a victim from another earthquake, the one in Managua or the one in Guatemala, in order to deceive their helpless audience of robots" (34).[27] In many ways Eleanore is herself one of those robots, who has fallen in love with an image on a screen, an image that creates a mirror in which she can perceive only the possibility of a new self that will move her beyond a moment of existential crisis.

As a short story, "Helpless Roger" performs what anthropologist Renato Rosaldo in *Truth and Culture: Remaking Social Analysis* calls "narrative analysis." The text tells a story that reveals the complex interplay of values, desires, and motivations as identity works out and reveals itself. More recently, anthropologist Pablo Vila has worked on such analytical strategies to examine the "narrative identities" and "constructions of others" that compete discursively in the stories and explanations given by inhabitants of Ciudad Juárez, Chihuahua, and El Paso, Texas: "People generally act (or fail to act) at least partly according to how they understand their place in any number of social relations whose meaning—however fragmented, contradictory, or partial—is narratively constructed" ("Polysemy of the Label" 106). Besides important tropes of identity, Vila here analyzes the "different systems of classification and plots to make sense of the perceived 'other' " (107). In a similar manner, Morris's *Gringolandia* maps the discursive fields in Mexico that systematically classify and emplot identities; the representations in these fields both construct the United States as Mexico's other and also give insights into constructions of national identity and possible self-perceptions by Mexicans. In literary texts, in particular, Morris notes, "Mexican thinkers have not only crafted a particular image of the U.S., . . . but have often portrayed and defined the Mexican through a contrast with his or her U.S. counterpart" (159). Morris emphasizes the Mexican discursive field as being organized around binary contrasts that privilege "deep human values" in Mexico and criticize the United States as "excessively materialistic, nihilistic, and lacking in 'true,' 'superior' values of family, faith, meaningful human relationships and high culture" (281). Viewed through this perspective, "Helpless Roger" neatly fits within the pattern of Mexican discursive fields and their representations of the United States. As Pablo Vila contends in *Crossing Borders, Reinforcing Borders*, such images may ratify identities across borders of difference.

But "Helpless Roger" does more than establish a simple cultural contrast between Mexico and the United States. Viewed hermeneutically, Eleanore Wharton poses a challenge for readers in both countries. Reading is not a neutral or abstract practice. As Patrocinio P. Schweickart and Elizabeth A. Flynn have noted, reading engages us "in particular contexts" and in relations "that involve social hierarchy and difference" (3): "The activity of reading is one of the ways of securing our consent, if we belong to the privileged group, and our acquiescence, if we belong to the inferiorized group, to the terms of the social contracts that maintain these unequal relations" (34). We all read in situated and embodied ways, sensuously holding the book in our hands, listening "in the lair of the skull" (Anderson 35) to the play of voice between narrator and character, perhaps imaging Eleanore Wharton against the background of the profoundly moving images of the Mexico City earthquake (a tragedy which did rally international support in a time of dire need), and probably responding to the uncomfortable details of her characterization. Do we read as men or as women when we imagine Eleanore's aging body, her unfulfilled maternal yearnings, and her desire for a "change of skin"? Do we read as Mexicans or as "gringos" when we reject her sad geographical, cultural, and linguistic deficiencies as well as her racist logic? Is race an element in Eleanore Wharton's own identity, and is Ivan Illich correct in seeing U.S. do-gooders as "White Americans (or cultural White Americans)" (319)? How do we identify, reject, or negotiate the complex interpellations that the text offers all readers?

For most readers in both Mexico and the United States, the black humor of Serna's writing provides a role-distancing mechanism. Both Eleanore Wharton as a gringa and the other characters as Mexicans are subjected to Serna's "ethnographic gaze." On the one hand, the short story reinscribes the binary difference analyzed by Morris, constructing a certain sense of Mexican national identity that contrasts with the spiritual deficits of northern neighbors. Such a reinscription of difference also repeats the failure of cross-cultural understanding: Eleanore Wharton cannot see past the projection of her own cultural preconceptions, and "Helpless Roger" repeats a recognizable series of generalized cultural preconceptions. Viewed in another perspective, however, "Helpless Roger," through both its humor and its portrayal of national difference as a structure of feeling, creates an opportunity for Mexican and U.S. readers alike to question stereotypes. As Raquel Mosqueda notes, in all his writings Serna "has turned cruel humor into an antidote against the constant temptation of taking ourselves too seriously" (118).[28] Eleanore Wharton does take herself quite seriously and she might never read or understand "Helpless Roger," in part because she does not know Spanish but also because, even in translation, the short story would never be published for the subscribers of *Reader's Digest*. Such recognition, however, also points toward the possibility for other identities among readers who have learned Spanish and who can perceive the social, cultural, and racial hierarchy at work in Eleanore's judgments. The distance opened by the black humor in "Helpless Roger" also invites readers to imagine other ways of feeling and thinking about cultural difference and the motivations for doing good.

Eleanore Wharton is a curious mirror for national character (flaws) through the limitations of her ability to justify her values, her choices, and her life. Although grotesquely exaggerated, she is not unlike the "Americans" analyzed in *Habits of the Heart: Individualism and Commitment in American Life* by Robert N. Bellah, Richard Madsen, William M. Sullivan, Ann Swidler, and Steven M. Tipton. Published in 1985, the year of Eleanore's trip to Mexico, *Habits of the Heart* is also a "character study"; it examines the American structure of feeling as a "moral vocabulary" related to the ways that individuals "use private and public life to make sense of their lives" (20). And like Eleanore Wharton, in *Habits of the Heart* individuals experience "limitations in the common tradition of moral discourse" and reveal that "it is easier to think about how to get what we want than to know what exactly we should want" (21). In this sense, the characterization in "Helpless Roger" signals a structure of feeling that supposedly motivates some U.S. citizens and invites readers to consider, however uncomfortably, the ways in which we identify with her and in which she represents aspects of U.S. altruism.

In "Helpless Roger," narrative strategies and textual order invite readers into Eleanore Wharton's personal world in a moment of crisis in order to see, within the flow of narrative movement, how a supposedly selfless feeling motivates her choices and emplots her future actions. As readers we view the world, momentarily, through a specific set of mental classifications and perceptions of others that reveals the contradictions in her thinking as felt and in her feelings as thought during her misguided mission to become an adoptive mother. This imagined structure of feeling represents what it means to be a U.S. citizen who thinks, feels, and sometimes chooses to act because of his or her uninformed or even misinformed ideas about life in other countries. By moving through this reading experience, those from the United States who can read in Spanish are invited into a border-crossing relationship to understand the nature of Serna's "ethnographic gaze" when it is directed upon aspects of North America. As Mexico's northern neighbors, such readers may negotiate the uncomfortable space between rejecting Eleanore Wharton as their representative and accepting the misguided aspects of her character that might have been lived out otherwise. Readers see one view of the do-gooder through Serna's narrative lens as Eleanore Wharton takes her place within an international repertoire of ugly Americans.

Los gringos en la literatura mexicana

Though I never was able to locate the anthology *Los gringos en la literatura mexicana*, I expect that in an up-to-date edition with a section on altruists, Eleanore Wharton would stand out. At first blush, she may seem an easy target for Serna's narrative sensibility, a grotesque exaggeration far removed from reality. She is a conglomeration of politically incorrect stereotypes that are challenging to analyze in a sensitive manner. She brings up a variety of topics that are often bitterly discussed in the United States: the politics of adoption by a single parent, by gay or lesbian couples, or by any family that does not fit the heteronormative model; international adoptions from Latin America by U.S. citizens; emergent reactions to international competitiveness during an age of rapid technological innovation and globalization; nationalist values of self-reliance and self-discipline; the dismal educational achievement of schoolchildren and adults regarding knowledge of geography, history, international cultures, and modern languages; the repertoires of racial and ethnic stereotypes; and finally, cultural preference for goal-oriented, pragmatic thinking and efficient problem solving as a national characteristic. Eleanore represents the U.S. citizen who gullibly buys into the simulacra of publications and fails to analyze critically: She believes naively the representations in *Reader's Digest*, the NBC news, and Hollywood road movies (Serna, "El desvalido Roger" 36). Without the insight of critical thinking, Eleanore's self-confident pragmatism quickly leads her down dead-end paths. This list of character traits, although tedious and embarrassing, includes the key elements of the archive of knowledge with which Eleanore feels, thinks, and actively constructs her reality.

Viewed historically, Eleanore Wharton represents one aspect of altruism identified decades earlier by Ivan Illich: She holds a misguided desire to share her middle-class values in order to make herself feel better. She also represents a certain role that belongs within Mexico's contributions to an international archive of representations that question the U.S. sphere of influence abroad: She stands for the self-satisfied philanthropists who are content with the pride they have in their generosity toward others. She remains oblivious to the other side of doing good that Illich evokes at both the beginning and the end of his speech. At the beginning, in his prefatory remarks, he notes that "the only thing you can legitimately volunteer for in Latin America might be voluntary powerlessness, voluntary presence as receivers, as such, as hopefully beloved or adopted ones without any way of returning the gift. . . . Even North Americans can receive the gift of hospitality without the slightest ability to pay for it; the awareness that for some gifts one cannot even say 'thank you' " (315). At the end of the presentation, Illich returns to these same ideas:

> It is incredibly unfair for you to impose yourselves on a village where you are so linguistically deaf and dumb that you don't even understand what you are doing, or what people think of you. And it is profoundly damaging to yourselves when you define something that you want to do as "good," a "sacrifice" and help.
>
> I am here to suggest that you voluntarily renounce exercising the power which being an American gives you. I am here to entreat you to freely, consciously, and humbly give up the legal right you have to impose your benevolence on Mexico. I am here to challenge you to recognize your inability, your powerlessness and your incapacity to do the "good" which you intended to do. (320)

In the world created by contemporary globalization, our international alliances and responses to each other's needs are not only important but also unavoidable and have immediate influence and consequences. Both Illich and Serna identify individuals who know little about the communities they seek to serve, individuals who have little interest in expanding their linguistic boundaries in order to communicate, individuals dedicated to making themselves feel better about their own privileges by seeking to help others become more like them. In the end, "Helpless Roger" raises the question of ethics in pushing readers to recognize the intentional fallacy that drives Eleanore Wharton's choices and actions, which is the belief that the meaning of her choices and actions is determined by her intentions. "Helpless Roger" in a sense responds to Illich's call by allowing U.S. readers to consider one version of "what people think of you," a reading experience that may inform the process of making choices and taking actions motivated by unselfish impulses. Serna's short story and Illich's lecture call upon idealists to listen to others, to become altruists not through good intentions and pride but through accepting their identities as responsive interlocutors when addressed by others.

NOTES

1. Morris, a political scientist, includes a chapter about literature, but he examines mainly essays about identity written by Mexico's intellectual elite and makes only a few references to narrative works, such as the novels by Carlos Fuentes *Where the Air Is Clear* (1958), *The Old Gringo* (1985), and *Christopher Unborn* (1987).

2. Serna is the author of two collections of short stories, *Amores de segunda mano* (Secondhand Loves; 1991) and *El orgasmógrafo* (The Orgasmographer; 2001); one collection of essays, *Las caricaturas me hacen llorar* (Cartoons Make Me Cry; 1996); a biography of Mexican movie star Jorge Negrete, *Jorge el bueno* (The Good Jorge; 1993); and six novels: *Uno soñaba que era rey* (One Dreamed of Being King; 1989), *Señorita México* (Miss Mexico; 1993), *El miedo a los animales* (Fear of Animals; 1995), *El seductor de la patria* (He Who Seduced the Homeland; 1999), *Los ángeles del abismo* (Angels of the Abyss; 2004), and *Fruta verde* (Unripened Fruit; 2006). In contrast with the satirical view of contemporary consumer society in his earlier works, *El seductor de la patria* and *Los ángeles del abismo* demonstrate Serna's ability to use humor in creating historical novels. His most recent novel, *Fruta verde*, explores sexualities and intimate relationships in Mexico.

3. All translations are mine unless otherwise indicated. "Identifican cadáver en Obispado: se trata de Danny Anderson, un norteamericano de cuarentaicuatro años, profesor de la Universidad de Kansas, casado y con dos hijos. Se encontraba en Monterrey acompañando a una delegación de estudiantes que visitaría durante una semana el Instituto Tecnológico como parte de sus programas de intercambio cultural. La víctima habría sido asesinada con un objeto punzocortante de suficiente longitud para atravesarle el cuerpo."

4. "[no] por ser un profesor ni por ser Danny Anderson ni por tener cuarentaicuatro años; lo hizo porque era un pinche gringo."

5. Paul Filmer provides a systematic assessment of "structure of feeling" in Williams's theoretical models. Whereas Williams generally uses the concept to explore the relationship between literary works and sociohistorical reality, I am using the concept to analyze the interplay between private feelings and thought, on the one hand, and public choices and actions, on the other, within the experience of a literary character. Although I do not follow their work in an exact manner, my own explorations are indebted to the ways that Laura Podalsky and Anne Cvetkovich have recast the concept of "structure of feeling" in their own scholarship. For an example of Cvetkovich's work, see her introduction with Ann Pellegrini to a special issue of the *Scholar and Feminist Online* dedicated to "public sentiments."

6. "Su individualismo lindaba con la misantropía. Se guarecía de la vida tras una coraza inexpugnable y rechazaba cualquier demostración de afecto que pudiese resquebrajarla. Odiaba ser así, pero ¿cómo podía remediarlo? ¿Tomando un curso de meditación trascendental? Corría el peligro de encontrarse a sí misma, cuando lo que más deseaba era perderse de vista. No, la meditación y el psicoanálisis eran supercherías,

trucos de maquillaje para tapar las arrugas del alma . . . y ella necesitaba una restauración completa, un cambio de piel. Eleanore Wharton era un costal de fobias."

7. "Niños como éste buscan desesperadamente a sus padres . . . sin sospechar que nunca volverán a encontrarlos."

8. "¿Con qué derecho permanecía en la cama lamiéndose las heridas mientras había en el mundo tantos niños infelices y dignos de compasión. . . . Estaba enternecida. El pequeño damnificado le había devuelto las ganas de luchar. . . . Saltó de la cama con el amor propio revitalizado. Eso era lo que necesitaba para sentirse viva: una emoción pura."

9. "producto imperfecto y deforme del coito visual entre su Polaroid y la pantalla televisiva."

10. "Si es verdad que tiene tan buen corazón adopte a otro niño. ¿Por qué a fuerza quiere adoptar a ése?"

11. "¿Sabe una cosa? Usted está loca. Métase, ándele, haga su escenita y ojalá que de una vez le pongan camisa de fuerza."

12. "los afectos unipersonales y exclusivos."

13. "El niño en quien vería encarnado lo más noble y lo más tierno de su neurosis."

14. "El capricho de buscar específicamente al niño del noticiero sólo podía echar raíces en un cerebro enfermo. A las personas normales que adoptaban niños las animaba la generosidad. Lo suyo era vil y sórdido. Roger no le importaba, eso tenía que admitirlo. Simplemente se gustaba en el papel de madre adoptiva. Y creyendo ingenuamente que prolongaría ese idilio consigo misma si encontraba al niño, había venido a México."

15. "Si algo la motivaba a llegar hasta el final en su misión filantrópica era demostrarle a ese país de borregos, a esa colmena sin individuos, que Eleanore Wharton tenía ideas propias, que sus extravagancias eran muy suyas, y que si jamás había renunciado a su independencia de criterio mucho menos cambiaría a Roger por un huerfanito cualquiera."

16. "punks del subdesarollo"; "para adoptar un pigmeo que además era un llorón horrible."

17. "como si fuere el niño sueco."

18. "No tenía remordimientos pero había sufrido una decepción. La de no haber atropellado al inocente, al tierno, al adorable y desvalido Roger."

19. "Puñal con que solían ir armadas los caballeros de la Edad Media para dar el golpe de gracia al enemigo."

20. "nuevos y más intensos pálpitos de misericordia."

21. James Creechan's Web site for the Conference on Inter-American Studies Projects, in the notes to the online version of Illich's speech, points out that whereas most individuals identify this event as occurring in Cuernavaca, it took place in Illinois.

22. The published version of Illich's talk, widely available on the Internet, has taken a place in the late twentieth-century canon of English-language texts often read in order to prepare individuals for international volunteer experiences and service learning opportunities.

23. "No le gustaba nada tener que hablar con un judío."

24. "el país de los mariachis que cantaban tango."

25. "Tenía el pelo envaselinado, el bigote canoso y los modales de un galán otoñal."

26. "Sus galanterías y sus manoseos de *latin lover*. Sabía perfectamente bien que había venido a México en busca de un niño pero la trataba como a una mujerzuela en busca de aventuras."

27. "La NBC pudo mentir acerca de su orfandad, o incluso, a falta de imágenes amarillistas, mostrar a una víctima de otro terremoto, el de Managua o el de Guatemala, para engañar a su indefenso auditorio de robots."

28. "ha hecho del humor cruel un antídoto contra la constante tentación de tomarnos demasiado en serio."

WORKS CITED

Anderson, Benedict. *Imagined Communities: Reflections on the Origins and Spread of Nationalism.* Rev. ed. London: Verso, 1991.

Bellah, Robert N., Richard Madsen, William M. Sullivan, Ann Swidler, and Steven M. Tipton. *Habits of the Heart: Individualism and Commitment in American Life.* New York: Harper and Row, 1985.

Blanco, José Joaquín. "Enrique Serna y sus silbatazos." *La Jornada*, 24 July 1996. *www.jornada.unam.mx.*

Brushwood, John S. *Los ricos en la prosa mexicana.* Mexico: Editorial Diógenes, 1970.

Carballo, Emmanuel, and Pablo Piccato, eds. *¿Qué país es éste? Los Estados Unidos y los gringos vistos por escritores mexicanos en los siglos XIX y XX.* Mexico: Consejo Nacional para la Cultura y las Artes; Sello Bermejo, 1996.

Carrera, Mauricio, and Betina Keizman. "Enrique Serna: prefecto del instituto patria." *El minotauro y la sirena: entrevistas-ensayos con nuevos narradores mexicanos.* Mexico: Lectorum, 2001. 13–33.

Creechan, James. Conference on Inter-American Student Projects Web site. *www.ciasp.ca.*

Cvetkovich, Anne, and Ann Pellegrini. "Public Sentiments: Introduction." *Scholar and Feminist Online* 2.1 (2003). *www.barnard.edu/sfonline.*

Equivel, Laura. *Like Water for Chocolate.* Trans. Carol Christensen and Thomas Christensen. New York: Doubleday, 1992.

Filmer, Paul. "Structures of Feeling and Socio-Cultural Formations: The Significance of Literature and Experience to Raymond Williams's Sociology of Culture." *British Journal of Sociology* 52.2 (2003): 199–219.

Fuentes, Carlos. *Christopher Unborn.* Trans. Alfred MacAdam and Carlos Fuentes. New York: Farrar, Straus and Giroux, 1989.

———. *Constancia and Other Stories for Virgins.* Trans. Thomas Christensen. New York: Farrar, Straus and Giroux, 1990.

———. *The Old Gringo.* Trans. Margaret Sayers Peden. New York: Farrar, Straus and Giroux, 1985.

———. *Where the Air Is Clear.* Trans. Sam Hileman. New York: Farrar, Straus and Giroux, 1960.

García Ramírez, Fernando. Review of *Amores de segunda mano*, by Enrique Serna. *La Palabra y el Hombre* 78 (1991): 259–60.

Hernández Cabrera, Miguel. "Una literatura del escarnio: entrevista con Enrique Serna." *La Jornada Semanal*, 21 June 1992.

Illich, Ivan. "To Hell with Good Intentions." *Combining Service and Learning: A Resource Book for Community and Public Service.* Vol. 1. Ed. Jane C. Kendall. Raleigh, N.C.: National Society for Internships and Experiential Education, 1990. 314–20.

Márquez, Celina. Review of *Amores de segunda mano*, by Enrique Serna. *La Palabra y el Hombre* 78 (1991): 266–67.

Martínez Ramírez, Fernando. "Serna: el fin justifica los medios." *Casa del tiempo*, 3rd ser., 6.70 (2004): 63–65.

Morris, Stephen D. *Gringolandia: Mexican Identity and Perceptions of the United States.* Lanham, Md.: Rowman and Littlefield, 2005.

Mosqueda, Raquel. "Los muchos modos del esperpento: la narrativa de Enrique Serna." *Literatura Mexicana* 12.1 (2001): 115–39.

Pérez Gay, Rafael. "Entre las ruinas y el jardín: trazos de la cultura en México, 1978–2002." *Nexos* 25.302 (2003): 30–47.

Pliego, Roberto. Review of *Amores de segunda mano* by Enrique Serna. *Nexos* 14.167 (1991): 86.

Podalsky, Laura. "Affecting Legacies: Historical Memory and Contemporary Structures of Feeling in *Madagascar* and *Amores perros*." *Screen* 44.3 (2003): 277–94.

Pogolotti, Marcello, ed. *La clase media en México.* Mexico: Editorial Diógenes, 1972.

———, ed. *Los pobres en la prosa mexicana.* Mexico: Editorial Diógenes, 1978.

Rosaldo, Renato. *Culture and Truth: The Remaking of Social Analysis.* Boston: Beacon Press, 1989.

Schweickart, Patrocinio P., and Elizabeth A. Flynn, eds. *Reading Sites: Social Difference and Reader Response.* New York: Modern Language Association, 2004.

Serna, Enrique. *Angeles del abismo.* Mexico City: Joaquín Mortiz, 2004.

———. "El desvalido Roger." *Amores de segunda mano.* Xalapa: Universidad Veracruzana, 1991. 17–38.

———. *Fruta verde.* Mexico: Planeta, 2006.

———. *El miedo a los animales.* Mexico: Joaquín Mortiz, 1995.

———. *El orgasmógrafo.* Mexico: Plaza y Janés, 2001.

———. *El seductor de la patria.* Mexico: Joaquín Mortiz, 1999.

———. *Las caricaturas me hacen reír.* Mexico: Joaquín Mortiz, 1996.

———. *Señorita México.* Mexico: Plaza y Valdés, 1993.

———. *Uno soñaba que era rey.* Mexico: Plaza y Valdés, 1989.

Torres, Vicente Francisco. Review of *Amores de segunda mano* by Enrique Serna. *La Palabra y el Hombre* 78 (1991): 239–40.

Toscana, David. *Duelo por Miguel Pruneda.* Mexico: Plaza y Janés, 2002.

Usigli, Rodolfo. *Impostor: A Play for Demagogues.* Trans. Ramón Layera with Dan Rosenberg. Pittsburgh: Latin American Literary Review Press, 2005.

Vila, Pablo. *Crossing Borders, Reinforcing Borders: Social Categories, Metaphors, and Narrative Identities on the U.S.-Mexico Frontier.* Austin: University of Texas Press, 2000.

———. "The Polysemy of the Label 'Mexican' on the Border." *Ethnography at the Border.* Minnesota: University of Minneapolis Press, 2003. 105–40.

Volpi, Jorge. *No será la Tierra.* Mexico: Alfaguara, 2006.

Williams, Raymond. *Marxism and Literature.* Oxford: Oxford University Press, 1977.

CHAPTER 8

"La pura gringuez"

The Essential United States in José Agustín, Carlos Fuentes, and Ricardo Aguilar Melantzón

Maarten van Delden

In a well-known passage from *El laberinto de la soledad* (The Labyrinth of Solitude; 1950), Octavio Paz describes how his approximately two-year sojourn in the United States in the 1940s produced an encounter not only with the way of life of Mexico's northern neighbor but also with his own identity as a Mexican. "I remember," he writes, "that whenever I attempted to examine North American life, anxious to discover its meaning, I encountered my own questioning image. That image, seen against the glittering background of the United States, was the first and perhaps the profoundest answer which that country gave to my questions" (12).[1] Paz suggests that a national identity takes shape against the background of other national identities, through a process of differentiation that involves contrasting one country with another. The English define themselves through their differences from the French, America fashioned its identity out of its break with Europe, and the Mexicans see themselves as one pole of a binary opposition with the United States. One consequence of this, as Stephen Morris points out in his book *Gringolandia*, is that the way in which Mexicans perceive the United States will often tell us something about the way in which they perceive themselves (10). Another result of the tendency to think in terms of polar opposites is that national identities come to be viewed largely as fixed entities. In the opening pages of *The Labyrinth of Solitude*, Paz concedes that his inquiry into the Mexican character and its differences from a North American identity may at some future time lose its relevance: "The questions we all ask ourselves today will probably be incomprehensible fifty years from now" (11).[2] In the meantime, however, his portrait of the Mexicans as one side of a dichotomy distinguishing them from the citizens of the United States produces a largely static, essentialist vision.

But what happens to this binary structure when social, cultural, and economic processes begin to erase the boundaries between countries? In an era of globalization, with the nation-state appearing less and less secure and the very notion of fixed, unalterable national identities more and more open to question, is it still possible to uphold the view of Mexico and the United States as polar opposites? Can one still define Mexico as everything the United States is not, and vice-versa? The three authors I study in this chapter—José Agustín, Carlos Fuentes, and Ricardo Aguilar Melantzón—all exemplify in their lives and in their work the apparently fluid nature of international cultural relations in the late twentieth century. All three lived and worked in the United States for extended periods of time, and all three register in their writings the influence of American culture. And yet we will see even in a period of increased cultural exchange—not to mention social and economic integration—that these three authors continue to uphold the view that the United States is fundamentally different from Mexico.[3]

José Agustín: Culture/Counterculture

After spending several years in the late 1970s and early 1980s teaching and writing at universities in the United States, José Agustín in 1982 published *Ciudades desiertas* (Deserted Cities), a novel about a Mexican couple experiencing a marital crisis during a sojourn in the United States. Agustín decided to write the novel after translating Ronald G. Walker's *Infernal Paradise: Mexico and the Modern English Novel* into Spanish. He saw his novel about the United States as a retort to the stereotypical foreigner's perception of Mexico as an "infernal paradise." *Ciudades desiertas* was, he said, his "little Montezuma's revenge" (cited in Calvillo 182). Indeed, the novel offers a sharply satirical reading of life in the United States. And yet, as we will see, Agustín's novel at the same time registers a sensibility that has been profoundly shaped by U.S. culture.

Ciudades desiertas tells the story of Susana, a Mexican writer who travels to the United States to participate in a writer's program at the University of Arcadia, a fictional town somewhere in the Midwest, and her husband, Eligio, who follows her north only to find that she has become involved with another man, a dark, brooding poet from Poland. Agustín's novel is concerned as much, if not more, with the American setting in which the couple's matrimonial difficulties develop as it is with Eligio's efforts to regain Susana's affections. The novel treats the American backdrop to the plot in a tone of mockery and astonishment. Again and again, Susana and Eligio lambaste what they regard as the outlandish way of life of their neighbors to the north. Their complaints are aimed primarily at what they view as the soullessness of life in the United States and at the arrogance of the Americans, who are convinced that they are living in the greatest country on earth.

The first person Susana meets when she arrives in the United States is Becky, an assistant with the writer's program at the University of Arcadia whose task it is to familiarize the visitors from abroad with their new surroundings. Agustín uses Becky to illustrate his view of Americans as a people lacking in human warmth and naturalness. The narrator describes Becky as "a cold and talkative girl with large glasses and a gift-wrapped friendliness" (13).[4] Her friendly veneer masks an authoritarian mentality. While she tries to appear cordial and helpful, she comes across as rigid and condescending. She is extremely keen on explaining the rules of life in the United States to her foreign charges, and on making sure that they're followed. When she accompanies a group of writers to the supermarket, she is horrified when they decide to eat their sandwiches in the parking lot. Becky explains that in the United States "we have parks and specially designated areas for picnics, with tables, trash cans, restrooms—everything you need for a clean, hygienic picnic" (77).[5] When she takes the writers to the bank to deposit their checks, she informs them, in a tone that brooks no disagreement, that "*under no circumstances*" should they fold their checks, for if they do the bank will not accept them (18).[6] At the airport, she describes, with a certain relish, the possible consequences for travelers who fail to follow proper protocol: "All travelers have to state whether they're carrying a firearm, and there's always some joker, I'm afraid it's usually someone from *our* program, who answers yes, and the security guards take them away and give them *a very hard time*" (13).[7] All her comments and actions reveal Becky's humorless and coercive mindset. Her controlling, inflexible personality makes a mockery of the myth of the United States as "the land of the free." And Becky is clearly no anomaly. Eligio speaks of a general loss of humanity in American society: "People here have turned into little robots, their souls are dying" (105).[8] He complains about the lack of warmth and authenticity in ordinary human interactions: People don't shake hands when they meet, their smiles seem fake, their actions programmed like computers (183). In sum, Agustín's vision of the United States is part of a tradition in Latin American literature that goes back as far as José Enrique Rodó's *Ariel* (1900), with its view of the United States as a materialistic nation lacking in spiritual depth. In *Ciudades desiertas*, this reading of the United States emerges not only from the depiction of characters like Becky, but also from a series of descriptions of emblematic locations in the modern American landscape.

In response to the local view that Arcadia is a genuine paradise, Altagracia, a Filipina writer, informs a group of newcomers to the program that "there is truly nothing in this hamlet" (25).[9] The novel repeatedly takes up this idea of the American void, the country's lack of depth, the "there is no there there" famously alluded to by Gertrude Stein when in Oakland, California. When he arrives at the Chicago airport, Eligio is struck by the eerie silence in the terminal: "There was something abnormal about the Chicago airport . . . There was a very strange silence in the air, how could that vast, terrifyingly long terminal, with its bars, restaurants and telephone booths, its boring shops selling gringo curios, its loudspeakers and incomprehensible machines, be so silent? . . . It was as if there was nothing there: The place felt like a huge freezer" (51–52).[10] It is not that there are no people about; on the contrary, the terminal is crowded: "So many people, and yet such silence!"[11] What is missing, however, is a sense of human contact: People "wandered from here to there, in a hurry, without looking at anyone, with the air of serious and

efficient executives" (52).[12] The scene concludes with a disturbing vision of prolif-
erating machines: "machines on all sides, machines selling cigarettes, candy, chocolates, stamps, sodas, the newspaper, machines for making change, machines for
depositing or withdrawing money from your bank account, machines that sold tea
or coffee or hot chocolate, machines for shining your shoes" (53).[13] The only person who approaches Eligio in the terminal is a rather menacing Hare Krishna who
tries to sell him a copy of the Bhagavad Gita for an exorbitant twenty-five dollars.
Evidently, in this world, even the realm of the spiritual appears only in a degraded
and commercialized form.

Susana comments that in the United States "nothing is sacred, everything is
empty" (77).[14] As he drives through the outskirts of Santa Fe, New Mexico, Eligio
is struck by how devoid the urban landscape is of a sense of history, a feeling for
beauty, or even a simple sense of human vibrancy: "Everywhere the same wide
avenues . . . as usual, no roundabouts or dividers, no flowers or statues, only kilo-
meters of asphalt . . . , empty parks, streets used only by cars, without pedestrians
or dogs or cats or street vendors or small stores" (178–79).[15] It is significant, of
course, that Eligio's list of missing items evokes a typically Mexican street scene,
for which he has begun to feel increasingly nostalgic. Back in Arcadia, the lack of
pedestrians in the streets had already troubled Susana and Eligio. In one of their
conversations, Susana observes jokingly that people here take the car even to go to
the bathroom (79). To Eligio, Arcadia seems too clean and tidy; what this place
needs, he says, is "a nice dog; dead, of course, his body decomposing in the street"
(82).[16] He wonders, sarcastically, whether the authorities in Arcadia sterilize the
sidewalks. And when Susana and Eligio leave the town and drive into the countryside, the monotony of the Midwestern landscape seems to echo the boredom of
the town itself (86).

Whereas the encounter with U.S. culture has left the Mexican characters in
Ciudades desiertas frankly aghast, their American hosts are convinced that they are
living in the greatest country on earth. All the people running the writers' program
at the University of Arcadia are constantly reminding their guests of how fortunate they are to be there—and of how much it is costing to pay for their stay. The
Americans believe that they have done the visiting writers a huge favor in inviting
them to participate in their program, and they are sure that the foreigners would
desire nothing more than to remain in the United States. But Rick, one of the program's directors, warns them that staying in the United States is "*incredibly difficult*
to arrange . . . in case one of those present here has already thought of trying to
remain permanently in this great country" (20–21).[17] In a scene that takes place at
the home of a wealthy donor to the writers' program at the University of Arcadia,
an elderly American couple approaches Susana and Eligio to chat, but they seem
less interested in learning about the visitors from abroad than in congratulating
them on being there: "what a great opportunity for you to have been able to come
here!" (122).[18] In response, Susana dryly suggests that it is a great opportunity for

them as well. Eligio wonders why all the writers in the program are from "the good ol' Third World" and suggests that it is probably because it is so much easier for the Americans to revel in a sense of their superiority with visitors from poor rather than rich countries (87). As Ramón, a writer from Argentina, points out, "These Yankees are constantly telling you that you are so lucky to be here, but they never say that they are lucky to have us here. What a bunch of nouveau riches!" (120).[19] The Americans are confident that they can impress their guests with their technology, their prosperity, and their efficiency. They are truly persuaded that their country is "the navel of the world" (104).[20] Toward the end of the novel, when Eligio falls in with a group of young Americans in Santa Fe who are highly critical of their own country, his sympathy for their views—they complain about Ronald Reagan and denounce the creeping fascism they see in the United States—does not diminish Eligio's annoyance at their conviction that America is the most important nation in the world: "Deep down, Eligio thought, these kids still think that this immense refrigerator is the true center of the world, and that this is the way it will be forever, poor fools" (182).[21] Eligio simply cannot understand the all-encompassing American arrogance. Susana, for her part, sneeringly suggests that Arcadia is not the world's navel, but its asshole (104).

Eligio's numerous and increasingly vehement tirades against all things American should not, however, lead the reader to believe that Agustín has produced a one-sided and simplistic act of literary revenge. For one thing, the novel's anti-American diatribes are always attributed to particular individuals. And Agustín makes it very clear that these individuals—especially Eligio—express highly subjective, even visceral, opinions that ought not to be taken entirely at face value. Eligio is an incisive and often hilarious observer of American mores and customs, but he is not meant to be regarded as a wholly reliable guide to the country he is visiting. He himself is aware of the distortions produced by his emotional state (he is deeply distraught over his abandonment by Susana). Toward the end of his stay in the United States, his distress has become so acute that the mere sound of English being spoken throws him into a rage. Still, a moment later we see Eligio feeling dismayed by his own intolerance (183). There is always an element of performance and exaggeration to his behavior, and everything he says needs to be taken with a grain of salt. Moreover, the author pointedly draws the reader's attention to Eligio's contradictions: He may despise the United States for its materialism and consumerism, but he keeps his savings in U.S. currency, and when the opportunity presents itself, he and Susana go on a "typically American" shopping spree at the local mall in Arcadia. The hypocrisy is not hard to miss.

To further elucidate the complexity of Agustín's vision of the United States, it may help to look at his depiction of a different type of American character: not the American who believes that the United States is the greatest country on earth, but instead the self-critical American who repudiates her own country and idealizes others, especially those regarded as primitive or premodern. As he pursues his wife across the United States, Eligio becomes involved with Irene, a young American woman who reflects this alternative outlook. Irene falls for Eligio because of his Indian looks: "She said that Eligio looked like an *Aztec idol*, an obsidian sculpture, she had never met anyone with such a pure and handsome Indian look" (100).[22] Her views of Mexico have been shaped by her readings of Malcolm Lowry, D. H. Lawrence, Graham Greene, Ben Traven, Antonin Artaud, and Carlos Castaneda, all of whom she has read with "true devotion" (173).[23] From these books, Irene has constructed a romanticized view of Mexico as a country that, unlike the United States, has remained connected to its indigenous roots.

The relationship between Eligio and Irene is rife with irony. To begin with, Eligio practically chokes on his drink when he finds out that Irene has fallen for him because he looks so Indian. He explains that in Mexico girls avoid him for that very same reason (100). Even though Irene has never been to Mexico, she lectures Eligio on how "he, and *all Mexicans*, were making a *big mistake* in not *valuing* their indigenous heritage" (173).[24] But what does she know about Mexico? At one point, she muses about her desire to visit Mexico City and meet famous writers like Gabriel García Márquez and Octavio Paz, who, she adds, "must be really good friends, no?" (174).[25] Still, even though Agustín gleefully exposes Irene's ignorance of the politics of Mexico City's elite intellectuals, it is certainly not the case that she is simply a butt of his mockery. Eligio is irritated by what he calls "all these wretched stereotypes of Mexico-as-land-of-death-infernal-paradise" (176) to which Irene seems so attached, but there are many things about her he likes and admires.[26] When it comes to Mexico, she's a hopeless romantic; in her daily life, however, she's a very practical and straightforward woman (174). Eligio also approvingly notes her strength of character, decisiveness, and independence (171). And he finds her physically very attractive: "She was very pretty, with a splendid body, truly more delectable and ripe than Susana's" (171).[27] In this novel, where personal identity is always closely tied to national identity, Irene's beautiful body clearly does credit to her country, as well as herself.

Irene is a complicated character, whose presence in the novel captures the complexity of Agustín's relationship to the United States. She represents the American counterculture of the 1960s and after—precisely the dimension of American culture to which Agustín himself was drawn. In his history of the counterculture in Mexico, Agustín makes it clear that many of the figures he examines—such as the pachucos, rebels without a cause, beatniks, and hippies—originated in the United States (*La contracultura en México* [The Counterculture in Mexico]). In *Ciudades desiertas*, Agustín offers a satirical perspective on the American counterculture, but there is no doubt that he prefers it over the mainstream. Note also that the novel's epigraph comes from a song by the 1960s rock band Cream—a British band to be sure, but one that was heavily influenced by the blues, a distinctly American form of music. In addition, the colloquial style, the loose narrative structure, and the travelogue elements in the novel are reminiscent of the very American genre of the road novel, especially the classic of the genre, Jack Kerouac's *On the Road* (1957). In sum, José Agustín's critical view of the United States is part of a longstanding Mexican and Latin American tradition of representations of the neighbor to the north. Yet there are also significant differences between Agustín and precursors such as Rodó, José Vasconcelos, and, to some extent, Octavio Paz and Fuentes. *Ciudades desiertas* disdains the United States for its materialism, its soullessness, and its cultural arrogance, but it does not do so from an aestheticist and aristocratic point of view. Instead, it draws at least some of the inspiration for its critique from the new, popular, and antielitist cultural trends emanating from the United States itself. Moreover, the very plot of *Ciudades desiertas* suggests that the United States is a place where a woman like Susana can free herself from some of the constraints of her marriage. Even though the couple is reunited at the end of the novel, the reader is meant to understand that the experience of leaving Mexico and spending a period of time in the United States has forced a readjustment for the good in relations between Eligio and Susana. This would seem to imply a favorable comment on the social and cultural values of Mexico's northern neighbor.[28]

Carlos Fuentes: Fear and Loathing on the U.S.-Mexican Border

Having lived in the United States as a child in the 1930s, and with his extensive experience teaching and lecturing at U.S. universities, Carlos Fuentes is an exceptionally knowledgeable observer of the culture, politics, and society of Mexico's northern neighbor. Throughout his career he has commented repeatedly in essays and newspaper articles on the relationship between the two nations. He has also used his fiction to delve into this contentious subject, perhaps most notably in two novels from the 1980s, *Gringo Viejo* (Old Gringo; 1985) and *Cristóbal nonato* (Christopher Unborn; 1987). In the early 1990s, with the two countries engaged in a historic effort to strengthen their ties, an effort that culminated in the North American Free Trade Agreement (NAFTA), a vast new free-trade zone linking Mexico, the United States, and Canada, Fuentes was once again drawn to this topic, writing a series of interlinked narratives about the U.S.-Mexico border— both in the literal and the metaphorical sense—published in 1995 as *La frontera de cristal: una novela en nueve cuentos* (The Crystal Frontier: A Novel in Nine Stories). But whereas Fuentes expressed his support for NAFTA in his essays and public statements, he used his fiction to put forward a very negative view of Mexico's new partner in the free-trade agreement.[29] In the stories of *The Crystal Frontier*, Fuentes presents Mexico as the victim of a long history of exploitation and aggression on the part of the United States. In addition, he characterizes the United States primarily by its lack of culture, taste, and sophistication. Americans are bullies and racists, generally ignorant of anything occurring beyond the borders of their own country. In Fuentes's stories, Mexican characters are sometimes seduced by the United States, but the seduction generally rings false. On the few occasions when Mexicans and Americans become romantically or sexually involved with each other, things do not turn out well. And yet, in spite of the almost Manichaean vision he presents in *The Crystal Frontier*, Fuentes introduces, at one point in the narrative, a character who expresses an optimistic, almost utopian, view of the possibilities of cross-border contact and mutual understanding.

Fuentes addresses U.S. aggression against Mexico in "Río Grande, Río Bravo," the concluding story of *The Crystal Frontier*. The tale's title refers to the two names—the American and the Mexican—of the river that marks the boundary between Mexico and the United States from the twin cities of El Paso and Ciudad Juárez to the Gulf of Mexico. The two names are an apt symbol of the strained and dissonant relationship between these two nations. The story alternates between sections of straightforward narrative describing the experiences of a range of characters living on the U.S.-Mexican border, and passages that poetically evoke the region's history, from the era of the first migrations into the Americas (222–24) to the days of the Mexican Revolution (260–61). The arrival of the first Americans is described in a tone of horrified astonishment: "The gringos came (who are they, who are they, for God's sake, how can they exist, who invented them?)" (247).[30] The narrator chronicles Mexico's loss of Texas in 1836 as well as the loss of additional territories to the United States following the U.S. invasion of Mexico during the 1846–48 war. Fuentes emphasizes the aggressive nationalist ideology infusing the U.S. drive to war, as well as the racist attitudes of Americans toward Mexicans. Earlier in the collection, he refers to Mexico's loss of half its territory to the United States as a "terrible despojo" [terrible despoiling] noting, furthermore, that "the gringos didn't even remember that war, much less know its unfairness" (57).[31] In "Río Grande, Río Bravo," the narrator pointedly contrasts the American ideology of Manifest Destiny with the ongoing search of the Mexicans for "their own destiny, not manifest but uncertain human destiny, to sculpt slowly, not to reveal providentially" (255).[32] The narrative subsequently moves on to the era of the Porfiriato, during which U.S. interests take over large chunks of the Mexican economy, and to the period of the Mexican Revolution, a key episode in Mexico's journey of self-discovery, which Fuentes accuses the Americans of having misunderstood (261).[33]

In contemplating the present state of relations between the two countries, Fuentes depicts the Americans as, in essence, exploitative and even abusive neighbors. In "Río Grande, Río Bravo," he introduces his readers to Dan Polonsky, a border patrol agent who regards Mexicans as "mosquitoes that sucked the blood of the USA and ran back home to support their lazy countrymen" (225).[34] The narrative mercilessly exposes Polonsky's contradictions: his own grandparents, immigrants from Europe, had themselves suffered discrimination upon coming to the United States, and Polonsky's wife hires an undocumented worker as a nanny. Furthermore, many of Polonsky's fellow border patrol agents are Mexican Americans, although Polonsky predictably questions their loyalty to the United States.

Other figures in *The Crystal Frontier* who capture the current state of U.S.-Mexican relations are the American businessmen in "Malintzin de las maquilas" (Malintzin of the Maquilas), who move their factories south of the border to take advantage of the cheap labor available there, and the elderly and wealthy American lady in "Las Amigas" who abuses her Mexican housekeeper. Such characters amount to not-very-subtle versions of the stereotypical figure of the "ugly American."[35] One should not overlook, however, Fuentes's pinpointing of the role played by Mexicans in the exploitation of their own country. After all, one of the key characters in the book is Leonardo Barroso, a prosperous businessman who owes his fortune primarily to his skill at negotiating cross-border deals.

The view that Americans lack culture, taste, and sophistication appears in several stories in *The Crystal Frontier*. The main character of "El despojo" (Spoils) is Dionisio "Baco" Rangel, a successful author of cookbooks and much in demand on the U.S. lecture circuit. The irony is that Rangel is deeply disdainful of the very country that celebrates him—and makes him rich. The United States has no culinary tradition whatsoever, and Rangel must suffer the horrible fate of having "to preach fine cooking in a country incapable of understanding or practicing it" (56).[36] The American inability to appreciate excellent cuisine is part of the overall thinness of the nation's cultural life. Rangel laments the country's lack of historical memory (57), its celebration of ignorance (60), and the obscene and wasteful abundance of its consumer culture (61–62). In "La pena" (Pain), a story about a young Mexican who receives a scholarship to study at Cornell, the narrator, clearly appalled, describes the radical informality of the American students: "They wear baseball caps they don't even take off indoors or when they greet a woman. They rarely shave completely. They drink beer straight from the bottle. They wear sleeveless T-shirts, revealing at all hours their hairy underarms. Their jeans have torn knees, and at times they wear them cut off at the thigh and unraveling" (36–37).[37] What is even more bizarre to Juan Zamora, the story's protagonist, is that the youths acting in this uncivilized manner are all from rich families (37). Dionisio Rangel believes that the essential difference between Mexico and the United States is that whereas Americans may have all the power in the world, Mexicans can take pride in the refinement of their culture: "Mexico also had conventions, manners, tastes, subtleties that confirmed her aristocratic culture. . . . In Mexico even a thief was courteous, even an illiterate was cultured, even a child knew how to say hello, even a maid knew how to walk gracefully" (65–66).[38] In "Malintzin of the Maquilas" the main character is a young Mexican woman who works in an assembly plant in Ciudad Juárez. In spite of her modest circumstances, she insists on traveling to work in her high heels, "unlike the gringas, who walked to work in Keds and put on their high heels in the office" (115).[39] In Fuentes's narrative world, to opt for style over practicality is a sign of one's Mexicanness, and one's difference from the Americans.

In a "nation the size of the universe" (184) like the United States, it is perhaps not surprising that people know very little of what is happening beyond the borders of their own country.[40] This does not, however, diminish the dismay Fuentes's stories convey upon contemplating the consequences of this ignorance. Consider, for example, Tarleton Wingate and his family, who act as hosts to Juan Zamora, the Cornell medical student from Mexico in "Pain." In his description of Tarleton, Fuentes evokes the widespread view of Americans as childlike, describing him as a "likable giant" with a "fresh, juvenile face" (34).[41] And like children, these Americans are uninformed. They know so little of the countries south of the border that Tarleton's wife, Charlotte, refrains from calling Juan a Mexican because she is afraid he might be offended! Given that the Wingates recoil from the very word "Mexican," how could one possibly expect them to know anything about Mexican politics? Juan notes, for example, that "the Wingates don't know that oil is the property of the state in Mexico," an ignorance that is presented as part of a larger ideological simplemindedness: "Dogmatically but innocently, the Wingates believe that the expression *free world* is synonymous with *free enterprise*" (35).[42] The narrative reveals a sinister side to this naiveté. It turns out that Tarleton had once worked for an arms factory in Ithaca and is now a consultant in the defense contracting industry. The story takes place in the early years of the Reagan administration, as the U.S. government was increasing its efforts to "stop the advances of Communism in Central America," efforts heartily applauded by the Wingates. But what leaves Juan thoroughly disconcerted is their indifference to the images of the war in El Salvador appearing on the nightly news: "He doesn't understand if they are pained when terrible pictures of the war in El Salvador appear—nuns murdered along the roadside, rebels murdered by paramilitary death squads, an entire village machine-gunned by the army as the people flee across a river" (34).[43] Evidently, the Wingates are unable to make the connection between Tarleton's work for the defense industry, Reagan's anti-Communist rhetoric, and the human rights abuses perpetrated by a Salvadoran military being propped up by the United States government.

Literary works concerned with cross-cultural or transnational encounters have often resorted to plots centered on romantic or sexual love as a way of exploring their themes. Fuentes's *The Crystal Frontier* is no exception in this regard. Juan Zamora in "Pain" falls for a fellow student named Jim Rowlands, who helps him discover his homosexuality. A beautiful love affair blossoms between the Mexican and the American: "The young men, a contrast of light and dark, looked good together. At first, they attracted attention on campus, then they were accepted and even admired for the obvious affection they showed for each other and the spontaneity of their relationship" (41).[44] But it turns out that Jim does not take his relationship with Juan all that seriously: After a period of romantic bliss, Jim suddenly informs Juan that he has all along been engaged to marry a woman back in Seattle, where his family is from. Juan is devastated by the loss, and returns to Mexico City. In "Malintzin of the Maquilas," a key scene takes place in a Juárez nightclub patronized primarily by female workers who enjoy a performance by a group of American male strippers known as the Chippendale Boys. The strippers sport tattoos on their bodies of both the Mexican and U.S. flags, suggesting a possible cultural (and sexual, given the setting) intertwining of the two countries. But the story makes it clear that the encounter between the Mexican women and the American dancers is of an utterly superficial nature. For one thing, the Chippendale Boys, with "their assembly-line smiles," are completely lacking in human warmth and authenticity. When they parade across the stage at the end of the performance, one of the Mexican women notes their bored, indifferent, even cruel expressions, concluding that these men would be incapable of feeling love for a woman (137).[45] The narrative most concerned with the possibility of U.S.-Mexican romance is the collection's title story, in which a Mexican worker in New York has a romantic encounter of sorts with an American executive. She is spending her Saturday at the office and he is cleaning the building's windows when their eyes meet through the glass, and they apparently feel an instantaneous attraction toward each other. She writes her name on the window, and he responds, before disappearing from view, by writing the word "Mexican" on the glass. The fleeting nature of the encounter, in combination with the fact that the Mexican character cannot—in the context of a meeting with an American woman—conceive of himself as an individual, instead reducing himself to a representative of a country, captures the impossibility of cross-border communication.

In spite of Fuentes's bleak assessment of the state of Mexican-U.S. relations, *The Crystal Frontier* does include a character who expresses a hopeful vision of the new culture emerging on the border between the two nations: José Francisco, the Chicano writer who appears in "Río Grande, Río Bravo." Having attended school on the northern side of the border, he is thoroughly familiar with the discrimination suffered by Mexicans in the United States. He recalls that as a child he was forbidden to speak Spanish—a prohibition to which he responded by singing songs in his native language during recess. He remembers losing a friend who had said that José Francisco could come to his house only if he pretended not to be Mexican. At school, he wages a successful battle to have students assigned to their seats by alphabetical order, instead of grouped by race and ethnicity (250). Still, in spite of this difficult history, José Francisco is an optimist. As a writer he sees it as his task to give voice to all the stories he has heard since his childhood: "stories about immigrants, illegals, Mexican poverty, Yankee prosperity, but most of all stories about families, that was the wealth of the border world, the quantity of unburied stories that refused to die" (251).[46] He is also an anthologist who believes that literature can help to create a transnational community in the Juárez/El Paso area: "José Francisco brought Chicano manuscripts to Mexico and Mexican manuscripts to Texas. . . . That was José Francisco's contraband, literature from both sides so that everyone would get to know one another better, he said, so that everyone would love one another a little more, so that there would be a 'we' on both sides of the border" (252).[47] The section of "Río Grande, Río Bravo" devoted to José Francisco concludes with a scene in which he is stopped at the border and checked for contraband, whereupon he begins to cast the manuscripts he is carrying with him to the winds, confident that they will end up in the right place: "tossing manuscripts into the air . . . convinced that the words would fly until they found their destination, their readers, their listeners, their tongues, their eyes." As the pages sail through the air, Fuentes's Chicano author expresses a rare sense of joy as he contemplates the momentary disappearance of the border between Mexico and the US: "José Francisco gave a victory shout that forever broke the crystal frontier" (253).[48]

Ricardo Aguilar Melantzón:
A Tale of Two Countries

José Francisco is a fictional character, but he did have a real-life model: Ricardo Aguilar Melantzón (1947–2004), a poet, critic, anthologist, testimonialist, short-story writer, and novelist who lived and worked for most of his life in the Ciudad Juárez/El Paso metropolitan area. Aguilar alludes to Fuentes's reference to him, noting at one point in his 1999 autobiographical novel *A barlovento* (Windward) that Fuentes, whom he calls "Charlie Fountains," "mentions your humble servant" in *The Crystal Frontier* (208).[49] The connection between the real Aguilar and Fuentes's fictional version of him can also be established from the prominent role accorded in both narratives to the character's motorbike. Aguilar devotes long passages of *Windward* to expressing his love of his bike, while Fuentes treats José Francisco's bike in "Río Grande, Río Bravo" as a key symbol of the border writer's mobility. However, if we compare Fuentes's presentation of José Francisco in *The Crystal Frontier* with Aguilar's self-presentation in *Windward*, a striking contrast emerges; instead of depicting the exhilaration provoked by the possibility of creating a transborder community, Aguilar offers a lengthy meditation, oscillating between the comic and the melancholic, on the huge gulf separating the two countries. *Windward* distances itself from the celebratory vision of the border as a deterritorialized space;[50] instead, it views the U.S. side of the border from a perspective of anguished alienation, while it approaches the Mexican side with a deep sense of identification and nostalgia.

Aguilar takes pains to emphasize the personal and intimate nature of his acquaintance with the border. At one point in his narrative, he complains about the invasion of outsiders (especially people from Mexico City) pontificating about the border experience, and contrasts the self-promoting agendas of these so-called experts with his own direct, detailed, and meticulous knowledge of the subject: "People talk a lot about what the border is and isn't and even more if you're the beenthere-donethat and knowitall-betterthananyone from Mexico City to puff themselves up in front of everyone else, the truth is if you really know the border first, very firsthand, you find her in the minutiae" (349).[51] In referring to his firsthand knowledge of the border, Aguilar is offering an astute defense of his own book. Much of what has been written in Mexico about the United States and its differences from its southern neighbor makes use of broad categories, such as the oppositions between future-oriented and traditionalist societies, between communitarian and individualistic cultures, or between spiritual and materialistic nations.[52] Many of Aguilar's opinions about the United States resemble the views put forward by Agustín and Fuentes, as well as numerous other Mexican authors. The difference is that *Windward*—and herein lies Aguilar's contribution to the tradition of Mexican readings of the United States—depicts the contrast between the two nations in exquisitely detailed and sensorial terms. For Aguilar, living in the United States as opposed to Mexico is literally a different bodily experience.

When *Windward*'s narrator moves to Las Cruces to take up a teaching position at New Mexico State University, he soon begins to suffer from a loss of literary inspiration: "For the past two years I've been asking myself what am I going to write about here." (305).[53] He attributes his inability to find anything to write about to the social and cultural void he perceives in the United States. Aguilar relates the sense of emptiness he experiences on the north side of the border to the utterly different organization of social life there. To begin with, it has to do with the absence of vibrant public spaces in the vast majority of American communities. In Las Cruces, for instance, there is absolutely no street life. The narrator's wife can't figure out why there are never any people about in the neighborhood where they live: "Rosi asks me what's up, what's with these people here, are they dead or what, what's up that at eight or nine in the evening they're already inside their house or under their blankets or whatever" (305).[54] When the narrator and his wife go for a stroll one evening in search of a cantina or café, the neighbors look at them as if they were creatures from outer space: "The neighbors hide as we walk by or they stand staring at us as if to ask what we're doing walking around in the street in the dark" (305).[55] In the United States, "Folks don't walk in the street; they get in their cars and drive wherever they're going" (306).[56] The contrast with Mexico could not be more striking. Remembering his life in Juárez, the narrator stresses the sense of constant activity, as well as the sheer objecthood, of the world that surrounded him: "There I was saturated with comings and goings . . . , soaked with humanity, plant, urban, with faces, trees and nopales, sidewalks, streets, parks, houses and buildings, friezes, Carpentieresque columns, deteriorated and deteriorating walls, with aromas, flavors, noises, lights and darkness, and the laughter of uniformed schoolgirls walking to school along freshly swept sidewalks" (305).[57] The narrator's use of the verbs "saturated" and "soaked" evokes the vibrant, dense reality of life in Mexico, which the narrator finds fulfilling in a way that life in the United States is not.

In Mexico, things literally have a stronger flavor than in the United States. Like many other foreign observers, Aguilar takes up the theme of the poor quality of the food and drink in the United States. He complains about the watery beer: "The damn gringo beer tastes like vile water" (308).[58] Even worse is the produce sold in the United States: "Now things from over there taste different, it's the very same corn, beans or chili, the same fruits or whatever you like but here it all tastes like a dish rag, the bananas are green, very green, like *guanábanas*, the apples taste like sand, the green lemons which in my opinion they confuse with yellow limes, the chili is sweet, can you believe it?" (308).[59] Later in the novel, he reflects on the antiseptic atmosphere in an American supermarket: "Here it's neither fish nor fowl. Yesterday I stopped to check out the supermarket, and I asked myself, what does it smell like? And I had to answer that it didn't smell like anything, not even at the fish counter . . . , unless it's a smell, like that of a deodorant, that serves to cover up other smells" (365).[60] In Mexico, by contrast, the streets are filled with rich and natural odors: "Over there, I've been getting used again to normal smells, of ink, of fresh and overripe oranges, roasted chile, freshly baked bread, corn tortillas, shoe polish and Oso brand oil, to cowhide, freshly cut wood, to creosote and oil near the train tracks" (365).[61] It is significant, in this regard, that the novel's concluding scene takes place in a Ciudad Juárez bakery, where several customers, including a young girl in her school uniform, wait to purchase some freshly baked rolls. The scene closes with the girl leaving the store: "The little girl pays, picks up her bag of bread and leaves skipping with joy as all children should" (369).[62] The Juárez bakery stands in for the notions of naturalness and authenticity Aguilar associates with the Mexican city. The young girl in the scene reinforces these connotations through her obvious innocence. Thus, at a time when Ciudad Juárez was linked in the public mind to profound processes of social disintegration—related in the first place to the still unsolved mystery of the hundreds of murdered women in the city—Aguilar chooses to underline the thoroughgoing *normality* of life in the Mexican city.[63]

The focus on the quality of the food and drink in the United States reveals Aguilar's predilection for sensory experiences as a way of capturing the differences between the two countries. Yet critiques of American cuisine are of course nothing new. More interesting, and certainly more surprising and unusual, are Aguilar's discussions of a number of other features of American life—and their differences from Mexico—all of which reveal how it *feels* different to be in one country rather than the other. Consider Aguilar's observations about what it is like to sleep in the United States ("there") as opposed to Mexico ("here"): "It's that the beds are different, the one there is hard as a plank of wood and we're in the habit of each one sleeping on his/her side; here the bed is softer and our spots are on opposite sides" (351).[64] But it is not just the mattresses that are different; each country also possesses its own peculiar aural environment influencing one's ability to sleep at night: "There you don't hear a thing, after all, we're living in the country, like they say we're only three blocks from the desert; here the train whistle blows at three o'clock in the morning and at six . . . ; there the highway is about two blocks away and we don't hear a thing, here the traffic on the other block is constant and you always hear everything" (351–52).[65]

Architectural details are also a good indicator of a country's character. Aguilar devotes a fascinating passage to discussing the differences in what he calls "the physiognomies of the buildings" (348), focusing in particular on the omnipresent window bars of Ciudad Juárez, and their complete absence in the United States. Aguilar humorously suggests how an architectural feature—or more precisely, its absence—changes its meaning when it crosses the border.[66] After describing Juárez as a "grilleworked city," he goes on to observe: "Here you see windows without grilles and you begin to think: 'Yikes, someone can get in here.' There you see a house with iron grilles and you say: 'Yikes, how dangerous. In case of a fire, how are they going to get out?'" (348).[67] In one country, the focus is on impeding burglaries (and on ornamentation); in the other, it is on accident prevention. The result is that the urbanized areas of Mexico and the United States look utterly different from each other. But even walking around a town or city in one country or the other can produce an entirely different experience. In Mexico, the sidewalks are generally in poor shape: "I don't know why people don't have more accidents when they walk, it's more like a balancing exercise than walking" (346–47).[68] In Las Cruces, by contrast, the sidewalks are models of sophisticated and socially conscious design: "There the majority are perfect, newly built, very smooth with entrances for cars and dips perfectly laid out for wheelchairs" (347).[69] In Mexico, when you go for a walk, you have to be careful not to put your foot in a pile of dog feces: "Here the dogs don't respect anybody or anything, they crap anywhere they like on the cement and you are the one who needs to smarten up so you don't step in it" (348).[70] In the United States, they order these matters differently: "There you don't see dogs on the street, the law prohibits it, unless they're leashed or chained to their owners and they should crap in places where there is no sidewalk, if they crap on the sidewalk their owners are responsible for picking up the turds" (348).[71] In sum, the United States feels like a quieter, safer, cleaner, and more comfortable place than its neighbor to the south. And yet, it is clear that the narrator of *Windward* much prefers the sensory overload of Mexico to the "quiet, tranquil, stealthy way of life" of the United States (306).[72]

Although the most distinctive and memorable passages in Aguilar's novel treat the differences between the two countries by means of a series of highly concrete and meticulously detailed impressions, *Windward* also includes sections that discuss the less tangible dimensions of U.S. culture. One argument the novel develops is that what characterizes this culture is precisely its *lack* of a spiritual dimension. One character refers to the "total cultural void" of the United States (363).[73] Elsewhere, the narrator refers with great disdain to the United States' leading cultural export: "the poorly translated and even worse dubbed trash Hollywood dumps on us" (361–62).[74] The novel includes a long and vehement tirade against U.S. prejudices toward Mexico, what Aguilar calls "Anglo-Saxon, Southern, Texan racism and ignorance" (322).[75] Perhaps what the narrator finds most distressing is the in-comprehension displayed by his American colleagues at the University of Texas at El Paso. They regard Mexico as a hopelessly violent and corrupt country, and they simply cannot understand why the narrator chooses to live there, when, as a U.S. citizen, he could be living on this side of the border (322). Perhaps the most devas-tating diagnosis of the spiritual condition of Mexico's northern neighbor comes in a passage describing the narrator's American students: "I hate it that my students from over here on this side are so closed, so tame, so sleepy and uninterested in everything that isn't partying and having fun and that they don't want to under-stand anything about the world in which they live" (327).[76] Aguilar goes on to describe his students—many of whom are Mexican American—as victims of "the waltdisneyesque tendencies of the cultural void in which they've grown up" (328).[77] In sum, in these passages Aguilar reiterates the view of U.S. culture as superficial and self-absorbed that we have already encountered in Agustín and Fuentes.[78]

Back to Mexico

Ties between Mexico and the United States have become closer and stronger than ever during the past quarter century. Increased Mexican migration to the United States, higher levels of integration of the two countries' economies, and more rapid circulation of cultural goods across the border are some of the factors that have contributed to the deepening interconnectedness of the two countries. The biog-raphies of the authors studied here confirm this historical trend. Both Agustín and Fuentes have spent extended periods living and working in the United States. And in Aguilar's case we must confront the remarkable fact that this profoundly Mexican writer was a U.S. citizen. Still, even though these three authors exem-plify in their careers the strengthening of the ties between the two nations in the late twentieth- and early twenty-first centuries, their views of the United States do not break with the dominant and long-standing historical tendency in Mexican literary representations of the "monster of the North." Like the majority of their precursors in the Mexican literary and intellectual tradition, Agustín, Fuentes, and Aguilar end up repudiating the United States.[79] True, each of these authors rec-ognizes that the United States is a large, diverse, and multifaceted country, with some positive aspects to balance the negative. In *Ciudades desiertas*, New York rep-resents the country's other dimension, a vibrant city with immense cultural riches to which the foreign writers in Arcadia hope to escape as soon as they get a chance. In "Spoils," from the collection *The Crystal Frontier*, Dionisio Rangel mentions his admiration for "American culture—sports, movies, gringo literature" (79).[80] Curiously, Aguilar seems the least inclined to highlight the positive aspects of U.S. society, although his reference to the higher salaries on the north side of the border probably explains why he finally chooses to live there. However, in spite of these concessions, the overall perspective is highly critical. In each of the three novels examined here, the encounter with the United States ultimately provokes in the Mexican characters an overwhelming urge to return as fast as possible to Mexico. Toward the end of his stay in the United States, Eligio in *Ciudades desiertas* begins to feel "a burning desire to be back in Mexico" (183).[81] Fuentes's "Spoils" similarly concludes with a scene in which the protagonist rushes back to Mexico, shedding all his gringo possessions, even his clothes, so as to reenter his home country in a state of naked authenticity (87–88). In *Windward*, the magnetic force of Mexico, repeatedly drawing the protagonist back across the border, is one of the novel's central motifs. In each case, the return to Mexico involves a rejection of the United States. And this repudiation is presented by all three authors in a confident, assertive manner, without much self-questioning. In their criticisms of the United States, Agustín, Fuentes, and Aguilar clearly presume not that they have captured just some aspect of U.S. society, but rather that they have delved into the essence of the country—what Agustín, in referring to one of his American characters, calls "la pura gringuez" [pure gringohood].

So how does one account for these three authors continuing the tradition of denigrating the United States while longing for Mexico? Why has the increased social, cultural, and economic contact and exchange between the two countries not brought about a change in Mexican literary representations of the United States? How is it that these representations continue to rely so heavily on a view of the two countries as polar opposites? One might regard the antagonism toward the United States in the work of Agustín, Fuentes, and Aguilar as particularly surprising given the success these authors have enjoyed in U.S. academic circles. A number of possible explanations for their anti-Americanism come to mind. To begin with, it is worth taking into account the specifically literary dimension of their portrayals of the United States. The truth of the matter is that an often vehement and satirical reading of U.S. culture and society has far more literary appeal than a cautious, balanced assessment of the pros and cons of life in this country. At the same time, one should not overlook the possibility that these authors are simply telling the truth about the United States as they see it. It is worth remembering that the anti-American views put forward by Agustín, Fuentes, and Aguilar are, in some form or another, widespread in the United States itself. Perhaps the portraits painted by these three authors are partial and exaggerated, but it would be difficult to argue that they have no basis in reality at all. Finally, one can also regard the hostility Agustín, Fuentes, and Aguilar express toward the United States as a response to the biased and denigrating view of Mexico that is so widespread on the U.S. side of the border—a kind of literary tit for tat. All three authors home in on the U.S. sense of superiority with regard to Mexico, and on the profound ignorance of most Americans about their neighbor to the south. Agustín, as we saw, explicitly described *Ciudades desiertas* as an act of vengeance aimed at the distorted perceptions that foreigners have of Mexico. Fuentes and Aguilar, no doubt, could have made the same claim about their depictions of the United States.

Still, it would be a mistake to conclude without noting that there are also significant differences among the three authors. What distinguishes *Ciudades desiertas* is the novel's comic tone, as well as the thoroughly de-idealized style in which Eligio expresses his love and nostalgia for Mexico (he longs for all that is *ugly* about his native country). Such elements have a somewhat relativizing effect on the novel's diatribes against the United States, making them appear at least in part the product of a highly individual perspective. Aguilar, as we have seen, repeats some standard motifs in the tradition of Mexican writings on the United States, but he also adds a new dimension to this tradition with his richly sensorial and highly personal account of what it is like for a Mexican to live in the United States. Fuentes is the most abstract and propositional of the three—the most concerned with making broad, historical statements about the United States and its relations with Mexico. In sum, the shared drive to define the essential United States ends up pointing each author in a slightly different direction.

NOTES

1. "Recuerdo que cada vez que me inclinaba sobre la vida norteamericana, deseoso de encontrarle sentido, me encontraba con mi imagen interrogante. Esa imagen, destacada sobre el fondo reluciente de los Estados Unidos, fue la primera y quizá la más profunda de las respuestas que dio ese país a mis preguntas" (14–15). For this work, the quotations and page numbers in the notes are from Paz's *El laberinto de la soledad*; the English quotations and page numbers in the text come from Lysander Kemp's translation.

2. "Las preguntas que todos nos hacemos ahora probablemente resulten incomprensibles dentro de cincuenta años" (13).

3. For an earlier attempt on my part to discuss the representation of the United States in Agustín and Aguilar, see Van Delden, "How American Is It?"

4. "una muchacha fría y locuaz, de grandes anteojos y cordialidad envuelta para regalo." All translations of passages from *Ciudades desiertas* are mine.

5. "había parques o áreas especiales para meriendas, con mesas y botes de basura y baños y todo lo necesario para que las cosas sean limpias, higiénicas."

6. "*por ningún motivo.*"

7. "a cada viajero se le pregunta si no lleva armas de fuego y nunca faltan los bromistas, me temo que por lo general gente de *nuestro* programa, que dice que sí, y los agentes de seguridad se los llevan y los hacen pasar *un muy mal rato.*"

8. "la gente se ha convertido en robotcitos, se les está muriendo el alma."

9. "en ese caserío de veras no había *nada.*"

10. "en el aeropuerto de Chicago ocurría algo anormal . . . lo que había allí era un silencio extrañísimo, ¿cómo era posible que en ese enorme hangar, terriblemente largo, con bares, restoranes, cabinas telefónicas, tiendas anodinas de gringo curios, altoparlantes y máquinas incomprensibles pudiera haber tal silencio? . . . Era como si no hubiese nada: un congelador inmenso."

11. "¡Y tanta gente, tan silenciosa!"

12. "Deambulaban de aquí a allá, con prisa, sin ver a los demás, con aire de ejecutivos serios y eficientes."

13. "máquinas por doquier, máquinas para comprar cigarros, dulces, chocolates, timbres postales, refrescos, periódicos, para cambiar billetes por moneda fraccionaria, para depositar o retirar dinero de cuentas bancarias, para beber té o café o chocolate caliente o frío, para lustrar los zapatos."

14. "nada es sagrado, todo es vacío."

15. "Por doquier eran las mismas avenidas amplísimas . . . como siempre, ni una glorieta, ni un camellón, ninguna flor, ninguna estatua, sólo kilómetros de asfalto . . . , parques vacíos, calles recorridas sólo por automóviles, sin peatones, sin perros, sin gatos, sin vendedores ambulantes, sin comercios pequeños."

16. "un buen perro; muerto, claro, pudriéndose en la calle."

17. "*increíblemente difícil de conseguir* . . . por si a alguno de los presentes ya se le había ocurrido tratar de quedarse definitivamente en ese gran país."

18. "¡qué inmensa oportunidad para ustedes de haber podido venir aquí!"

19. "esos yanquis siempre te dicen que *tú* eres afortunadísimo de estar aquí, y jamás dicen que *ellos* tiene la fortuna de contar con nosotros, ¡qué nuevorriquismo!"

20. "el ombligo del mundo."

21. "Estos niños, pensó Eligio, en el fondo siguen creyendo que este inmenso refrigerador es el mero cabezón del mundo, y que así ha de ser por siempre, pobres pendejos."

22. "dijo que Eligio le parecía un *ídolo azteca*, una escultura de obsidiana, nunca había conocido a nadie con un corte indígena tan puro y tan hermoso."

23. "verdadera devoción."

24. "él, y *todos los mexicanos*, hacían *muy mal* en no *valorar* su herencia indígena."

25. "deben ser muy amigos, ¿no?"

26. "todos esos pinches estereotipos de México-como-país-de-la-muerte-paraíso-infernal."

27. "era muy guapa y de cuerpo espléndido, realmente más rico y maduro que el de Susana."

28. Fernando García Nuñez observes that Eligio, a typical Mexican macho, is transformed by his journey to the United States. His American experiences help him overcome his macho prejudices and teach him to recognize his own wife as a human being and individual. Such a reading suggests that Agustín—perhaps involuntarily, according to García Nuñez—views the United States in a much more favorable light than one might at first realize, since he presents it as a country where relations between men and women have reached a stage of greater equality and maturity (162–64).

29. In *Nuevo tiempo mexicano* (1995), Fuentes asserts that Mexico made the right decision in joining NAFTA (107). In an essay from the same collection, written before the treaty was approved, he describes NAFTA as the first constructive initiative undertaken in a very long time by the United States in its relations with Latin America (99).

30. "llegaron los gringos (¿quiénes son, quiénes son, por Dios, cómo pueden existir, quién los inventó?)" (275). For this work, I provide in the notes the original Spanish and page numbers. The English quotations and page numbers in the text come from MacAdam's translation.

31. "los gringos ni se acordaban de esa guerra, ni sabían que era injusta" (69).

32. "su propio destino, no manifiesto, sino incierto, humano, a esculpir lentamente, no a revelar providencialmente" (284).

33. See Hart's *Revolutionary Mexico* and *Empire and Revolution* for detailed and informative accounts of the historical background Fuentes evokes in these passages.

34. "mosquitos que le chupaban la sangre a los USA y se regresaban corriendo a mantener a sus indolentes paisanos" (253).

35. Steven Boldy views the seeming caricatures in *The Crystal Frontier* as self-conscious stylizations of the clash of cultures between Mexico and the United States. Boldy's reading devises a Fuentes who is much less crude in his depiction of the United States than we might be inclined to think (233–35).

36. "predicar la buena cocina en un país incapaz de entenderla o practicarla" (68).

37. "Usan gorras de béisbol que no se quitan en el interior ni para saludar a las mujeres. Rara vez se rasuran por completo. Beben la cerveza empinando la botella sobre los labios. Usan camisetas sin mangas, mostrando a todas horas el vello de las axilas. Lucen rasgaduras en las rodillas de sus blue jeans y a veces andan con éstos cortados a la altura de los muslos, deshebrándose" (46).

38. "México también tenía formas, maneras, gustos, sutilezas que confirmaban una cultura aristocrática . . . en México hasta un bandido era cortés, hasta un analfabeta, culto, hasta un niño sabía decir buenos días, hasta una criada sabía caminar con gracia" (78).

39. "al contrario de las gringas que caminaban al trabajo con kedds y en la oficina se ponían los tacones altos" (132).

40. "país del tamaño del universo" (205).

41. "simpático gigantón"; "fresca cara juvenil" (44). See Jullien (33–40) for a discussion of the *topos* in French writings about the United States of the Americans as "un peuple enfant" [a childlike people].

42. "los Wingate ignoran que el petróleo es propiedad del Estado en México." "Dogmática, aunque inocentemente, creen que la expresión 'mundo libre' es idéntica a 'libre empresa.' "

43. "detener los avances del comunismo en Centroamérica." "Él no entiende si les apena cuando salen imágenes terribles de la guerra en El Salvador, monjas asesinadas a la vera del camino, rebeldes asesinados por los batallones paramilitares, un pueblo entero ametrallado por el ejército al huir cruzando un río" (44).

44. "Contrastaban los dos hombres jóvenes y se veían bien juntos, el rubio y el moreno. Primero llamaron la atención en el campus, luego fueron aceptados e incluso admirados por el cariño obvio que se profesaban y la manera espontánea de su relación" (51).

45. "sonrisa fabricada en serie" (153). See Van Delden, "Aux confins," for a more detailed discussion of this scene.

46. "historias de inmigrantes, de ilegales, de pobreza mexicana, de prosperidad yanqui, pero historias sobre todo de familias, ésta era la riqueza del mundo fronterizo, la cantidad de historias insepultas, que se negaban a morir" (251).

47. "José Francisco llevaba manuscritos chicanos a México y manuscritos mexicanos a Texas . . . ése era el contrabando de José Francisco, literatura de los dos lados, para que todos se conocieran mejor, decía, para que todos se quisieran un poquito más, para que hubiera 'un nosotros' de los dos lados de la frontera" (281).

48. "arrojando manuscritos al aire . . . convencido de que las palabras volarían hasta encontrar su destino, sus lectores, sus auditores, sus lenguas, sus ojos." "José Francisco lanzó un grito de victoria que rompió para siempre el cristal de la frontera" (282).

49. "menciona a tu servilleta" (236). In some of the passages I quote from *A barlovento*, I have made changes to Beth Pollack's translation of the novel.

50. See García Canclini and Gómez Peña for influential expressions—one scholarly, the other artistic—of this point of view.

51. "la gente habla mucho de lo que es o no es la frontera y más si es chilanga descúbrelotodo y sábelomejorquenadie para engrandecerse ante los demás, la verdad es que uno que de veras la conoce de primera y muy primera mano se da cuenta de ella, aquí, en la minucia" (390).

52. The consummate expression of these views of the differences between Mexico and the United States can be found in the work of Octavio Paz. Some of his most significant essays on the topic are "La democracia imperial," "El espejo indiscreto," "México y Estados Unidos," and "La mesa y el lecho." For a discussion of Paz's writings on the United States and Mexico, see Van Delden, "¿Dentro o fuera de la historia?"

53. "Ya tengo dos años preguntándome de qué voy a escribir por acá" (343).

54. "La Rosi me pregunta que qué ondas, que si la raza acá esta muerta o qué, que qué hacen a las ocho o a las nueve ya metidos en el chante, o bajo las colchas o en dónde" (344).

55. "los vecinos se nos esconden al paso o se nos quedan viendo como preguntándose qué andamos haciendo al caminar por las calles en la oscuridad" (344).

56. "La raza no camina por la calle. Se sube en su ranfla y jala para cualquier lado que vaya" (344).

57. "Allá estaba empapado del ir y venir . . . saturado de geografía humana, vegetal, urbana, de caras, árboles y nopales, banquetas, calles, parques, casas y edificios, frisos, columnas a los Carpentier, paredes derruidas o en derrumbe, de olores, sabores, ruidos, luces, oscuridades, de las risas de las niñas uniformadas que caminan a la escuela sobre banquetas recién barridas" (343).

58. "la pinche cerveza gabacha es agua vil" (346).

59. "Ahora las cosas de allá me saben diferentes, será el mismísimo maíz, frijol o chile, las mismas frutas o lo que quieras pero se me hace que acá saben como a trapo, los plátanos verdes verdes, como guanábanas, las manzanas arenosas, los limones verdes según yo, los confunden con limas amarillas, el chile dulce ¿puedes creerlo?" (346).

60. "Acá ni fu ni fa. Ayer me puse a ver en el super, ¿a qué huele? Y me tuve que contestar que a nada, ni en la sección de pescado . . . a menos de que sea un olor para esconder los olores como los de los desodorantes" (407).

61. "Allá he estado reacostumbrándome a los olores normales, a tinta, a naranjas pasadas y frescas, a chile tostado, a pan recién horneado, a tortilla de maíz, a bolo de zapatos y grasa marcas Oso, a vaqueta, a madera recién cortada, a creosota y aceite cerca de los rieles del tren" (407).

62. "la nena toma su pan, paga, toma la bolsa y sale brincando y arrastrando el pie de contento como deben hacerlo todos los niños" (411).

63. For accounts of developments over the past decade and a half or so in Ciudad Juárez, see Bowden and Loret de Melo.

64. "es que las camas son muy distintas, la de allá es dura como un palo y ya tenemos la costumbre de que cada quien duerme para su lado, acá la cama es más blandita y estamos alrevesados de posición."

65. "allá no se oye nada, como estamos en el campo, como quien dice a unas tres cuadras está el desierto, acá pita el tren a las tres de la mañana y a las seis . . . allá pasa la autopista a unas dos cuadras y no oímos nada, acá el tráfico de la otra cuadra es constante y se oye todo siempre" (393).

66. "las fisonomías de las construcciones" (389).

67. "una ciudad enrejada"; "acá luego que ves unas ventanas sin rejas te pones a pensar: 'Chin, por allí se pueden meter.' Allá ves una casa con rejas y dices: 'Chin, qué peligroso. A la hora de un incendio, ¿por dónde se van a salir?'" (390)

68. "No sé cómo la gente no sufre más accidentes cuando camina pues más que caminar se trata de un ejercicio de balanceo" (388).

69. "allá la mayor parte son perfectas, recién construidas, muy aerodinámicas con sus entradas para carros y sus bajadas para sillas de ruedas perfectamente trazadas" (388).

70. "acá los perros no respetan a nadie ni a nada, se cagan sobre el cemento en cualquier lugar y tú eres quien debe ir muy avispado para no meter la pata" (389).

71. "allá no hay perros en la calle, la ley lo prohíbe, a menos de que vayan amarrados de un cinto o de una cadena a sus amos y deben de cagar sobre lugares no abanquetados, si se cagan sobre la banqueta los amos son responsables de recogerles los mojones" (389).

72. "vida callada, sigilosa, calmada" (344).

73. "vacío absoluto de cultura" (405).

74. "la porquería traducida mal y doblada peor de la escoria de Hollywood que nos exportan, que nos dompean" (401–2).

75. "el racismo y la ignorancia anglosajona, sureña, tejana" (361).

76. "Me da mucha flojera que mis alumnos de acá de este lado estén tan tapados, tan domesticados, tan dormidos y desinteresados de todo lo que no sea la parranda y el desmadre y que no quieran comprender nada del mundo en que vivimos" (367).

77. "las tendencias waltdisneyescas del vacío cultural en que se han desarrollado" (368).

78. It appears that the real Ricardo Aguilar—as opposed to the persona he constructs for himself in *Windward*—held quite different views of the United States. In Oscar Martínez's very useful ethnography of life in the U.S.-Mexico borderlands, Aguilar appears (under the pseudonym Roberto Carrasco) as a representative of the figure of the binationalist. As such, he speaks of his mixed feelings about the United States: While he complains about the country's lack of culture, he also states that he likes the United States "for its people, its modernity, its inventiveness, its technology, its recognition of the contributions of people like me" (Martínez 88). Professor Martínez was kind enough to confirm that the Roberto Carrasco of his book is indeed Ricardo Aguilar (e-mail to the author, 23 April 2007).

79. See Carballo for a useful anthology of writings by Mexicans about the United States.

80. "la cultura, los deportes, el cine, la literatura de los gringos" (92).

81. "un deseo ardiente por estar en México."

WORKS CITED

Aguilar Melantzón, Ricardo. *Windward*. Trans. Beth Pollack. *Puerto del Sol* 37.2 (2002): 185–369 (trans. of *A barlovento* [Torreón, Coahuila: Editorial del Norte; Mexicano, 1999], 2d ed., published in Ricardo Aguilar Melantzón, *Que es un soplo la vida: trilogía de la frontera* [Mexico: Ediciones Eón, 2003], 203–411).

Agustín, José. *Ciudades desiertas*. Mexico: Alfaguara, 1995.

———. *La contracultura en México: la historia y el significado de los rebeldes sin causa, los jipitecas, los punks y las bandas*. Mexico: Grijalbo, 1996.

Boldy, Steven. *The Narrative of Carlos Fuentes: Family, Text, Nation*. Durham, Eng.: Durham Modern Language Series, 2002.

Bowden, Charles. *Juárez: The Laboratory of Our Future*. New York: Aperture, 1998.

Calvillo, Ana Luisa. *José Agustín: una biografía de perfil*. Mexico: Blanco y Negro Editores, 1998.

Carballo, Emmanuel, ed. *¿Qué país es éste? Los Estados Unidos y los gringos vistos por escritores mexicanos de los siglos XIX y XX*. Mexico: Consejo Nacional para la Cultura y las Artes, 1996.

Fuentes, Carlos. *Cristóbal nonato*. Mexico: Fondo de Cultura Económica, 1987.

———. *The Crystal Frontier: A Novel in Nine Stories*. Trans. Alfred MacAdam. New York:

Harcourt/Harvest, 1997 (trans. of *La frontera de cristal: una novela en nueve cuentos* [Mexico: Alfaguara, 1995]).

———. *Gringo viejo*. Mexico: Fondo de Cultura Económica, 1985.

———. *Nuevo tiempo mexicano*. Mexico: Aguilar, 1995.

García Canclini, Néstor. *Culturas híbridas: estrategias para entrar y salir de la modernidad*. Mexico: Grijalbo, 1990.

García Nuñez, Fernando. "Notas sobre la frontera norte en la novela mexicana." *Cuadernos Americanos* 2.4 (1988): 159–68.

Gómez Peña, Guillermo. *Border Brujo*. Auth. and perf. Guillermo Gómez Peña. Prod. and dir. Isaac Artenstein. Videocassette. Third World Newsreel, 1991.

Hart, John Mason. *Empire and Revolution: The Americans in Mexico since the Civil War*. Berkeley: University of California Press, 2002.

———. *Revolutionary Mexico: The Coming and Process of the Mexican Revolution*. Berkeley: University of California Press, 1987.

Kerouac, Jack. *On the Road*. New York: Viking Press, 1957.

Jullien, Dominique. *Récits du nouveau monde: les voyageurs français en Amérique de Chateaubriand a nos tours*. Paris: Editions Nathan, 1992.

Loret de Melo, Rafael. *Ciudad Juárez*. Mexico: Océano, 2005.

Martínez, Oscar J. *Border People: Life and Society in the U.S.-Mexico Borderlands*. Tucson: University of Arizona Press, 1994.

Morris, Stephen. *Gringolandia: Mexican Identity and Perceptions of the United States*. Lanham, Md.: Rowman and Littlefield, 2005.

Paz, Octavio. "La democracia imperial." Paz, *Tiempo nublado* 29–58.

———. "El espejo indiscreto." Paz, *Ogro* 53–69.

———. *El laberinto de la soledad, Posdata y Vuelta a El laberinto de la soledad*. Mexico: Fondo de Cultura Económica, 1999.

———. *The Labyrinth of Solitude*. Trans. Lysander Kemp. New York: Grove Press, 1985.

———. "La mesa y el lecho." Paz, *Ogro* 212–34.

———. "México y Estados Unidos: posiciones y contraposiciones." Paz, *Tiempo nublado* 139–59.

———. *El ogro filantrópico: historia y política, 1971–1978*. Mexico: Joaquín Mortiz, 1979.

———. *Tiempo nublado*. Barcelona: Seix Barral, 1986.

Rodó, José Enrique. *Ariel*. Ed. Castro Belén. Madrid: Cátedra, 2000.

Van Delden, Maarten. "Aux confins des États-Unis et du Mexique: traversée ou enforcement des frontières? Sur deux récits récents de Carlos Fuentes et de Ricardo Aguilar." Trans. Pierre Zoberman. *Qu'est-ce qu'un espace littéraire?* Ed. Xavier Garnier and Pierre Zoberman. Paris: Presses Universitaires de Vincennes, 2006. 173–90.

———. "¿Dentro o fuera de la historia? El pensamiento de Octavio Paz en torno a México y los Estados Unidos." Trans. Alvaro Uribe. *Anuario de la Fundación Octavio Paz* 2 (2000): 88–99.

———. "How American Is It? Three American Writers Look North." *Literal: Latin American Voices* 4 (2006): 26–29.

Walker, Ronald G. *Infernal Paradise: Mexico and the Modern English Novel*. Berkeley: University of California Press, 1978.

PART III

At Home with the Other

Mexico Deals with Virtual Nationhood into the Twenty-first Century

CHAPTER 9

If North Were South

Traps of Cultural Hybridity
in Xavier Velasco's *Diablo Guardián*

Oswaldo Estrada

My family es singular, ninguno habla español,
nos teñimos to' de rubio, olemos a Christian Dior.
— "Violetta," rap by Pedro Antonio Valdez

Although several critics have praised Mexican writer Xavier Velasco for his innovative contributions to Latin American literature—his unconventional essays, chronicles, and fictional narratives—little attention has been paid to his novel, *Diablo Guardián*. Until now only Gabriel Cabello has approached the ambiguity of this literary work and the development of its characters as a fictional necessity.[1] Surprisingly, the best tribute to the novel appeared shortly after the presentation of *Diablo Guardián* in Santo Domingo, when Dominican writer Pedro Antonio Valdez dedicated a satirical rap to the protagonist (Rufinelli 13). Perhaps the lack of critical studies on the novel that won the Alfaguara Prize in 2003 originates from its hybrid nature. The text presents itself as a riddle of almost six hundred pages of bicultural and bilingual prose, written in a Spanish language that amalgamates Mexican colloquialisms with English expressions in a kind of code switching. The characters' identities have also been crafted on the border of these two languages, between Mexico and the United States, or on the bridge of a Mexican reality and the fallacy of an American dream predicated on media images. Velasco's irreverent writing style is that of a Bakhtinian fool or a judge in disguise, one who ridicules equally the North and the South, as well as their inevitable interaction, from an outsider's perspective. Hiding behind the plot and the narrators, the author manipulates a group of Mexican characters who undergo multiple transculturations to reconcile their inferiority complex and hopeless orientations toward Anglo America, only to remain metaphorically trapped in the same labyrinth of solitude that Octavio Paz delineated more than fifty years ago.

The action of the novel revolves around the confessions that Violetta, like a postmodern heiress of *Lazarillo de Tormes*, makes about her picaresque life to one of her colleagues, only this time the (pseudo)autobiographical memoirs are dictated in a series of audiotapes. Recognizing the dark side of her confidant, who is also an outcast of Mexican society, she will see him not as a guardian angel, but as a genuine guardian devil. Through this interlocutor, translator, or transcriber in charge of writing down her life, whom we know only by the derogatory nickname of Pig, we digest the hybrid essence of a protagonist made up of cultures in conflict. The novelistic pact between the main narrator and her virtual listener or reader, a distinctive trademark of some of Carlos Fuentes's novels, such as *Cristóbal nonato* (Christopher Unborn) and *El naranjo* (The Orange Tree), is not a mere prelude to but the foundation of the narrative. As if we were on the other side of a confessional, before long we learn that the central character is incapable of finding a place of her own within her society. Violetta, whose real name is Rosalba Rosas Valdivia, is the unfortunate daughter of a middle-class Mexican family of the 1990s who rejects everything that represents Mexico and dreams of belonging to the American world. This personal incongruity will make her diminish the women of her own mestizo ethnicity, classifying them as *lambisconas, pendejas,* or *hijas de la chingada*. Employing similar words, Rosalba will refer to all the members of her family and her Mexican roots as *coatlicues, tlahuicas, nacas,* and *pirujas,* cultural terms that, loosely speaking, categorize members of her society and family as ignorant savages, streetwalkers, and bastards.[2]

As I illustrate throughout this essay, the cultural hybridity of the protagonist evolves from her eagerness to live a distorted American life that she has absorbed from U.S. TV, movies, and comic books popular in a contemporary Mexico of the last decade. I use the term "hybridization" to outline what Néstor García Canclini considers "socio-cultural processes in which discrete structures or practices that existed separately, combine to generate new structures, objects and practices" (iii).[3] Since cultural purity is an illusion that does not fit in our history, it is in our best interest to refer to discrete rather than "pure" structures or practices, for we transition from more heterogeneous cycles to others that are more homogeneous and then to others that are relatively more heterogeneous, with neither being wholly one thing. "Migrations, the mixing of high-tech and 'primitive,' of mass-mediated and oral culture, the scrambling of social classes who can no longer be securely stratified except through taste," explains Jean Franco: "all this has seriously compromised any notion of an undiluted popular culture."[4] Nonetheless, in a world dominated by globalization and identities that are formed with the Internet, hybridization does not always mean "fusion, cohesion, osmosis, but rather confrontation and dialogue" (García Canclini ix).[5] This is particularly true in Rosalba's case and that of her guardian devil. There are parts of their identities that resist hybridization, even as they face the inevitable Latinization of the United States or the Americanization of Latin America.[6]

The cultural impurity of the protagonist in *Diablo Guardián* is sketched out from the very first pages of the novel. Although she is born and bred Mexican, Rosalba situates herself as a "misplaced individual" in her own country, as one who lives within a superficial world that imitates another.[7] This is evident in her initial self-description. "I was blonde since I was very little," she explains. "Every Sunday, before breakfast, the whole family had to step in front of the sink. Can you believe they dyed our hair with cold water even when we had a cold and a fever?" (37)[8] The mandatory hair dye that transforms her black hair is an obvious sign of her family's wannabe aspirations, but it also portrays her cultural awkwardness or the false construction of a foreign identity. At Rosalba's house, not one doll is brown skinned. Her parents make a conscientious effort to speak English between themselves, even if they can never eliminate their noticeable accent from Tlalnepantla. The children in the family read magazines in English and, consequently, learn to picture themselves in Disney World, with Anglo-American artists, in the fantastical world of Hollywood, and surrounded by the skyscrapers of large U.S. cities. This cultural contradiction of living in the South with eyes focused on the North has a lot to do with a Latin American reality that suffers from "the impact of cultural and economic globalizing forces" (Schelling 197). As Stephen Morris indicates, the "omnipresence" of the United States in the vast majority of visual images that wander about Mexican cities—various film productions, magazines, and television—always indicate that white and a state of whiteness are the ideal (168). This limited conception of the United States as the land of progress and modernity, power, independent life, and individualist mentality runs throughout the novel, even when Rosalba fights against the farce of being a foreigner in her native country. At the age of fifteen she is determined to stop being a fake blonde and to have "black hair," but what she wants most is "to speak English" in order to live in the United States. Her plan of finding a supposedly more authentic identity only orients her in the same direction as her parents.

Freedom and separation from her family become a reality when Rosalba steals more than a hundred thousand dollars from her parents to escape to the United States. With no regrets and comforting herself with the popular saying that "a thief who steals from a thief will be pardoned a hundred years," Rosalba takes the money that her parents had previously stolen from the collection boxes of the Mexican Red Cross.[9] The most blatant feature of this first cultural transition, which entails escaping from a false environment to acquire a new, and possibly more legitimate, identity, is that she detects traits of her *Mexicanness* that keep her from becoming an*other* American. While she narrates her voyage in Spanglish to the man who acts as her evil confessor, an ashamed Rosalba admits: "My God, I'm a *naca* . . . I come from a cheesy, cheap family. I'm a run-away from fucking Woolworth" (53, 87).[10] Wrapped in black humor, her words force us to revise Carlos Monsiváis's analysis of the *nacos*, marginalized in Mexico for being the plebes, "the coppertoned masses" that form a "genuine urban stain" ("Léperos y catrines" 170).[11] The protagonist of this story, however, gives an interesting twist to the pejorative term that derives from *totonaco*. By calling herself a *naca*, Rosalba accepts the usual "prevailing disdain" and the "oppression" toward herself, as well as the "interiorized image of a minor country" (Monsiváis, *Escenas* 238).[12] But her cultural complex and the stigma of being peripheral within Mexico do not stop her from doing something to alleviate her ambivalent situation: She defines herself as a "súper naca . . . en upgrade process" (144).

This willingness to develop a new and perhaps improved self away from all that represents the upwardly yearning Mexican middle class has the opposite effect on Rosalba. By wanting to be someone else, diminishing herself and those of her social and ethnic condition, she reaffirms her indelible Mexicanness. As Velasco explains in one of his recent chronicles: "No Mexican would feel completely satisfied with his life if he could not count on at least one kindred spirit on whom to dump the most shocking of national insults, one that has like so many words only four letters: n-a-c-o. That's why every Mexican lives and dies to preserve or acquire proof that *he is not naco*" (*Luna llena* 65).[13] Rosalba's ambition to become the subject of her own desire transforms her into an impoverished or ridiculous cartoon figure of the American other, in a world of masks and solitude.[14] Against all her calculations, she has begun to live the elaborate fiction of her parents: She goes to the supermarket to buy magazines and postcards in English, listens to Iggy Pop's music, and counts down the minutes and hours that separate her from the United States.

It is precisely then that Rosalba devises a strategic plan to stop being Mexican and to become American. First, she thinks: "I will go to New York" (53).[15] Later her fantasy transports her to the North of her dreams: "I clipped newspapers, pasted photos of skyscrapers in my notebooks, I even had a little map of the subway lines. I imagined myself going from store to store with my super-black hair, almost blue, singing: I need some loving, like a fastball needs control. I laughed to imagine my dad serving me a hot dog and stealing the change from my ten dollars" (53).[16] The description of this future hybridization reveals more than ever her "colonized mind," for its exposition portrays the marginalization of her self, class, race, and gender, within and outside Latin America.[17] Rosalba's behavior reflects a state of mind that several Mexican intellectuals, such as Fuentes, Monsiváis and Bartra, have emphasized for several decades in their writings. It is a Mexican attitude that considers the United States a model that ought to be imitated.[18] In *Diablo Guardián*, as in everyday reality, the economic and political example of the United States is seen as an essential ingredient of triumph or personal modernity. As a consequence, "English expressions, clothes sporting U.S. icons, and even dreams of working in America and participating in the consumer society, all become personal manifestations of imitation and a basic part of Mexican popular nationalism" (Morris 168).

Driven by the mentality that forces her to situate herself in the atlas of Anglo-

American culture, Rosalba resorts to filmic images, cartoons, and stories from the North in order to feel like Wonder Woman (91), capable of crossing the barriers of her origin and adopting a second citizenship. This is how she "will eventually define herself more by what she wants to be than by who she really is" (Cabello).[19] The layout of this paradox in *Diablo Guardián* renovates in novelistic fashion the Mexican notion of *malinchismo*, defined by Agustín Basave Fernández del Valle as the social complex of loving what is foreign, with a profound rejection of what is yours (746). At least implicitly, Xavier Velasco assigns to Rosalba Rosas Valdivia the term *malinchista*, disseminated in Mexico since the 1930s. Monsiváis wrote of the people who carry this label: "In every circumstance and with nothing to justify themselves, they prefer strangers, they overvalue them, consider them naturally superior, they 'get in bed' with them" ("La Malinche" 190–91).[20] Even against her will, Rosalba establishes her close relationship with Malinche and the origin of Mexicanness when she displays the attitude of a traitor toward her country, her evident national preference, her disdain for Mexico, and her almost childish and irrational infatuation with the United States.

Infected by the virus that attacks thousands of Latin Americans, for whom the "center of the world has moved, with all of its symbols and order," to the large Latino cities of the United States, such as Miami, Los Angeles, and New York (Bryce Echenique 72), Rosalba prepares herself to enter the world of her dreams and enjoy all of its cultural artifacts.[21] Since she is a runaway and does not have a passport, a visa, or a birth certificate, the protagonist relies on her made-up standards of U.S. living to enter the United States like any other American. Influenced by numerous North American films that invade Mexican television screens, Rosalba chooses to copy and interiorize one of the many stereotypical images of the U.S. world: She buys a red wig and dresses up like a tennis player. Behaving like a picaresque narrator of her own adventures and misfortunes, she tells us of her eventful crossing to the state of Texas: "I crossed over at the river, like any other fucked up bastard. With over a hundred thousand in my suitcase, clinging to an inflatable raft, the *coyote* pulling me and me like an idiot there, just floating. . . . Anyway, I crossed over and I reached firm ground hugging my suitcase. It was one of those horrendous old valises that would make anyone who saw it swear that its owner was a country bumpkin" (119).[22] After this comic entrance to the United States, Rosalba begins to reconstruct her life from scratch, trying to leave behind every distinctive trait that would associate her with Mexico.

Against all her plans, crossing the border as an illegal immigrant not only turns her automatically into a wetback (*mojada*), but also affects her at a deeper level.[23] The physical action of passing from Mexico to the United States psychologically transforms Rosalba into a new person. Sitting at the edge of a park, with her suitcase under her arm, she realizes, "I'm a worthless mouse trapped in a huge cage," but immediately tries to convince herself, "I'm a gringa, right? I'm American" (119).[24] In the first place, the move north of the border that separates her country from the U.S. empire implies the immediate adoption of English as a second language. At the same time, this passage to the United States allows her to embrace a foreign citizenship that nevertheless offers her the opportunity to be more like the person she wants to be. The ambivalence of this cultural metamorphosis is that her desire to become the other by imitating an American model requires "a negation of self" and, to some extent, a "loss of identity" (Morris 176). This incongruity mirrors another facet of her *malinchismo*, one that is closely linked to her ambivalent *mexicanidad*. By wanting to be another person, radically different from who she really is, Rosalba places herself in the battleground of both cultures, giving birth to a new individual who does not belong to either side.

The internal conflict of a subject of Latin American descent who finds herself between two cultural legacies and sees the United States as a stepparent—a characteristic that is often portrayed in the prose of Latino writers like Miguel Elías Muñoz, Julia Álvarez, Esmeralda Santiago, Ana Castillo, and Sandra Cisneros— permeates the narrative when Rosalba thinks that she is living in one of the many American stories that she has read in Mexico.[25] Imagining that the United States is populated by movie stars and animated characters, she decides to see life through rose-colored glasses The fantasy begins when, as she is on the verge of repentance for crossing the U.S. border illegally, Eric comes to her rescue. He is an average eighteen-year-old Texan dressed in his baseball uniform, but Rosalba sees him as her savior Superman. She describes him as "tall, blonde, thin, a well-made gringo" (120).[26] In order to get rid of a Mexican heritage that clearly clashes with the present situation, she behaves like Lois Lane and presents herself as a fragile and delicate person in desperate need of deliverance by the American hero of her distorted world (123). By means of this mental alteration, Rosalba feels that her American dream is a tangible reality, even though she has to create a fiction and develop a double personality to produce it.

The journey to the North only deepens her sociocultural contradictions. The American space allows the *pícara* (rascally wanderer) of *Diablo Guardián* to transform herself into another woman with the aid of wigs, elegant dresses, and foreign names. Apparently, she has left behind her former identity, that "*muñequita* [little doll] made in Mexico" (388), and all that culturally ties her to that country. Likewise, the North of her dreams allows her to abandon what she considers third-world traditions, with the intention of adopting other accents and behaving in such a way that she can temporarily cover her marginal origin. What Rosalba fails to anticipate in her attempt to be the other is that the search for and adoption of an alien identity does not eliminate the Mexicanness that she profoundly rejects. With regard to this cultural hybridity, Alfonso de Toro would certainly state that her "*transculturalidad*" makes her resort to "cultural models, fragments or consumer goods that are generated neither within one's own cultural context (local or base culture) nor by one's own cultural identity, but instead come from external cultures and belong to another identity and language" (214).[27] In this arena of heterogeneous action, Rosalba will suffer the tragic consequences of fabricating herself of imported materials.

Although this new comic-book heroine soon exchanges Superman for Batman, Spiderman, Super Mario, or Silver Surfer in a long chain of prostitution, what matters here is how she constructs her life according to the "*transmedialidad*" that includes "diverse forms of hybrid expression and representation, such as the dialog between different 'media' (video, films, television), . . . between electronic, filmic and textual media" (De Toro 221).[28] For this young Mexican woman, the United States has to be the way she has seen it on television. When Rosalba finds herself alone in a dramatically different world than the one she had imagined, her best solution to this problem is to readjust her perception. Therefore, she mentally blocks out her surrounding reality and sees only what she wants to see, or at least she gives us this impression in her confessions to Pig. (This strategy of giving life to personal dreams, myths, or legends in foreign territory is not as irrational as it seems. As we all know, the first conquistadors of indigenous America also created a New World according to their readings, popular stories, and personal convictions.)[29] Once recovered from the initial clash of perceptions and helped by Superman and other antiheroes of real life, Rosalba develops a transient identity between two cultures that involves an almost unknown Mexico and New York, Miami, or Las Vegas. From that moment on, hers will be the uncertainty of living "in the middle" or "on the border." She is now tied to the magic of various U.S. cultural icons (the comic books, the movies, the videogames); she tries to absorb the experiences of the U.S. middle class (the fast food, the mall, the taxis, the subway); and she rejects everything that ties her to Mexico (her idiosyncrasy, her indigenous roots, her English with a Mexican accent).

Seen as a "nomadic, recodifying and innovating movement of cultural phenomena in regard to the 'Other' and 'Otherness' . . . between 'local' and 'external' " (De Toro 217), the hybridity of the protagonist of *Diablo Guardián* is much more evident in her self-reflections.[30] Perhaps we do not know what kind of bilingual social audience is supposed to read this novel (Corral 94), but it is clear to us that Rosalba is a combination of the world she abominates and the one she desires. She embodies the love/hate relationship that most, if not all, foreigners develop toward their country of adoption. For instance, she feels that she speaks "with a terrible accent, except now with the contractions I had learned from comic books in English. Gonna, wanna, gimme, gotta. You feel really gringa when you use them. Then you get used to them, like any good social climber. . . . Every bit of me is *wannabe*, what can I say" (135–36).[31] And she is right. Even though she cleverly combines her English and Spanish, from the start she recognizes that "my gringo accent has never come out. My r's are too strong, I think in Spanish, I stutter. It's not that I don't enjoy speaking English, but I get tongue-tied" (119).[32] This sensation of otherness, the "strange heritage of those who live on the cultural margins, even though they seem to be assimilated" (Rivero 717), makes Rosalba truly uncomfortable.[33] "I like beginnings," she declares, "endings, basements, the penthouse, prostitutes, nuns, but everything in the middle stinks" (228–29).[34]

Imprisoned in this intermediate chamber, Rosalba manufactures for her guardian devil a critical image of the United States and its inhabitants. Without resorting to the American stereotypes that proliferate in Mexican films, such as the gringo tourist, the blonde, the explorer, or the racist (Morris 196–200), the *pícara* nonetheless carries out stereotypical readings of *gringolandia*. On one hand, she admires Americans' organization, their "always seeming to have an impressive agenda in mind" (141), as well as their early promiscuity ("gringos start bed-hopping when they're fourteen" [154]).[35] But on the other hand, Rosalba quickly criticizes their lack of sexual passion. She may, for instance, describe Eric as Superman, but she is never reluctant to point out the unfavorable effects of his deficient kryptonite in bed: "Stupid, she thought. Idiot, little faggot, useless jerk, animal. There I am sweating ice in the bathroom, making up my eyes and face and taking it off who knows how many times. Putting on the perfume he had bought me, trying on a bathrobe, then a towel, you don't know what all. And Superman out there drooling on his big pillow. Not even a smack, a good night, a goddamned It's been such a crazy day" (155).[36] Later on, when Rosalba is determined to get rid of her uncomfortable virginity, she is the one who pulls him by the hair to the Saks fitting room. As we anticipate, his masculinity does not measure up to Rosalba's expectations this time, either. Resentful of his lack of manliness in that crucial moment, she tells us: "The jerk didn't have a clue what to do; just imagine, I was the rapist, I was the one assaulting a nun. Just so you get the picture, he only lifted a finger in order to fend me off" (157).[37] Because of this unfortunate experience, she will see every American who passes through her body as a financial enterprise and will describe him as a usable, interchangeable, and disposable object.

Likewise, the U.S. world is reduced to the social sphere of large cities like New York, where the cost of living is extremely high and people spend "a hundred bucks for an airport limo, four hundred more for a room at the Plaza with no view of Central Park, fifteen hundred [for] two skirts from Saks" (183).[38] The place that Rosalba describes devours personal identity, is consumed by materialism, and cannot escape from the tornado of dollars and luxurious stores. If the proud *mexicas* and their conquered descendants considered the old city of Tenochtitlan the moon's bellybutton, New York represents a lot more than that for Rosalba; it is "the bellybutton of the world," and she does not intend to leave the magic of the city for any "fucking village" (184).[39] This representative capital of modernity and progress, she explains, "screws anyone without a home. Cheap hotels are infectious caves, and those that seem more or less decent never cost you less than an expensive sweater. It's a rip-off everywhere you go" (194).[40] Acting as the leading protagonist of an action film and wanting to "tour her own Disneyland" (201), Rosalba takes us closer to this degraded world by showing us its pornography and prostitution, where she believes herself to be successful at taking advantage of silly

Americans.[41] She even ventures a title for it, "Farm Girl Discovers Manhattan" (231), admitting to her evil partner in crime that she exploits the sentimentalism of those Americans who cannot stand her suffering.[42] She thinks they are dumb and gullible, dupes of her incredible stories. Rosalba concludes that most Americans "like to see people suffer, that it makes them feel safe and important, fortunate, good. In fact, you're not asking them to give you anything; you're selling them peace of mind" (265).[43]

The originality of these passages in which Rosalba reads and interprets U.S. culture comes from the fact that her reflections convey the same message presented by numerous stereotypical U.S. images in Mexican films. In other words, her speculations on the American world "tell us little about the *gringo*, but much about the Mexican" (Morris 200). Simply stated, when she defines Americans, Rosalba exposes distinctive traits of her Mexicanness. By describing the United States as a modern and powerful emporium where people spend thousands of dollars on appearances and banalities, Rosalba highlights her inferiority complex, her shame for being the product of an underdeveloped Mexico, and her desperate desire to belong to a first world. Feeling completely hopeless and inferior to others, she can only confess to her guardian devil: "Someone had made a mistake in maternity and I, who was born to be a millionaire, ended up in a family belonging to the circus class. But that damned luck had run out, and the proof was that I was walking around New York" (267).[44] At the same time, when Rosalba depicts American males as cold individuals who are rather feminine and sentimental, not sufficiently macho in front of an innocent prostitute like herself, she reaffirms that the image of the United States helps to define Mexican national culture. New York might have everything—money, sex, drugs, short-lived adventures, and hallucinatory excursions—but it is this middle-class Mexican immigrant who prostitutes herself who gives the impression of benefiting from this world.

In this turbulent windstorm that travels from North to South, Rosalba's body is stranded in the ambivalent and contradictory space of those who live in the middle of two worlds. Even unconsciously or against her will, she has become the revised and improved version of the "nueva mestiza" portrayed by Gloria Anzaldúa in the midst of two cultures in perpetual duel:

> Because I, a *mestiza*,
> continually walk out of one culture
> and into another,
> because I am in all cultures at the same time,
> *alma entre dos mundos, tres, cuatro,*
> *me zumba la cabeza con lo contradictorio.*
> *Estoy norteada por todas las voces que me hablan*
> *simultáneamente.*[45]

The difference between Rosalba and the mestizas for whom the Chicana poet writes is that Xavier Velasco's character does not fight for any social or political cause, does not carry the banner of the Virgin of Guadalupe, and does not wave the flag of her indigenous roots. Her hybrid nature makes her a mestiza, but, more significantly, she is Latina. However, Rosalba does not use this term charged with political, social, and ethnic connotations; rather, she identifies as "Mexicana y newyorka" (Mexican and New Yorker) (388). In order to take on this role, Rosalba adopts a new name and, thanks to it, gives another twist to her fragile identity. Since she does not have any personal documents, she takes the German passport of an Ulrik Schmidt and scribbles with childish handwriting her nom de guerre over his: "Violetta Schmidt . . . Mexican in New York, the daughter of a German father and a Canadian mother" (245, 269).[46] Unfortunately, this mask with which she deserts Rosalba Rosas Valdivia will force her to share the destiny of many Latinos who live in the United States as "second-class citizens" (Rivero 723).[47]

Although Rosalba asserts that she studies business administration at Columbia University, that she lives on Claremont Avenue, and that her father is a prosperous businessman (253), she never stops being an outsider within the U.S. culture. The stolen money allows her to stay at luxury hotels, to travel, and, above all, to buy clothes at the most expensive boutiques in New York, but it does not make her 100 percent American. With the sole purpose of staying in the United States and away from Mexico, Violetta prostitutes herself in some of the best presidential suites of the city and enjoys the material goods that the American world can offer in combination with money: illegal cravings, twenty-thousand-dollar watches, rides in the most costly cars, and other unnecessary expenditures. She suffers from a hysterical materialism that makes her behave like a "Venus de los cheques" or like "Ifigenia en *Disneyland*," two characters who reveal their hunger for money in "fables putrefied by greed and revenge" also written by Velasco.[48] Yet Violetta knows better than anyone else that her stay in the United States is a piece that does not fit within the American puzzle. She does not have any friends; her habits of eating, dressing, walking, and thinking remind her that she is a foreigner; and sometimes, even if it hurts to admit it, she feels an uncontrollable anxiety to go back to Mexico. This is how Violetta "will keep moving constantly between two worlds without identifying fully with either: the world of the prefabricated woman, of kitsch and the media, of the zigzag world of oral culture" (Cabello).[49]

She narrates her journey with clarity: "I was fed up with being the wretched daughter of a ruinous family, and I jumped. First over the dollars and then over the border, and then suddenly I was in New York feeling as though I had to jump again, and I swear to you that I wouldn't have known in which direction" (229).[50] It is true. Although Rosalba tries to assimilate and be assimilated by an American world of sexual freedom, fast food, brand-name clothes, expensive hotel rooms, and drug abuse, she always feels that she does not fit in because she cannot stop being a Mexican-American who spends her days comparing prices and imitating others. Simply put: "My problem is that I'm a product of Sears determined to make it into a Saks display counter. . . . I'm a low-class Mexican, I know it. . . . Always Sears, never Saks. What can I do, Woolworth doesn't fit in Tiffany's" (227–28).[51] Regardless of her external American conversion, her transculturation "does not imply the loss or annulment of [her] culture nor a definitive homogeneous result, but a continuous and hybrid process" (De Toro 215).[52] Instead of transforming Violetta into a new person, this process of Latinization, most evident in the lives of U.S. Latinos, draws attention to the violent contact of Mexico and the United States within her own self. For that reason she will have to live with one foot here and another one there, as the permanent resident of an "intermediate" space (De Toro 223) where her Mexican complex of inferiority will collide with her marginal position in the United States.

In general, we tend to think positively about the hybridization of plants and animals, because these "enhance the genetic variety of the species and improve their survival rate in new habitats and climates" (García Canclini v).[53] But when the object of hybridization is the human being, the result is usually uncertain, complicated. Violetta, for example, does not know where to go with her identity. Tired of insulting Mexican women, she finally recognizes that she is herself "una hija de la chingada" [a daughter of Malinche, the emblematic first "screwed" woman of Mexico] (186). She is so desperate to find a place of her own that sometimes she wants to go back to Mexico and live in "any little old town. Rent a tiny house with a chicken coop, braid my hair and dress like a servant" (211).[54] More often than not she diminishes herself and admits with resignation her cultural *mestizaje*: "Even today I feel like I'm living the life of a little sweet-water fish that who knows who tossed into saltwater" (328).[55] These features of her wavering identity expose her ambiguous relation to both cultures—Mexican and American—but they also highlight that a great deal of her Mexicanness cannot be nor will ever be completely erased. The outfits, the wigs, the imitation of the American accent with its proper contractions, her New Yorker ways, her comic inventions, and even her one-night stands with ephemeral American lovers who, within her world of fantasy, take her to the apex of an imagined American glory—all are just parts of a composite mask or a colorful façade with a skeletal smile. In fact, when she evaluates her life in the United States, Rosalba Violetta can only conclude: "I was there without being present" (378).[56] The constant feeling of being a stranger, different, from an underdeveloped world, tied against her will to Latin America and wanting to belong to the language, culture, and society of her (permanent or temporary) residence, incorporates Rosalba within the genealogical tree of the vast Latin family of the United States.

Situated in the last decade of the twentieth century, Xavier Velasco's novel lets the main character travel to the American world, makes her suffer the cultural transformations of the Latino in the United States, and finally returns her to Mexico. In abject contradiction to the euphoria of her four years in New York,

Violetta goes back to her parents' house like a prodigal daughter to accept her former job as a maid without salary. She allows her family and other men to use her,
while she tries to pay back the stolen money. Her previously fantastical discourse is
now filled with a grief that leads us through the labyrinth of her solitude: "I always
say that I escaped from home looking for freedom, but that isn't true. . . . I left
home to create my own enslavements. More perfect, more solid" (417).[57] In spite
of the fact that Violetta has lived in hybrid and heterogeneous environments—
Mexico, a country bombarded by American images, and New York, a multiethnic
and multicultural city—she cannot discard her Mexicanness. Like the Mexican
who sings, shouts, and whistles during a day of celebration only to maintain absolute silence the rest of the year (Paz 53), Violetta enjoys a prolonged American
weekend or cocktail party, but as soon as she returns to Mexico, her figure disinte-
grates in the outskirts of the city.

In this marginal zone, Violetta finds the man who will become her lover and
guardian devil. From the moment they meet at a newspaper press, where she takes
a second job, the two characters form a perfect duo. A Mexican citizen like her,
Pig is also an "outsider" in Mexico, where he publishes his frustrated fantasies and
lives comfortably without love or friends. Pig tells us that he populated his childhood with imaginary "gringas musas" [gringa muses] (56) until he acquired the
"mania of speaking alone in English" (398).[58] As if he were unconsciously imitating his informant's personal habits, "he had discovered in English an interminable
source of analgesics. Harsh and judgmental, corpulent and granite hard, Castilian
words seemed too pitiable, pompous, corporeal, to undertake with them any form
of dialogue with oneself. Thus, without giving it a second thought, he acquired
the vice of speaking to himself only in English" (398).[59] But the secrecy of this
strategy does not fulfill his life either. The English language only transports him to
another world and opens up the possibility of invading a forbidden space, different from the reality at work but still ultimately a mask, like one of the many that
Violetta wears to disguise her true self. As an individual lost in the magic of this
second language or in the pseudonyms that he uses as a news reporter, Pig is the
ideal victim for Violetta's trap. He follows her in silence like a lapdog, memorizes
her anecdotes, and internalizes her bilingual and mysterious voice, until he finally
makes her disappear.

Ironically, then, the novel's message with respect to cultural hybridization is
profoundly negative. It shows that Rosalba has gained nothing from her long travels or from escaping her house and the weekly dye jobs in the family bathroom.
Nor has she benefited from the experience of living an American illusion in which
she becomes a "nueva Malinche," fluent and influential in two languages.[60] At the
end of her multiple acculturations in her native Mexico, Texas, New York, and Las
Vegas, the protagonist of this story admits that she is her own Barbie doll, always
dressed up for an intimate or public occasion. Her strategies as a bicultural prostitute, her destiny as a disposable object, the constant abuses of a family that now

expects to auction her to the best bidder, as well as the mental assault of her self by known or unknown individuals—all make of her another "Chingada." Violetta is not, of course, "the mother who has suffered, metaphorically or in fact, the corrosive and shameful act implicit in the word that gives her the name" (Paz 83).[61] In contrast to the one who is usually associated with the mother of all Mexicans, the transculturated woman in *Diablo Guardián* is more like the Malinche that Monsiváis imagines in the twenty-first century: "freed of her ideological chains . . . perhaps with the hope of updating herself and shedding her identity as a traitor" ("Malinche" 193).[62] As expected, her hopefulness originates from a profound frustration with respect to her multiple identities:

> Violetta, Rosalba, Rosa del Alba: by now none of these was me. I lived divided all the time. Rosalba in the office, Rosa del Alba at home (they called me that to fuck with me, that was completely clear) and Violetta in the mirror. I looked at myself for hours, sometimes seated in the car, others before the bathroom mirror, still others at my little bureau mirror. I would say: Where could I be? In my eyes, in my lips, in my forehead? Almost all my life was happening behind my own back. I, Violetta, was not to be found in any of the personages she represented every day. (Velasco, *Diablo Guardián* 546–47)[63]

Tired of not fitting anywhere, not in the North or the South, at home or at work, as daddy's little girl or as a country girl, "prófuga del metate" [deserter of the grindstone] (417), Violetta decides to eliminate herself. "I can't stand this anymore, I'm fucking tired," she admits. "These are way too many masks for someone who has never known who the fuck she is, where she comes from, or where she's going. I don't know and I don't care, but I can't go on carrying these little suitcases" (570).[64] The most practical solution is to disappear. She stage-manages her own death, leaving at the scene of an accident a bracelet, a pendant with her initials, a blouse stained with her own blood, and three locks of hair. Her only assistant will be her guardian devil, the man who gives us her story as an autobiographical novel from the perspective of a first-person narrator. And nobody better than he to carry out this task, since he also suffers from the illness of living in the middle of two cultures, belonging to neither. As we have seen in the case of Rosalba Violetta, her cultural *mestizajes* push her farther away from the two societies where she belongs—the inherited Mexican one, and the adopted American. Accordingly, her death might indicate that only in this dubious zone will she be able to reconcile the contradictions of living, as Gloria Anzaldúa describes it, "in the Borderlands," "without any barriers," at an eternal "crossroads."[65] At any rate, Violetta begs her evil writer: "Kill me. Yank me out of this story, help me burn this shitty witch, before she ends up burning me" (571).[66]

The paradox of this grand—or pathetic—finale is that Rosalba or Violetta falls again into one of her many traps. From her fictional deathbed, she will have to reinvent, for the tenth time, another identity, in order to spend—we already know how—the two million dollars that she steals from her boss. In spite of her powerful impulse to "deterritorialize" herself from Mexico and "reterritorialize" herself in the United States, Rosalba Rosas or Violetta Schmidt follows the fate of her Aztec ancestors, who began their eternal voyage to the underworld with obsidian masks adorned with precious gemstones.[67] This is how the protagonist of *Diablo Guardián* remains trapped in her own lonely maze. With a newly fabricated face, Rosalba initiates the journey of many Mexicans, portrayed by Octavio Paz as being distant from the world and everyone (32). Although highly fictional, Rosalba's life exemplifies various cultural trends of contemporary Latin America. It exposes, among other topics, the failure to fit in the space of origin due to social discrimination based on ethnicity, on being a marginal mestiza, or a *naca* who remains peripheral. Rosalba's voyage to the United States and her temporary stay in this country is also part of the "Latin American exodus" that has populated sectors of the United States in the last ten years (Suárez-Orozco 13). Her metafictional death makes us reconsider the positive, negative, or ambiguous effect of the uncontainable cultural hybridization that currently dominates Latin America and the United States.

The development of these ideas in *Diablo Guardián* transports us to the axis of Latin American cultural studies. Although it is increasingly true that we live in a world where cultural hybridity takes the place of national patrimony, it is still important to document this contemporary process of transculturation in fictions or chronicles, not to change the impossible but at least to better understand it. To a certain extent, we must accept the impossibility of there being a single culture, "the fact that its authentic 'content' is never anything more than a myth, exploded as soon as one cultural form encounters another, or as soon as such a form crosses the 'border' of country and city, North and South, etc." (Larsen 91). This overt hybridization, however, has its flaws. There are cultural ingredients that refuse to mix; they remain separate substances, like water and oil. They happen to be incompatible and unmistakable, even within a globalizing atmosphere.

NOTES

1. In his article "*Diablo guardián* o la necesidad de la ficción," Cabello explains that the narrator and her interlocutor live through the magic of fiction: She invents a foreign reality, and he writes down his fantasies.

2. The first three words of this derogatory rosary of Mexican women degrade the indigenous element present in every mestizo. Rosalba's pejorative reference to Coatlicue reminds us of the monstrous goddess of the Aztec world, and her numerous references to the Tlahuicas and Nacas (Totonacs) revive the pre-Columbian cultures that once inhabited the valley of Mexico (Townsend 41, 58).

3. "procesos socioculturales en los que estructuras o prácticas discretas, que existían en

forma separada, se combinan para generar nuevas estructuras, objetos y prácticas." I wrote this article in Spanish and translated it, along with all citations, into English myself. I am grateful to Linda Egan for her careful review and final correction of this translation.

4. From Franco's study "Globalization and the Crisis of the Popular," cited by Vivian Schelling (197).

5. "la fusión, la cohesión, la osmosis, sino la confrontación y el diálogo."

6. It is appropriate to talk about both trends. Between 1995 and 2000 the United States has received more than 1.2 million immigrants, many of whom come from Latin America (Suárez-Orozco 13).

7. I speak of Rosalba as a "misplaced individual," taking into account the theoretical postulates that Roberto Schwarz puts forth in his book *Misplaced Ideas*. The Brazilian critic explains how Latin Americans "constantly experience the artificial, inauthentic and imitative nature of our cultural life" (1).

8. "Yo fui rubia desde muy chiquita. . . . Todos los domingos, antes del desayuno, tanto mis papás como nosotros teníamos que pasar lista en el lavabo. ¿Creerás que hasta cuando teníamos catarro y calentura nos teñían el pelo con agua fría?"

9. "Ladrón que roba a ladrón, tiene cien años de perdón."

10. "My God, soy una naca . . . vengo de una familia cheesy. Plasticosa. Baratona. Rascuache. Prófuga del pinche Woolworth."

11. "las masas cobrizas . . . genuina mancha urbana."

12. "desprecio imperante . . . opresión . . . la imagen interiorizada de un país menor." For a complete analysis of the emergence in Mexico of the term "*naco*" during the mid-1950s, see both of Monsiváis's articles.

13. "Ningún mexicano sentiríase plenamente contento con la vida si no contara con al menos un semejante en quien descargar el más contundente de los insultos nacionales, mismo que como tantas palabras contiene solamente cuatro letras: n-a-c-o. De ahí que cada mexicano viva y se desviva para conservar o conseguir un certificado de que *no es naco*."

14. I am referring to *El laberinto de la soledad*, especially to the first two essays, "El pachuco" and "Máscaras mexicanas," in which Octavio Paz defines essential elements of the Mexican identity.

15. "Me voy a ir a New York."

16. "Recortaba periódicos, pegaba en mis cuadernos fotos de rascacielos, tenía hasta un mapita con las líneas del *subway*. Me imaginaba recorriendo tiendas, con el pelo negrísimo, ya mero azul, cantando: *I need some loving, like a fastball needs control*. Me reía de imaginarme a mi papá sirviéndome un *hot dog* y robándose el cambio de mis diez dólares."

17. On numerous occasions, Edward Said elaborates on the theme of psychological colonization and its representation in writing. See, for instance, his essay "Representing the Colonized," included in his book *Reflections on Exile* (293–316).

18. For a detailed analysis of the critical readings that these and other Mexican intellectuals make of the United States and its influence in Mexico, see Morris's fifth chapter, "Gringolandia in the Writings of the Intellectual Elite."

19. "irá definiéndose a sí misma más por lo que quiere ser que por aquello que verdaderamente es."

20. "En todo y sin motivos que los justifiquen, prefieren a los extranjeros, los sobrevalúan, los consideran naturalmente superiores, se 'amanceban' con ellos."

21. "el centro del mundo se ha desplazado, con todos sus símbolos y su orden."

22. "Me pasé por el río, como cualquier jodida. Con más de cien mil dólares en la

maleta, trepada en un colchón inflable, el pollero jalándome y yo como pendeja allí, flotando. . . . Total que me cruzó y yo me bajé abrazada a la maleta. Era de esos velices viejos horrorosos, que cualquiera los ve y jura que la dueña es una palurda."

23. Gloria Anzaldúa defines this term with accuracy, particularly in her book *Borderlands*: "Without benefit of bridges, the '*mojados*' (wetbacks) float on inflatable rafts across el *río Grande*, or wade or swim across naked, clutching their clothes over their heads. Holding onto the grass, they pull themselves along the banks" (11).

24. "Soy un pinche ratón en tamaña ratonera. . . . Soy gringa, ¿sí?, I'm American."

25. Eliana Rivero studies some of these authors who use their writing to come to terms with an ambiguous U.S. identity and culture ("Latinounidenses").

26. "alto, rubio, delgado, un gringazo bien hecho."

27. "a modelos, a fragmentos o a bienes culturales que no son generados ni en el propio contexto cultural (cultura local o de base) ni por una propia identidad cultural, sino que provienen de culturas externas y corresponden a otra identidad y lengua."

28. "diversas formas de expresión y representaciones híbridas como el diálogo entre distintos 'medios' (video, películas, televisión), . . . entre medios electrónicos, fílmicos y textuales." Taking as a point of departure the concepts of hybridity and "*transversalidad*," De Toro refers to the process of "*transmedialidad*," since it implies the exchange of multiple forms in the media (221).

29. Influenced by myths, legends, and fairy-tales, most Spanish conquistadors expected to find a marvelous reality in the New World. According to their readings and popular stories, this vast and unknown territory had to contain giants, wizards, dwarfs, enchanted islands, Amazons, and fountains of youth. When the American reality proved radically different from their original expectations, these conquistadors adjusted their perceptions to see what they wanted to find in the first place (Leonard 37).

30. "movimiento nómada de fenómenos culturales con respecto al 'Otro' y a la 'Otredad' . . . recodificador e innovador entre lo 'local' y 'lo externo.' "

31. "con un acento terrible, pero ya con las contracciones que me había aprendido en las historietas en inglés. *Gonna, wanna, gimme, gotta*. Se siente una gringuísima cuando las usa. Ya luego te acostumbras, como buena arribista. . . . Toda mi sangre es *wannabe*, qué quieres que haga."

32. "el acento gringo nunca me ha salido. Mis erres son muy fuertes, pienso en español, tartamudeo. No es que no me divierta hablar inglés, pero me atoro."

33. "herencia extraña de los que viven en los márgenes culturales aunque parezcan asimilados."

34. "Me gustan los principios . . . los finales, los sótanos, el penthouse, las pirujas, las monjas, pero lo que hay en medio es apestoso."

35. "mente de agenda impresionante"; "los gringos ya andan saltando camas desde los catorce años."

36. "*Estúpido*, pensaba. *Pendejo, mariquita, inútil, bestia*. Yo sudando de frío en el baño, pintándome los ojos y la cara y despintándome quién sabe cuántas veces. Poniéndome el perfume que me había comprado, probándome la bata, la toallita, no sabes. Y Supermán babeando su almohadota. Ni siquiera un *smack*, un *buenas noches*, un maldito *It's been such a crazy day*."

37. "El güey no supo ni qué hacer, haz de cuenta que yo era un violador y me estaba tronchiplanchando a una monjita. Pa que mejor me entiendas, sólo metió las manos para zafarse de mí."

38. "Cien *bucks* por una *limo* del aeropuerto, cuatrocientos más por un cuarto en el Plaza sin vista al Central Park, mil quinientos [por] dos faldas en Saks."

39. "el ombligo del mundo . . . pinche pueblo."

40. "se ensaña con quien no tiene casa. Los hoteles baratos son unas cuevas infectas, y los que te parecen más o menos decentes nunca te cuestan menos que un súper suéter. Un robo en todas partes."

41. "dar una vuelta por [su] propia Disneylandia."

42. "*Chica de rancho descubre Manhattan.*"

43. "les gusta ver sufrir a la gente, les da seguridad, se sienten importantes, afortunados, buenos. En realidad no les estás pidiendo que te regalen nada; les vendes la tranquilidad de su conciencia."

44. "Alguien había cometido un error en la maternidad y yo, que había nacido para millonaria, fui a dar a una familia de clase maromera. Pero esa puta suerte ya se había terminado, la prueba era que yo andaba en New York."

45. "Una lucha de fronteras / A struggle of Borders," cited in the chapter "La conciencia de la mestiza" of Anzaldúa's *Borderlands* (77).

46. "Violetta Schmidt . . . mexicana en New York, hija de padre alemán y madre canadiense."

47. "ciudadana de segunda clase."

48. "fábulas putrefactas de avidez y revancha." This is a collection of various short stories gathered under the title *El materialismo histérico* and populated by all sorts of people whose primary goal in life is to acquire money.

49. "permanecerá moviéndose constantemente entre dos mundos sin identificarse plenamente con ninguno: el mundo de la mujer prefabricada, del *kitsch* y de los media, y el mundo en zigzag de la cultura oral."

50. "Yo estaba harta de ser una jodida hija de familia jodida, y salté. Primero sobre los dólares, luego sobre la frontera, y de repente estaba en New York sintiendo como que otra vez tenía que saltar, y te juro que no sabía para dónde."

51. "Mi problema está en que soy una mercancía de Sears empeñada en llegar a un aparador de Saks. . . . Soy una naca, ya sé. . . . Siempre Sears, nunca Saks. Qué le vamos a hacer, Woolworth no cabe en Tiffany."

52. "no implica pérdida ni cancelación de lo propio ni tampoco resultado definitivo sintético homogeneizante de la cultura, sino un proceso continuo e híbrido."

53. "acrecientan la variedad genética de las especies y mejoran su sobrevivencia ante cambios de hábitat o climáticos."

54. "cualquier pueblo méndigo. Rentar una casita con gallinero, hacerme trenzas y vestirme con ropa de sirvienta."

55. "Todavía hoy siento que mi vida es la de un pececito de agua dulce al que quién sabe quién echó al agua salada."

56. "Estuve allí sin estar."

57. "Siempre digo que me escapé de mi casa buscando libertad, pero no es cierto. . . . Me escapé de la casa para criar mis propias esclavitudes. Más perfectas, más sólidas."

58. "Manía de hablar solo y en inglés."

59. "Había descubierto en el inglés un surtido interminable de analgésicos. Ásperas y juiciosas, corpulentas, graníticas, las palabras castellanas le parecían demasiado dolorosas, ampulosas, corpóreas, para emprender con ellas cualquier forma de diálogo consigo mismo. De ahí que sin pensarlo contrajera el vicio de hablarse en puro inglés."

60. I take the term from Marisa Belausteguigoitia. See her article "Las nuevas Malinches."

61. "la madre que ha sufrido, metafórica o realmente, la acción corrosiva e infamante implícita en el verbo que le da nombre."

62. "librada de sus cadenas ideológicas . . . tal vez con la esperanza de ponerse al día y mudar su condición de traidora."

63. "Violetta, Rosalba, Rosa del Alba: ya ninguna era yo. Vivía dividida todo el tiempo. Rosalba en la oficina, Rosa del Alba en la casa (me lo decían por joder, eso estaba clarísimo) y Violetta en el espejo. Me miraba por horas, unas veces sentada dentro del coche, otras en el espejo del baño, otras en mi espejito del buró. Decía: ¿Dónde estaré yo? ¿En los ojos, en los labios, en la frente? Casi toda mi vida sucedía a espaldas de mí misma. Yo, Violetta, no estaba en ninguno de los personajes que representaba a diario."

64. "Ya no lo soporto, ya me pinche cansé . . . Son demasiadas máscaras para alguien que nunca ha sabido quién chingados es, ni de dónde viene, ni para dónde va. No lo sé y no me importa, pero lo que no puedo es seguir cargando maletitas."

65. In her poem "To Live in the Borderlands" Anzaldúa proposes these metaphors to conjugate the ambiguity of all Latinos who live with one foot in and one foot out of American culture. This poem is included in her book *Borderlands* (194–95).

66. "Mátame. Sácame de este cuento, ayúdame a quemar a esta bruja de mierda, antes de que ella acabe de quemarme a mí."

67. I borrow these two terms from García Canclini to explain "the loss of a culture's 'natural' relation to its geographical and social territories, as well as partial territorial relocations of old and new symbolic productions" (288).

WORKS CITED

Anzaldúa, Gloria. *Borderlands / La Frontera: The New Mestiza*. San Francisco: Aunt Lute Books, 1987.

Basave Fernández del Valle, Agustín. *Vocación y estilo de México: fundamentos de la mexicanidad*. Mexico: Limusa, 1990.

Belausteguigoitia, Marisa. "Las nuevas Malinches: mujeres fronterizas." *Nexos* 314 (2004): 28–30.

Bryce Echenique, Alfredo. "La Plaza de Armas." *Nexos* 332 (2005): 71–72.

Cabello, Gabriel. "Una estética para el vacío: *Diablo Guardián* o la necesidad de la ficción." *Ciberletras* 11 (2004): np.

Corral, Wilfrido H. "Y tus padres también: testamento de los nuevos narradores hispanoamericanos." *Cuadernos Hispanoamericanos* 663 (2005): 89–95.

De Toro, Alfonso. "Hacia una teoría de la cultura de la 'hibridez' como sistema científico transrelacional, 'transversal' y 'transmedial.' " *Nuevo Texto Crítico* 25/28 (2000–2001): 197–234.

García Canclini, Néstor. *Culturas híbridas: estrategias para entrar y salir de la modernidad*. Mexico: Grijalbo, 2001.

Larsen, Neil. *Determinations: Essays on Theory, Narrative, and Nation in the Americas*. London and New York: Verso, 2001.

Leonard, Irving A. *Los libros del conquistador*. Trans. Mario Monteforte Toledo. Mexico: Fondo de Cultura Económica, 1996.

Monsiváis, Carlos. *Escenas de pudor y liviandad*. Mexico: Grijalbo, 1981.

———. "La Malinche y el Malinchismo." *La Malinche, sus padres y sus hijos*. Ed. Margo Glantz. Mexico: Taurus, 2001. 183–93.

———. "Léperos y catrines, nacos y yupis." *Mitos mexicanos*. Ed. Enrique Florescano. Mexico: Aguilar, 1995. 165–72.

Morris, Stephen D. *Gringolandia: Mexican Identity and Perceptions of the United States.* Lanham, Md.: Rowman and Littlefield, 2005.

Paz, Octavio. *El laberinto de la soledad.* Mexico: Fondo de Cultura Económica, 1999.

Rivero, Eliana. "Latinounidenses: identidad, cultura, textos." *Revista Iberoamericana* 71 (2005): 711–29.

Rufinelli, Jorge. "Parricidios, filicidios, matricidios, fratricidios." *Quimera* 245 (2004): 10–13.

Said, Edward. *Reflections on Exile and Other Essays.* Cambridge, Mass.: Harvard University Press, 2002.

Schelling, Vivian. "Popular Culture in Latin America." *The Cambridge Companion to Modern Latin American Culture.* Ed. John King. Cambridge: Cambridge University Press, 2004. 171–201.

Schwarz, Roberto. *Misplaced Ideas: Essays on Brazilian Culture.* London and New York: Verso, 1992.

Suárez-Orozco, Marcelo. "Some Thoughts on Migration Studies and the Latin American Éxodo." *Latin American Studies Association Forum* 37 (2006): 13.

Townsend, Richard F. *The Aztecs.* New York: Thames and Hudson, 1992.

Velasco, Xavier. *Diablo Guardián.* Argentina: Alfaguara, 2003.

———. *El materialismo histérico.* Mexico: Alfaguara, 2004.

———. *Luna llena en las rocas.* Mexico: Alfaguara, 2005.

CHAPTER 10

"Mexican" Novels on the Lesser United States

Works by Andrés Acosta, Juvenal Acosta, Boullosa, Puga, Servín, and Xoconostle

Emily Hind

The popularity of nonfiction genres in the United States and Mexico, including documentaries and reality TV, corresponds to an inverse distaste for literal-minded terminology and reality-based images in recent presidential practice. Whether with respect to the self-perpetuating war on drugs, the euphemistic "war on terror," or the proposed wall on the Mexican border, governmental policy seems to operate as theory divided from practice, as a sign infused with superficial symbolism but divorced from aesthetic and even legal coherence. Similar to the news under George W. Bush's presidential tenure, during Vicente Fox's presidency the media based in Mexico City broke political scandals related to the Mexican government with a regularity that defied verisimilitude. Some highlights include the ruling of human rights lawyer Digna Ochoa's death as suicide despite bullet wounds in her thigh and head (the left side—an odd choice for a right-handed person) and the almost countless assassinations of journalists, police, and other officials who had pledged to combat the drug trade. The new millennium occasionally saw the Mexican press report on the notion of law and order as a kind of joke that added bitter humor to the scandals, in the same way that off-the-wall coverage in the United States of the proposed border fence tips the news toward the ludicrous and reveals the northern government's inability to discuss rationally the scale and causes of undocumented migration. By March 2005, that scale included more than six million Mexicans working in the United States without proper documentation, according to estimates informed by the U.S. Census Bureau and the Department of Labor (Passel 1).

The coincidence of scandals and bizarre governmental projects with the popularity of nonfiction genres in both countries suggests a public taste for truth hunting. This aesthetic turn away from "fiction" and toward "reality" presents a challenge for novelists, who are largely still stuck with the task of drafting acknowledged fictions. Among the contemporary novelists writing in North America today, Mexican-born writers who contemplate the United States show special concern for the ungrounded nature of images in the media and the currently free-floating definition of Mexico. As those novelists know, since 1 January 1994, Mexico and the United States are joined by more than a border and a shared population. The North American Free Trade Agreement (NAFTA, or TLC, Tratado de Libre Comercio) came into effect on that date, and over the years following its ratification the incremental design of the treaty has eased tariffs and other bureaucratic processes that separate trade and workers across Canada, the United States, and Mexico.

The agreements that form NAFTA mean that Mexico faces a split between traditional rhetoric and current policy, to extrapolate from Sergio Aguayo Quezada's claim that postrevolutionary Mexican nationalism posed the United States as the dominant potential threat to Mexican sovereignty (162). Now that the northern threat operates as a free trade business partner, Mexican officials risk overt hypocrisy if they cast the United States as an opponent.[1] U.S.-based intellectuals, such as José Limón, Héctor Calderón, Colin MacLachlan, and William Beezley, summarize the historically mobile border and ceaseless cultural flow across it with the phrase "Greater Mexico," which in Limón's definition refers to "all Mexicans, beyond Laredo and from either side, with all their commonalities and differences" (3). In the first footnote of his study, Limón acknowledges that he borrows the term "Greater Mexico" from Américo Paredes (215). Ramón Saldívar's recent study of Paredes cites the Chicano thinker's definition of the famous phrase: "Greater Mexico begins at the border of Guatemala and extends all the way to the Great Lakes, to New York, or wherever there are *mexicanos*. They vary from one place to another, but to my mind, they're basically the same. The differences are in degree of acculturation" (141–42). Like NAFTA, the term "Greater Mexico" defies the official and traditional Mexican insistence that Mexico differs fundamentally from the United States, and it defies the U.S. logic of a fenced border. On the positive side, then, the term "Greater Mexico" presses the two countries to recognize social reality. On the other hand, the phrase captures only one side of a complex story by fudging the fact that at the turn of the millennium México is still not the United States, nor vice versa.

Greater Mexico's bid to set aside the North American presence within the latter's national borders potentially leads to what George Yúdice has called the "blindness" of contemporary American studies practitioners "in imagining that adoption of multiculturalism is somehow beyond the national [U.S.] frame" (263). Indeed, the term "Greater Mexico" hints—somewhat paradoxically given its framing in English—that exchange across the border takes place with a minimum of cultural adjustment. Studies of Greater Mexico sometimes incorporate a Chicano experience, which is, I would argue, still distinguishable from the non-Chicano Mexican experience. It is difficult, after all, to discriminate against people in Mexico simply for being Mexicans, while the Chicano/Chicana political identity recognizes that it is not difficult at all to discriminate against Mexicans in the United States.[2] This is why the term "Greater Mexico" offers a neat revenge to those who identify with Mexico in some way but live in the United States. The territorial marker does not necessarily offer the same comfort to those who live within the official borders of Mexico.

Accordingly, a glimpse of the shadow that Greater Mexico casts over mapped Mexico appears with the difficulty of translating the descriptor. In response to my lazy casting about for another authority on the topic, my husband, a native of Mexico City who currently resides most of the year in Northern Mexico, obliged my request for a translation of "Greater Mexico." During his latest U.S. visit, he proposed "el México del más allá" [the Mexico over there/beyond here] and "el México más grande" [the Bigger Mexico] which led me to wonder what that other Mexico might be, the smaller one that stayed "acá." But wait, I am "here," which turns my husband's "here" into my "there." How to speak of a Mexico over "there" (south of the U.S. border) if "there" is "here" for someone who sees the world from Mexico even when standing in my kitchen in Wyoming? How different is the mental Mexico from the "real" one inhabited within Mexican borders? A realistic answer to that question takes into account pervasive U.S. influence in Mexico, and there arises the complexity of "reading the United States from Mexico."

Frustratingly for a U.S.-born critic seeking to duck cultural imperialism, Mexican-born writers who at one time might have been expected to serve as outsiders to the United States today deliver the musings of knowledgeable insiders on the subject. The Mexican-born authors of the texts published in Mexico City from 1998 to 2006 examined here enjoy keen authority to comment on the United States because, like many contemporary, university-educated Mexicans, they are—figuratively speaking—U.S. citizens-in-law. Rather than blood ties, these Mexicans seem bound by legal agreement, for instance, NAFTA, and this formal relationship often involves tense marital relations. Most of the authors have lectured or taught at U.S. universities, read North American literature in English, and traveled the country. The novelists react to north-of-the-border influence in ways that test without necessarily triumphing over the asymmetry of the binational exchange. Given the international inequality, it proves much more difficult to argue that wide portions of the non-Hispanic U.S. population are Mexico's citizens-in-law. Though NAFTA may bind U.S. citizens to Mexicans, the English-speaking population probably does not watch Mexican film or Mexican television, or listen to Mexican songs, or pursue a graduate degree in Mexico, or even take a job in Mexico in the same numbers that create the Mexican-born, U.S. citizens-in-law. The unbalanced international relationship may lend the Mexican-born writers' observations political urgency, as well as encourage an air of resignation or even cynicism regarding possibilities for Mexico's autonomous cultural future.

I here refer to this almost inescapable U.S. influence in Mexico as the "Lesser United States." The discomfort of that term is immediate. In contrast to Limón's

expansionist theory of Mexico, the notion of a Lesser United States strikes a politically incorrect chord for its connotations of U.S. cultural imperialism and Mexico's
smaller geographic size. Though neither of those factors is up for debate, the term
"Lesser United States" annoys and even angers not just because it acknowledges a
discouraging state of affairs for a Mexican/ist, but also because it might perpetuate
the historical reality of North America's and Mexico's lopsided mutual influence.
Admittedly, tempering the idea of Greater Mexico with that of the Lesser United
States illustrates the contradiction that plagues my thinking, as I at once rely on a
difference between Mexico and the United States in order to justify my activities
as a critic who studies "Mexican" literature *and* as I claim that this difference is
disappearing. Hence, despite my argument that the texts I analyze here are concerned with Mexico as the Lesser United States more than with Mexico as Greater
Mexico, for many critics the novels will fit the category of Chicana literature.

These gooey interactions between Greater Mexico and the Lesser United
States, between Chicanos/Chicanas and U.S. citizens-in-law, and between free
trade and asymmetrical markets make for rich confusion—a problem similar to
the overlapping terminology and categories that Michel Foucault describes in
his preface to the study of, as the translation from French has it, "the order of
things." There, Foucault notes that his earlier treatise on the history of madness
reflects views of the "Other" and by comparison his examination of the ordering of
knowledge reflects views of the "Same" (xxiv). To borrow from Foucault's musings,
I can hypothesize that the categories United States and Mexico pose a problem
because it is an arbitrary task to divide the same. After all, even the differences
between the countries often point to their sameness. To the extent that the two
countries are non-Asian, non-African, and non-European, they are both American
with Asian, African, and European influences. In view of the blatant cultural realities in Mexico, including widespread commercial celebration of Santa Claus and
Halloween, the categories for "Mexican" fiction writers and "Mexicanist" critics
threaten to collapse in the same way that categories for Foucault's natural scientists
threaten to overlap, and thus the U.S.-based query, "What does Mexico take from
America?" (obvious answers: Starbucks, a movie, or graduate study) gives way to
the less taxonomical question regarding what contemporary Mexico might *do* with
the U.S.-originated phenomena that it has already consumed.

A clear-cut answer to these contradictions and imbalances that would tidily
enumerate what "Mexico" does with U.S. cultural production eludes me. Fortu-
nately, a neat answer is, at least from one perspective, unnecessary. The urge to
advance an optimistic, rational reading—one that would expect progress and solutions—would probably stem from the U.S.-based reading that I wish to avoid or
at least temper. According to the aforementioned cultural critic Aguayo Quezada,
U.S. citizens are so confident in technology and action that "they expect to find the
solution to any problem, as long as they approach it with the proper technique and
method and they set themselves quickly to 'doing something' to solve it" (47). A

consciously non-U.S. or Mexican-sympathetic attitude might refuse the principles of action, optimism, rationality, progress, and technology without suggesting a solution to these habits. In other words, residence in the Lesser United States does not mean that constant exposure to and consumption of U.S. cultural production requires Mexicans to think like U.S. citizens, which in turn means that observers need not recommend that Mexicans engage in optimistic, active, or organized rebellion against U.S. cultural influence. Those values might promote something like a triumphant Greater Mexico that assimilates certain U.S. ideals in order to assert its sovereignty. Rather than solutions, the reaction to the Lesser United States in works by Mexican-born writers exhibits the complexity that relative ideological autonomy allows. The innovative, loose, somewhat rough or spontaneous-feeling literature displays a mixture of assimilation and criticism without attempting to dictate a pragmatic direction for "progress."

Now to put names behind the theory: María Luisa Puga (1944–2004), Andrés Acosta (1964–), and Ruy Xoconostle (1973–) set their texts in a Mexico that is already U.S.-inized. Carmen Boullosa (1954–), Juvenal Acosta (1961–), and J. M. Servín (1962–) place characters on the other side of the border. These novelists register social changes in novels that display equal interest in defending the legitimacy of fiction. For these authors, the very notion of the novel responds to some sort of perceived crisis. It is not just that the Spanish-language "nation-building" novel of the nineteenth century and the national identity–affirming novel of the twentieth century have become less relevant in an age that undermines the ideological basis for Mexican nationality, it is also that in an age of NAFTA the very relationship of the novel with nationality throws the literary genre into question. The birth of the Lesser United States has seen the problematization of allegories regarding the national future.

Importantly, characters' location and status on one side or the other of the Río Bravo/Rio Grande offer an unreliable register of where they are at any given moment, in psychological terms. Boullosa's *La novela perfecta* (The Perfect Novel) describes the phenomenon of residing mentally in the Mexico that existed before the advent of the Lesser United States, even while narrating from the U.S. East Coast, which becomes a sort of Greater Mexico because of the Mexican lens. As the narrator admits: "I compare everything, from the sunlight to the smell of people on the subway. With Mexico, of course. I haven't lived there for twelve years, but I keep doing it. Shoes, bags, gestures, homes. . . . Not only here, in my Brooklyn or in detestable Manhattan: also in Paris, wherever we are. I compare everything, I measure everything with my Mexico . . . as if we were the universal parameter" (115).[3]

"My Brooklyn" and "my Mexico" in this passage signal the cultural straddle involved in Greater Mexican positioning, a straddle that parallels the author's residence in Brooklyn and her marriage to a non-Spanish-speaking U.S. citizen. Boullosa's narrator does not express a desire to return to Mexico, and so this straddle assumes the sustainable pose of a Mexican residing in permanent and not unpleasant displacement, rather than preparing the reader for a move. A return to "my Mexico" for the protagonist would probably be impossible anyway, since with long-term residence in the "real Mexico" the narrator would likely find not the authentic root of Greater Mexico, but the cosmopolitan base of the Lesser United States.

Despite the willful application of a nostalgic and possibly apocryphal "Mexican" viewpoint, Boullosa's character participates in a defense of the novel as a genre capable of the truth telling that eludes reality-based genres. The "perfect novel" anticipated in the title turns out to be a machine that translates writerly thought into three-dimensional images complete with scent. In *La novela perfecta*, the machine eventually spins out of control and kills the U.S. creator of the technology, leaving the Mexican-born author, Boullosa's male narrator-protagonist, unharmed but wiser. In the process of technological meltdown, the protagonist witnesses how the images of characters become nightmarish permutations with exchanged limbs and facial features that can be stopped only by an interruption in Brooklyn's electrical grid. Those deformed creatures recall the physically malleable posthuman characters in Boullosa's earlier novel, *Cielos de la Tierra* (Heavens on Earth), a fragmented text that moves from narrative of Mexico's colonial past to postapocalyptic science fiction. Although *La novela perfecta* does not imagine planetary destruction, it does suggest that a cultural collapse might result from the empty materialism of the United States.

Per Boullosa's penchant for allegory, this stern warning appears in *La novela perfecta* with the narrator's assertion that the fake, dead-end lies of the "perfect novel" represent the figurative essence of contemporary "man": "Broken all, like disposable beings, repeated, ignorant that [contemporary humans] are each one an initerable world, they ended up murdered by that fabulous machinery, the vertigo of diamonds, the vertigo of money, the splendor of money" (150).[4] This statement converts Boullosa's narrative into allegory by decoding the false characters' second-order meaning and the symbolism of their deaths. The empty characters of the perfect novel's machinery represent contemporary humans, and their downfall corresponds to an unfortunate attraction to material values. The narrator's subsequent epiphany causes him to reject the "perfect novel" and its vacuous visual signs in favor of language-based, literary "lies" that offer not so much untruths as the construction of a possible world (120).

These literary lies relate to the emptiness of the cultural phenomena that Boullosa discovers in New York. In her long narrative poem "Los nuevos" (The New Ones), published a few years before *La novela perfecta*, she criticizes Manhattan publicity for excluding love and coherence and promoting excess and "perfect poetry": "metaphor *per se*" (158). In *La novela perfecta*, Boullosa avoids the "metaphor per se" not only through the aforementioned vertically thick allegorical technique, but also by distinguishing fiction from the false: the insincerely told and the image without an author (144). At first, this last point seems to contain a contradiction, given that the protagonist did create the plot and characters contained in the machinery of "la novela perfecta." However, he is careful to deny authorship of the images once he realizes that the machine is broken (143). *La novela perfecta* proposes that image-based reality can take on a mindless, zombielike life of its own in a way that written texts and paintings (such as the Remedios Varos mentioned in the novel) do not because writing depends on mindful interpretation before it can "come alive." This distinction between fiction and falsity, between the depth of authentic art like writing and painting and the superficiality of computer-mediated, three-dimensional images, criticizes future technology and implicitly questions the supposed spontaneity and validity of imaged-based genres like reality television.

If Mexico as a lost cause can no longer be defended as something other than an imagined rule of comparison, in its place the literary text can still demarcate worthy territory. Boullosa redefines the genre of the novel in order to concentrate on the importance of narrative intention, coherence, and meaningfulness by attaching a subtitle, *Un cuento largo* (A Long [Short] Story). In the manner of a short story, *La novela perfecta* focuses on one principal aspect of the protagonist's life, the experience with the "perfect novel." Once the ultimately imperfect machine breaks down, the "perfect novel" becomes by implication Boullosa's "long short story," whose tight focus in the main story line restores a stable hierarchy between character and author. This coherence supplies an implicit contrast with the empty variety in U.S. culture. In the paradoxical space of Boullosa's "long short story," the States can exist as subordinate to the protagonist's mental Mexico, and within that literary territory a displaced Mexican can refuse to see himself as Latino, Chicano, or some other identity framed in English. *La novela perfecta* does not suggest a need to forge a new or compromised identity, because tightly drawn if dysfunctional perfection does not require compromise. This transcendence from the national to the aesthetic ideal restores the novel's place in transnational society as a privileged space for authentic fictions.

Boullosa's plainly stated defense of fiction finds a match in J. M. Servín's *Por amor al dólar* (For Love of Money). This autobiographically informed text describes protagonist Servín's employment history as an undocumented worker in the United States and during a brief stint in Ireland. Supporting black-and-white photographs and reproductions of identity documents in the novel stake a truth claim to lived experience. The amateurish photographs recode the text by giving exact images of many characters in the novel. Thus, the photos constitute a small-scale assimilation of the technology of realism that frightens Boullosa's protagonist, and they serve as an analogy of reality television: The plot of day-by-day immigrant experience is so natural, so artless, so gray, it must be real. In other words, a reader may suppose that if the photos were staged, they would surely display greater aesthetic complexity. Almost all the photographs are of immigrants, and by implication the resented gringo bosses are not authentic enough to merit a picture. Still, many of Servín's photos function ironically, because the reader has no way of corroborating their accuracy. Are the people identified and the backdrops really what the captions claim? The migrant world becomes still more literary, which in the context of the present analysis means more authentic, when protagonist Servín hints that literature offers a coherent, applicable version of real life.

Main character Juan Servín reads Raymond Carver, calls himself Gatsby in a gas station, and recounts a tenuously relevant anecdote about F. Scott Fitzgerald and Ring Lardner (128–29). The vague relevance of at least some of these references indicates that the realm of literature grants us valid experience, even if the literary anecdotes that form that realm diverge substantially from the character's lived experience. If the reader understands the allusions as an inverse model, then the relevance of *The Great Gatsby*, for example, emerges through its very irrelevance. Unlike Gatsby, Servín does not seem destined to amass a fortune in the deluded belief that the American dream lies within his grasp, both because hardworking Servín is not a gangster, a point made more sardonic in view of his undocumented status, and because the American dream is not viable for those caught in a perpetual struggle for day-to-day survival. The goal-oriented behavior that drives Gatsby's determined fantasy recalls Aguayo Quezada's comment about the U.S. belief in the value of expecting to find the solution to any problem and "doing something" to solve it. In contrast to Gatsby, Servín prefers to read and drink after work rather than lay plans for a brilliant future. That last difference marks the gap between Servín and many of the insensitive and unobservant U.S. characters in *Por amor al dólar*; the latter, like Gatsby, might have a library but do not seem to read much.

Author Servín also uses an untranslated epigraph from Nelson Algren and translated epigraphs by Henry Miller and Don Delillo. In light of the non-literary-anecdote-dropping U.S. public that protagonist Servín must serve, the epigraphs point out the migrant protagonist's perception of a richer, truer cultural environment than the one that the native, largely nonreading U.S. residents believe themselves to inhabit. Beyond workplaces and rented rooms where the protagonist may temporarily lay his head, the place that protagonist Servín finds worthy of cultivating parallels the literary territory of Boullosa's *La novela perfecta*. Servín's carefully demarcated literary territory does not concern itself with Mexican nationalism and, because of the U.S. authors cited, distances itself even from notions of a literary Greater Mexico. In the context of North American racial discrimination, there is a troubling choice in an undocumented migrant protagonist electing to narrate observations about the United States through white male–authored U.S. literature. Nevertheless, the white male authority implicit in quoted authors Algren, Delillo, and Miller sanctions author Servín's literary efforts and suggests the presence of a Lesser United States in the protagonist's literary terrain as he reads his life through such texts as reproductions of U.S.-issued identity cards and white male writers from the United States.

This erudite space grants the protagonist belonging in a literary Lesser United States a province that transcends nationality by welcoming a migrating Mexican and centers itself on a canon seen strangely, first from the outside in and then, as Servín continues reading from Raymond Carver to the other authors, from the inside out, a position that allows Servín to imply his connection with fetishistic details regarding Fitzgerald and Ring Lardner. This literary consumption takes place not as an assumption of presupposed cultural heritage but as a self-assigned labor of assimilation that leads to inverting the tradition and placing Gatsby in a gas station. There is little, if any, allowance for women intellectuals in this literary realm, but that exclusion may provide one of the character Servín's claims to status. The bridge called Servín's back that links undocumented, blue-collar work with U.S. intellectual elitism is buttressed by machismo. Without it, the protagonist might fall from a livable literary terrain into asphyxiating despair.

Protagonist Servín's inclination to live through literary references recalls María Luisa Puga's *Nueve madrugadas y media* (Nine Dawns and a Half), with the difference that Servín's male-dominated environment gives way to Puga's sexless character Hernández, a twenty-four-year-old gender-neutral virgin with an anonymous voice whose principal activity in life is reading (Puga 14). Realistically or not, Mexico City native Hernández claims to have lived, through the written word, more in English than in Spanish (104). Like Servín's text then, Puga's novel refers mostly to non-Mexican writers, especially Dostoyevsky and Delillo. The conceit that drives *Nueve madrugadas y media* has Hernández carrying out a grant project and staying as a houseguest with select authors, the first of whom is "Puga." The novel reproduces the dialogue between Hernández and Puga during the wee hours of each morning in the author's home for some "nine and a half dawns." The unembellished script between interlocutors helps circumvent a would-be narrator's need to apply gender-marked pronouns and adjectives to Hernández. The untraditional novel format also points to the increasingly transnational literary and decreasingly nationalistic context that Hernández inhabits.

As might be expected of a genderless character, Hernández exhibits a personality by embodying a different sort of stereotype, a generational one. With the progression of the dialogues, Hernández begins to resemble a rhetorical tool meant to typify contemporary Mexican-born young adults. The driving complaint of the work might be summarized in Puga's description of Hernández's generation as "the half Mexicans half Gringos" (72). Hernández explains the dynamic of Greater Mexico and the Lesser United States as an exercise in crossing an imperceptible border: "We didn't even see the Gringos. We were taken to the United States since we were kids . . . but, like I say, we didn't leave the country. We weren't in another country, in another culture. We were still here [in Mexico]" (49).[5] Though the ability to view the United States as Greater Mexico may seem a tactic of resistance, Hernández does not express solidarity with Chicanos: "A thousand times better to be of the illegals' ilk. Never that of the 'grin car' [green card]" (72).[6] Undifferentiated travel from Mexico across the border in the context of a rejected Chicano identity indicates the presence of the Lesser United States in Mexico, and it signals the loss of an earlier version of Mexican nationalism.

Puga resents that loss and the encroaching U.S. influence. For example, she decries Mexico's addiction to the United States' "artificial dream" (48). In times of a criticized addiction to simulated dreams, the novelistic reaction of elaborating more fictions may seem tongue in cheek, but Puga, like Boullosa and Servín, works to defend fiction as less artificial than U.S.-originated deceits. Notwithstanding Puga's impatience with Hernández's combined gringo-mexicana culture, she eventually admits that the purer national identity for which she feels nostalgia never existed (92). Puga hardly operates as a nationalist herself, in view of her disinterest in the PRI and PAN parties and her rejection of "this structure called country of Mexico," a rejection motivated at least in part by the lack of integrity of that structure (100).[7]

Although Puga decries Hernández's generation for its acquiescence to membership in what I term the Lesser United States, she identifies her interlocutor's greatest fault not as just hybrid nationalism, but as a resistance to all particular identities. In an articulation of this resistance, Hernández sets anonymity as a life goal: "[I wish t]o be a run-of-the-mill person. . . . I want to walk around the world without feeling part of any generation, without being young, leftist, postmodern, new age, all those things; . . . I try to be a person who journeys through the world, who lives it, who experiences it, and nothing more" (32).[8] Despite the desire to avoid belonging to a generation, Hernández does describe the one that belongs to him/her: "We are *fake*. We are Mexican-Gringos" (85).[9] Hernández's inauthenticity conditions his/her supreme interest in literature over life beyond the text. Hernández admits: "It's not that I'm *so* interested in reading; it's not that I think it's a good thing, but it's the only thing I know how to do now. What else can I do" (124).[10] This last idea is not phrased as a genuine question, because Hernández does not seek freedom from his reading habit and even expresses a preference for literary characters over people because only characters are "real" (120). In lieu of any particular identity, whether nationalist Mexican, reformed Chicano or some other variation on the Mexican/U.S. continuum, Hernández prefers the land of literature. Puga, notwithstanding her nostalgia for bygone Mexico, also resides in that literary territory.

The protagonist Puga comes to seem more like the author Puga with every additional biographical detail, but an ironic reading allows for the possibility that she, like Hernández, is "fake." After all, Puga assigns herself two different ages: fifty-five and fifty-two (27, 79). The "no-one's-land" (105) comprised of the wee morning hours during which she writes and talks to Hernández facilitates her freedom in identity, a freedom from precise age as well as from gender expectations. The "tierra de nadie" thus hosts an inhabitable Mexico of the mind devoid of the rejected "structure called country of Mexico" (100). The freedom of "no one's land" also allows Puga to redefine the role of woman intellectual. She disdains any responsibility to act as a surrogate mother and proudly points out that she never gave birth and will not use Hernández to realize her potential for motherhood (79). Instead of playing the maternal role for Hernández, Puga acts aggressively and at novel's end orders Hernández out of her home so that she can sleep. Before that brusque dismissal, Puga flatly informs Hernández that she does not like his/her project and adds: "Let me tell you something else: I don't like you much. Apparently independent, intellectual of the 90s. Young, free, but not really. You depend on your parents, even if you build your world in a rooftop studio. You're one of the atrocious Mexico City gang. You haven't understood yet what it is not to live in the center. Under it all, you and I don't have anything to talk about" (108).[11] This refusal to admit Hernández as an equal to the "nobody's land" of freed literary time/territory means that Puga does not accept Gringo-Mexicans into her supposedly apolitical literary space—remember her previously cited rejection of the PRI and the PAN during one of the dialogues.

Although María Luisa Puga discusses the erasure of difference in this novel, and although both she and Boullosa explore compulsive nostalgia for it in their works, neither Puga nor Boullosa, nor for that matter Servín, offers the U.S. way of life as a neat substitute for formerly Mexican nationalist identity, largely because the gringa culture seems fake, dead, or lobotomized in the novels. Interestingly, Andrés Acosta's *Dr. Simulacro* (Dr. Simulacrum) proposes a similar exploration of artificiality in the context of a problematic Mexican identity, but without mentioning any connection with U.S.-bequeathed cultural emptiness, unless protagonist Dr. Simulacro's true-crime TV show is taken as a reference to northern culture. The show could just as easily reveal connections to European reality television. I suspect that the Lesser United States takes such root in the Mexico City depicted in *Dr. Simulacro* that it becomes unnecessary to mention the phenomenon as such.

The cultural assessment delivered in Acosta's novel focuses on Mexican politics, and in a fictional critique of Vicente Fox, Acosta has the unnamed president of Mexico ask Dr. Simulacro to star in a reality TV show that will decide cases of Mexican justice by re-creating them on the program, then deliver the "truth" of the case based on the re-creation, and finally react to the validation of the verdict with tallies of audience phone calls. The title *Dr. Simulacro* inevitably leads to theorist Jean Baudrillard's notion of simulacra as ailments of commodity culture, a topic that relates to Puga's critique of the United States for exporting its "artificial dream" and Boullosa's displeasure with North America's celebration of "metaphor per se." Of course, the Mexican-born authors' complaints regarding materialism and emptiness stemming from U.S.-influenced cultural developments are hardly new. The most famous criticism of shallow, cold, Anglo materialism, predicted to fail before Hispanic warmth and spiritual superiority, is the century-old *Ariel* (1900) by José Enrique Rodó. Baudrillard's work greatly expands the possibilities of lambasting the United States for its materialism by reaching beyond the material and describing the existence of signs that relate to one another in ways that create alternative realities without necessarily preserving a relationship with a known and original reality.

In his introduction to Baudrillard's selected works, Mark Poster explains that when "distinctions between object and representation, thing and idea," lose validity, then Baudrillard's simulacra, or models "which have no referent or ground in any 'reality' except their own," come to construct the world. Poster clarifies: "Simulations are different from fictions or lies in that the former not only present an absence as a presence, the imaginary as the real. They also undermine any contrast to the real, absorbing the real within [themselves]" (6). When the simulacra begin to compose a system unto themselves, Baudrillard claims the existence of "hyperreality" or a world of self-referential signs. Baudrillard illustrates the latter concept with Disneyland as a site of grand-scale intertwined and ungrounded cultural references (Baudrillard 12).

Andrés Acosta's *Dr. Simulacro* may signal the presence in Mexico of hyperreality with a portrait of the Fox administration that recalls the theatrics and possibilities for inconsequential behavior suggested in the notion of Disneyland/world, including the (Clinton-reminiscent) tendency to make policy decisions based on opinion polls. Showing the limits of satire, as well as the public's credulity, Acosta has Dr. Simulacro's audience set a control on the public lie when callers reject the verdict delivered on his last program, a Digna Ochoa–like murder that Dr. Simulacro rules "suicide." This outrageous yet historically recognizable ruling marks the end of Dr. Simulacro's career and his own disappearance as a suicide, which concludes the novel. The foregone fact of U.S. cultural influence in contemporary Mexico, along with Baudrillard's globally applicable theory of simulacra, releases present-day Mexican-born writers from Rodó's responsibility of forecasting solutions and triumphs. Instead, the novelists experiment with versions of the Lesser United States without the constraints of optimism. Still, the writers reflect awareness that the novelistic genre must renew itself if their work is to remain relevant to the reality-obsessed audience, even if that audience has already fallen prey to the Lesser United States' emptiness and English-language preferences.

As I earlier stated, for Servín, Boullosa and Puga, literature combats that U.S.-related emptiness by providing a space of "true lies" or an authentic life-in-literature. The motivation behind these authors' defense of fiction finds its articulation in *Dr. Simulacro*, when Andrés Acosta acknowledges the pressure to cave in to the inauthentic aesthetics that true fiction opposes. The narrator of *Dr. Simulacro* explains: "Today the preamble should reassure the reader that the story is effectively real, that it took place a short time ago, and in fact, very possibly in the neighbor's house" (141).[12] This preference for the "real" story seems to demand the impossible: an unplotted narrative, or unstoried story line. Given this audience preference for veracity, it is no wonder that Acosta's narrator declares that his text is not a novel. In a further connection with nonfictional genres, Acosta manages to stage the performance of a text in *Dr. Simulacro* by beginning the work with the narrator's explanation that armed men have broken into his home and are forcing him to write an account of Dr. Simulacro's exploits. In this way, the narrator denies the fictional nature of his writing and claims to draft the text in real time without regard for aesthetic value: precisely the qualities of a would-be factual report drafted according to the design of reality television, which in turn is precisely the sort of television that *Dr. Simulacro* will come to show as theatrical and illegitimately authoritative. On the other hand, Dr. Simulacro upholds the prospect of discovering truth through fiction, and so Acosta undertakes the defense of literature that interests the other Mexican-born authors (141).

Acosta's defense incorporates contradictions, however, because the lying, artificial character who is Dr. Simulacro can hardly be trusted to reveal truth of any kind, whether through fiction or without it. As his name indicates, Simulacro is the very definition of an unreliable character. Apparently, the character trusts that reality is universal rather than particular, legible in analogies and anagrams, and thus Simulacro believes that the empty symbols, the simulacra referenced in his name, will somehow echo others in sensible relationships. Therefore, he confidently intuits what might be taken for the truth of his social surroundings: the outline of the Virgin of Guadalupe resembles that of a vagina, for example, and anagrams for the name Ronald Reagan include "a darn long era" and "an oral danger" (52, 130). The resulting tension between the untrustworthy protagonist and his belief in symbolically coherent, grounded reality-through-fiction remains unresolved if Acosta means to argue the truth-value of literary devices even as he criticizes Simulacro's tactics. Nevertheless, the ultimate point of the novel argues that in the face of the threatening hyperreality facing Mexican citizens who might come to live in unrelieved artificiality through shallow media and ungrounded policy decisions, literature can serve as a corrective. By drafting a novel that mimics the conventions of reality programming even as it debunks the truth-claim behind that televised genre, Acosta suggests that literature can play the reality game, too, and in the process restore authenticity, that is, realize a distrustful and grounding critique of official reality.

As with Puga's attempt to define the genderless character Hernández and Servín's reliance on bibliographical details, Andrés Acosta resorts to a description of Dr. Simulacro's education in order to sketch out the character. Dr. Simulacro, as a self-creation, *is* his education, despite his shady techniques for earning graduate degrees, which include plagiarism and forgery. In fact, all the novels discussed in the present analysis take care to provide details regarding characters' intellectual backgrounds. In transnational times, education reveals more about identity than does birthplace. Besides establishing identity, the details about education point to the source of characters' authority. For instance, Servín's protagonist drinks too much and suffers social discrimination, but he is usually more polite than the gringos are, and he often seems to read more than they do. The relationship between politeness and education recalls the dual sense of the Spanish-language term *educación* as both schooling and good manners.

Under conditions of increasing international migration and facilitated free trade, it is no surprise that rules of etiquette may become difficult to discern as two or more codes come into play: Is a student's hello kiss to a professor cheerful courtesy (Mexico) or sexual harassment (United States)? When eating, should elbows rest on the table (Mexico) or remain off the table with one hand in one's lap (United States)? When residing in Greater Mexico or the Lesser United States, should residents alternate customs or pick one set and ignore the resulting cultural confusion? In addition to teasing out the rules of *educación*, Mexican-born novelists who incorporate allegory and analogy in their technical repertoire suggest that understanding the contemporary state of affairs corresponds to a relatively simple decoding of one's surroundings through proper education. This championing of acculturation suggests that the veracity-claiming genres are not as self-evident, nor as guilelessly apprehensible, as they would present themselves to be.

In order to discuss the matter of education and allegory, I turn to a pair of Mexican-born writers interested in the Lesser United States; Ruy Xoconostle and Juvenal Acosta each write allegorical novels that take care to describe the protagonists' education. Although in the original draft of his first novel, *El cazador de los tatuajes* (The Tattoo Hunter), Juvenal Acosta's autobiographically inspired Julián Cáceres is a graduate student living in San Francisco, California, the second edition of the same title marks the author's professional development and converts Julián into a university professor in the same state. This gesture recalls the autobiographical turn practiced in the texts by Boullosa, Puga, and Servín. Despite his interest in Mexican-born authors, literary critic Julián notes that his move to the United States coincided with the shedding of his national identity: "I stripped off that official homeland like someone rejecting an unwanted embrace. I left that idea of Mexicanness behind me as if it were a possessive mother, blackmailing, manipulating, selfish. I wanted to change skins and I ended up empty" (*El cazador de tatuajes* 1998, 33; 2004, 32).[13]

By posing emptiness (*vacío*) as the absence of Mexicanness (*mexicanidad*), Acosta clears the space previously occupied by nationalism. What fills that gap relates to the erotic quest. As the title and opening paragraphs signal, a tattoo hunt registers "tribal" affiliations in lieu of national identity. Nonetheless, Juvenal Acosta despises a Mexico that waves megaflags and shops at Wal-Mart (1998, 77), or as the second edition of *El cazador de tatuajes* rewrites the passage, a Mexican stock market that sells off the country (2004, 75), and both his novels indicate that simulacra are natural in any city.[14] Acosta's novel mentions Baudrillard by name, and the reader may understand the protagonist to engage in the creation of a literary reality that makes his life interpretable and even unique.

As mention of Baudrillard and use of the term "simulacra" anticipate, Acosta drafts academically informed prose. The self-conscious intellectual stance does not allow Julián to define himself in a secure Mexican identity or to place himself in an overtly recognized identification with Chicanos (gender-inclusive language is unnecessary for this character). Instead, Acosta describes a return to tribalism for his

protagonist and even hints at an accompanying primitivism by relating objectifying descriptions of women's bodies as cities and maps (see *El cazador de tatuajes*).
This macho reaction to the challenges of living in the United States avoids mention
of critics famous for their feminism. In turn, the machismo recalls J. M. Servín's
protagonist's reach to a male constituency in his creation of a transcendent literary
terrain where readers, regardless of their migratory status, comprise the privileged
members. Thus, in Andrés Acosta's work, the crisis of communal identity that appears to relate to simulacra and that spurs the search for tribes in the absence of
nations also involves a crisis of men's roles. In defense of his masculinity, Acosta's
protagonist dedicates himself in an almost professional way to sexual conquests.

The machismo of Acosta's thematic parallels Ruy Xoconostle's protagonist
Cuki's crisis of nationality and masculinity. If Juvenal Acosta's Julián tends to drop
intellectuals' names and academic titles, Cuki prefers to pepper his discourse with
pop culture references. When he decides to set aside professional goals despite his
high-paying employment, Cuki consciously imitates Kevin Spacey's movie character in *American Beauty* and takes a minimum wage job at a supermarket. The
reference to the U.S. film supplies only one of innumerable allusions to North
American culture in Xoconostle's work. Rather than effect an unnuanced criticism
of U.S. cultural production as superficial or artificial, Xoconostle embraces it and
achieves a satirical revitalization of the gringo with relatively flat secondary characters in an impossibly inventive Mexico already subsumed by U.S. culture. Along-
side his vertiginous use of neologisms and defiant phonetic spellings of English-
pronounced-through-Spanish, Xoconostle has his characters consume in dollars,
though they live and work in Naucalpan and various cities in northern Mexico,
including Ramos Arizpe and Saltillo.[15] Protagonist Cuki's apartment complex is
nicknamed "Melrose Place" and complements characters' frequent comparisons of
Cuki's ex-wife, Midyet, with the U.S. actress Jennifer Connelly.

This inventive culture provides at once a celebratory autopsy on the former
country of Mexico and a cynical birth certificate for the Lesser United States. In
Xoconostle's "Mexico," the top national universities produce lawyers and accoun-
tants who stock VHS tapes in Blockbuster, assemble Whoppers, and wash cars
outside Target (*Pixie en los suburbios* [Pixie in the Suburbs] 17). Target stores do
not exist in Mexico, and the juxtaposition of imaginary Targets and obsolete VHS
cassettes represents a "Mexico" that is neither pure nor purely real, though this
play with temporal, linguistic, and cultural boundaries seems to identify some of
Mexico's actual problems. Xoconostle's funky chronology mixes the 1980s culture
(e.g., Atari and VHS tapes) with postmillennial effects (e.g., housecleaning robots).
This combination of periods and cultures—this simulated Mexico—supports Xoconostle's interest in the vastly disparate economic experiences present there. His
protagonist identifies first and fifth worlds in Mexico—Coahuila and Naucalpan
respectively (170). In recognition of the fifth world, Xoconostle's repeated reference
to a robot that cleans house and prepares meals might actually refer to members of

the Mexican lower class, an implication that the narrator never addresses. Broadly speaking, Xoconostle's brand of humor constructs a kitschy science fiction concerned with political commentary, linguistic originality, and a gross, even adolescent, sense of humor.

Despite the teenage crudity, Xoconostle takes pains to describe Cuki's impressive résumé, though the protagonist laments having studied in a Mexican university that was not quite as good as the Tec de Monterrey, a prestigious Mexican university organized in the style of U.S. institutions, complete with a series of ads at the turn of the millennium that featured student sports and computer-filled classrooms. Perhaps in evidence of his appreciation for pop culture, Cuki expresses cynicism regarding the excessive formal education that he believes causes dysfunctionality in his generation: "Can someone be overeducated? Yes. Us. My generation. We are the Overeducated Generation. The Overinformed Generation. The Overrated Generation. They have told us so much shit, they have filled us with so many lies through newspapers and magazines and radio and *fido* [neologism for TV] that, by force of repetition, we have believed them" (*Pixie* 191).[16]

In Xoconostle's work, side effects of formal education are conformity and undue respect for questionable categories. This intellectual paralysis born of too much education echoes the plight of Puga's Hernández, who has no interests aside from studying, yet does not apply the knowledge gained as much as collect it. Such antipragmatism, of course, rejects the U.S. values that would recommend "doing something" with erudition. Xoconostle's Cuki does write a book that his friends read as a roman à clef, but he does not seem to make any particular "progress" by doing so.

In evidence of a rejection of U.S. values even as they demonstrate expert familiarity with American cultural production, Ruy Xoconostle and Juvenal Acosta reject the pragmatic urge to "do something" with their novels by making a transition from one novel to the next that manages to undo the idea of progress in the plots. In a confusing technique related to my understanding of allegory in the novels, the first novels supply the characters for the second novels, which in turn rewrite and reinterpret the circumstances of the first. The characters' unexpected defiance of the first novels' plots demonstrates the by now familiar theme regarding the possibilities for discovering truth in fiction. When characters in the second novels reinterpret the events of the first narratives, it appears that the characters correct the authors and their original protagonists as would-be authorities. In other words, Ruy Xoconostle and Juvenal Acosta hint that literary creations can gain reality and even autonomy, and in the process can reveal their own independent truths. This gesture also alerts the reader that the characters have no stable content in themselves and that it is the narrative context that determines the course of action. Again, this gesture of cultivating a literary realm corresponds to the decidedly non-Mexican-nationalist literary spaces created in novels by Boullosa, Puga, Servín, and Andrés Acosta.

To elucidate the allegory, I will note that the female characters in the first novels, Xoconostle's *Pixie* and Juvenal Acosta's *Condesa*, appear in the second novels on an altered plane of reality. By way of a talk-show exposé, Xoconostle uses the second novel, *La vida sin Pixie* (Life without Pixie), to investigate which, if any, elements remain once the reality of the first novel, *Pixie en los suburbios*, is consumed and reinterpreted. In greater detail, *La vida sin Pixie* centers on Cuki's appearance on a "Mexican" talk show where the "truth" (its falsity) of his successful novel will be revealed: What Cuki had imagined as an incarnation of his ex-wife's all-consuming career, "Hank," the figure who takes her away from Cuki in the first novel, comes back in the second novel as a normatively human lover. Hank appears on a talk show and narrates his side of the story as Midyet's other man. Conversely, in the second text, *La vida sin Pixie*, Midyet's sister Pixie is revealed as Cuki's idealized version of his ex-wife and not a mysterious and desirable stranger, as she was depicted in the original *Pixie en los suburbios*. The effort to reduce the women— real and imaginary—to manageable scale in the first novel (ex-wife "Midyet" and imaginary lover and sister-in-law "Pixie") does not tame them.

Juvenal Acosta's second novel, *Terciopelo violento* (Violent Velvet), allows one of the protagonist's lovers, Ángela Caín, known as "La Condesa" in the first novel, to narrate part of the second text, which tends to fill in explanatory details related to *El cazador de los tatuajes*. Like Xoconostle's Pixie/Midyet, in Acosta's second novel Condesa/Ángela Caín upsets the male narrator's original, preferred plot. This development contrasts with the nineteenth-century nation-building allegories that employed women characters as representatives of the nation and as land to be fertilized.[17] Rather than a feminist message, however, Xoconostle's and Juvenal Acosta's quirky allegories created by the revisited plots may indicate that the characters merely serve as symbolic markers, in the way that chess pieces represent patterned moves on a game board. When one character makes a move, the outcome of the game appears to shift; thus, secondary characters come to trump the authority of the protagonist as narrator.

In other words, melodramatic allegory of the sort employed in nineteenth-century nation-building novels becomes unstable when the "good" Pixie proves a figment of Cuki's imagination, and Acosta's mysterious "bad" Condesa comes to narrate the adolescent trauma that informs her sexual pursuits as an adult. The characters' instability from one novel to the next suggests that in a hypothetical third novel, they might reposition themselves once again. In this manner, Acosta's and Xoconostle's allegories resist final, secure interpretation, and community threatens to reveal itself as an illusion. Ultimately, the repetition of plots allows Acosta's and Xoconostle's protagonists to live out an interrogation of borders and an unstable no-longer-national allegory that demonstrates how the *interpretation* of action, rather than action alone, affects the plot. This potentially infinite rewriting of events points to a condition of the nonnationalist literary terrain as a place of freedom but also of contingency.

In her study of allegory in transnational Spanish-language literature, albeit by way of distinct texts and authors, Debra Castillo discovers a machismo that Xoconostle's and Juvenal Acosta's second texts manage to temper. According to Castillo, texts by Ariel Dorfman, Boris Salazar, and Gustavo Sainz have in common a non-U.S.-born protagonist and a stereotypical woman character that functions as a culturally overdetermined symbol. Although like Castillo's texts, many of the "Mexican" texts that I analyze here practice allegory, they tend to show how women characters *resist* male control. The crisis of masculinity that Xoconostle and Juvenal Acosta explore through a machista protagonist and the second novels that allow the female characters greater independence defies the trend that Castillo describes, then.

In fact, the irrelevance of the nineteenth-century nationalist, heterosexual allegories from a Latin American other emerges in a further trait common to texts by Boullosa, Puga, Juvenal Acosta, Xoconostle, Servín, and even Andrés Acosta. This trait has to do with the insistent presentation of queer sex—the scenes of imaginary infidelity and an orgy (Xoconostle); sadomasochism and bisexuality (Juvenal Acosta); a sexless, genderless character (Puga); and the metrosexual and probable homosexual Simulacro (Andrés Acosta)—and complements the fact that *none* of the eight novels gives the protagonists children. This end-of-the-line depiction may point out the irrelevance of reproductive sex to abstract literary spaces that replace national territories, or it may signal the lack of projected future for the nations at hand. Yet another motive for omitting a future generation in the novels may correspond to the critique of U.S.-related artificiality. Simulacra derived from North American culture could make "Mexican authenticity" impossible, because the characters' would-be national identities might come to exist only in quotation marks. Unlike Baudrillard's simulacra, reproductions of already false characters might lead not to identical copies but to ever more blurry reproductions that lose legibility. (Recall the earlier mention of Boullosa's interest in distorted posthuman or simulated bodies.)

Debra Castillo's transnational literary study also highlights criticism that finds fault with the new styles of fiction. For example, Castillo collects negative criticism of Puerto Rican Gianinna Braschi's bilingual *Yo Yo Boing!* that rejects the text for flaunting "unfinished business," being "undisciplined," proving that "narrative" need not depend on "plot," and including "one genre too many." Castillo cleverly parallels these opinions by translating Braschi's "huevos" [balls (testicles)/eggs] manifesto in order to show that by the author's own words her work is "chock-full of poetic flaws" (182). Turning back to my own study, I note that the oddness of repeating a plot over Xoconostle's and Juvenal Acosta's twinned novels resists academic expectations for educated or mannered writing. And certainly, across the eight novels the stylistic experiments fail to achieve perfection when compared to the style of literary plenitude dominant in modernist and Boom novels and in many of today's English-language prize-winning best sellers. Due to the narrative loose ends and rough edges—which imply disdain for literature valued according to the impression that the author invests considerable time in its drafting and the reader invests considerable professionalism in deciphering it—I am hesitant to assign the novels that I discuss here in a university classroom. What if I discover that the novels are so raw that I cannot sustain the typical academic discourse apt for modernist texts that registers hidden meanings and tightly woven, resonating structures?

It would seem that the asymmetrical assimilation between Mexico and the United States inspires unfamiliar, asymmetrical texts. If even one of the eight works reviewed here becomes routine material for university classroom analysis, then critical standards for "polished" and "deep" contemporary novels will have changed along with the rhetoric of national identity. In that event, the possible literary flaws of the eight novels by Mexican-born authors will have been judged not flaws at all, but rather a new literature that requires a new critical etiquette, a new *educación*. Certainly, an inevitable challenge to the reader's education arises when languages begin to mix, not in the least because monolingual audiences may suffer alienation. In the event that education and etiquette will not align themselves into a practice satisfactory for Mexican-born intellectuals who also act as U.S. citizens-in-law, there remains the promise of regrounding the inheritance of U.S. artificiality in a literary space that allows a glimpse of truth through fiction. The literary approaches that claim truth through allegory, analogy, and anagram, as well as photographs and autobiographical details, tend to require a legible, stable world that supports echoing designs—perhaps the very opposite of the vertiginous reality of ungrounded claims repeated in much of the media in Mexico and the United States today. The literary space that embraces protagonists without a viable sense of nationalism—and in some cases without reliable authority or stable identity—hosts a realm of experimentation where literatures talk, languages mix, and truthful fictions rule.

NOTES

1. All translations are mine unless otherwise indicated. For discussion of shifts in official Mexican rhetoric, see Vizcaíno.

2. Mexicans of the United States who claim a Chicano/Chicana identity mostly or frequently do so in English, which does not recognize the linguistic gender rules of Spanish, among which the masculine plural includes both male and female. Chicanos have deliberately chosen to keep male and female identities separate in verbal expression, which renders necessary the wordy but inclusive term "Chicano/Chicana."

3. "Comparo todo, desde la luz hasta el olor de la gente en el metro. Con México, por supuesto. Hace doce años que no vivo allá, pero lo sigo haciendo. Los zapatos, las bolsas, los gestos, las casas. . . . No sólo aquí, en mi Brooklyn o en la destestable Manhattan: también en París, donde estemos. Comparo todo, mido todo con mi México . . . como si fuésemos el parámetro universal."

4. "Rotos todos, como seres desechables, repetidos, olvidados de que [los seres contem-

poráneos] son cada uno un mundo irrepetible, terminaban por ser asesinados por esa maquinaria fabulosa, el vértigo de los diamantes, el vértigo del dinero, el esplendor del dinero."

5. "Nosotros ni vimos a los gringos. Fuimos llevados a Estados Unidos desde niños . . . pero, como te digo, no salíamos del país. No estábamos en otro país, en otra cultura. Seguíamos aquí [en México]."

6. "¿Los chicanos? No, afortunadamente. Mil veces mejor ser de la estirpe de los ilegales. Nunca los de la grin car. Esos no" (72).

7. The ostensibly secular PRI (Party of the Institutional Revolution) employed leftist so-cialist policies along with violent coercion to maintain political dominance in Mexico for more than half a century. The more conservative, religiously backed PAN (Party of National Action) triumphed at the presidential level over the PRI with Vicente Fox's precedent-setting win in 2000. The second PAN-ista president of the new mil-lennium, Felipe Calderón, has continued his predecessors' conservative economic policies. Thus, the PAN has offered Mexican politics more of the same neoliberal tactics fostered under the PRI-orities set in the 1980s and 1990s.

8. "[Quisiera] [s]er una persona común y corriente. . . . Quiero andar por el mundo sin sentirme generación de nada, sin ser joven, izquierdista, posmoderno, nueva era, todas esas cosas; . . . busco ser una persona que transita por el mundo, que lo vive, que lo experimenta y ya."

9. "Nosotros somos *fake*. Somos mexicanos-gringos."

10. "No es que me interese *tanto* leer; no es que crea que es algo bueno, pero es lo único que sé hacer ahora. Qué más puedo hacer" (124).

11. "Déjame decirte más: tú no me gustas mucho. Dizque independiente, intelectual de los 90. Joven, libre, pero no tanto. Dependes de tus padres, aunque construyas tu mundo en una azotea. Eres de una chilanguería atroz. Tú no has entendido todavía lo que es no vivir en el centro. En el fondo, tú y yo no tenemos nada de qué hablar."

12. "Hoy el preámbulo debe asegurar al lector que el relato es efectivamente real, que sucedió hace poco y, de hecho, muy posiblemente en la casa de su propio vecino."

13. "Me despojé de esa patria oficial como quien rechaza un abrazo indeseado. Dejé esa idea de mexicanidad atrás de mí como si se tratara de una madre posesiva, chantajista, manipuladora, egoísta. Quise cambiar de piel y me quedé vacío."

14. In *El cazador de tatuajes*, Acosta propone que the only natural aspect of the contem-porary city is simulacrum or artifice (1998, 17), and in *Terciopelo violento* (Violent Velvet), he describes a traffic in simulacra that the city reinvents each day (67).

15. In Xoconostle's first collection of short stories, a glossary deciphers the terms, but by the publication of the novels, the reader must surmise from context that, for example, "fido" is a TV, "ptitsa" is a woman, and "tich" is an interjectory "güey," or "dude." As for the phonetic games, Ruffles potato chips become *rófols* (*Pixie* 86–87), newlyweds go on *jánimuns* (110), visitors go to the city's *dauntaun*, the protagonist recalls his "año *sofmor*" (15), and so forth.

16. "¿Alguien puede estar sobreeducado? Sí. Nosotros. Mi generación. Somos la Generación Sobreeducada. La Generación Sobreinformada. La Generación Sobrevalorada. Nos han dicho tanta mierda, nos han metido tantas mentiras a punta de diarios y revistas y radio y fido que, a fuerza de repetirse, nos las hemos creído."

17. Mention of (trans)national allegory brings to mind earlier Spanish American, nation-building novels that Doris Sommer analyzes in *Foundational Fictions*. Sommer exam-ines allegorical political views in novels such as *Amalia* (1851–1855) and *Doña Bárbara* (1929) that make use of heterosexual couples as a model for emerging Latin American nations.

WORKS CITED

Acosta, Andrés. *Doctor Simulacro*. Mexico: Joaquín Mortiz, 2005.

Acosta, Juvenal. *El cazador de tatuajes*. Mexico: Sansores y Aljure Editores, 1998. Rev. ed. Mexico: Joaquín Mortiz, 2004.

———. *Terciopelo violento*. Mexico: Joaquín Mortiz, 2003.

Aguayo Quezada, Sergio. *El panteón de los mitos: Estados Unidos y el nacionalismo mexicano*. Mexico: Grijalbo, 1998.

Baudrillard, Jean. *Simulacra and Simulation*. Trans. Shiela Faria Glaser. Ann Arbor: University of Michigan Press, 1994.

Boullosa, Carmen. *Cielos de la Tierra*. Mexico: Alfaguara, 1997.

———. *La novela perfecta*. Mexico: Alfaguara, 2006.

———. "Los nuevos [Part One]." *Salto de mantarraya (y otros dos)*. Mexico: Fondo de Cultura Económica, 2004. 87–162.

Calderón, Héctor. *Narratives of Greater Mexico: Essays on Chicano Literary History, Genre, and Borders*. Austin: University of Texas Press, 2004.

Castillo, Debra A. *Redreaming America: Toward a Bilingual American Culture*. Albany: State University of New York Press, 2005.

Foucault, Michel. *The Order of Things: An Archeology of the Human Sciences*. Trans. unknown. New York: Vintage, 1994.

Limón, José E. *American Encounters: Greater Mexico, the United States, and the Erotics of Culture*. Boston: Beacon Press, 1998.

MacLachlan, Colin M., and William H. Beezley. *El Gran Pueblo: A History of Greater Mexico*. 3rd ed. Upper Saddle River, N.J.: Prentice Hall, 2004.

Passel, Jeffrey S. "Estimates of the Size and Characteristics of the Undocumented Population." Pew Hispanic Center Report. 21 March 2005. Washington, D.C. *pewhispanic.org/files/reports/44.pdf*. 29 October 2006.

Poster, Mark. Introduction to *Selected Writings* by Jean Baudrillard. 2d ed. rev. and expanded. Stanford: Stanford University Press, 2001. 1–12.

Puga, María Luisa. *Nueve madrugadas y media*. Mexico: Alfaguara, 2003.

Saldívar, Ramón. *The Borderlands of Culture: Américo Paredes and the Transnational Imaginary*. Durham and London: Duke University Press, 2006.

Servín, J. M. *Por amor al dólar*. Mexico: Joaquín Mortiz, 2005.

Sommer, Doris. *Foundational Fictions: The National Romances of Latin America*. Berkeley: University of California Press, 1991.

Vizcaíno, Fernando. *El nacionalismo mexicano en los tiempos de la globalización y el multiculturalismo*. Mexico: Universidad Nacional Autónoma de México, 2004.

Xoconostle, Ruy. *La vida sin Pixie (una comedia)*. Mexico: Joaquín Mortiz, 2005.

———. *Pixie en los suburbios*. Mexico: Joaquín Mortiz, 2001.

Yúdice, George. *The Expediency of Culture: Uses of Culture in the Global Era*. Durham: Duke University Press, 2003.

CHAPTER II

Political Cartoons in Cyberspace

Rearticulating Mexican and U.S. Cultural Identity in the Global Era

Hilda Chacón

This chapter explores how Mexican political cartoons in cyberspace interrogate Mexican and U.S. cultural identity during the post-NAFTA period.[1] The signing of the North America Free Trade Agreement on 1 January 1994 by the United States, Mexico, and Canada marked the official entrance of Mexico into the global market. On the same date, the Mayan Zapatistas announced their uprising against the neoliberal project pursued by the power elite and the seventy-five-year ruling government, the PRI (Partido Revolucionario Institucional), headed by then-president Carlos Salinas de Gortari. From that moment on, diverse Mexican groups would further their examination of the country's position in the global era and especially scrutinize their country's relationship with the United States, perceived as the driving force of NAFTA. Diverse cultural artifacts produced after the signature of the agreement, such as urban chronicles, art projects, journalistic essays, narrative and theatrical works, and cyberblogs, attest to this transnational questioning. I focus here on contemporary political cartoons posted in cyberspace that, in my view, not only reassess Mexico's role in the global partnership but also reshape in unique ways the signs of national cultural identity for both Mexico and the United States. I examine cartoons published in the three most-visited Mexican media in cyberspace: *La Jornada*, *El Universal*, and *Milenio*.[2]

In the global era, political cartoons posted in cyberspace are a particularly potent critical tool that transcends both national territory and time. Cyberspace, as Fredric Jameson stated in his well-known treatise *The Postmodern*, is indeed the main cultural medium of the global era (38). Furthermore, I consider the Internet *the* transnational medium, because it possesses the capacity to boycott its own global project, as I established in a previous work.[3] Because the logic of the Internet itself involves new ways of creating meaning, it deserves closer analysis, such as the one I am proposing.

I concentrate on cybercartoons produced in Mexico during four key moments of the Mexican-U.S. relationship at the turn of the twenty-first century: first, the 9/11 attacks on the World Trade Center, the Pentagon, and the downed airplane in Pennsylvania; second, the beginning of the war in Afghanistan in October 2001 and of the war in Iraq in March 2003; third, the ongoing debate in various forums on border-control issues (as of October 2006); and fourth, the "moment" in which Mexico asserts that it is forced to adapt to the U.S. lead in the global era. These milestones have generated a large volume of cartoons in Mexican media, restating that nation's long bittersweet relationship with North America. For the sake of my argument, I have chosen to examine drawings that offer "ruptures" and "interstices," as Homi H. Bhabha proposes in *The Location of Culture*, where an adversarial notion of identity has been posited to shift signs of power and domination. The cybercartoons produced in the aforementioned moments are intense and even harsh; in them, Mexican artists displace assumed notions of power and cultural identity, contesting the overtly dominant role of the United States.

The cartoons generated in response to the four time periods shake up both Mexican and U.S. self-definitions in the late capitalist era, which, per Jameson's theory, highlights the predominant role of computers and "hyperspace" (38). Identifiable traits of the new Information Age—Jameson's "discontinuities" (29), "collage" (31), "disjunctions" (41), "fragments" (25), "simulacrum" (6, 9, 21, 46), and "masks" (17)—can be found in Mexican political cartoons in cyberspace; it is for this reason that I see these online caricatures as pertinent to contemporary analysis. Further, in the ruptures or ideological fissures detectable in them, we can discern their criticism of the global project, a decidedly self-referential (postmodern) gesture. However, these inversions of the expected disrupt fixed notions of identity and, following a concept of Bhabha's, open spaces of negotiation "of the 'in-between' " (148) that offer both societies an opportunity to change their historical and contemporary relationship. These cybercartoons are examples of "nonsynchronous temporality of global and national cultures . . . [that] open a cultural space—a third space—where the negotiation of incommensurable differences" may occur (218).

Why Cybercartoons?

Mexican political cartoons have been the subject of recent scholarly analysis by Stephen Morris in *Gringolandia* (129–58), but although I share some of Morris's premises, I propose that the Internet as the medium of late capitalism allows for a larger and more geographically dispersed audience and thus for an expanded range of possible readers for the questions posed in printed political cartoons.[4] This idea builds on the assertion that George Landow makes in his 1994 essay "What's a Critic to Do?" that "the very speed of networked electronic communications changes our experience of publication" (13). Speed, as Landow proposes (and simultaneity, I add), makes the Internet a unique communicative tool because it instantaneously links geographically disconnected populations.

The Internet is also a medium of another kind of displacement: "Disconti-nuity—the jump—the sudden displacement of the user's position in the text" is a main feature of "hypertext," according to Aarseth, who offers a threefold defini-tion of the word (69). He moves freely among the three: first and most general, hypertext as "a direct connection from one position in a text to another" (67); second, hypertext as the implementation of the first, "usually a computer applica-tion called a hypertext system, with idiosyncrasies and enhancements that make it different from other systems" (67); and third, hypertext as a "a text embedded in (and defined by) such a system" (68). All three of Aarseth's definitions assume that the reader is viewing the hypertext on the Web, and thus the technological envi-ronment is key to its understanding (68).

Gunnar Liestøl points out another feature of Internet reading: "Hypermedia creates new conditions for experiencing information and meaning" (116). In his view, the reader of cybernetic information has to (re)create a discourse from the stored information, resulting in what Liestøl identifies as "constant recontextualiza-tion" (116), which generates an oscillating relationship between "a flexible, unstable whole" (such as the Internet as a medium) and the space created by the interaction between the "reader" and the hypertext (117).[5]

The Internet, as the medium capable of instantly publishing globally any con-tent, has profound and powerful implications. Its worldwide coverage, as well as its impression of immediacy and connectedness, allow readers to transcend geo-graphical isolation, thus creating a virtual world community that can react instantly and without the hindrance of traditional publishing—or national boundary—lim-itations. The cybercartoons that I analyze in this chapter perform, in my view, the opportunity for what Homi Bhabha identifies as "disintegrative moment[s], even moment[s], of enunciation," constituting "sudden disjunction[s] of the present" (217) where "collective experiences of *nationness*, community interest, or cultural value are negotiated" (2).

Scholars interested in Mexican political cartoons have not thoroughly explored this possibility. For example, Morris states that Mexican "caricatures focusing on the U.S. . . . . offer a distinct discourse on the nation" and that "in many ways these interwoven themes . . . on the U.S. serve to define Mexico" (143). In fact, through its online political cartoons, Mexico today frequently switches from its traditional role of exotic object of study to an equal and active political subject capable of questioning traditional arbiters of power. Some might posit that Mexican political cartoons published in newspapers do the same thing, if to a smaller audience, be-cause the cartoonists are still actively exercising their authority as subjects to ques-tion traditional arbiters of power. The point here, however, is not simply that the Internet authorizes Mexican cartoonists to criticize U.S. power or that it merely amplifies their voices. Rather, when read on the Internet, these cartoons take on more complex meanings due to the nonlinear and simultaneous ways of creating meaning that the Internet permits, as well as because the Internet reaches audi-ences beyond national territories.

Mexican cybercartoon criticism is contradictory, ambiguous, and, at times, unclear. But its power to question accepted notions of cultural identity resides precisely in this lack of clarity, in the gaps where the renegotiation of identities takes place. In these interstices, or "Third Spaces" (36, 218), or "in-betweenness" (217), as Bhabha might term them, Mexican political cartoonists in cyberspace reappropriate and redefine icons of national identity from both Mexico and the United States, reallocating their traditional meaning and thus creating new connotations. In the process, they use the playful and slippery ways of constructing meaning in the global or the postmodern (Jameson) era to question Mexico's and the United States' positions within that era. No icon seems to be totally "Mexican" or wholly "U.S. American" in these cybercartoons. Besides, the cartoonists' criticism is available at any time on any day of the week on any page in the newspaper or on the Web. Furthermore, since cybermedia create a massive global community, which includes Mexico as well as the United States, the assumption that the United States serves "to define Mexico" in oppositional terms, as Morris proposes, is not accurate. In some of these cartoons in cyberspace, Mexico slips out of its historical role as "the subaltern" of the United States (Morris 154) to portray itself as an empowered judge, for example, of the war in Iraq that followed the 9/11 attacks on the United States; in other poignant illustrations, Mexico in solidarity shares the pain and sorrow of the United States. Simple binary/oppositional categories are thus insufficient to analyze the complexities involved in the construction of cultural identities and political agency proposed by these cybercartoons.

Bypassing the binary, I focus on the intricacy and rapidity of contemporary human exchange and the slippery business of renegotiating cultural signifiers. In my analysis, "constant recontextualization" (Liestøl) in the assignment of cultural identity is the norm, through a relentless acceptance of indefinition and redefinition, in which what has just been stated may be immediately contested. The result is a constant dislocation of meaning that simultaneously incorporates and rejects elements of each culture. The Internet is key in this process because it is where power and domination are fluidly and freely interrogated as fixed cultural identities are unhinged.

The Cybercartoon's Ancestor in Mexico

Political cartoons have been a key element in the establishment of freedom of speech in Mexico since nineteenth-century cartoonists began to question the elite's privileges within the chaotic nation-building project. Mexican cartoonists were frequently incarcerated by conservative and liberal government officials who were the focus of their harsh criticism; political cartoonists would not let the errors and contradictions committed by the oligarchy go unnoticed (Barajas, *El país* 25–29). José Guadalupe Posada (1852–1913) is probably the best-known Mexican political cartoonist of the nineteenth century. Posada's drawings in *La Gaceta Callejera*

(Street Gazette) ceaselessly challenged the dictatorial rule of Porfirio Díaz (1876–1911). However, his criticism of the burgeoning national project as conceived by the first ruling elite of the criollos began only in the mid-nineteenth century; as a genre, political cartoons in Mexico appear as early as 1826 (Barajas, *Historia* 19).[6]

Mexican audiences have historically appreciated political cartoons that denounced the corruption of national politicians and continue to heed cartoons that daily interrogate their political views. Of course, contemporary cartoonists have access to the Internet and an audience that may expand within the country, as the Mexican public's computer use grows, as well as beyond its borders. And it is not only the reader in Mexico who is of interest in this scenario, but also the Mexican outside Mexico, who through the Internet can still imagine himself or herself reading from within what has been termed "Greater Mexico"—the vast territory from Central America to Canada ever more densely populated by Mexican immigrants who maintain contact with their country of origin in part through the Internet. If they are moved through study of cartoons with an oppositional slant to rethink their own or their nation's traditional sociopolitical stance on many issues, historically accepted notions of Mexican and U.S. cultural identity may also be subject to (perhaps radical) change. Cybercartoons may also inspire collective political activism, such as support for the Zapatista movement or opposition to privatization of the Mexican petroleum industry.[7]

Contemporary Mexican Cybercartoons

Today, users of the Internet can bear witness as world cultures fragment, reshape themselves, give up traditional features, or take on borrowed characteristics across the global transcape as humorists sketch metaphoric challenges to any short- or long-lived status quo. Among other comments on the political arena, the cybercartoons I analyze here challenge the icons of authority traditionally attached to the United States; they also question their own government's role. An important element of this process is a recognizable desire to rearrange Mexican and U.S. markers of cultural individuality; in the drawings, the sites for these signs are full of contradictions, ambiguities, overlappings, disjunctions, reinscriptions, and erasures that weaken U.S. power while elevating Mexico to a position of authority over the United States. One typical gesture is to move icons of national and cultural identity across the border, thus satisfying, in virtual reality, their nation's enduring desire for recognition as of equal worth with the United States.

Because the Internet erases the borderlines between private and public spaces—between the outer world and the privacy of the viewers' homes—and between present, past, and future, it opens gaps wherein users temporarily inhabit the rim of an in-between space created in cyberspace by Mexican cartoonists who temporarily have conferred special political and cultural powers on their country and on fellow Internet users.

9/11 and Afghanistan 2001

Mexican political cartoons reacting to the tragic events of 9/11 in 2001 appeared in various Mexican media online almost immediately after the attack on the World Trade Center and the Pentagon, and the crash of a fourth hijacked airplane in a Pennsylvania field. Although some cybercartoons immediately conveyed Mexico's solidarity, as if the attacks had taken place on Mexican soil, others demonstrated an ambiguous position. A cybercartoon published two days after the 9/11 attack suggests its similitude to previous attacks—on Hiroshima and Nagasaki (1940s), Vietnam (1960s), Panama (late 1980s), and Baghdad (Kuwaiti-Iraqi war 1980s), all perpetrated by the United States (figure 1). There is ambiguity in acknowledging the horror of current events on the one hand, and on the other suggesting a parallel (poetic justice?) with attacks led by the United States against other cities in the past. In fact, the cybercartoon is entitled "¿Y por qué?" (And Why?) and implies a connection between the attacks on 9/11 and the U.S.-led bombarding of Hiroshima and Nagasaki, Vietnam, Panama, and Baghdad. It is not an open accusation. However, it displaces the attacks of 9/11 and problematizes them to contest U.S. military actions elsewhere, in other moments of history. In this cybercartoon, the cartoonist overlays moments in history and displaces the North American position from victimizer to victim. There is an implied minimization of the suffering inflicted on the United States in this treatment, a pain transformed into something else: perhaps an earned punishment. I see such a transformation in the role of the United States, from victimizer to victim, as proof of the reinscribing of the "historic commonality" (Bhabha 7): Now the United States and the countries it has attacked share the historic common factor of having suffered military attack by foreign forces; now the United States has stopped being the sole uncontested military power on the planet. The reshuffling of historical bombardments aims to "resettle" the reach of the Mexican neighbor's calamity. In this ambiguous vision of the attacks of 9/11, cartoonist "El Fisgón" of *La Jornada* proffers a complex notion of justice in which the United States is not only a victim but also a perpetrator of the current tragedy. While the criticism is not completely clear—it is more a blurry suggestion—we witness in this cybercartoon the presence of an absence, an example of what Derrida identifies as a metonymic logic of displacement (cited in Bhabha 55): Here the colonial subject has been suddenly presented with an absence; if the United States is not a "victim" anymore, then . . . what is its identity vis-à-vis the 9/11 attacks? In this cybercartoon, what has already been stated—a sympathetic sentiment and the recognition of the horror of the attack—is immediately denied and replaced with an implied accusation: The United States may now be justly suffering the same horrors that it has perpetrated in the past against other nations.

On 7 October 2001, shortly after the 9/11 attacks, the Bush administration launched a war against Afghanistan, whose Taliban government was allegedly har-

Figure 1: Fisgón, "¿Y por qué?" (And Why?), *La Jornada*, 13 September 2001. Reprinted by permission of *La Jornada*.

boring Osama Bin Laden, the presumed principal architect of the attacks. A fundamentalist Muslim, Bin Laden had received training from the CIA and participated in destabilizing the Soviet government when its troops were fighting against the Afghani people in Afghanistan during the 1980s. (As readers know, Bin Laden still has not been found.) Less than two years after 9/11, the U.S. government extended the war to Iraq, where U.S. troops are still deployed. The weapons of mass destruction that President Bush alleged were hidden in Iraq were never found. Nevertheless, the first vow to launch a war against Iraq was uttered as early as September 2001; this promise appears in some Mexican political cybercartoons, which exhibit features of unclear meaning common in the global era. In one cartoon, for example, the Spanish saying "estar en pie de guerra" [to be on a war footing/ standing] is represented by a boot that replaces the head of a military figure (figure 2). The image also suggests another Spanish saying, "pensar con los pies" [to think with your feet], to express the senselessness of the imminent wars in Iraq and Afghanistan. In addition, the absurdity of the upside-down boot substituted for a head negates the authority represented by the U.S. military uniform. Through this

Figure 2: Ahumada, "En pie de guerra" (On a War Footing/Standing), *La Jornada*, 26 September 2001. Reprinted by permission of *La Jornada*.

strategy, cartoonist Ahumada from *La Jornada* mocks the authority of the United States to pursue an additional war in Iraq.

A cartoon posted on 11 September 2004, the third anniversary of the 9/11 attacks, presents a disturbing and confusing position regarding the war against terrorism led by the United States (figure 3). Here the image of jail bars tangled from an explosion confronts viewers online; two are still smoking, resembling the Twin Towers after the attack on 9/11. Two huge footprints outside the bars are presumably those of the escapee, and on the jail's bottom wall appears the Spanish word "*Terrorismo*." Angel Boligán from *El Universal* thus presents Internet viewers with an imprecise message: The geographical space occupied by the World Trade Center has been moved from New York City to a jail, and the tragedy of the Twin Towers converted into a part of that jail. Blowing up the bars (the Twin Towers) actually has allowed the escape of an unidentified detainee: Is this an innocent person who has been unjustly incarcerated, an attacker who will continue setting up bombs in public areas, a fundamentalist Muslim, or even a U.S. soldier? Does the cartoonist suggest that the Bush government's war on terror is itself "terrorism"? Here we can

Figure 3: Boligán, "Tres años suelto" (Free for Three Years), *El Universal*, 11 September 2004. Reprinted by permission of the artist.

perceive a slippery, mobile representation of meaning in which the events that occurred on 9/11/2001 overlap the present in an obscure way. The cartoon may even
imply some reference to the Abu Ghraib scandal, for accusations of violations of
the human rights of Arab prisoners kept in the U.S.-run penitentiary became public around May 2004. On 13 January 2004, Spc. Joseph Darby had handed over
some alarming pictures to the Army's Criminal Investigation Command (CID)
denouncing abuses committed by U.S. soldiers against Arab prisoners. The CID
reportedly launched an investigation immediately, and about three and a half
months later, CBS News and the *New Yorker* published disturbing images and stories of the incident, which is still under investigation (Walsh). It is even possible to
assume that the cartoonist is referring to the United States as a potential criminal
who has escaped confinement and is now free and capable of committing terrorist
acts.

This is another example of how cybercartoons manage to "resettle borders"
(Bhabha 9), in this instance through a reconfiguration of the U.S. tragedy in a way
that appears to turn the victim of terrorism into a source of terrorism; also, the 9/11
attack on the Twin Towers has transcended U.S. national borders to spread into
Mexico and, indeed, because the Internet is a world without borders, throughout
the globe. Further, this cybercartoon attests to what Liestøl calls a "constant recontextualization" of meaning between the readers and the Internet (116): The 9/11
attack on the Twin Towers and the Abu Ghraib scandal have been reconstrued to
suggest a new interpretation of the U.S.-led war against terrorism, in which we can
glimpse proof of what Bhabha has identified as a use of the past to create a new
understanding shared by all in the present (7). With the power conferred on it by
the Internet, Mexico suggestively and subtly holds the United States accountable
both for its military actions and for its own victimization. The notions of "home"
(the United States) and history (the 9/11 attack on the Twin Towers) overlap in an
interpretation that leeches sovereign sanctity from the United States.

March 2003: Beginning of the War in Iraq

In March 2003 the Bush administration broadened its search for Bin Laden to
include the capture of a longtime enemy and one-time ally in the Middle East:
Saddam Hussein, then president of Iraq. This new priority culminated in the
bombing of Baghdad. Once Hussein was apprehended on 13 December 2003, the
mass media forgot about Bin Laden. As Mexican political cartoonists dragged the
U.S. war in Iraq over to the online battlefield, Boligán portrayed the U.S. Army's
entrance into Baghdad as a gigantic soldier's boot about to step into a trap (figure
4), with the city situated on the edges of the device. At first, the outsize propor-
tions of the soldier's body, in comparison to the trap's dimension, fill our eyes.
However, a second look reveals the entire city of Baghdad poised at the edges of
the trap in a way that seems to allow this small and thin device to ensnare the

Figure 4: Boligán, "Trampa" (Trap). This cartoon appears in several publications online with diverse titles and in *El Universal*, 17 March 2003. Reprinted by permission of the artist.

American soldier, who had earlier appeared dominant. The trap's thinness becomes its strength: Baghdad at the edge, now a fanged predator, may at any time trap and destroy the invader, who in this cybercartoon has also become its prey. Thinness has mutated; weakness has become potential strength, or the possibility to respond in a lethal way to defend Baghdad against the invaders. In this deceptive drawing, the Mexican political cybercartoonist empowers himself to displace images of power and domination distinctive to the United States; in doing this, the satirist also assumes a virtual identity, positioning himself as a hypothetical witness in Baghdad to judge U.S. (mis)steps there.

Another disturbing image about the war on Iraq is an Arab Statue of Liberty, also by Boligán and published in *El Universal* (figure 5). The image trespasses gender and ethnic markers by portraying the statue as an Arab man, a cultural gap that forces viewers to observe a primordial icon of U.S. national identity saying something unexpected about the role of the United States in Iraq. Here the United States is robed like an Arab and taking possession of a destroyed Iraq, perhaps suggesting that the local government is responsible for the destruction of that country in the name of liberty, or maybe that the Arabs still hope to attain the same liberty that the statue in New York City represents. At the same time, it could invite global audiences and especially Americans to rethink the significance of "liberty" for Arabs. Or is it implying that the United States is using Iraqi hopes of liberty as a pretext to destroy their country? The unclear and ironic "hybridity" (Bhabha 14) of markers of national identity radiate worldwide in this distorted emblem of U.S. generosity and hope. Nevertheless, I recognize its drive to put Mexico on an equal level with the United States by questioning the implications of the U.S- led war. Yet another illustration by Boligán from *El Universal* questions the United States' role in the world community, especially in Iraq, from still a different angle (figure 6). In it a soldier whose nationality is unspecified lies in a pool of blood that we take to be the locus of personal journals that will never be published; all that viewers can perceive are fragmented sentences. These are not random: They are unfinished sentences recalling pain, solitude, and daily events in the war—untold stories inscribed in blood and now on the Internet. This cybercartoon may be revealing by what it conceals: The silence of the dead soldier invokes a collage of voices muffled by a vast historical error.

With dark humor, the same cartoonist juxtaposes the presence of U.S. soldiers in Iraq with that of undocumented Mexican workers in the United States (figure 7). A group of U.S. soldiers crowds on top of a sign that says "Iraq"; they comment about the latest events in the United States and refer to President Bush's failed Immigration Reform Bill to legalize the nation's estimated eleven million undocumented immigrants.[8] In the sardonic drawing, one of the U.S. soldiers says, "The Immigration Reform Bill was not approved!" and another answers, "Oh, good! I hope that no more illegal foreigners will be permitted to enter into our territory!" in a metonymic displacement of the situation of Mexican workers in the

Figure 5: Boligán, "Oh, sorpresa" (Oh, Surprise), *El Universal*, 3 May 2003. Reprinted by permission of the artist.

Figure 6: Boligán, "Representaciones de la guerra" (Representations of War), *El Universal*, 30 March 2003. Reprinted by permission of the artist.

United States to the current presence of U.S. soldiers in Iraq.[9] By overlapping the U.S. troops' "migration" to Iraq with their apparently sincere concern about undocumented Mexicans coming into the United States, the cartoonist mocks U.S. attempts to impose on other nations migration policies that its own government is not willing to follow. The cartoonist is stretching the parallel, however, for it is evident that Mexican immigrants intend to work, live, and remain in the United States, whereas the vast majority of U.S. soldiers in Iraq have no intention of doing more than follow military orders during a prescribed tour of duty before returning home for good. In a humorous way, however, the Mexican political cartoonist attacks U.S. policy on border-control issues by pointing out, with satiric distortions

Figure 7: Boligán, "Ilegales" (Illegals), *El Universal*, 10 April 2006.
Reprinted by permission of the artist.

of the concepts of "migrancy" and "undocumented," that, for whatever reason people cross uninvited into a foreign land, there's not much the receiving territory can do to keep them out.

Debates on Border Control in the United States

Debates on immigration in the U.S. House of Representatives and Senate not surprisingly have generated an abundance of cartoons in Mexican cybermedia. One of the most ambiguous, and therefore interesting, is Boligán's caricature from *El Universal* entitled "¿Qué sucedió el 2 de octubre de 1968?" (What Happened on

2 October 1968?), which to Mexican viewers clearly recalls the night the Mexican Army killed Mexican students in Tlatelolco Square during a peaceful demonstration (figure 8). In the cartoon, that tragic event has been transferred to the present and placed at the border between Mexico and the United States. Adding a further degree of ambiguity, the Grim Reaper is perched on a cross on the U.S. side of the border. The Mexican flag witnesses the Grim Reaper and its cemetery from the other side of the border wall. At first glance, there seems no connection between the massacre by the Mexican government of its own citizens in 1968 and the current situation at the border between Mexico and the United States. Death and the crosses that seem to symbolize the massacre of students in Tlatelolco have been shifted to the U.S. side of the border, a site and concept that have themselves been given new meaning: An event in Mexican history now alludes to the death of Mexican workers who cross the border during the global era, a gesture that would appear to equate a Mexican president's massacre of his own society's innocent students with a U.S. president's inhumane treatment of innocent Mexicans fleeing joblessness in their society. Or is the cartoonist blaming the United States for its support of the Mexican government during the massacre of students in 1968? Is he accusing the United States as well of not protecting the Mexicans who cross the border from a terrible death in the desert? Or is he underlining the Mexican government's betrayal of its own citizens in 1968 as a watershed moment in which the Mexican government abandoned its duty to its people, an abandonment that created a chain of political and economic failures in Mexico that have subsequently exposed its citizens to the abuses and tragedies on the border? It is unclear why the cartoonist juxtaposes these events so separate in history—and political context—at the border between Mexico and the United States. However, I perceive the assertion of Mexican cultural identity as an iterated performance, Mexican history at the border between the first world and the third. The borderlines of national identity have been fluidly intertwined and, thus, resettled.

Boligán directly addresses the strong and dignified presence of undocumented Mexican workers in the United States in a cartoon in which thousands of workers form a giant agricultural or migrant worker looming over Uncle Sam, who ignores the giant to chase stray workers with a broom, as if trying to shoo away insects (figure 9). Through collective engagement, powerlessness has become strength, giving political leverage to the united migrant workers, whose numbers in the millions alone make them adversaries impossible to defeat. Of course, the proposed construction of meaning in this cybercartoon is so ambiguous that it can also be interpreted as workers whose numbers overwhelm the border patrol's capacity to "swat" them away. Once again, the ambivalent policy of the United States when dealing with migrant workers is onstage here in cyberspace. The cartoon could also invoke the political organization of migrant workers within the United States, documented or not, who demonstrated in response to immigration legislation debates. We can also find cartoons of a more explicitly severe tone: In a drawing by

Figure 8: Boligán, "¿Qué sucedió el 2 de octubre de 1968?" (What Happened on 2 October 1968?), *El Universal*, 27 July 2003. Reprinted by permission of the artist.

Figure 9: Boligán, "El gigante" (The Giant), *El Universal*, 13 April 2006. Reprinted by permission of the artist.

Antonio Neri Licón, Uncle Sam has taken a few construction blocks from the Statue of Liberty to build a border wall to separate Mexico from the United States, in accordance with statements in the Secure Fence Act, which aims to erect a wall between the two countries (figure 10).[10] The reinvention of the Statue of Liberty in material terms—the historic concept of U.S. liberty is "under (re)construction" here—is a crucial element of the cartoonist's pointed comment. The Statue of Liberty, located on Liberty Island next to Ellis Island in New York, has been since the nineteenth century the first icon to greet thousands of hopeful émigrés as they approached a nation that received immigrants pursuing a better life for themselves and their families. Now the Statue of Liberty's meaning as a cultural marker for freedom has been reconstituted. The "fragments" of a fundamental sign of U.S. national identity, the bricks taken off the Statue of Liberty, appear to deconstruct America's image and the hopes of contemporary migrant workers.

The border wall appears in yet another of Boligán's cybercartoons from *El Universal* (figure 11); this time the wall that the Bush administration is determined to build across the border is a metaphor for the TLC (Tratado de Libre Comercio, the

Figure 10: Nerilicón, "En construcción" (Under Construction), *Milenio*, 27 October 2006. Reprinted by permission of the artist.

Spanish name for NAFTA). According to my reading, the wall has displaced the TLC in an evocative way: The cybercartoon implies that the "free trade agreement" became a one-way deal. Although the criticism may seem clear at first sight, the supposed copy of the narrative of the TLC that the Mexican peasant holds in his hands does not show the text of this international trade agreement. Instead, the TLC sheet exhibits a map of Mexico, perhaps suggesting that the trade pact is a bill of sale for the whole country, a gap in the trade pact that contests the supposedly multilateral benefits of the treaty.

Humor can also be a means to displace authority and mainstream assumptions in these political cartoons, as in Patricio's drawing entitled "La enchilada completa: primera tira cómica binacional e indocumentada" (The Whole Enchilada: First Binational and Undocumented Comic), in which two migrant workers try to go across the new border wall (figure 12). Eventually, they pass to the other side when they find a tunnel built by the *narco* traffickers who smuggle drugs into the United States. The dialogue reads: "Now what the hell are you doing, you f—Saturnino?" / "Looking for water? We don't need water; we need to get to the other side! Dollars!

Figure 11: Boligán, "El muro" (The Wall; document reads "NAFTA"),
El Universal, 18 January 2005. Reprinted by permission of the artist.

Figure 12: Patricio, "La Enchilada completa" (The Whole Enchilada), *Milenio*, 28 September 2006. Reprinted by permission of the artist.

Money!" / "There it is!" / "What are you doing standing there? Help me to push this huge stone!" / "Oh, you!" / "C'mon, then! Isn't it true that you needed to get to the other side urgently? Let's go!" / "What is the number one rule that every migrant must learn?" / "There is always a *narco* tunnel nearby."

Mexico's Nation-Building Project in the Global Era

The globalization process is perceived in Mexico, and generally throughout Latin America, as a project launched mainly by the United States, since the World Bank and the International Monetary Fund have their headquarters in Washington, D.C. The tendency to reduce the involvement of the state in national economies, as well as in social services such as education and health care, has grown in Latin America since the early 1980s in a process that is generally referred to now as neoliberalism. Privatization of the southern hemisphere's economies was carried out in good part through the U.S. Agency for International Development (USAID), whose loans and aid packages were managed by U.S. embassies throughout Latin America. Therefore, it is not surprising that the all-pervasive effects of globalization are perceived in Mexico as intimately connected to the political objectives of the United States. Neoliberal globalization is a constant theme of today's Mexican political cartoonists. In a cartoon that depicts the U.S. and Mexican governments as one entity, for example, Magú from *La Jornada*, uses the United States' leading role in the war against terrorism to denounce the Mexican government's abuses of civil rights—a criticism of the universal governmental abuse of power (figure 13). Here the cartoonist addresses the U.S. Patriot Act of 2001, enacted on 26 October 2001; this law was followed by the Patriot Act Improvement and Reauthorization Act of 2005, signed by President Bush on 9 March 2006. The cartoonist lampoons the alleged erroneous application of the Patriot Act in a planetary representation of Mexico and the United States in order to denounce inappropriate judicial practices in Mexico and to delegitimize both U.S. and Mexican governments. The figure of Uncle Sam as a Republican elephant tramples the whole planet as it approaches the Mexican Judicial Authority. (Interestingly enough, this building is located beyond the Mexican territory represented by the map.) Uncle Sam says, "I want to tap telephones, use electric torture, and spray soda water in their noses." The caption reads: "As world police in the new millennium the United States is vindicating judicial methods used in Mexico since the last century."[11] Here the cultural markers of identity (worldwide, U.S., Mexican) have been aligned in the caricaturized planet to challenge the abuses committed by both states, independent of nationality: The United States and Mexico are capable of violating the human rights of prisoners; thus, the two countries act as equals in the global era. Here the official discourses on democracy of Mexico and the United States jointly collapse, and citizens in both countries experience the destruction of their human rights by their mutual governments. So what is authentically Mexican or U.S. American when

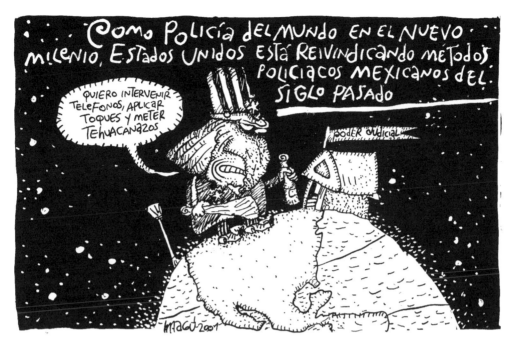

Figure 13: Magu, "Razones de seguridad" (Security Reasons), *La Jornada*, 26 September 2001. Reprinted by permission of *La Jornada*.

it comes to respect for citizens' human rights in the global era? The cartoonist seems to suggest that the two governments' national identities have merged into one global identity that disregards human rights in any national territory.

Even as they rely on visual media to reach their audiences, Mexican political cartoonists criticize the heavy reliance of contemporary societies on image and media, as we see in a Boligán cartoon from *El Universal* entitled, "The One Who Kills with TV Sound Bites, Dies from TV Sound Bites" (figure 14).[12] Boligán presents Adam and Eve watching a TV screen. The biblical serpent is offering them the apple on the "Tree of Science and Knowledge" through the mediation of a TV monitor. The cartoonist is mocking the advancement in Mexico of evangelical religious groups who aim to impose unilateral interpretations of biblical texts. Right-wing religious groups currently wield strong influence in the Mexican media; the cartoonist seems to point out how nonsensical it would be to have television mediate Adam and Eve's encounter with the serpent or, maybe, any other biblical passage. In this piece the artist fractures a straightforward reading of the Bible with the presence of a TV monitor that, instead of showing commercials, presents the serpent's offer in a close-up shot. In spite of the apparent mockery, the role of the TV monitor is ambiguous: Does it help to close the gap between the message and the audience, or does it permit by its own merit greater credibility for that message? Is the artist ironically suggesting that visual media allow biblical discourse to

Figure 14: Boligán, "El que a spot mata, a spot muere" (The One Who Kills with TV Sound Bites, Dies from TV Sound Bites), *El Universal*, 18 September 2005. Reprinted by permission of the artist.

be kept at a safe distance? Or is he instead ridiculing ownership of the media that does not allow questioning of religious principles? Or does this cybercartoon suggest what would happen if religion took over the media? It is unclear. However, here the monitor opens a gap in biblical discourse that permits the artist to mock fundamentalist groups in power.

Mexican political cartoonists in cyberspace also explore the increasing con-

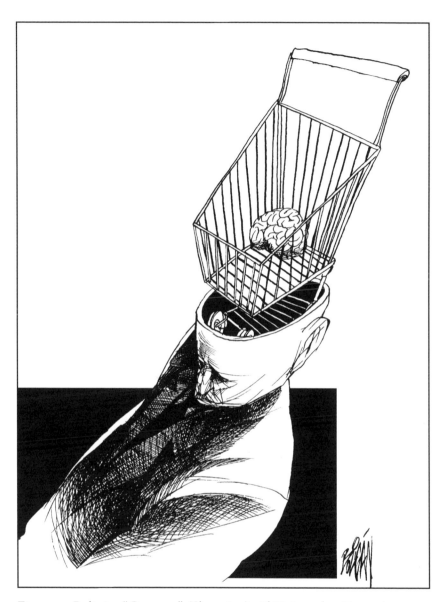

Figure 15: Boligán, "Compras" (Shopping), *El Universal*, 31 December 2005. Reprinted by permission of the artist.

sumerism of the global era. For example, a cartoon by Boligán shows a fragmented human body of undeclared gender with a shopping cart embedded in its skull and its brain inside the cart (figure 15). The perspective of the sketch invites Internet viewers to observe the contents from above. Readers are confronted again with "fragments" of an entity (Jameson) that reduce the significance of a whole human body, a coherent shopping activity, and the entire brain to provoke us into reconsidering their meaning. The representation of consumers as disjointed pieces of an unassembled whole asks us to question the merits of consumerism in the global era—which is to say, to question our main activity, which is shopping, a great deal of which we do online: consumers from everywhere on earth buying products made from everywhere on earth and paying with seemingly one virtual monetary unit. In this cybercartoon, shopping is not only a U.S. cultural marker, but also a Mexican cultural trait; both countries have merged their cultural markers of identity and have become indistinct in the global era.

Another aspect that Mexican political cybercartoons address is the project of the nation in Mexico, or the "imagined community," as Anderson proposes, and recently the contested outcome of the last Mexican presidential election, 6 July 2006.[13] Political cartoonists in cybermedia have pleaded for the necessity of civil engagement in societal solidarity during the transnational era. For example, in a drawing by Bolígan from *El Universal*, fragmentation of the whole—the human body, in this case—becomes, paradoxically, a way of maintaining societal unity and a Mexican sense of belonging to a shared cultural identity (figure 16). A human being, gender undeclared, has cut off one arm in order to elongate the other arm to rescue a person drowning, of whom we see only a hand coming from the water. In this cartoon, Bolígan is in fact praising the successful experience of civil organization that resulted from the earthquake that struck Mexico City on 19 September 1985; it was produced on the anniversary of the tragedy in 2002. The most interesting aspect of this cartoon is that in addition to using the aforementioned postmodern/postindustrial—and, in the context of this study, we might say postnationalist—strategies to convey meaning, it also brings the past experiences of civil organization to a present in which competition is backgrounded in favor of a more cooperative, democratic, societal body.

The Power of the Internet

In the contemporary political cartoons that I have analyzed, Mexican and U.S. cultural identities collapse, interdict, silence, and dialogue with each other—even if not necessarily in friendly terms. I have followed Homi H. Bhabha's invitation to resist binary oppositions (10), as well as to "think beyond narratives of originary and initial subjectivities," and concentrated "on those moments or processes that are produced in the articulation of cultural differences" (1); moments in which "plural" cultural translations occur (223) on the "non-synchronous" temporalities of global and national cultures where "historical time . . . jumps back and forth" (218). It is in the gaps between where changes in cultural identity and negotiations of power take place in the international community we all now inhabit.

Although the globalization process is tying together the national economies of the whole planet, it yields particular side effects in economies such as Mexico's that on some levels could be considered peripheral to the U.S. economy. Al-

Figure 16: Boligán, "El terremoto y la sociedad civil" (The Earthquake and Civil Society), *El Universal*, 22 September 2002. Reprinted by permission of the artist.

though some official data from institutions like the World Bank rank the Mexican economy within the top half of income per capita on the planet, these numbers can be deceptive. According to a joint report elaborated by the World Bank and the United Nations Development Program, the income of Mexican multimillionaires is fourteen thousand times higher than that of the average of the Mexican population during former president Vicente Fox's administration, and his economic decisions generated higher societal inequality and deterred further growth of the Mexican economy (González, "Grandes"). Danny Leipziger, vice president of the World Bank, announced two days later that NAFTA is not an option for Mexico's economic development and advised Mexico to divert its exports to European markets (González, "El TLC"). The Mexican government has repeatedly admitted to depending for the stability of the Mexican economy mainly on Mexican workers' *remesas* (remittances) sent to Mexico from the United States. According to official Mexican government data, the remittances sent by the workers abroad reached a record $24 billion dollars in 2006 (González, "Remesas"). Also, according to a study by the Center for Integration and Development of North America at the University of California at Los Angeles, migrant Mexican workers produce more money than that generated by NAFTA itself (Brooks, "Migrantes"). In view of this information, I refer to the Mexican economy as peripheral to that of the United States.

Financial consortiums have reached out beyond national capitals, thus blurring traditional markers of national economies. Financial transactions occur at vertiginous speed across the planet, mainly via the Internet. The very concept of currency worldwide has mutated from a tangible, concrete artifact to a virtual concept that travels as a cybernetic message: Money, as some of us used to know it, is being transformed into fiber-optic waves. In fact, economies can be impacted in seconds by these virtual transactions at any time, a circumstance that exposes a vulnerability of this medium. This is how critical the Internet has become. What we are presently witnessing is the rapid traffic of uncensored worldwide cultural transactions on the Internet, as well as the conversion of economic codes into cybernetic conventions. Certainly, the vast majority of the world's population bears witness to the great spectacle of the globalization process without an apparent direct participation in the decision-making process; however, I argue that massive public access to the Internet—an access that is difficult to control—potentially empowers the audiences of viewers across the planet. Viewers could, for example, boycott patterns of consumption; therefore, viewers globally have the potential to massively impact a given economy or political project.

Jameson asserts that the globalization process somehow implies the "Americanization" of other economies (xx). But Mexican critic Carlos Monsiváis defines the process for Mexico as instead "the psychological adaptation of Mexicans to a game that has been imposed on them from abroad" (132). Monsiváis concurs with Jameson that the twentieth century was, overall, the century of the "Americanization" of Mexico. However, for Monsiváis this trait does not necessarily mean the loss of Mexicanness. He vows that at the turn of the twenty-first century, "we are still Mexicans, and proudly so, as they used to say in the forties, *but a different kind of Mexicans*" (140; my emphasis). In his view, the notion of *mexicanidad* is, as it always was and will be, a "cultural creation" (134) and, as I have been arguing throughout this chapter, what can be made can be unmade, and with particular ease and speed through the Internet.

Benedict Anderson highlights the key role of print capitalism as the foremost technological medium for the creation of the "imagined communities" that later became the nations that separated themselves from Europe in the nineteenth century, in the case of Latin America. This capitalistic technological device, in Anderson's view, was eventually responsible for the spread of national sentiments that permitted the creation of nation-states as we currently know them. Anderson's proposal can be expanded in the global era, when national icons and other markers of cultural identity (as well as financial transactions) could not be further away from the print concept. Homi Bhabha questions Anderson's assumption of an " 'imagined community' rooted in a 'homogenous empty time' of modernity and progress" (6) and proposes a "radical revision" of such a "geopolitical space" so the entire national and international community confronts "its influx of postwar migrants and refugees, as an indigenous or native narrative *internal to its national identity*," with the aim to "deploy the cultural hybridity of their borderline conditions to 'translate,' and therefore reinscribe, the social imaginary of both metropolis and modernity" (6). In Bhabha's view, the new critiques of our times should "dwell 'in the beyond,' " a process that he defines as "a return to the present to redescribe our cultural contemporaneity; to reinscribe our human, historic commonality; *to touch the future on its hither side*. In that sense, the intervening space 'beyond,' becomes a space of intervention in the here and now" (7). We can find evidence of Bhabha's assertion in Mexican contemporary political cartoons in cyberspace, as I have argued.

Peripheral Contestatory Power and Globalization

I think that cybermedia can produce new meanings that transcend the original source of utterance and generate new uncensored modes of meaning. Internet users can perceive this potential power in the kind of online discourse I have analyzed in this essay. What Jameson could not anticipate at the time of his proposal of "the postmodern" are the contradictions that characterize "present-day multinational capitalism" (37) in peripheral economies like Mexico's. Although I agree that the Internet offers only a virtual representation of late capitalism phenomena, I also believe that, paradoxically, this medium can actively boycott assumptions of the current leading economic project—one of these assumptions being the notion of cultural identity. As I have discussed in this essay, cultural influences "imposed from abroad" (Monsiváis 132) are adapted with uncensored new meanings that are multiplied in simultaneous and multidirectional ways.

This potential ability of the Internet to achieve planetary coverage and its ability to merge past and present in the here and now, as I have argued, is the main point of entry into the global medium, the gap through which a sophisticated public could take back the power that, ironically, was wrested from it by the self-same medium. Jameson foresees that the cultural logic of late capitalism has the ability "to expand our sensorium and our body to some new, yet unimaginable, perhaps ultimately impossible, dimensions" (39), which is an ability that the Internet has taken to its maximum level. I have argued that it is possible for Mexican cybercartoonists to articulate such notions, in particular about Mexican and U.S. cultural identity, concepts that challenge traditional markers of power and domination, and to achieve some inroads into the U.S.-led global era's supremacy over the Mexican population. In this refreshing exercise of the imagination and freedom of expression, contemporary Mexican cartoonists in cyberspace demonstrate that they know the language of the global era and that they are able to use it to contest the location of Mexico as a nation within this new planetary trend. They have recast notions of Mexican and U.S. cultural images to indicate ways to potentially empower Mexican society to develop new roles in a world whose physical boundaries have been at least partly evaporated by the Internet. Because of its transborder, transtemporal nature, the Internet can reach more informed and thinking Mexican citizens with the hope of adjusting both the country's historical cultural notion of self and its contemporary stance with regard to action in the world and at home. As I have suggested, Mexican contemporary cartoonists in cyberspace accomplish these goals by questioning the binary oppositions that have dominated the scholarly debate about the Mexican-U.S. relationship.

NOTES

1.   I use the words "cyberspace," "cybermedia," "cybercartoons," "hypermedia," "hyperspace," interchangeably, following Fredric Jameson's trend in *The Postmodern, or the Cultural Logic of Late Capitalism*, where he uses the terms "hyperspace" (38, 44) and "cyberpunk" (38).

2.   *La Jornada* is the medium with by far the most updated and extensive archives on the Internet. It is also the most visited Mexican medium in cyberspace. *El Universal* also has an archive of previous editions, although not as extensive as *La Jornada*'s, which goes back to 29 March 1996. *Milenio* posts only the cartoons of the week on its site and does not keep an accessible archive of past publications. I have excluded *Proceso* and *Reforma* since they charge to access previous publications in cyberspace and do not keep archives of older political cartoons. Neither *El Heraldo de México* nor *Novedades* have cartoon archives online, as is the case for *El Economista*, *El financiero*, and *La crónica de hoy*. Since an important aspect of my rationale is easy, public access

to political cartoons through the Internet, I have excluded these media from my analysis.

3. See my article "¿Puede Internet?" translated into Portuguese as "Poderia Internet?"

4. In reflecting upon the analyses of political cartoons by Rosaura Sánchez and Beatrice Pita, and quoting Naomi Lindstrom's article "The Single-Panel Cartoon," Morris affirms that for political caricature to be understood it "must be anchored in popular culture while at the same time *shaping perceptions* and popular narratives" (130; my emphasis). Morris also proposes that Mexican caricatures focusing on the United States offer a "distinct discourse on the nation" and "serve to define Mexico" (163); I agree with this premise. I propose that Mexican political cartoons in cyberspace, due to its larger and unrestricted audience reach, also serve to redefine the cultural identity of the United States—within Mexican society, at least—in the global era. Another premise that my essay shares with Morris's work is his recognition of the "asymmetry" of the relationship between Mexico and the United States (135, 145, 147).

5. I share Liestøl's view and expand his notion of the "reader" to incorporate "users" or "consumers" of information in cybermedia. The complex and paradoxical features of cyberspace are further highlighted by Mireille Rosello in *The Screener's Maps*, where she states that the Internet—paradoxically, because it is a medium that can store "millions of bytes of information . . . instantaneously"—might end up turning literature into "a variation of oral performance" (147). I contend that Rosello's assumption about literary works in cyberspace can be extended to other genres on the Web, such as political cartoons. In Mexico, these inject an intense oral performativity into the political contextualization that cybermedia invite the reader to rearticulate.

6. By "criollos" I refer to the sons (and daughters, absent in this historical account) of Spaniards born in the Americas, who launched the independence struggle. Place of birth was at the core of the insurrection, since criollos could not hold the positions of political power and representation that Peninsulars could from the beginning of the colonization process until around 1824, when independence was mainly consolidated throughout the countries that now constitute Latin America. However, the criollos did not create a nation/state project inclusive of other groups, especially those marked by ethnic differences—including mestizos (those of ethnic mixture, such as of European and indigenous natives), native indigenous, or Afro descendants also born in the Americas (Anderson 49, 81, 150, 192, 203).

7. As I elaborate elsewhere, it is evident that the EZLN presence on the Internet has, at a minimum, reinforced survival of the Zapatistas through the years. To cite but one other example of cyberspace's contestatory potential, recent massive demonstrations in Mexico City against the law meant to further privatize PEMEX were reportedly organized through the Internet and cell phones (*La Jornada* online, 14 April 2008, *elsenderocontraelfraude2006.blogspot.com/*; *kikka-roja.blogspot.com/*), or even YouTube videos.

8. This bill, approved by the Senate Judiciary Committee on 27 March 2006 (*www.whitehouse.gov/news/releases/2006/03/20060327–1.html*), has a follow-up bill, the Border Security and Immigration Reform Act of 2007, introduced in the U.S. Senate on 18 January 2007 (*www.whitehouse.gov/infocus/immigration/*).

9. "¡Que no se aprobó la reforma migratoria! . . . ¡Qué bueno, que no permitan más extranjeros ilegales en nuestro territorio!"

10. President Bush signed a bill to construct this wall on 26 October 2006. See *www.whitehouse.gov/news/releases/2006/10/20061026.html*.

11. "Quiero intervenir teléfonos, aplicar toques y meter tehuacanazos." "Como policía

del mundo en el nuevo milenio, Estados Unidos está reivindicando métodos policía-
cos mexicanos del siglo pasado."

12. "El que a spots mata, a spots muere."

13. It is widely believed that fraud granted the presidency to the right-wing representative of the currently ruling PAN (Partido de Acción Nacional/National Action Party),
Felipe Calderón, who won the election in July 2006 by a margin of about 0.6 percent
(244,000 votes at the national level) over the leftist candidate of the PRD (Partido
Revolucionario Democrático/Democratic Revolutionary Party), Andrés Manuel
López Obrador, commonly known as AMLO. Cartoonists in cybermedia have
portrayed the outcome of these elections as a questionable process that has deterred
democracy in Mexico. Some of these cartoonists openly depict electoral fraud, a
political practice that in their view has become a national institution. Another topic
for recent cartoons online is the elite's longtime maintenance of the indigenous
populations of Mexico in oblivion. On this issue, cartoonists have addressed the
recent teachers' association uprising to demand better salaries in Oaxaca, a southern
Mexican state characterized by its combative indigenous populations. The government, along with the ruling elite in the cartoonists' portrayal, have ignored popular
demands until they became nationally known around June 2006. The government's
lack of response and the teachers' escalating anger provoked the threat of military
intervention by the Mexican Army, according to Mexican media reports. The threat
turned into tangible danger on 28 October 2006, when military troops of the state of
Oaxaca opened fire against civilians and international journalists on the streets. This
military action resulted in the killing of U.S. American videographer Bradley Roland
Will, thirty-six years old, from IndyMedia. Also Policía Federal Preventiva [Preventive
Federal Police] troops entered the main square of Oaxaca City on 30 October 2006,
just as I was finishing this essay; civil demonstrators were gathered at this central location. Other national concerns that have drawn the attention of Mexican political cartoonists in cyberspace include Mexico's involvement in *narco* trafficking; the killing of
women in Ciudad Juárez, Chihuahua, across from El Paso, Texas; domestic violence
and the rising censorship of human sexual behavior promoted by the Opus Dei right-
wingers in positions of power in Mexico's PAN-lead government; and, lately, freedom
of speech and respect for the physical safety of journalists.

WORKS CITED

Anderson, Benedict. *Imagined Communities: Reflections on the Origin and Spread of
      Nationalism.* New York: Verso, 1983.

Aarseth, Espen J. "Nonlinearity and Literary Theory." Landow 51–86.

Barajas, Rafael (el Fisgón). *El país de 'El Ahuizote': la caricatura mexicana de oposición du-
      rante el gobierno de Sebastián Lerdo de Tejada (1872–1876).* Mexico: Fondo de Cultura
      Económica, 2005.

——. *La historia de un país en caricatura: caricatura mexicana de combate (1826–1872).*
      Mexico: Arte e Imagen; Consejo Nacional para la Cultura y las Artes, 2000.

Bhabha, Homi H. *The Location of Culture.* New York: Routledge, 1994.

Brooks, David. "Migrantes contribuyen con más fondos a las economías de México y EU
      que el TLC." *La Jornada,* 18 January 2007.
      www.jornada.unam.mx/2007/01/18/index.php?section=politica.

Chacón, Hilda. "¿Puede Internet (ó la lógica del capitalismo avanzado) subvertir el proyecto de la globalización?" *CiberLetras: Revista de Crítica Literaria y de Cultura / Journal of Literary Criticism and Culture* 4 (2001) ISSN: 1523–1720. *www.lehman.edu/ciberletras/* or *www.lehman.cuny.edu/ciberletras/.*

———. "Poderia Internet (ou lógica do capitalismo avançado) subverter o projeto de globalização?" *DataGramaZero: Revista de Ciência da Informaçã* 2.3 (2001) ISSN 1517–3801. *www.dgz.org.br/* or *www.dgzero.org/.*

González Amador, Roberto. "El TLC no es opción de crecimiento para México." *La Jornada*, 29 November 2006. *www.jornada.unam.mx/2006/11/29/index. php?section=economia.*

———. "Grandes empresarios frenan el crecimiento de México: BM." *La Jornada*, 27 November 2006. *www.jornada.unam.mx/2006/11/27/index.php?section=economia.*

———. "Remesas, motor de la economía: respaldan consumo de mexicanos." *La Jornada*, 30 August 2006. *www.jornada.unam.mx/2006/08/30/030n1eco.php.*

Jameson, Fredric. *The Postmodern, or the Cultural Logic of Late Capitalism.* Durham: Duke University Press, 1994.

Joysmith, Claire, and Clara Lomas, eds. *One Wound for Another. Una herida por otra. Testimonios de Latin@s in the U.S. through Cyberspace. 11 de septiembre de 11 marzo de 2002.* Mexico: Universidad Nacional Autónoma de México, 2005.

Landow, George P., ed. *Hyper/Text/Theory.* Baltimore: Johns Hopkins University Press, 1994.

———. "What's a Critic to Do?" Landow 1–48.

Liestøl, Gunnar. "The Reader's Narrative in Hypertext." Landow 87–120.

Minh-ha, Trinh. *Woman, Native, Other: Writing Postcoloniality and Feminism.* Bloomington: Indiana University Press, 1989.

Morris, Stephen D. *Gringolandia: Mexican Identity and Perceptions of the United States.* Oxford: Rowman and Littlefield, 2005.

Monsiváis, Carlos. "Will Nationalism Be Bilingual?" *Mass Media and Free Trade: NAFTA and the Cultural Industries.* Austin: University of Texas Press, 1997. 131–41.

Rosello, Mireille. "The Screener's Maps." Landow 121–58.

Said, Edward. *Orientalism.* New York: Knopf, 1979.

U.S. Congress. USA Patriot Act. 26 October 2001. *www.gpoaccess.gov/topics/military.html.*

Walsh, Joan. "The Abu Ghraib Files." Salon.com. 14 March 2006. *www.salon.com/news/abu_ghraib/2006/03/14/introduction/.*

White House. "President Bush Signs Secure Fence Act." News release. 26 October 2006. *www.whitehouse.gov/news/releases/2006/10/20061026.html.*

CHAPTER 12

A Clash of Civilizing Gestures

Mexican Intellectuals
Confront a Harvard Scholar

Ignacio Corona

Welcome to the Alamo, Mr. Huntington!
—Pat Buchanan

Partial truths or half-truths are often more insidious
than total falsehoods.
—Samuel P. Huntington

Modern political thought has striven to differentiate the properly politi-cal issues from the ethnocultural ones, often embedded in the process of nation building. Some conceptions have underscored the priority of the cultural community over the political one, while others—specifically that conception known as republican nationalism—have held that the political com-munity is or should be privileged over the cultural one (Bauböck). The global phe-nomenon of migration, with its increased contact among cultural communities and ethnicities, has often provided a motive for the ethnocultural elements to be-come more salient within the receiving countries. In effect, groups opposed to migration resort to an ethnocultural definition of the nation to reclaim it or save it from the recent arrivals. While up to this point anti-immigrant manifestations have not reached a critical level in the United States, the country has not been an exception to this worldwide phenomenon, as evidenced by a variety of expressions, from the collective actions of self-appointed border vigilantes to the publication of books or manifestos. One such text is *Who Are We? The Challenges to America's Na-tional Identity* (2004) by Samuel P. Huntington, which underscores the importance of those ethnocultural elements for the viability of the nation as it warns about the dangers facing American national identity due to the increase of Hispanic—in particular Mexican—migration. In spite of a well-orchestrated publicity cam-paign, as represented by its preview in *Foreign Policy*, the journal of the Council on Foreign Relations—the most influential private organization on the subject in the country—the book has failed to become a best seller. And yet, due to its confrontational position, alarmist tone, and the academic notoriety of its author, it has prompted numerous responses in the media, as well as in academic circles, in both Mexico and the United States.[1] Considering Huntington's background as former presidential advisor (for two years he served on the National Security Council during President Carter's administration), but most importantly because of the lessons of history, his critics have argued that such a book provides a rationalization for a potentially dangerous xenophobic discourse (Galindo Quiñónez).

While the primary context in which *Who Are We?* inscribes itself is that of the national debate on migration, I propose that it is the larger context of cultural responses to the social, economic, and cultural impact of globalization, with their manifest interest in the notions of national or group identities, that can provide the most comprehensive perspective regarding the book's public intervention. Indeed, the diverse effects of globalization continue to be a source of anxiety in the U.S. academic world, as the sociologist Arjun Appadurai observed more than a decade ago (1). In this essay, I explore the reception of *Who Are We?* among Mexican intellectuals, especially in relation to the long tradition of meditations on the Mexican character and national identity. This reception reveals that the identitarian politics at the basis of Mexican nationalism (and related cultural discourses) is seemingly undergoing a mutation. In that sense, some intellectuals are carrying out complex ideological maneuvers to establish unprecedented levels of connection with the Anglo-Protestant ethos, while making an effort to salvage the cultural difference model implemented by postrevolutionary nationalism since the early 1920s. At the same time—as Mexican philosopher José Vasconcelos did early in the twentieth century—some Mexican critics propose cultural *mestizaje* (crossbreeding) as a more suitable model than the puritanical politics of exclusion and purity for responding to the quandaries posed by the social and cultural effects of globalization. And yet the prevailing culturalist focus of both the book and most of its critiques deflects attention from other political, social, and economic issues at the forefront of the complex relationship between Mexico and the United States.

The Apocalypse's Harbinger Visits Veracruz

A recognized expert on foreign policy and national security, Huntington committed what could be considered a diplomatic faux pas during his intervention at a business summit, not long after the publication of his controversial book. He declared that Mexican migrants, who annually remit more than twenty billion dollars to Mexico, constituted "a serious threat to the U.S. national security," as they could introduce into that country weapons of mass destruction. His recommendation was that the U.S./Mexico border be further militarized or closed altogether. While his remarks did not necessarily require a neutral audience, given that the event was held in the city of Veracruz and, naturally, most of those present were

Mexicans, the journalists covering the event considered his comments a provocation. Mexico City's newspaper *La Crónica* reported the incident online with the following headline: "According to Huntington, Mexicans can introduce weapons of mass destruction in the U.S.; national intellectuals refute him."[2] Spain's *El País* informed readers: "Mexico rebels against Huntington. Mexican intellectuals denounce the demagogy and ignorance of a text by the American political scientist" (Aznárez).[3] According to the *La Crónica* article, political analyst Jesús Silva-Herzog Márquez openly criticized Huntington's thesis by observing that in the writings of the "Stephen King of U.S. political science" there is always "a tone of alarm to catch the attention of an academic community that is not aware of what is really occurring."[4] What seemingly bothered the audience most was not the content of a statement clearly in tune with Huntington's writings on "the Mexican problem" and his known knack for grandiose announcements and controversy, but his refusal to engage in an open dialogue with them, which came to represent for many at the event an example of the arrogance associated with U.S. foreign policy in its political and commercial dealings with its neighbor to the south (Ruíz Mondragón).

Huntington's implied transfer of the U.S. conflict with Islamic fundamentalists toward the border with Mexico is far from an innocent geopolitical slippage. The unexpected linkage of undocumented migration with Islamic terrorism alludes to a comparable source of fear and anger. Furthermore, it suggests that these phenomena are the most important threats the United States faces at this juncture: Both forces are equally destructive. If terrorism attacks U.S. economic interests and human lives, Huntington sees Mexican migration as the only threat capable of destroying the nation's inner fabric, the Anglo-Protestant core of values that constitutes the "American national identity" (*Who Are We?* xvi).

This figurative association may also explain the underlying continuity between his two most recent books, *The Clash of Civilizations and the Remaking of World Order* (1996), in which he elaborates on the irreducible differences between Muslims and Westerners, and *Who Are We? The Challenges to America's National Identity*. Just as *The Clash of Civilizations* identifies unbridgeable cultural fault lines to "predict" an unavoidable East-West confrontation, in *Who Are We?* the author identifies a similar cultural conflict, this time taking place inside the country. This book reinforces a strand of U.S. public opinion that espouses a strong nativist stance in the debate on migration by articulating a structure of xenophobic feelings against a background of an imminent apocalyptic scenario. In that sense, Huntington's scholarship is put at the service of political positions to rationalize personal motivations.[5]

Just as in *The Clash of Civilizations*, instead of dissecting and explaining the phenomenon at hand from its multiple angles, Huntington reinforces his anti-Hispanic rhetoric in *Who Are We?* with a peculiar combination of statistics, personal observations, and citations to "demonstrate" how Hispanic culture imperils America's culture.[6] As an extended meditation on the origin and nature of national (American) identity and how it is threatened by several cultural challenges, the author upholds three main theses in this book. Thesis 1: The meaning and saliency of identity has varied over time. There have been moments in U.S. history in which national identity has been unquestioned. However, beginning in the 1960s, "subnational, dual-national, and transnational identities began to rival and erode the preeminence of national identity" (xv). Thesis 2: "The American Creed," the product of the distinctive Anglo-Protestant culture of the founding settlers, is "the crucial defining element of American identity" (xv). The key elements of that culture include: "the English language; Christianity; religious commitment; English concepts of the rule of law, the responsibility of rulers, and the rights of individuals; and dissenting Protestant values of individualism, the work ethic, and the belief that humans have the ability and the duty to try to create a heaven on earth, a 'city on a hill' " (xvi). This subordination of the country's democratic foundations—synthesized by the American Creed—to an implicit ethnocultural hierarchy is in conflict with the credo as a set of values shared on political grounds. Although Huntington states that in studying the American identity he has left behind "the racial and ethnic component" (xvii), his claim that a core culture is more important than others in the constitution of a national identity definitely involves a "strong conception" of ethnicity (Glazer 109–10). Thesis 3: Anglo-Protestant culture has been crucial to American identity for three centuries. For the first time in history, this identity has been challenged by the dissemination of the doctrines of multiculturalism and diversity and, particularly, by the spread of Spanish "as the second American language and the Hispanization trends in American society" (xv–xvi). Among Hispanics, Mexicans are the least inclined to assimilation: "The driving force behind this Hispanization, the Mexican influx, shows no signs of weakening" (317). The author agrees with Morris Janowitz, for whom "the Mexicans are unique as an immigrant group in the persistent strength of their communal bonds" (cited in *Who Are We?* 245). Huntington identifies six factors that explain why Mexicans have failed to assimilate and why they present a problem of integration: geographical proximity, large numbers, illegality, regional concentration, persistence, and historical presence (222–30). These six factors, however, are secondary with respect to the main difference he finds between the two groups: Anglo-Protestant and Mexican cultural values. This difference is what constitutes a danger for "American" identity and culture.

As could be expected, the publication of Huntington's article and subsequent book triggered a firestorm of critical response in the Mexican media, a clear indication that the professor of political science had touched a sensitive collective fiber. The condemnation of the book's xenophobic premises was unanimous; what was diverse was the expression of the responses, from a sort of *ninguneo* (pretending to ignore the interlocutor and his diatribes as a way to diminish his importance), to name-calling ("learned ignorant"; "masked racist"), to implicit celebrations of the impact of Mexican culture abroad, of which the scholar's anxiety was a clear symptom.

In the first group of responses, Huntington appeared as just one more anti-immigrant and anti-Mexican academic, and the best solution was simply to ignore his book. Political commentator Denise Dresser considered that Huntington had become "a dreadful analyst for which he should not be read, but confronted." In a second group of responses, the tone was harsher. Some commentators hardly disguised their anger, aiming charges of ignorance and racism at the controversial author. Writer José María Pérez Gay identified "ridiculous and incredible absurdities" in the text and added that "[the author's ignorance] knows no limits."[7] For the novelist Fernando del Paso, "to talk about a Latin American civilization contrary to Western civilization—that is, in a present or future, ongoing or probable clash—is a folly that could be understandable in an Italian laborer, but which is inexcusable stated by an American scholar."[8] Adolfo Aguilar Zínser, former Mexican ambassador to the United Nations, considered the text "offensive and degrading" in a piece he wrote for *Reforma*.[9] Carlos Fuentes considered that Huntington's tactics against the spread of Spanish in the United States amounted to "fear of the 'other,' so favored by fascist mentalities" (81). Others accused Huntington of dishonesty in the use of references, sources, and quotes—phrases taken out of context. Some made it a priority to defend national culture by inverting the terms and the implicit hierarchies employed by the Harvard professor. Enrique Krauze, for instance, defended the virtues of cultural mestizaje, which he positioned as far superior to the exclusionary and divisive Puritanical roots that still shape U.S. mainstream culture: "Mexicans understand the advantages and satisfactions of ethnic assimilation very well, because for centuries (in fact, since pre-Hispanic times) their history has been spectacularly inclusive. Not just ethnic mixing, but cultural mixing especially, is the gift of Mexico, a country in which Indians, blacks, Spaniards, and other Europeans have mingled and been able to live together through centuries" (*Identity* 31–32). Nowhere in Krauze's text is there a hint of irony in his proposition, as if he ignored or downplayed "the darker side of *mestizaje*" (Miller 4). This selective amnesia, which erases the implicit violence of mestizaje, withdraws the concept from any colonialist connotation and therefore from actual asymmetries of power in its colonial and postcolonial occurrence. As exemplified by these critics, Mexican intellectuals were responding to Huntington with their own civilizing model, a corollary of which would be that U.S. society could eradicate racism by promoting "nonpure ethnics" (mulatto, mestizo, etc.) as the ideal type of U.S. citizen.

Finally, a third group of critics, espousing a recalcitrant nationalist position, celebrated the vitality of Mexican culture and the "challenge" it represented to U.S. culture and identity. Mexicans could well represent the role of uncivilized barbarians, speaking their own tongue and maintaining their barbarian customs, as long as they did not surrender to or were not assimilated (and ontologically wiped out) by the dominant society. Like the *rudos* (bad guys or rule benders) in the sport of *lucha libre* (Mexican wrestling), this group found a sort of symbolical reward and a sense of self-importance in being considered *rudo* (rough) in contrast to the *técnicos* (good guys, technicians, or rule abiders)—just in the fact of being different, in their anti-character, which while in action makes irrelevant the fact of being the target of the insults and whistles of the public. In a way, this nonassimilationist posture derives from the sense of uniqueness crafted by postrevolutionary nationalism and further elaborated by the philosophers of *la mexicanidad* (Mexicanness).

In the wake of the visceral criticism in the printed and electronic media, some scholars have since provided a more in-depth analysis of the polemical book by orienting their responses toward its political implications; such writings include those published by scholars associated with CIDE (Centro de Investigación y Docencia Económicas / Center of Economic Research and Teaching) and El Colegio de México. These essays have taken the discussion out of the essentialist arena by examining the text's ideological and political underpinnings, as represented by Fernando Escalante Gonzalbo's essay published by the South American journal *Nueva Sociedad* in an issue titled "Latino Culture in the United States."[10] Escalante also edited *Otro sueño americano* (Another American Dream), a collection of essays that beyond its dominant satirical tone insightfully detects the grave misconceptions and methodological faults found in Huntington's book. In an interview with Ariel Ruiz Mondragón that appeared online just months after the publication of *Who Are We?* Escalante questioned the book's value and its author's apparent intentions:

> Independently from the book's academic value, which is not much, from a political perspective it is an important book, and hence my interest in discussing it. I am not interested in Professor Huntington's opinions: this fellow is an evangelical protestant and believes that everyone should be an evangelical protestant. That is his own problem, as is the fact that he does not like Mexicans. The real problem of the text lies in the fact that he tries to justify, establish and disseminate these opinions as if they were the result of scientific findings. There lies an imposture.[11]

The semantic relationship between "imposture" and "impostor" could well summarize the critical reception of Huntington's arguments among Mexican intellectuals. That many voices in the United States and throughout the Hispanic communities joined the chorus of critical responses was also due to the vagueness of the term "national challenge" in such a text. In effect, Mexican migration appears as only one element of the multifarious "Hispanic challenge." The referent is multiple: Latino migrants in general; Hispanics in the United States; Hispanic culture; Mexicans in general; Catholics; even advocates of multiculturalism, and so on. While this semantic elasticity may be methodologically flawed, it is rhetorically important to the author's key populist denunciation: the danger of an unprecedented collapse and the urgent need to rescue and reconstruct the nation and its true identity from the "silent invasion."[12]

Trojan Burritos and the Obsessive Search for an Enemy

Who Are We? continues Huntington's career-long search for national enemies, perhaps as a personal legacy of the cold-war era. In a Nietzschean perspective that conceives war as the prime engine of history, enemies are as feared as desired (inasmuch as they are useful for reinforcing group cohesion and producing group identity). In that way, they are needed for the country's survival; otherwise, "national consciousness can get unfocused and national identity eroded [and, in their absence], Americans can turn against each other" (*Who Are We?* 120). If up to *The Clash of Civilizations* the author had found those enemies of America abroad, the relative novelty in *Who Are We?* is that he finds them at home. An apparently innocuous enemy lurks within the alleged "Hispanization" of the country. Mexican migrants, in particular, operate as Trojan horses, or rather, as Jay M. Sepúlveda playfully puts it, as "Trojan burritos" (4). The culinary aspect—in this allusion to the ubiquitous Mexican cuisine-based creation—is at the heart of the danger that Huntington perceives. In effect, not only the physical presence of migrants, but also their culture—including their food, music, language, and so on—is a threat to the (dominant) national identity. This enemy is especially dangerous, because his friendly face is only a mask. "They are among us, but they are not like us. Hispanic immigrants are loyal to their original countries, as they are to their culture, religion, and language"—this seems to be the author's message.

In supporting his argument regarding the Mexican threat, Huntington suggests that migration amounts to a "silent invasion," a "reconquista" [reconquest]: "No other immigrant group in American history has asserted or has been able to assert a historical claim to American territory. Mexicans and Mexican Americans can and do make that claim. Almost all of Texas, New Mexico, Arizona, California, Nevada, and Utah was part of Mexico . . . [and] Mexicans do not forget these events. Quite understandably, they feel that they have special rights in these territories" (*Who Are We?* 229–30). In an ironic bout of guilty conscience the author seems to be interpreting the spatial concentration of migrants—in decades-old traditional destinations (Arizona, Texas, California)—through a kind of palimpsest with the episode of the founding of the Republic of Texas.[13] Enrique Krauze, discards the idea as an absurdity:

> The obvious question is: who made this claim, and when? No serious (or unserious) figure of the twentieth century, political or intellectual—at least, none that I know of—ever proposed something so absurd. . . . Indeed, during the first decades of the century, the prevailing sentiment was nearer the reverse: a Mexican fear—not unfounded, at least until 1927, when President Coolidge was a step away from declaring war on "Soviet Mexico"—of a new invasion by the United States. Huntington maintains that Mexicans "haven't forgotten" the war of 1847, and warns that our plan is to turn California

into "Mexifornia" or the "Northern Republic." . . . Basing his judgment on anecdotal evidence (the booing of the American team at a soccer game in Los Angeles) and the sentimental or rhetorical declarations of Mexican politicians (intended for their constituencies in Mexico), without offering a single serious or reliable example, Huntington feeds the false notion that Mexicans harbor a historic grievance against the United States—for which the migrants, moved by some kind of blind collective subconscious, are now exacting payment. It looks like Manifest Destiny revisited and reversed. But it is simply not true. Anti-Americanism, at least of the raging kind that is so common around the world today, is far from being a popular sentiment in Mexico. (*Identity* 29–30)

To feed the xenophobia that underlies his claims, Huntington relies on myths rather than facts. To this end, he refers to an argument that has circulated in and out of academia since at least the emergence of the Chicano movement of Aztlán and is somehow related to the internal colonialism thesis defended by some Chicano historians (i.e., Rodolfo Acuña), which Huntington does not include in his speculation. According to this argument, Mexicans are going to claim the territories the United States took by force in the nineteenth century. The migrants would be, therefore, pawns within this grand conspiracy between Mexicans and Mexican Americans. For this assertion, Huntington seemingly relies on David Hanson's *Mexifornia: A State of Becoming*, a book that launches a vitriolic attack on Mexican migration and Mexicans in general.

Hanson is one of Huntington's intellectual companions in the ideological battle for radicalizing public opinion, as they conceive the Mexican problem in identical terms. Chapter 1 in Hanson's book, "What Is So Different about Mexican Immigration?" becomes "Why Mexican Immigration Differs," as a subsection of chapter nine in *Who Are We?* It is not a coincidence, then, that the two writers (uncritically) cite the same sources. For instance, Huntington quotes the professor to whom Hanson also gives authority to predict the formation of an independent Hispanic republic, "La República del Norte," encompassing the entire southwest United States by 2080.[14] More interested in producing an impact on the media than in a fair and substantial discussion of the subject, these authors seem intent on reinforcing prejudice and negative attitudes, especially among less-informed readers.[15] The social implications are potentially damaging for the group that now occupies the category of "national enemy" in Huntington's framework, because it becomes, as never before, the receptacle of social phobias and anxieties. If ideology can be a fantasy, a social fantasy (Escalante, *Enemigo* 57), even a paranoid scheme, it can also produce real effects and filter the way reality is seen and understood.

The publicized "prophetic" qualities of Huntington's *The Clash of Civilizations* can best be understood in this light not as a reading of the future, but as a rationale for a particular political or military agenda. Similarly, *Who Are We?* may not predict an immigration backlash or an attack on the Latino community, but it justifies actions that could be taken—for instance, raids against undocumented or suspected undocumented Latino workers—or anti-Mexican provisions, such as the one recently proposed by the Appropriations Committee of the Arizona House of Representatives.[16] More than a prediction, the text provides a set of "motives and justifications" for possible action from governmental agencies or even from mere groups of citizens. A more recent complement to Huntington's anti-immigrant argument comes via another Harvard scholar, Robert D. Putnam.[17] Focusing on the concept of "social capital" and using categories such as "trust or distrust of neighbors" in his surveys, Putnam and his associates make the "discovery" that, in the "short and medium run," immigration and ethnic diversity challenge social solidarity and inhibit social capital. What comes as a surprise is the naiveté of researchers who apparently had expected that complete assimilation and effective intercultural knowledge and communication occur instantly upon contact with other groups by a sort of social osmosis. Their study does not hypothesize how the inhibition of social capital they find, if verified by other studies, can be diminished by the adequate participation of a diversity of social and political actors. Just like Huntington, Putnam recommends constructing a new, broader sense of WE to dampen the negative effects of "diversity," although he imagines such an entity as transformative and not merely "given" (138–39).

The interventions of Hanson, Putnam, and Huntington in ongoing debates over migration, however, obscure the role they inadvertently perform: that of reflecting indirectly on the impact of globalization in the United States, of which migration is a by-product. But they do so by treating these effects as isolated social phenomena and focusing on immediate demographic consequences and supposed corrosive cultural impact. The result of this methodological procedure is a total erasure of the economic, which coincidentally is one of the common rhetorical procedures of "conservative populism" (Frank 242). In consequence, neither Huntington's nor Putnam's approach to the subject reflects on the U.S. role in "worldwide" globalization and its strong impact south of the border, which subsequently increases the possibility of migration, let alone proposes relevant legislation on the main issues discussed.

Huntington displaces the socioeconomic problematic of migration to work with imaginary constructs such as identity. His culturalist approach is channeled by preconceived notions and stereotypes that reaffirm the migrants' otherness to conclude, beforehand, that their ethnocultural difference is precisely the main obstacle against their assimilation. By metonymically subsuming the phenomenon of migration in the figure of the migrant, he constructs an ideological (or cultural) enemy out of the unsuspecting (documented or undocumented) worker. Huntington endows this "enemy" with the unprecedented power of corroding the "essential and homogeneous" core of U.S. society and national identity, regardless of the marginal place the migrants may occupy in that society.[18] In that sense, his entire theoretical construction in *Who Are We?*—not unlike that in his *The Clash of Civilizations*—constitutes an elaborate rationalization of the primal instincts: fear and aggression. This seems to be Carlos Fuentes's interpretation when, playing along with the paranoid fear of a supposed clash between Anglo and Hispanic "civilizations," he bluntly states that "we [Mexicans] are winners, not losers; the loser is Huntington, isolated in his imaginary land of Anglo speaking, white, and Protestant racial purity" (81). In any case, constructing positive international relationships is evidently not on Huntington's academic or political agenda. Searching for ways to deter conflict or devising strategies of cooperation among nations or communities is not part of his intellectual project, not even as a counterpart to the manifest impulse to detect "national enemies." It is possible to suspect, from a national security standpoint, that if an enemy is detected, the next step will be to neutralize it or, if possible, eliminate it altogether.

Identity, a Nontransferable Object

A fundamental aspect of *Who Are We?* that Mexican scholars have paid particular attention to is its underlying mythopoetic character. In effect, Huntington delimits and prescribes a certain normativity without making sure that what he describes exists. On this precise point, the culturalist approach turns naturalist by objectifying and trying to demonstrate that national identity can be proved scientifically. Such a proposition reminds us of Néstor García Canclini's observation that "the ultimate end of culture is to convert itself into nature" (*Culturas* 154). Although Huntington's analysis of identity follows a historical examination "to find meaning and virtue in America's past and in its possible future" (*Who Are We?* xvii), his discussion remains in the abstract due to his conviction that the core of U.S. identity has remained unchanged since the eighteenth century and has not been substantially affected by other (non-Anglo/Protestant) influences. This is one of the typical methodological errors of culturalism, a wishful desire for a nonexistent coherence (Bayart 63). Without connections among identity, culture, and historical circumstance, Huntington works with prepackaged monolithic notions and ethnocentric hierarchies in which one culture is inherently superior to others. Escalante Gonzalbo wonders in his interview with Ruiz Mondragón if Huntington has read anything written on the subject in the past century:

> Reading Huntington's book, observing his ignorance of all twentieth-century anthropology, and his contempt for the most elementary discretion and sobriety in the use of statistics, confronts us with a very delicate disjunctive: either the professor does not really know what anthropologists have written about, does not know what identity is, does not know how to use statistics, and therefore he is naïve or ignorant, or he does it in bad faith, deliberately concealing that [information]. In principle, I do not want to

attribute to him bad faith. I suppose he does not know, that indeed he has not read [about it].[19]

Huntington defends a ferocious monolingualism and a monotheist (Christian) culturalism, into which the other groups have to assimilate. He rejects hybridity or intercultural contact. Therefore, the "we" of the title establishes rules of membership to differentiate and exclude the "they," which encompasses not only the cultural others, but also those academics who supposedly have betrayed the values of national identity (*Who Are We?* 270). Such intolerant irrationalism forms the basis of all ultranationalisms and fundamentalisms, Escalante Gonzalbo writes: "Just like all culturalist arguments, Huntington's has a blind spot which reveals his political nature, given that it is contrary to reason: he cannot even admit that the existence of a collective subject as such, as subject with a fixed and unique identity, can be questioned. He does not discuss it or explain it. He takes it for granted as an absolute obviousness" (*Enemigo* 54).[20]

Huntington encompasses the political and ethnocultural senses of identity by basing his conception of identity on two fundamental characteristics: accepting the American creed (with its principles of liberty, equality, individualism, representative government, and private property) and sharing the core values of the Anglo-Protestant culture (*Who Are We?* 40–41). If, politically speaking, it is not necessary to be Anglo to accept the ideology of the American creed, the ethnocultural element establishes internal boundaries, because then the issue is not only a matter of sharing a given set of values. The moral superiority of Anglo-Protestant culture is the privilege of a group or a majority of its population. While Huntington does not explicitly use the term "race," his overt emphasis on the (idealized) recovery of the Anglo-Saxon ethos in the contemporary United States implies the inherent "benefit" of ethnic homogeneity. This is another way to frame the race issue: Transfer some of its properties to the culture of a group.

A Postnational Revelation

Huntington's cultural concerns with the homogeneous nature of the nation-state and the cohesion of a national identity are not detached from the material socioeconomic transformations taking place during the 1980s and 1990s, most of them—including increased Mexican migration—a direct or indirect impact of globalization. Jorge Larraín Ibáñez has convincingly argued that "the process of globalization has clearly eroded colonial or imperial identities" and that "it is possible to argue that due to this phenomenon of globalization and the growing dissolution of the ancient boundaries and barriers, all national identities are under pressure" (23). Therefore, the debate between (ultra)nationalist ideologies, such as the one represented by Huntington, and multiculturalism in the United States can be linked to those transformations and their cultural aftereffects as much as to the political legacy of the civil rights era. Beyond multiculturalism's properly representational demands, its crucial compensative aspects ultimately transmit the aspiration for social equality from a diversity of groups that address historical injustices and denounce socioeconomic and educational gaps. Against this move, *Who Are We?* aspires to defend unity as much as purity. In his emphasis on a national identity and a specific culture—the core culture—that Huntington perceives threatened by the mentioned demands, he attempts to delay the configuration of a more multicultural polity in U.S. society. As cultural critic Néstor García Canclini points out: "A defense of purity is imposed in many countries to counter modern tendencies to put specific elements of each ethnic group or nation into a relative context in order to construct democratic means of coexistence, complementarity, and multicultural forms of governing" ("North Americans" 145). Beneath Huntington's argument, it is possible to sense a resistance to political change, which is a common feature of both "the two Americas" literature and the literature of national decadence (Allan Bloom's *The Closing of the American Mind*, Dinesh D'Souza's *Illiberal Education: The Politics of Race and Sex on Campus*, and many others). Such a negation of social change is based more on ideology (or nostalgia) than on an accurate depiction of society, which, as a historical entity, changes and evolves.

In the same decades that the debates on multiculturalism were occurring in the United States, a profound revision of the tenets of the dominant cultural discourse took place in Mexico. Amid an acute economic crisis, the ideology of state protectionism—as much an economic as a political policy—was abandoned in favor of the neoliberal model. The application of this paradigm directly shook the decades-old corporatist system and impacted established sociocultural forms and patterns of interaction at all levels. These events renovated a critical interest in such anchors of individual and collective forms of identity as nationalism, language, and culture. Mexico's social scientists and cultural critics attempted to produce interpretive frameworks to create meaning out of the new sociocultural realities: a country that underwent the crisis of legitimacy and ultimately loss of the power of the single-party system—the main axis of social articulation throughout the twentieth century; that was traversed by demographic flows; and that experienced an increasingly deterritorialized economy, which now depended on the income generated by its migrants as much as by the country's own productive apparatus, excepting revenue from oil. In this context, an essayistic discourse about post- and transnationalism emerged to fill the gaps opened by the new realities in the nationalist edifice.[21]

While the intensification of a redemptive identitarian politics in the United States might be different from the demands for a more effective pluralism in Mexico, there are important parallels. In both countries, those demands have confirmed the homogenizing and normative nature of national discourse. In the case of multiculturalism, one of its main arguments has been that the history of the United States and its narrative of social, economic, and political progress have traditionally focused on the majority, ignoring the contributions and the particular histories of marginalized groups.

The correspondent discourse in Mexican society is the recognition of its cultural plurality beyond its mestizo identity, and new legislation concerning gender and Indian rights—the latter evidently a direct response to the antiglobalization Zapatista uprising. In synthesis, cultural differences had been suppressed in favor of a unified ideological vision in the respective national histories. Intellectuals in Mexico have looked for a way to recognize such differences without undermining the concept of national identity.[22] They have yet to produce an alternative to the inherent identitarian problematic, and their work remains mostly corrective in nature, based on a critique of the essentialist subterfuges of hegemonic cultural discourse.

The introduction of such essentialism in what became Mexico's official cultural discourse after the 1910 Revolution was an ideological maneuvering to construct "a national identity"—an imagined collective being—in order to represent the country in "the concert of modern nations," to use an epochal expression. The resultant cultural difference, embedded in the concept of mestizaje, apparently conflicted with the universalizing project of modernity. However, such a difference, with respect to a "universal contemporary subject," constituted only the symbolization of a unified national culture, which in turn represented a territorialized and sovereign modern state. An aspiration to difference (the cultural uniqueness of the mestizo being) then complemented aspirations of independence and modernity. Significantly, in his *Labyrinth of Solitude* Paz writes about a desire to be "for the first time in our history, contemporary with the rest of men" (226).[23]

In consequence, the notion of mestizaje does not contradict that aspiration of modernity but enhances it, because it tries to eliminate all ethnic and class conflicts—and competing concepts of culture—that might become obstacles to a national reconstruction project. In that sense, it does not constitute a "regressive form of modernity," as has been recently argued for other national contexts (Bayart 38). The idea of a modern nation harmonically resolving its ethnic, cultural, and class differences in the master trope of mestizaje became the keystone of Mexico's modernization project. In consequence, modernization and national (mestizo) essence became indissolubly interrelated. As evidenced in the promotion of Mexico's tourism industry since the 1950s, the introspective search for the sources of the national character was a cultural reaction as much as a complement to the modernization project. With elements derived from positivism and psychoanalysis, an undeniable essentialism resulted inherent to constructions of *la mexicanidad* by Samuel Ramos, Octavio Paz, the Hiperión group, Jorge Carrión, and many others.

Such an essentialization is not too different from Huntington's musings about a homogeneous and transhistorical Anglo-Protestant Americanness. The essential *mexicanidad* and its related cultural nationalism articulate a system of inclusions and exclusions. Historical determinism, another evil, lurks nearby as well.

In effect, if culture is determined by those essences, change—or at least profound change—is not possible. That is why a given cultural essence persists through time. In consequence, political citizenship becomes subordinated to cultural citizenship; innate membership in a determined group becomes prevalent. For Huntington, true Americans are those close to the ethnocultural Anglo-Protestant eighteenth-century ideal. In the case of Mexico, essential Mexicans would be the mestizos tormented in their collective unconscious by the country's history and myths, the sons of La Malinche. If so, and despite the generous virtues attributed to the concept of mestizaje, other groups of Mexicans, like recent immigrants and their progeny, may be politically Mexican but not partake of or be marginal to that cultural essence. Because of this restrictive condition, there is a nativism common to both constructions of national identity.[24] If applied to cultural configurations rather than to ethnic-based notions of identity and understood as an evolving or flexible cultural process not unlike that of hybridity, a benign interpretation of mestizaje appears more predisposed to cultural exchange and acceptance of the other.[25] Seemingly unaware of the ambivalence of their generalizations in choosing specific features and dichotomies from the mass of existing cultural patterns and behaviors, cultural agents shaped—much more than "revealed"—an essential Mexican character.[26] In effect, within the cultural difference model, virtues—but also peculiarities and generalizations (most of them too stereotypical to begin with, but considered folksy, innocuous, and even colorful)—were mythologized, objecti-fied, and profusely reproduced throughout the twentieth century by a diversity of cultural agencies, Mexican and foreign alike. Ideal or not—within certain human-istic parameters—the importance lay in uniqueness: "¡Como México no hay dos!" [Mexico has no equal!].

Ironically, *Who Are We?* posits those cultural features and dichotomies as the reasons Mexican migrants are rejected as inassimilable subjects. If, in the "peda-gogic function" (in Homi Bhabha's term) of Mexican cultural discourse, the im-portance of history had been underscored as a way to instill a sense of nation-ality, in Huntington's view Mexican migrants appear too obsessed with the past and, therefore, as inadequate beings in a capitalist system oriented toward endless progression and requiring future-oriented subjects. Likewise, whereas family and communal bonds had been considered compatible with and even essential to the needs of the Mexican state, given the mutual reinforcement existing between state and family structures of control in Mexican society, in Huntington's controversial treatise the migrants appear unable to function in more abstract or impersonal organizational systems. And so on.

Huntington argues that the cultural values and traits that shape the migrants' mental and axiological schemes make them unfit to become true Americans. Their cultural predispositions impede their full assimilation into U.S. society (*Who Are We?* 244). Huntington has held up an ethnocentric (Anglo-Saxon) mirror in which these elements—such as Jorge Castañeda's "*mañana* syndrome" and what the for-

mer Mexican foreign affairs minister deems "ferocious differences" with the United
States—become unredeemable vices or ethnocultural (racial) defects (*Who Are
We?* 254). A generalization, cliché, or stereotype faces itself, but the mirror has
distorted the image. Huntington quotes Mexican and Mexican American intellectuals, researchers, businessmen (out of context and in a slanted manner, in most
cases) to make this "mirror operation" more effective and insidious; the message is:
"These are not my words, but their own words and characterizations of their own
people."[27] Taken aback by this "seemingly twisted" interpretation of the usual essentialist clichés of cultural texts, some Mexican intellectuals now finally realize the
problematic of sustaining dichotomies and characterizations of that nature. These
had seemingly served the purpose of constructing cultural difference, but stereo-
typing was built into the process. Many had forgotten about that underside of essentialism until *Foreign Policy* published Huntington's "The Hispanic Challenge."

For the neoliberals and technocrats who during *salinismo* (Salinas de Gortari's six years in office) had crafted the "new" international image of Mexico and
had lobbied for closer business relationships with its neighbor to the north, Huntington's text should have been a huge disappointment. In its telling omission of
NAFTA (North American Free Trade Agreement among the United States, Canada,
and Mexico), *Who Are We?* certainly does not share the optimism of its promoters
regarding the underlying vision of the trade agreement. Speculating on this point,
they might be surprised to learn about the persistence of a certain race and class
dynamic in the United States (perhaps assuming that the history of discrimination against all things Mexican was a thing of the past) and to discover that the
U.S. ideological scenario is not only trade driven, but also traversed by isolationist,
supremacist, religious fundamentalist, and diverse retrograde views. Would they
perhaps wonder whether NAFTA was a mere façade, in which case the United
States would not consider Mexico an equal business partner? How was it possible
that from its most famous university—the same institution that had graduated and
legitimized the grand artificer of neoliberalism, Carlos Salinas de Gortari ("Mexico's
Kemal Ataturk": Huntington's label)—came a discourse that set the country back
in time to a land of siesta, fiesta, and mañana? How could one of its most famous
scholars produce a pseudoacademic discourse full of stereotypes and describe Mexicans in such hostile terms, that is, as ideological and cultural enemies?

The occasion demanded that a prestigious member of the Mexican intelligentsia intervene and respond in his own terms to the Harvard scholar. Unfortunately, the response came exactly in the terms established by Huntington. I specifically refer to Enrique Krauze's articles because they constitute a timely and forceful
response, but even more because of Krauze's position as heir to Octavio Paz's role
as one of the intellectual caudillos of the Mexican cultural scene. In "El falso profeta" (The False Prophet) Krauze criticizes Huntington's article, but he does not
defy the professor's premises and ends up falling prey to his ideological trap, that
of essentialism.[28] According to Krauze, Mexicans are fundamentally good-natured

and hardworking (as opposed to their association with terrorism in Huntington's statements in Veracruz). He goes so far as to represent them as ideal subjects of economic exploitation, in a tacit agreement with Mexico's place in globalization as a huge reservoir of cheap labor ("Mexicans are not the 'enemy within': Simply stated, they are many and soon they will be more"). He even compares them favorably with the migrants that European countries receive ("So what's the problem? France and Germany can only dream of such immigrants") (*Identity* 32). While Krauze recognizes that migration is a "national shame," he does not deepen his critical assessment of Mexico's lack of economic growth and the pernicious social and economic effects of the model implemented by the latest administrations. His essay resembles former president Vicente Fox's emphasis on the importance of migration, as if this phenomenon was more than a temporary escape valve for the Mexican economy and was in fact a sound economic strategy of development for the country.

In this regard, Krauze's defense of the northbound migrants also belongs in the terrain of assimilationism. He tries to convince Huntington and the antimigration sector of U.S. society that the presence of the Mexican migrants not only is necessary for their economy, but should even be desired. He promotes a sort of affect theory of migration:

> Has Huntington ever seen the people he scorns? Has he spoken to them? No, he didn't feel the need to see them or to speak to them. . . . And the people are there, if he wishes to encounter them, in the restaurants of Manhattan, on the streets of Queens, in Central Park on Sundays. Quiet, obedient, cautious, law-abiding, peace-loving (above all peace-loving), they toil to send money to their families, and they dream (in Spanish or in English, what difference does it make?) about a better future. (*Identity* 32)

Supported by some of the same data that Huntington used to make the opposite point, Krauze is convinced that the migrant subject and his descendants will be loyal post-Mexicans:

> Mexicans will seek to become part of American culture (and American cultures: Korean, African, European, South American, Jewish, Anglo-Saxon), and to assimilate in the essential areas: language, business, politics, respect for the law, and, in the middle term, marriage. They will certainly maintain their differences in other areas: They will stick to their families if they can bring them; they will opt for citizenship, if they are allowed; they will miss the land they came from for a generation or two; they will cling quite wisely to their cuisine; they will continue to be Catholics and to celebrate the holidays of the civil and religious calendar. (*Identity* 32)

But like the Harvard scholar—and against the evidence provided by many studies that prove that most Mexican immigrants do not settle permanently in the United States—Krauze conceives migrants not as temporary migrants but as aspiring U.S. citizens escaping their own national citizenship.[29] Such a postnational view downplays the fact that migration is mostly a rational economic strategy propelled by the salary differential between the two countries. Migrants are then active economic agents (more salient in this regard than political subjects or cultural citizens) in the same way that they are also objects (often victims) of globalizing processes. Krauze does not take the discussion to other (less essentialist) grounds by analyzing, for instance, contradictions between the U.S. political legal framework and its own economy, which end up criminalizing migrants, or by commenting on the demand for workers and a visa system that exacerbates the problem. His efforts to accommodate the essential Mexican to the mold of the essential hard-working Anglo reveal the success of neoliberal ideology, and the anti- or postnational proposition of globalization, in modifying the premises of once hegemonic nationalist cultural discourse. The cultural difference model espoused by that discourse is thus subtly abandoned to produce a view in which the essential Mexican subject is almost identical to the essential Anglo national subject (apart from food and religion).[30]

This postnational turn of Mexican cultural discourse revives decades-old concerns with the Americanization of Mexican society due to the nonreflective adoption of customs, values, and patterns of consumption, not to mention cultural identity, but this time at the level of the cultural elites (Monsiváis, *Will* 131–32). Many Mexicans have shared such a fear in the antipode of Huntington's anxieties, as exemplified by an anecdote offered by Cuban-Spanish writer Carlos Alberto Montaner:

> A few years ago I gave a talk in Monterrey in northern Mexico. The theme was Europe before the American leadership in the twenty-first century. When I finished, a local political leader approached me and said: "My concern is not the American leadership in Europe, but the growing influence and admiration that our neighbors arouse among the people from Monterrey. For us, it is a danger that in the United States there are twenty-eight million Mexicans [*sic*] who produce as much as the one hundred million that there are in Mexico." "Why?"—I asked to him. "Because I'm afraid that all the North of Mexico, under the influence of Texan culture and of those Mexicans who live over there, will one day ask for annexation to the U.S. and that our country will divide in half again." My interlocutor thought the same as Huntington, but in reverse.[31]

In the metaphysical dispute about the essential Mexican character as different from (Huntington) or similar to (Krauze) the Anglo character, discussion of socioeconomic factors is mostly absent. It is possible to assume that Huntington's rant against Mexican migration is also a cover-up of two issues he does not talk about: the racialization of migration and the effects of U.S. economic and political policies on Latin America.[32] Indeed, *Who Are We?* ignores—as most of Huntington's Mexican critics also do—the underlying economic forces of globalization that alter cultural and social textures and in many cases increase social tensions, while in a few other cases produce a more positive and liberating social effect. The introduction of this factor in the debate on the "Mexican migration problem" presents another perspective: that of the active role of the receiving country, in this case the United States, either in the form of traditional pull factors or as a consequence of the effects of U.S. foreign policy (in its economic and political, and not only military, connotations) on the sending countries, including Mexico.[33] Whether this policy is seen as a destructive force or ambivalently as a necessary evil for countries always avid to attract foreign investment in their economies, the fact is that in the global scenario, the receiving countries are far from being the passive receptacles of the hungry hordes who, with proper documentation or not, enter their territories.

Beyond Cultural Dualisms

The Huntington episode has left Mexican intellectuals with a full agenda. At the level of discourse, there is first the need to confront essentialism and the other "isms" (e.g., classism, racism, sexism, authoritarianism, and even centralism) that, codified in language and other forms of expression, have often accompanied Mexican cultural discourses. The opportunity is bright not only to criticize the Harvard scholar's text (his views as well as those of the opinion trend that he represents can hardly be changed), but also to articulate new discourses more responsive to and perceptive of the cultural plurality and multiplicity of social perspectives that exist in Mexican society and communities abroad. Mexico's relationship with the United States has understandably been one of the permanent obsessions in Mexican cultural and political discourse.[34] In part because of this controversy, many intellectuals have been more willing to discuss the new sociodemographic configurations and issues that affect the Mexican population in the United States, and not only the impact this country has on Mexico. The notion of national interest—in a moment of postnationalism—is, in consequence, being expanded or even redefined.

Krauze's unfortunate defense of Mexican migrants—admitting the assimilationist gambit posited by Huntington's essentialist game—may have (accidentally or unconsciously) raised an important theme he has not yet exploited: surpassing the traditional dichotomies of culturalism. These dichotomies have been an integral part of cultural discourse in both Mexico and the United States. What Huntington attempts is to maintain the cultural difference model long implemented with respect to the Mexican other in order to reaffirm a sense of "national identity," a national identity "besieged" or "distorted" by new identitarian possibilities inside U.S. territory (i.e., the Latino, the borderlander, the Chicano, the new mestiza, etc.). In his antagonistic construction, he does not realize that Mexicans are as essential to his own sense of identity as Anglos are for Mexican culturalist discourse. As Jean-François Bayart has argued: "The production of identities, and thus also the production of cultures is relational; it reflects a relationship to the Other as much as a relationship to the Self" (96). There is an interdependence and interrelationship not easily recognized or even admissible. As in the case of its respective economies and societies amid globalization, there is an unavoidable interrelationship between Mexico and the United States often eluded in the act of entertaining and contrasting essentialist dichotomies or cultural differences. Krauze's rapprochement toward that "Anglo other," as mentioned earlier, might mark an incipient effort to go beyond these dichotomies and the habit of fixed identities embedded in the essentialist premises of Huntington and the thought of philosophers of *la mexicanidad*.

Future disquisitions on the subject will determine if in Krauze's civilizing gesture there is a mimicry—in the "colonized personality" or framework of mind (Fanon 182)—in search of a new behavioral model for the neoliberal post-Mexican citizen; a mere surrendering to the other's wishes to avoid the expression of his fear and anger against the national body, and therefore effacing a sense of autonomy; or the possibility of a more realistic way of thinking by admitting that culture is a process that never occurs in one direction only (be it northward or southward, eastward or westward) whose flow one must enter to find alternatives to the pernicious and trite dichotomies that have dominated the relationship between Mexico and the United States.

NOTES

1. One example is Amitai Etzioni's article "The Real Threat: An Essay on Samuel Huntington," which serves as both a review of Huntington's book and a systematic rebuttal of its main claims. Etzioni concludes that the book is hardly a work of social science, with its "highly tendentious and misleading" use of data (385).
2. "Según Huntington, mexicanos pueden meter a EU armas de destrucción masiva; intelectuales nacionales lo rebaten" (online *La Crónica* headline, 22 September 2004). All translations are mine unless otherwise indicated.
3. "México se rebela contra Huntington. Los intelectuales mexicanos denuncian la demagogia e ignorancia de un texto del politólogo estadounidense."
4. "un tono de alarma para llamar la atención de la comunidad académica que no ve lo que ocurre realmente."
5. In the book's foreword, Huntington excuses himself by saying that the "motives of patriotism and of scholarship . . . may conflict." In recognizing this problem, he claims: "I attempt to engage in as detached and thorough an analysis of the evidence as I can, while warning the reader that my selection and presentation of that evidence may well be influenced by my patriotic desire" (xvii). The overlapping of such a patriotic imperative with the analysis of the evidence he provides may explain the methodological and epistemological pitfalls detected by many critics.
6. Mexican critics observe that these two books contain conspicuous inaccuracies, simplifications, and contradictions that outweigh their insights and undermine

their epistemological contribution. Regarding *The Clash of Civilizations*, Fernando del Paso, for instance, argues that "although the book contains many interesting and accurate observations, it turns out that the principal among those theories, in the first place, was not invented, or rather, enunciated for the first time by Samuel Huntington, but by an ex prime minister of Canada, Lester B. Pearson, the Nobel Peace Prize winner of 1957—and whom Huntington had no choice but to cite—who almost half a century ago said that 'the most important and long-lasting conflicts' would no longer occur 'between nations belonging to the same civilization, but between civilizations themselves.' That is the origin not only of the article, but also of the book and Samuel Huntington's success" [aunque el libro contiene algunas cosas interesantes y atinadas, resulta que la principal de esas teorías, por principio de cuentas, no fue inventada o, digamos, enunciada por la vez primera por Samuel Huntington, sino por un ex primer ministro canadiense, Lester B. Pearson, Premio Nobel de la Paz 1957—y a quien Huntington no le queda más remedio que citar— quien hace casi medio siglo expresó que "los conflictos más importantes y de más largo alcance" no ocurrirían ya "entre las naciones pertenecientes a una misma civilización, sino entre las propias civilizaciones." Ese es el origen no sólo del artículo, sino también del libro y del éxito de Samuel Huntington].

7. "En uno de los disparates más chuscos e increíbles—el profesor de Harvard y director del Instituto de Estudios Estratégicos John Olin—compara al ex presidente Carlos Salinas de Gortari nada menos que con Kemal Ataturk (1881–1938), el creador de la Nueva Turquía, cuyas reformas impusieron la modernidad occidental: abolió el califato (1924), secularizó el Estado, estableció el sufragio universal, impuso el alfabeto latino, sus leyes emanciparon a las mujeres y el Estado apoyó el proceso de industrialización en Turquía. El profesor Huntington, que en verdad no conoce límites, llama a Salinas de Gortari "el Kemal Ataturk de México."

8. "hablar de una civilización latinoamericana en contraposición a la occidental—o sea en *clash*, presente o futuro, actual o probable—es un disparate que apenas sería comprensible si proviniera de un cargador italiano, pero que es inexcusable en un académico norteamericano."

9. "Lo que ha escrito Huntington es ciertamente ofensivo y denigrante, nos ubica por necesidad en la discusión del espinoso tema del patio trasero que nuestros actuales gobernantes quisieran eludir" (Aguilar Zínzer, paragraph 6).

10. To graphically illustrate the main topic of the dossier, the journal's cover provided yet one more visual re/construction of the most visible U.S. national symbol, the flag, by replacing the stars with small bright semi-peeled bananas and the red stripes with undulating chains of red chilies, in an interpretation of the process of Hispanization that Huntington talks about.

11. "Con independencia del valor académico del libro, que realmente no es mucho, políticamente es un libro importante, y de allí el interés de comentarlo. Las opiniones personales del profesor Huntington a mí, personalmente, no me importan: el señor es un protestante evangélico y cree que todos deberían ser protestantes evangélicos. Es su problema, al igual que no le simpaticen los mexicanos. Lo malo es que trata de justificar, fundamentar y difundir sus opiniones como si fuesen el resultado de hallazgos científicos. Allí es donde hay una impostura."

12. The implicit question the author might want to ask his readers is a familiar one: "What should patriots do with this silent invasion before they retake their lands and perhaps—already at that—take the rest of the country?"

13. Huntington explains: "History shows that serious potential for conflict exists when people in one country refer to territory in a neighboring country in proprietary terms

and assert special rights and claims to that territory" (230). The allusion to a "potential conflict" between Mexico and the United States clearly permeates the statement.

14. David Hanson, for instance, writes on this point: "So are we now a Mexifornia, Calexico, Aztlán, El Norte, Alta California, or just plain California with new faces and the same old customs? Many of us think about this in the abstract. Charles Truxillo, a Chicano studies professor at the University of New Mexico, for example, promises that some day we will all be part of a new sovereign Hispanic nation called "República del Norte" encompassing the entire Southwest" (x–xi). In his critical review of Hanson's book on the American Immigration Law Foundation Web site, Walter Ewing comments that "in Hanson's worldview, the Mexican-American War of 1846–1848 marked the last time the United States, or any other nation, had any influence on the course of Mexican economic and political development. Apparently, U.S. Cold War politics played no role in perpetuating decades of authoritarian one-party rule in Mexico, U.S. trade policies have had no impact on the Mexican agricultural sector, and [former] President Vicente Fox, a former Coca Cola executive, is simply a modern-day Pancho Villa obsessed with the *reconquista* of California. It is unfortunate that a historian such as Hanson so blatantly ignores over 150 years of modern U.S.-Mexican history."

15. In a disclaimer similar to Huntington's, Hanson confesses that "*Mexifornia* is about the nature of a new California and what it means for America—a reflection upon the strange society that is emerging as the result of a demographic and cultural revolution like no other in our times. Although I quote statistics gleaned from the U.S. Census and scholarly books on Mexican immigration into the United States, this is not an academic study with the usual extensive documentation. I write instead of what I have seen and heard living half a century in California's Central Valley, at the epicenter of the upheaval" (xii).

16. As reported by an independent publication, *La voz de Aztlán*, on 17 April 2008 the provisions of SB 1108, approved on 16 April 2008 and scheduled for a vote by the full house, "would withhold funding to schools whose courses 'denigrate American values and the teachings of European based civilization.' One section of SB 1108 would bar public schools, community colleges, and universities from allowing organizations to operate on campus if they are 'based in whole or in part on race-based criteria,' a provision Rep. Russell Pearce said is aimed at MEChA. 'Arizona legislation will outlaw MEChA and Mexican-American studies'" (*www.aztlan.net/arizona_targets_mecha.htm*, accessed 23 April 2008).

17. I thank Hiram José Irizarry Osorio, research fellow at the Kirwan Institute for the Study of Race and Ethnicity at the Ohio State University, for bringing this essay to my attention.

18. If granted these speculations, it might be one of the few cases in world history in which a cultural minority imposes its values on the dominant cultural majority, even without the control of the media and other forms of cultural production (perhaps not since the clandestine Christian groups abandoned the catacombs to "civilize" the profane Roman Empire).

19. "Leyendo el libro de Huntington, observando su desconocimiento de toda la antropología del siglo XX, el desconocimiento de la más elemental discreción y sobriedad en el uso de estadísticas, lo pone a uno en una disyuntiva muy delicada: o bien el profesor de verdad no sabe lo que han escrito los antropólogos, no sabe lo que es la identidad, no sabe cómo se usan las estadísticas, y entonces es ingenuo o ignorante, o bien lo hace de mala fe, ocultando deliberadamente aquello. De entrada, no quiero atribuirle mala fe. Supongo que no sabe, que de verdad no ha leído."

20. "Como todos los argumentos culturalistas, el de Huntington tiene un punto ciego en el que se pone de manifiesto su carácter político, porque es refractario a la razón: no puede siquiera admitir que se dude de la existencia del sujeto colectivo como tal, como sujeto con una identidad única e inmodificable. No lo discute ni lo explica, lo da por supuesto como si fuese una obviedad absoluta."

21. Among the texts that provide a diagnostics or propose new ways of understanding those realities are Bartra's *La jaula de la melancolía* (Melancholy's Cage) and *La sangre y la tinta* (Blood and Ink), Bonfil Batalla's *México profundo* (Deep Mexico), García Canclini's *Culturas híbridas* (Hybrid Cultures), Monsiváis's *Rituales del caos* (Rituals of Chaos), and Lomnitz's *Modernidad indiana* (Indigenous Modernity).

22. This tension is one of the main problems addressed by Roger Bartra's *La sangre y la tinta*, among other texts on contemporary Mexican history that bridge political and cultural analysis.

23. "Somos, por primera vez en nuestra historia, contemporáneos de todos los hombres."

24. As Judit Bokser states: "The concept of *mestizaje*, essentially ethnic, turned into a sign of unifying belonging that eventually opened out into a concept of Mexican nationhood that negated ethnic plurality and cultural diversity as contrary to national identity, thus fomenting a monolithic vision that aspired to nullify those divergent elements that truly do compose the nation. This functioned as the political and philosophical substratum that fed the migration politics of the time, which were restrictive with respect to Jews precisely when for this group the need to abandon the European continent was ever more imperative" [El concepto de mestizaje, esencialmente étnico, se convirtió en un instrumento para crear un marco de pertenencia unificador que desembocó en una concepción de la nación mexicana que negaba la pluralidad étnica y la diversidad cultural como contrarias a la identidad nacional, fomentando una visión monolítica que aspiró a anular los elementos diversos que realmente la componen. Esto actuó como el sustrato político-filosófico que nutrió las políticas migratorias de la época, que fueron restrictivas frente al grupo judío precisamente cuando la necesidad de abandonar el continente europeo resultaba cada vez más imperiosa] (cited in Aguilar Rivera 171).

25. The lack of a referent in English or direct translation of "mestizo" other than "half-breed" in old dictionaries clearly indicated a void of meaning tied to a certain cultural anxiety of miscegenation. Currently *Merriam-Webster's Collegiate Dictionary* defines "mestizo" as "a person of mixed blood," and more specifically, as "a person of mixed European and American Indian ancestry."

26. We have only to recall Octavio Paz's famous set of oppositions with respect to the "psychocultural" differences between Mexicans and North Americans: "They are optimistic, we are nihilists; . . . we are sad and sarcastic; . . . they are happy and humorous. North Americans want to understand; we want to contemplate. They are active; we are passive," and so on [Son optimistas; nosotros nihilistas—sólo que nuestro nihilismo no es intelectual, sino una reacción instintiva; . . . somos tristes y sarcásticos; ellos alegres y humorísticos. Los norteamericanos quieren comprender; nosotros contemplar. Son activos; nosotros quietistas] (45).

27. Soon after the publication of Huntington's *Foreign Policy* essay, several of the cited researchers (e.g., James P. Smith and Rodolfo O. de la Garza) expressed their concern about the conclusions Huntington had drawn, which were contrary to what they had concluded in their research. In an interview in Mexico City, Rodolfo O. de la Garza complained: "I am perhaps the person Huntington most cites to affirm things that I never said" [soy quizá la persona que más cita Huntington para afirmar cosas que yo nunca dije] (cited in Velasco 153). He concludes about Huntington's arguments

that they "more closely resemble nativist ravings than scholarly assessments" (cited in Glenn).

28. The article subsequently appeared in the *New Republic* as "Identity Fanaticism," 21 June 2004.

29. Several studies from the Mexican Migration Project based in Princeton University can offer relevant information on this regard. See B. Reyes, "Immigrant Trip Duration."

30. In further representing the importance of conformity in assimilating the values of the essential Anglo, the issue of *Letras Libres* includes an essay by Tamar Jacoby, a senior fellow at the Manhattan Institute, who on the cover of the Simon and Schuster edition of Huntington's *Who Are We?* is quoted as praising the author, but who in her essay for *Letras Libres* implicitly contradicts his findings and views. Through ethnographic studies, Jacoby concludes that the migrants are culturally transformed by their stay and with due time assimilate well into U.S. culture and society. She does not expect the Mexican migrants to form an ethnic enclave, a conclusion supported by research from other agencies that report the increase in the number of Mexican American households that have already achieved middle-class status. Her essay, like Krauze's, strongly supports the assimilationist perspective and the implicit superiority of one set of values over another: "What [migrants] most criticize about Mexico is the lack of cleanliness and punctuality and the corruption. The process of transformation they describe begins when they stop being demanding of themselves and start being exigent with everyone else. In their hearts, they all recognize that they have not stopped being Mexican, but not to the extent that they can resist assimilating to the adoptive culture" [Lo que más critican es la falta de limpieza, la impuntualidad y la corrupción. El proceso de transformación descrito por ellos mismos empieza con volverse exigentes consigo mismo para después volverse exigentes con los demás. En el fondo, todos reconocen que no dejan de ser mexicanos, pero no al nivel de resistir la asimilación de la cultura de adopción] (31–32).

31. "Hace unos años fui a dar una conferencia a Monterrey, en el norte de México. El tema era Europa ante el liderazgo norteamericano en el siglo XXI. Cuando terminé, se me acercó un dirigente político local y me dijo: 'Mi preocupación no es el liderazgo norteamericano en Europa, sino la creciente influencia y admiración que nuestros vecinos despiertan entre los regiomontanos. Para nosotros es un peligro que en Estados Unidos haya veintiocho [*sic*] millones de mexicanos que produzcan tanto como los cien que hay en México.' '¿Por qué?'—le pregunté. 'Porque me temo que todo el norte de México, bajo la influencia de la cultura texana y de esos mexicanos que allá viven, un día pidan la anexión a Estados Unidos y nuestro país vuelva a dividirse.' Mi interlocutor pensaba lo mismo que Huntington, pero al revés."

32. These issues remain hidden under the culturalist approach taken by Huntington and most of his critics: "Recognizing the racialization of immigration should help one understand that much of what we are witnessing is a scapegoating of Latinos for much larger forces and factors that are under way in U.S. society, . . . most especially the restructuring of capitalism that has been under way and [of which] immigrants are the victims rather than the source. . . . The scapegoating that we are seeing, including the rise of violent militias and public demonstrations against immigrant day laborers, tends to focus on the Latino as if it is the Latino who is the source of all of our problems" (Fletcher).

33. Fletcher alludes to this issue when he refers to "immigration to the USA as a major *result* of U.S. foreign policy that has destroyed the political and economic infrastructure of so many countries, e.g., El Salvador." In a sort of Newtonian opposing force,

migration would be the corresponding effect of the penetration of foreign capital and the alteration of the local economy and displacement of the local population.

34. Enrique Krauze's more recent article, "Mirándolos a ellos" (Looking at Them), published in his journal *Letras Libres*, provides a good summary of the difficult relationship between the two countries and the changing attitudes it has engendered throughout history.

WORKS CITED

Acuña, Rodolfo. *Occupied America: A History of Chicanos*. New York: Harper and Row, 1981.

Aguilar Rivera, José Antonio. *El Sonido y la furia: la persuasión multicultural en México y Estados Unidos*. México: Taurus, 2004.

Aguilar Zínser, Adolfo. "Huntington y el patio trasero." *Reforma*, 5 March 2004. *busquedas.gruporeforma.com/reforma/Documentos/*. 20 June 2006.

Anderson, Benedict. *Imagined Communities: Reflections on the Origin and Spread of Nationalism*. London: Verso, 1983.

Appadurai, Arjun. *Modernity at Large*. Minneapolis: University of Minnesota Press, 1996.

Aznárez, Juan Jesús. "México se rebela contra Huntington." *El País Plus*, 4 November 2004. *www.elpais.com/global/*. 11 April 2006.

Barber, Benjamin. *Jihad vs. McWorld*. New York: Ballantine Books, 1996.

Bartra, Roger. *La jaula de la melancolía: identidad y metamorfosis del mexicano*. Mexico: Grijalbo, 1996.

———. *La sangre y la tinta*. Mexico: Océano, 1999.

Bauböck, Rainer. "Citizenship and National Identities in the European Union." New York University School of Law Jean Monnet Center. Working Papers. *www.jeanmonnetprogram.org/papers/97/97–04–.html*. 10 April 2006.

Bayart, Jean-Francois. *The Illusion of Cultural Identity*. Trans. Steve Rendall. Chicago: University of Chicago Press, 2005.

Bhabha, Homi. "DissemiNation: Time, Narrative, and the Margins of the Modern Nation." *Nation and Narration*. Ed. Homi K. Bhabha. London: Routledge, 1993. 291–322.

Bloom, Allan. *The Closing of the American Mind*. New York: Simon and Schuster, 1987.

Bonfil Batalla, Guillermo. *México profundo: una civilización negada*. Mexico: Grijalbo, 1994.

Brooks, David. "The Americano Dream." *New York Times*. 24 February 2004.

Carrión, Jorge. *Mito y magia del mexicano*. Mexico: Editorial Nuestro Tiempo, 1970.

Cornelius, Wayne. "Ambivalent Reception: Mass Public Responses to the 'New' Latino Immigration to the United States." *Latinos: Remaking America*. Ed. Marcelo M. Suárez-Orozco and Mariela M. Páez. Berkeley: University of California Press, 2002. 165–89.

Del Paso, Fernando. "Samuel Huntington y el imperio de todos." *La hoja latinoamericana*. 11 March 2003. *www.rodelu.net/lahoja/lahoja82_3.htm*. 20 June 2006.

Dresser, Denise. "El americano amenazado." *Reforma*, 1 March 2004. *www.reforma.com*. 20 June 2006.

D'Souza, Dinesh. *Illiberal Education: The Politics of Race and Sex on Campus*. New York: Free Press, 1991.

Eilenberger, Wolfram. "Entrevista a Samuel P. Huntington, autor de 'El choque de Civilizaciones.'" *La Vanguardia*, 13 September 2006. *www.jordipujol.cat/files/articles/LVhuntington.pdf*. 20 July 2007.

Escalante Gonzalbo, Fernando, ed. "El enemigo en casa: huntington y la 'invasión latina.' " *Nueva Sociedad* 201 (2006): 46–60.

———. *Otro sueño americano: en torno a ¿Quiénes somos? de Samuel P. Huntington.* México: Paidós, 2004.

Estefan, Alberto. "La frontera invisible: la amenaza de la migración ilegal." *Istor* 5.19 (2004): 160–65.

Etzioni, Amitai. "The Real Threat: An Essay on Samuel Huntington." *Contemporary Sociology* 34.5 (2005): 477–85.

Ewing, Walter A. "Mexifornia: A State of Confusion." American Immigration Law Foundation Web site. 30 September 2003. *www.immigrationpolicy.org/index.php?content=fc030930 21 July 2007.*

Fanon, Frantz. *The Wretched of the Earth.* New York: Grove Press, 2004.

Fletcher, Bill, Jr. "Another Side to Race and Immigration." *Black Commentator,* 26 July 2007. *www.blackcommentator.com.* 27 July 2007.

Frank, Thomas. *What's the Matter with Kansas? How Conservatives Won the Heart of America.* New York: Metropolitan Books, 2004.

Fuentes, Carlos. "Huntington and the Mask of Racism." *New Perspectives Quarterly* 21.2 (2004): 77–81.

Galindo Quiñónez, Heriberto M. "Ni perros ni latinos." *El Correo en EU.* 1 April 2004. *www.elcorreo.eu.org/.* 27 July 2007.

Ganster, Paul, and David E. Lorey. *The U.S.-Mexican Border into the Twenty-first Century.* 2d ed. New York: Rowman and Littlefield, 2008.

García Canclini, Néstor. *Culturas híbridas: estrategias para entrar y salir de la modernidad.* México: Grijalbo, 1989.

———. "North Americans or Latin Americans? The Redefinition of Mexican Identity and the Free Trade Agreements." McAnany and Wilkinson 142–56.

Garza, Rodolfo O. de la, Ángelo Falcón, and F. Chris García. "Will the Real Americans Please Stand Up: Anglo and Mexican-American Support of Core American Political Values." *American Journal of Political Science* 40.2 (1996): 346–48.

Glazer, Nathan. "The Problem of Ethnic Studies." *Ethnic Dilemmas, 1964–1982.* Cambridge: Harvard University Press, 1983. 97–125.

Glenn, David. "Critics Assail Scholar's Article Arguing That Hispanic Immigration Threatens U.S." *Chronicle of Higher Education,* 24 February 2004. *chronicle.com/.* 19 June 2006.

Hannerz, Ulf. "Notes on the Global Ecumene." *The Anthropology of Globalization.* Ed. Jonathan Xavier Inda and Renato Rosaldo. Oxford: Blackwell, 2002. 37–45.

Hanson, Victor Davis. *Mexifornia: A State of Becoming.* San Francisco: Encounter Books, 2003.

Huntington, Samuel P. "Civilizations at Odds." *At Century's End: Great Minds Reflect on Our Times.* Ed. Nathan Gordels. La Jolla, Calif.: ALTI, 1995. 58–67.

———. *The Clash of Civilizations and the Remaking of World Order.* New York: Simon and Schuster, 1996.

———. *Who Are We? The Challenges to America's National Identity.* New York: Simon and Schuster, 2004.

Jacoby, Tamar. "La conexión mexicana: cómo Nueva York lleva las de ganar." *Letras Libres* 64 (2004): 30–32.

Krauze, Enrique. "Huntington: el falso profeta." *Letras Libres* 64 (2004): 24–26.

———. "Postdata a Huntington." *Letras Libres* 66 (2004). *www.letraslibres.com.* 20 June 2006.

———. "Identity Fanaticism." *New Republic* 230.23 (2004): 28–32.

———. "Mirándolos a ellos." *Letras Libres* 66 (2004). *www.letraslibres.com.* 20 June 2006.

Larraín Ibáñez, Jorge. "The Concept of Identity." *National Identities and Sociopolitical Changes in Latin America.* Ed. Mercedes F. Durán-Cogan and Antonio Gómez-Moriana. New York: Routledge, 2001. 1–29.

Lomnitz, Claudio. *Modernidad indiana: nación y mediación en México.* Mexico: Planeta, 1999.

McAnany, Emile G., and Kenton T. Wilkinson, eds. *Mass Media and Free Trade: NAFTA and the Cultural Industries.* Austin: University of Texas Press, 1996.

Miller, Marilyn Grace. *The Rise and Fall of the Cosmic Race.* Austin: University of Texas Press, 2004.

Monsiváis, Carlos. *Los rituales del caos.* Mexico: Ediciones Era, 1995.

———. "Will Nationalism Be Bilingual?" McAnany and Wilkinson 131–41.

Montaner, Carlos Alberto. "Los hispanos en EE UU, los cubanos y los errores de Huntington." *Firmas Press,* 4 January 2004. *www.firmaspress.com.* 15 May 2007.

Moya, Paula. "Introduction: Reclaiming Identity." *Reclaiming Identity: Realist Theory and the Predicament of Postmodernism.* Ed. Paula M. Moya and Michael R. Hames-García. Berkeley: University of California Press, 2000. 1–28.

Myrdal, Gunnar. *An American Dilemma: The Negro Problem and Modern Democracy.* New York: Pantheon Books, 1975.

Paz, Octavio. *El laberinto de la soledad y otras obras.* New York: Penguin Books, 1997.

Pérez Gay, José María. "El ocaso del futuro: Samuel P. Huntington: el ideólogo del miedo." *La Jornada,* 21 December 2005. *www.jornada.unam.mx/imprimir.php?fecha=2 005l221andnota=008a1pol.phpandseccion=nota.* 10 April 2006.

Pew Hispanic Center and Kaiser Family Foundation. *2002 National Survey of Latinos.* 2002. *pewhispanic.org/reports/report.php?ReportID=39.* 25 May 2007.

Putnam, Robert D. "E Pluribus Unum: Diversity and Community in the Twenty-first Century: The 2006 Johan Skytte Prize Lecture." *Scandinavian Political Studies* 30.2 (2007): 137–74.

Reyes, Belinda I. "Immigrant Trip Duration: The Case of Immigrants from Western Mexico." *International Migration Review* 35.4 (Winter 2001): 1185–1204.

Reyes, Raúl. "English Rates First in Latino Families." USA Today.com, 6 April 2007. *www.usatoday.com.* 6 April 2007.

Ruiz Mondragón, Ariel. "La impostura nacionalista de Huntington: entrevista con Fernando Escalante Gonzalbo." *La insignia,* 19 October 2004. *www.lainsignia.org/2004/octubre/cul_046.htm.* 10 April 2006.

Schlesinger, Arthur M., Jr. *The Disuniting of America: Reflections on a Multicultural Society.* New York: W. W. Norton, 1991.

Schwartz, Stephen. "Ser hispanófilo." *Letras Libres* 64 (2004): 28–29.

"Según Huntington, mexicanos pueden meter a EU armas de destrucción masiva; intelectuales nacionales lo rebaten." *La Crónica,* 22 September 2004. *www.cronica.com.mx/nota.php?id_nota=145032.* 13 April 2006.

Sepúlveda, Jay M. "The Trojan Burritos and the Burden of History: How Mexicans Are Coming Back for Their Lost Lands." *Litera* 1.6 (2006): 4–5.

Smith, James P. "Assimilation across the Latino Generations." *American Economic Review* 93.2 (2003): 315–19.

Velasco, Jesús. "Samuel Phillips Huntington: un antiinmigracionista más." *Istor* 5.19 (2004): 138–59.

CHAPTER 13

Jorge Ramos Reads North from South

Beth E. Jörgensen

This essay examines a popular journalistic perspective on contemporary U.S. society produced from within the United States by a Mexican national who has lived "north of the border" for more than twenty years. Journalism in all its print and electronic forms is without question the dominant public discourse of our time, and along with other mass media productions it has joined literary writing at the center of critical analysis and debate. Jorge Ramos Avalos lives and practices journalism across the borders of our neighboring nations, and also across the boundaries of distinct national and linguistic identities that are internal and not foreign to U.S. society. He exemplifies the notion of fluid, constructed individual and national identities that is prevalent in border studies and in contemporary theories of subjectivity. Writing from a place that is both inside and outside mainstream America, Ramos holds well-defined positions on the strengths and weaknesses of U.S. culture and politics today. He reaches a wide domestic and international audience as a broadcaster and as an author, thus playing a role in the formation of public opinion. This analysis of selected books and columns will treat his work as a chronicler of the Hispanic experience in the United States and secondarily as a journalist covering world events, with a focus on how Jorge Ramos reads the North from the South.

As the best-known voice and face of Spanish-language television and radio news in the United States, Jorge Ramos is both a creation of and a contributor to the pervasive presence of the mass media in contemporary culture and an example of the star status of key personalities in today's journalism. Ramos as media icon is impossible to avoid or overlook in his multiple roles as coanchor for the nightly Univisión news broadcast, cohost of a weekly news hour, *Aquí y Ahora* (Here and Now), prominent interviewer of Latin American and U.S. politicians, occasional on-location correspondent in the world's war zones and disaster areas, radio personality, newspaper and Web columnist, and author of numerous books. The name of this recipient of seven Grammy Awards, as well as multiple journalism prizes— including the prestigious Maria Moors Cabot Prize given by the Columbia University School of Journalism—frequently appears on lists of the most influential

Hispanics in the United States.[1] Ramos has a deep commitment to understanding U.S. society and to interpreting and critiquing it for a wide Spanish American and U.S.-Latino audience. He speaks and writes from the dual perspective of an insider and an outsider in the United States, having lived in North America full time since 1983 and yet having deliberately maintained Mexican citizenship and, perhaps less successfully, a claim on a Mexican cultural identity. Not willing to make himself completely at home in mainstream English-speaking America, he writes and conducts his broadcasts predominantly in Spanish and he personally identifies with his diverse Hispanic audience. However, as a Mexican, he feels himself to be a minority within the large and influential Cuban American population of southern Florida, where Univisión is located. Finally, he knows that he is less and less at home in an ever-changing Mexico, giving him a thrice-complicated experience of cultural identity. By remaining in the United States for more than two decades beyond the one year that he originally planned to stay, Ramos has become a self-styled man without a country—"un exiliado light" [lightweight exile], as he says—who has achieved extraordinary professional success and material privilege. Without rejecting the advantages of his successful integration into U.S. society, he nonetheless projects an attitude of responsibility and solidarity with other Hispanic immigrants in their more difficult struggle to survive and to thrive in the North.

Jorge Ramos's reading of the United States in his work as a journalist addresses three target audiences: Hispanics residing in the United States, Spanish Americans outside its borders, and non-Hispanics in the North. In the first two instances he engages very directly with the project of interpreting U.S. society for those who occupy a position that is in some way conceived as "outside" or "other than" American. In contrast, in his representation of the Latin wave of immigrants from the South for a non-Hispanic reader or viewer, his perspective on mainstream U.S. society is implicit because it is filtered through the lens of the Hispanic experience. In either case, the United States is a constant preoccupation at some level of all his journalistic work, regardless of the specific topic.

Journalism in the late twentieth and early twenty-first centuries, in spite of rapid changes in the structures of media ownership and the means of dissemination of the news, is still usually described in certain conventional terms by practicing journalists and by those who study mass media trends. The prominent media critics Bill Kovach and Tom Rosenstiel base their discussion of modern journalism on a tradition of public discourse that has its roots in the seventeenth and eighteenth centuries with the early newspapers published in England and debates over theories of free speech and a free press (21–22). Common to the norms of the journalistic enterprise in the West since that time has been the ideal of a provider of independent, reliable information that gives the public the knowledge it needs to participate in the institutions of self-government. Journalism and democracy are therefore inextricably linked, and this is a connection that Jorge Ramos repeatedly affirms. Accepted methods for the collection and verification of facts are assumed to ground the information communicated through media channels. Other conventional views hold that the media define community by creating a common language and a mutual knowledge of reality, they serve as a watchdog in the public interest, they speak on behalf of the powerless, and they challenge public complacency (17–18). The increasing commercialization and globalization of the media in the present time and the move toward a journalism of assertion rather than one of verification are, in the view of Kovach and Rosenstiel, threats to the model that they defend. It is also a commonplace today to acknowledge the prevailing atmosphere of doubt and mistrust toward the traditional discourses of truth in our age of skepticism, and to place journalists very low on the scale of relative trustworthiness. A frequently quoted study conducted in 1999 by the Pew Research Center for the People and the Press documents the deep loss of faith in the fourth estate among the American public.[2]

In comments scattered throughout Ramos's books and in several columns published in 2003, 2005, and 2006, a definition of journalism emerges that is largely in line with the heroic, civic-minded image evoked by Kovach and Rosenstiel, and he is aware of working both within the demands of the ideal model and against the very real erosion of public confidence that has taken place. In *No Borders*, his 2002 autobiography, Ramos explains that he came to journalism initially as an act of rebellion against parental authority when he chose to study communications rather than engineering at the UNAM (Universidad Nacional Autónoma de México, Mexico's national university). In the autobiography he also recalls a brush with newsroom censorship on his first job as a journalist, working for the XEW radio station in Mexico City. This personal experience, combined with his awareness of the strictures placed on press freedom in Mexico, explains his decision to study in the United States in 1983 and eventually to remain there to work.[3] Ramos particularly admires American democracy's assertion of freedom of the press in the context of a long history of limitations on free expression throughout Latin America. He firmly holds that the successful working of democracy requires an active and fearless press that takes seriously its obligation to tell the truth. The press's role in the dissemination of accurate information about the world is obviously one aspect of its contribution to society, but Ramos tends to emphasize that the most critical task of the journalist is not simply to inform but to serve as a counterbalance to those who hold power. Using the example of Bob Woodward and Carl Bernstein's historic investigative reporting on Watergate and the Nixon Whitehouse, Ramos claims in an online column from July 2005 entitled "Sólo queremos que nos crean" (We Just Want to Be Believed) that the journalist has the responsibility to question those in power and to denounce abuses of authority. In explaining his approach to interviewing political figures, he reiterates that "journalists are a counterweight to power. . . . The natural place for journalism is in opposition, always questioning, balancing power or fighting against it" (*A la caza del león* 21, 23).[4] Thus, he says, one frames questions very differently for a dictator than for a victim of dictatorship, or for a head of state than for a member of the opposition. He calls this "justicia periodística" [journalistic justice] and he takes the U.S. press to task for its post-9/11 reluctance to subject President George W. Bush to probing, challenging questions about the Iraq war.[5] The other key to his practice as an interviewer and a chronicle writer is a sense of social responsibility that pushes him toward advocacy journalism. Ramos frequently characterizes his role as that of a voice for those who are excluded or silenced by mainstream society, recalling his admiration for Elena Poniatowska and the late Orianna Fallaci, two prominent journalists from Mexico and Italy, respectively.[6] Ramos's writings on the struggles of Latino immigrants exemplify this stance, insofar as his own status as an immigrant and a Latino with privileged access to the media interpolates him into a position of identity-based advocacy.

Jorge Ramos's most visible work is as a TV news broadcaster, but he is also a prolific author, turning to writing as a vehicle for presenting in-depth reporting and expressing opinions that TV news and its sound bites do not allow (Ramos, *No Borders* 3).[7] In addition to a weekly column that is distributed to more than fifty newspapers in the United States and Spanish America and is made available in an archive on his Web site, Ramos has published seven books to date, all of them nonfiction. He writes and publishes in Spanish, but four of his titles have been translated into English, and throughout this study I quote from the published English translations when available. His first book, *Detrás de la máscara* (Behind the Mask), came out in 1998, and it collects twenty interviews of political figures and writers, including Bill Clinton, Subcomandante Marcos, and Octavio Paz. A second volume of his journalistic interviews entitled *A la caza del león* (Hunting the Lion) appeared in 2001. *Lo que vi* (What I Saw; 1999) compiles fifty articles on worldwide events that Ramos covered as a reporter: the war in El Salvador, the fall of the Berlin Wall, and the war in Kosovo, among others. *La otra cara de América*, published in 2000, chronicles the struggles and aspirations of recent Spanish American immigrants to the United States. It was translated into English in 2002 under the title *The Other Face of America*. Also in 2002 at the age of forty-six he published his autobiography, *Atravesando fronteras* (No Borders). *La ola latina* (The Latino Wave) came out in 2003 and presents Ramos's views on the rising political, economic, and cultural power—and influence—of the Hispanic population in the United States. Finally, *Morir en el intento* (Dying to Cross; 2005) is an example of investigative journalism about a notorious crime in the transport of undocumented immigrants that occurred in Texas in 2003: the death by suffocation of nineteen Mexicans and Central Americans who crossed the border in the locked and unventilated rear of a tractor trailer truck.

This is an impressive list of books for a full-time TV and radio journalist to have produced within the space of seven years. However, the number of titles is somewhat deceptive. Ramos writes on a limited number of themes, and his presentation of them is marked by an extraordinary amount of repetition. In compar-

ing one book to another and even within a single book, the attentive reader will
find that not only key ideas but entire passages of text are recycled virtually intact.
His writing is also remarkable for the relative simplicity of the narrative discourse,
which remains uncomplicated by elements of irony, intertextuality, ambiguity, self-
reflexivity, or other hallmarks of a more literary journalism. In carrying out his
advocacy mission on behalf of immigrants and in playing his role as a "voice for
the voiceless," he does not problematize the position of an intellectual speaking for
others in the ways that we are accustomed to seeing today, especially in the field of
anthropology, but also in journalism.[8] Nevertheless, from his vantage point "looking North" *from* the North's own increasingly Hispanic South, Ramos stakes out a
clear and energetic position on a variety of aspects of U.S. society, using a familiar,
albeit reduced, rhetorical repertoire to represent his views and to persuade his readers; despite its shortcomings, his journalism is widely read and plays a role in shaping public opinion.

Jorge Ramos reads the United States in highly positive terms overall, and compared to the Mexico that he left behind in 1983, he finds much to praise in the
North. Vastly greater economic opportunities, press freedom, superior education,
successful democratic institutions, liberal social mores, and the historically ener-
gizing forces of immigration and diversity are the nation's strengths—imperfectly
achieved but nonetheless significant and praiseworthy. At the same time, racism
and anti-immigrant attitudes and policies are constant targets of his criticism, with
racism being seen as the root cause of the other problems. As a consequence of his
conviction that the primary jobs of the journalist are to assume a critical stance
vis-à-vis those who occupy positions of power in society and to denounce social
ills, his writings focus more heavily on exposing the shortcomings of the United
States than on praising its virtues, without that emphasis obscuring his underlying
admiration and his fundamental desire to promote positive change. Racism and
anti-immigrant sentiment are particularly egregious in his view precisely because
they directly contradict the national virtues and the promise that the United States
seems to offer. In addition to stemming from his concept of the social role of the
journalist in a democracy, the tension in Ramos's work between praise and criticism of U.S. culture may be seen as a manifestation of an ambivalence that is well
documented in public opinion in Mexico. Stephen Morris's book *Gringolandia:
Mexican Identity and Perceptions of the United States* proposes that for many Mexicans the United States, to varying degrees, represents both a threat and an opportunity, and this dichotomy has shaped Mexican political and historical discourse for
many decades. In this regard, Morris's analysis of public school history texts, books
that Ramos must have read as a child, gives some insight into the foundations of
Ramos's perspective on the United States. Among the broad themes that define
the schoolbooks' representation of the United States are the nation's democratic
values and advanced economy (portrayed as positive attributes), as well as a negative assessment of its expansionist history and its historical exploitation of Latin

America's natural resources and hunger for foreign capital (Morris 87, 89–103). Interestingly, Ramos sees Hispanics viewed in the United States predominantly as a threat and not as an opportunity, and he seeks to correct that perception and show how the Hispanic presence may be one solution to declining American values, including the erosion in tolerance toward immigrants. In what follows, I have chosen three books, *No Borders*, *The Other Face of America*, and *The Latino Wave*, as well as a series of his columns on the Iraq war, to examine how Ramos reads America from his position as a Mexican living in Miami and working as a journalist for the Spanish-language media.

The unquestioned center of gravity for Jorge Ramos's vision of the United States—its past, its present, and its future—is the crucial significance that he attaches to its being a nation created by immigrants and therefore rightfully characterized by diversity of race and cultural heritage. Ramos understands the invention of the United States in the traditional terms taught to American schoolchildren: that all Americans are descendents of immigrants who left their places of birth and came to an adopted land in search of new opportunities, new freedoms, and a better future. Plymouth Rock and Ellis Island, for example, are universally known signs of America's immigrant past, and they are at the center of its most enduring and beloved myths: Tales of hardworking, freedom-seeking founders of the nation persist in the popular imagination, quite resistant to the complications posed by other equally foundational but less frequently told stories of American "origins," the Trail of Tears and the Middle Passage principal among them. Another myth of national origins and identity is expressed in the description of the United States as a melting pot, an idea that serves hegemonic cultural and political interests rather better than those of newly arriving groups, insofar as it privileges assimilation by immigrants to the dominant culture rather than continual transformation of society in response to changing demographics.

This myth has faced strong challenges recently in the popular discourse by the image of the United States as a salad bowl. Instead of undergoing the process of blending and breaking down of differences that serves up a cooked-down, homogenous stew, a salad is made out of many ingredients that retain their distinctive nature while contributing to the whole. Ramos both expressly and implicitly favors the salad bowl over the stewpot, as this anecdote from the book *The Other Face of America* illustrates: "I recently had the opportunity to visit an elementary school, and I noticed a drawing of an enormous salad on the blackboard. It was a social science class, and the name of the salad was the United States." He goes on to comment that schoolchildren are coming to understand what their elders are slow to appreciate: that "to be American is to be multicultural, multiethnic, and multiracial" (162).

Within the long history of the American immigrant experience, Ramos is most concerned to understand and to explain the late twentieth-century wave of Spanish American newcomers, both legal and undocumented. The Latino wave is the predominant theme of four of his seven books, and in his exploration of the meaning of the presence of thirty-five million Hispanics in the United States, he also reveals his perspective on the strengths and the weaknesses of American society. The three titles under analysis here address the immigrant experience and read the United States from three different angles. The autobiographical *No Borders* gives an inside view of Ramos's personal opinions about the United States and his own process of making a new life in the land of immigrants. *The Other Face of America* seeks to make Hispanics, America's largest minority, more visible to its majority citizens. *The Latino Wave* celebrates the growing political power and economic and cultural influence of U.S. Hispanics and predicts their continued growth and contributions to the future of the United States. Ramos's narrative about the growing Hispanic presence is always complemented by corresponding references to his interpretation of the United States as a nation of predominantly European origins. Self and other, Hispanic and Anglo, are represented as mutually defining and mutually resisting cultural and historical subjects.

Jorge Ramos frames *No Borders: A Journalist's Search for Home* as a conventional autobiography, according to the terms set out by Philippe Lejeune in his well-known study of the genre: "retrospective prose narrative written by a real person concerning his own existence, where the focus is his individual life, in particular the story of his personality" (4). As the title suggests, Ramos's focus is the question of home as a site of identity formation, self-affirmation, and attachment, and as a source of values. In the double move of leaving and arriving, emigrants/immigrants have a complicated relationship to multiple homes, the ones left behind and the ones settled in new places. It is no surprise, then, that Ramos organizes his life story under spatial rubrics. The thirteen chapters are divided into four sections entitled "My House," "The American Experience," "Going Global," and "The Eternal Return," which correspond respectively to his family home in Mexico City, the United States, the world, and again Mexico.

Ramos's autobiography conveys his perspective on American society in the process of narrating his upbringing, his move to Los Angeles in 1983, and his career as a journalist through the year 2002. His recounting of the attitudes that he absorbed as a child and as a university student, which were the attitudes that he took with him to California, closely mirror the results of the research Stephen Morris reports in *Gringolandia*, mentioned earlier. Ramos recalls being introduced to America through the filters of a childhood visit to Disneyland and through the popular music of the 1970s played on Mexico City radio shows. Imported popular culture products, whether they were music, clothing, or films, were highly valued by Mexican youths of the time, in spite of President Luis Echeverría's efforts to create a homegrown "cultural order that would oppose American influence" (*No Borders* 19). In the realm of politics, the young Ramos perceived the United States as "the giant of the north" (19) and as a power that Latin America had to confront. An anti-Yankee, anti-imperialist perspective was part of the student culture of the late 1970s and early 1980s, as Ramos attests, and he states that when he decided to leave Mexico after the censorship incident, he did not feel a strong pull from the north. England and France were appealing choices, but he went to California for practical reasons—his acceptance with scholarship aid to graduate school at UCLA.

The early years in California were characterized by his exposure to new freedoms, particularly permissiveness in personal behaviors such as drug use, sex, and fashion. More significant for his work as a journalist are two fundamental insights gleaned from "the American experience" that Ramos returns to again and again in his writings about the United States and the status of the immigrant. The first lesson, which he claims to be one of his mantras, was that "the best things about the United States are its opportunities; the worst thing is the racism" (107). This clearly reiterates the "opportunity and threat" conception that is prevalent among Mexicans, but it reverses its terms by shifting the focus and the location of the threat posed by the United States. That is, Hispanics who are reading the United States from the outside perceive the outer-directed threat of U.S. imperialism as primary, and it reinforces in them the idea of individual nations as separate spaces whose territorial integrity can (and must) be defended. For Ramos, reading America from the inside, the racism that originates within U.S. borders threatens its citizens and must be remedied by creating more fluid, permeable borders rather than by mounting a stronger defense of them. His second insight on American culture, closely related to the first, is that Latino, primarily Mexican, immigrants are repopulating and reconquering the American Southwest, and that their growing numbers and influence will, in Ramos's opinion, change the society irrevocably and for the better in twenty to thirty years.[9] Ramos is an enthusiastic proponent of this demographic and cultural shift, believing that Latinos bring sorely needed values such as racial tolerance and the importance of family and hard work into the ongoing transformation of American society. These values will help the United States address and overcome its internal racism. The chapter "News of the Reconquest" contains some of Ramos's most unreserved and optimistic statements about immigration and diversity in North America, as when he asserts: "The most defining factor of American society has two elements: tolerance toward diversity and acceptance of immigrants" (137). A few pages later, however, he warns against current, less tolerant trends such as English-only nativism and anti-Hispanic sentiments, but he concludes the passage with a hopeful alternative. "The cultures that have fought to maintain their purity tend to commit the greatest excesses and tend to be characterized by violence, racism and discrimination. On the other hand, when a nation accepts its 'multi' condition, the potential is great for that nation to invigorate ingenuity through tolerance and humanity" (140). All of Ramos's writings to some degree affirm this belief in tolerance at the same time that they address troubling policies and attitudes. A critique of racism and intolerance is inevitably evoked by a celebration of immigration and diversity.

The Other Face of America: Chronicles of the Immigrants Shaping Our Future
and *The Latino Wave: How Hispanics Will Elect the Next American President*, published only three years apart, provide two rather different images of the status and
the experience of Hispanics in the United States today. In the process of addressing the topics identified in the titles, the writings also provide direct and implied
commentary on the American society into which the Latino wave must integrate.
The first book offers a stark picture of the discrimination suffered by Latinos, especially those who are in the United States illegally. The stated purpose of the
chronicles that comprise the text is to combat widespread prejudice by making
their "Hispanic neighbors" visible and valuable in the eyes of non-Hispanic white
Americans. In this regard, the translation of the book into English in 2002 was
a necessary condition for reaching the majority of its target audience. The 2003
English-language paperback edition contains two introductions that provide a record of the changing context in which the text has been produced and received. In
early 2002, Ramos reflected on the impact of the events of 11 September 2001 on
the U.S. view of immigrants, concluding that the positive work toward significant
immigration reform of the previous few years had largely given way to a renewed
reaction against immigrants. He demonstrates and denounces U.S. racism, discrimination, and exploitation in the book by telling stories of Latino immigrants
and by documenting the "Latinization" of the United States. The new introduction
to the 2003 edition swings back to an optimistic tone based on Ramos's personal
opinion that a more positive, welcoming attitude toward newcomers is reemerging
two years after the 9/11 attacks. In both introductory pieces, Ramos prefigures the
advocacy journalism practiced in the chronicles to follow. In giving "the reason for
the book," he leans uncritically on the now-standard journalistic claim of being
"the voice of those who have none" (xxxvi).

Ramos's thesis is that twentieth-century immigrants from the South come to
the United States to work and they work hard, but they are discriminated against
based on their skin color and their pride in their language and their culture in a
way that earlier generations of immigrants coming from Europe were not.[10] He
declares the melting pot of the nineteenth century a dead concept, and he defends
the strength of Hispanic families who honor their national traditions while making
a significant positive contribution to North American culture. Ramos communi-
cates this message in *The Other Face of America* by using a variety of the conventional techniques found in journalistic and nonfiction writings. The book com-
prises forty-seven very brief chapters, some of which are mini–life narratives based
on Ramos's interviews with immigrants. Other chapters chronicle his own experiences, provide eyewitness reports of contemporary events and personalities, or take
the form of opinion pieces. The emphasis is on Mexican immigrants, although
Ramos devotes a number of chapters to portraying the diversity of the U.S.-Latino
community with its origins in many Spanish American nations. Ample statistics
and frequent citation of authority figures such as politicians, academics, and com-

munity activists interrupt the life stories, creating the hybrid discourse that is characteristic of the contemporary chronicle. There is a hierarchy of sources, however, that privileges the mediated speech and the attributed agency of the testimonial subjects—undocumented workers, male and female, who remain anonymous due to their legal status. The metonymic quality of testimonial narrative is thus reaffirmed. Ramos's interviewees matter because they serve as representative members of a socially excluded and largely invisible community and not primarily as unique protagonists of that community's struggle.[11]

The chapter entitled "Amelia and San Guivi" is a good example of Ramos's obsessive themes and characteristic rhetorical ploys in *The Other Face of America*. A first-person narrator identified as the journalist embarks on a criticism of former California governor Pete Wilson and his anti-immigrant policies of the 1990s. The narrator quickly establishes a relationship of sympathetic complicity with the reader through rhetorical questions, direct address, touches of humor, and knowing verbal winks, such as when he says, "Forgive me, but I'm going to have to do a bit of math." The overall strategy for persuasion in the chapter is to juxtapose the generalizations about undocumented immigrants that were circulated by the Wilson administration and the representative story of one immigrant, Amelia from Michoacán. The story of Amelia's struggle to enter and to survive in the United States, narrated as a true life story, is employed to discredit the "big lie" of Wilson's political propaganda that undocumented immigrants take more from society than they contribute. In a confrontation reminiscent of both the David and Goliath story and the history of the unequal relationship between Mexico and the United States, a hardworking, essentially defenseless woman is depicted as threatened by an aggressive male representative of the prevailing power structure. The question, "Why did Pete Wilson want to wage war against that woman?" (11) embodies the lopsided nature of the conflict. Throughout the chapter, Amelia is held up as one individual among "millions of others like her in the United States." Her value to Ramos's argument lies in her typicality and not in her exceptionality. In spite of having overcome formidable obstacles, she is not a superwoman, but an ordinary "courageous, hardworking, and dedicated" immigrant (13). Details of her family life and the interplay between maintaining old traditions and adapting to a new culture further personalize Amelia's experience in contrast to the impersonal and monolithic power of the state. The anecdote that explains the chapter's title is exemplary. Anyone who has tried to learn a new language as an adult can identify with the gaps in comprehension, the ingrained patterns of pronunciation, and the cultural factors that led Amelia to "hear" and translate the name of the holiday of Thanksgiving into just another fiesta for a saint, San Guivi. The chapter ends with a postscript, which is a common feature of many of the chronicles in the book. The postscript presents opinion poll data from 1993 and 1994 showing negative attitudes toward immigrants among the general population. However, the poll results, couched in quantitative language, have no persuasive power, following as they do the compelling human-interest story of Amelia, and their anti-immigrant message is thoroughly delegitimized in this final gesture by Ramos.

The Latino Wave is an extended essay on how "the United States is becoming a Latino nation" (xvii). Here the image is one of an increasingly powerful Hispanic community within a nation that is undergoing a process of "Latinization." The book's subtitle, *How Hispanics Will Elect the Next American President*, and the dedication—"To the first Latino U.S. president, who, surely, has already been born" (vii)—confidently make assumptions about the nation's changing demographics and about the power of Latinos as a voting bloc. Using current population growth data and patterns of language use among Hispanics, Ramos projects well into the future to imagine a majority Hispanic United States by the year 2125 in which Latinos will continue to speak Spanish—or Spanglish—and maintain traditional Hispanic customs, thus strengthening the nation in a variety of ways. Most notably, Ramos claims that Latinos exemplify the "tolerance for diversity" (xxii) that should be emulated by all Americans, and they also represent a renewing of morals and values, an issue that I address later in this essay. The only obstacles that Ramos concedes to this idealized, harmonious vision of the future are the forces of fear and ignorance that feed endemic racism, and his purpose in writing is in large part to provide an alternative, positive image to combat that ignorance.

The Latino Wave is somewhat less anecdotal and personal than *The Other Face of America*. Ramos makes a strong claim in the book to what Eric Heyne in his study of nonfiction literature calls "factual status" (480). Factual status refers to the ways in which a writer uses textual markers of factual discourse and incorporates evidence of verifiable persons and events into a narrative in order to invite its reading as nonfiction.[12] In the acknowledgments, Ramos provides an extensive list of the experts whom he consulted in preparing the book and the sources for the data that he cites (for example, the Pew Hispanic Center and the National Academy of Science), and he refers to several previously published titles on the topic of Hispanic immigration. The book's seven chapters are thoroughly documented with endnotes, ranging from fourteen to almost seventy in number. One striking aspect of the book's content, immediately apparent to those who are familiar with Ramos's work, is the enormous amount of material recycled from his previous publications. While the emphasis has shifted from a denunciation of anti-immigrant attitudes and policies to an affirmation of the political power—both realized and potential—of U.S. Hispanics, Ramos relies on familiar sources, statistics, historical and contemporary examples, and professional experiences to develop his argument.

Ramos's defense of his thesis that the United States is becoming an increasingly Latino nation inevitably reveals key elements of his overall perspective on American society. The workings of U.S. politics, both internal electoral politics and external or foreign policy; the fact of America's cultural heterogeneity; the historical resistance to acknowledging that heterogeneity; and perceived weaknesses in American social and moral values are all addressed in the process of examining the present and the future role of a growing Hispanic population. Chapters 1 and 4 treat electoral politics in the United States primarily by focusing on George W. Bush's victory over Al Gore in the 2000 presidential election. Ramos's analysis of the two candidates' campaigns arrives at a striking conclusion: Bush won the presidency due to his gaining an increased share of the Latino vote, which he had effectively courted through his attention to the Spanish-language media in the United States. His election represents for Ramos the crucial importance for both major political parties of taking the Hispanic vote into account, and the mistake of taking for granted the political loyalties of Hispanic voters.

The urgent need for immigration reform is another of Ramos's recurring concerns. He rejects the possibility of closing the borders to exclude immigrants, because the pull of economic opportunity is a powerful force for peoples from underdeveloped countries and it will continue to determine the flow of immigrants from south to north into the foreseeable future. He affirms the advantage of a more open border, seeing it as a means of increasing the opportunities for Hispanic immigrants to transform U.S. society in a positive direction. These same chapters also reflect on U.S. foreign policy as it pertains to Latin America. Ramos criticizes the alternating pattern of interest and ignorance that characterizes both official U.S. policy and popular consciousness about the region. In an increasingly globalized world, Ramos believes, the United States—which he calls an "imperial republic" extending itself through its military, trade, international corporations, technology, and exportation of culture—must learn to accept not only globalization's benefits (in terms of an increase in its geopolitical power), but also the consequences of its own "cultural invasion" by others.

Chapters 2, 3, and 5 represent the United States as a nation that is and has always been culturally, racially, and linguistically heterogeneous. Once again rejecting the myth of the melting pot, Ramos further complicates the image of American internal diversity by demonstrating that the Hispanic population is also heterogeneous and not uniform in its origins, traditions, racial composition, or economic status. Against this reality, Ramos observes the signs of a historical resistance to perceived "threats" to an idealized image of a homogeneous United States coming from the outside. He quotes Benjamin Franklin as having complained in 1751 about the "Germanization" of parts of colonial Anglo-America. As quoted by Ramos, Franklin wrote the following in an essay entitled "Observations Concerning the Increase of Mankind, Peopling of Countries, etc.": "Why should Pennsylvania, founded by the English, become a Colony of Aliens, who will shortly be so numerous as to Germanize us instead of our Anglifying them, and will never adopt our Language or Customs, anymore than they can acquire our Complexion" (*Latino Wave* 69). Ramos connects this concern to present-day fears of the Latinization of the United States, opposition to bilingual education, and growing xenophobia. Again, he holds up the threat from within of racism as a more serious problem for the nation's future than the changes introduced by immigrants.

What is interesting in Ramos's argument is that he does not draw the obvious historical lesson from Franklin's quote. That is, history has shown that America was not "Germanized" in terms of language, nor were English-origin customs and institutions supplanted by German ones, as Franklin feared, although a process of mutual influence did occur. It therefore stands to reason that the influx of Latinos in the late twentieth and early twenty-first centuries will not fundamentally and radically change the "complexion" of the United States, but rather the integration of new immigrants into the society will continue to result in a process of mutual transformation. Ramos's claim that Hispanics in the United States will, for example, speak Spanish for generations to come is open to counterarguments, and it is not supported by the historical experience of earlier waves of German, Italian, and Irish immigrants, to mention just three populations who arrived in large numbers in the nineteenth and early twentieth centuries. By means of illustration, German immigrants actively sought to create a place for themselves and to preserve their distinct culture by establishing social clubs, private schools, and German-language newspapers, but these efforts did not effect a long-lasting transformation of U.S. society. Therefore, it is questionable that even the different circumstances that now exist for the Latino wave, which include frequent contacts with the countries of origin, ease of travel back home, and the constant (for now) influx of newcomers, will be powerful enough to impede the tendency on the part of immigrants to adapt linguistically and culturally to the dominant culture while also contributing new elements to it. Regardless of evidence for and against Ramos's predictions, his presentation of his argument in these texts clearly has a wide appeal, and his views are granted some degree of privilege in the public discourse on immigration, as evidenced by the awards that he has won.[13]

Ramos is most hopeful about Hispanic influence on the United States in the realm of what he calls moral values and beliefs. Without directly accusing America of being a morally degenerate society, he suggests that if it accepts Latino values within the prevailing political and economic structures (which he views as models of success), it will "without a doubt, be a healthier and more humane society" (*Latino Wave* 86). For Ramos, these values include, first of all, the family values of keeping one's children living at home until they marry and taking care of elderly relatives in the family circle rather than sending them to retirement communities. He also mentions opposition to divorce, to abortion, and to homosexuality as predominant Hispanic values that will resist assimilation into the more liberal, secular U.S. culture. This part of Ramos's analysis invites a critical assessment that he does not provide. First, he concedes that these beliefs coincide with those of conservative Republicans (presumably majority white nonimmigrants), and yet he also claims them as a "unique [Latino] outlook on life" (85). There is an unrecognized irony in identifying shared values for Hispanics and Republicans, given conservative opposition to a reform of U.S. immigration policies. Second, one can only wonder what an "opposition to homosexuality" (corresponding to 72 percent of Hispanics, according to an unspecified poll) means for the embrace of diversity that Ramos praises so effusively when it concerns racial, linguistic, and cultural difference. Gender relations is an area that he does not touch upon when describing U.S. Latinos, and he avoids addressing whether the opposition to a woman's right to choose is properly seen as an affirmation of human rights and diversity of religious beliefs or as a threat to those very values. Like the generalizations about earlier immigrant groups that I have already commented upon, Ramos's treatment of values is far less systematic and well informed than his representation of other aspects of the presence of Latinos in the United States. Nevertheless, he uses the values issue to support the thesis, explicitly stated in *The Other Face of America* and, I believe, implicit to his argument in *The Latin Wave*, that Hispanic immigrants will "save America from itself" (*Other Face* xv). He cites the racial conflict of the civil rights movement and the "misdirected bloodshed" of the war in Vietnam as twentieth-century errors of a "confused and sometimes blind" country. Such errors may be avoided under the healthy influence of immigrants who "have chosen to leave home for a better life here" (xv).

A somewhat different dimension of Jorge Ramos's critical perspective on the United States appears in the weekly columns carried in more than fifty newspapers and published online at his Web site. These columns treat current events, and they combine the functions of reporting and editorializing. From December 2002 until March 2006, the columns' most frequent topic was the war in Iraq, with nineteen articles directly dedicated to the lead-up to the war, the invasion of March 2003, and the ongoing conflict. During the same period, Ramos wrote fifteen columns on immigrants and immigration policy and a handful each on many other issues and events affecting the United States and, secondarily, Latin America. Ramos's take on the Iraq war has been consistent throughout. He criticizes both President George W. Bush's motives for going to war and a too-complacent U.S. Congress, press, and public, and he decries what he sees to be a gross misuse of U.S. military power, resources, and political capital in the world. In what follows I briefly focus on his critique of Bush's motives insofar as it contains a critical view of U.S. electoral politics that can be applied to many other policy decisions.

American democracy and the freedoms and opportunities that it affords are among the principal strengths that Ramos admires as an immigrant from a country that endured one-party rule for seventy years in the twentieth century and, before that, a thirty-five year dictatorship. However, his discussion of the war in Iraq reveals his perception of a serious weakness in the American system: the undue power that electoral politics exercises in determining domestic and foreign policies. Ramos's portrayal of the decision to go to war in Iraq unequivocally and repeatedly attributes it to Bush's desire to be elected to a second term as president. "Las guerras que vienen" (The Coming Wars), an online column from 23 December 2002, states this clearly: "Peace does not suit the president of the United States George W. Bush at this time. It is through war that he is looking for his place in history, *his reelection in 2004* and also the strengthening of the U.S. as the only superpower in the face of the threat of terrorism" (my emphasis).[14] On 10 March 2003, shortly before the war began, Ramos reiterates this point in "El terror después de la guerra" (The Postwar Terror) to explain why Bush would not wait a few months more until the United Nations weapons inspectors completed their work. "The problem for the United States is not only the climate in Iraq—where it is practically impossible to fight during the summer—but the political calendar. Bush does not want to be involved in a war at the end of this year or the beginning of next when he will have to concentrate on his reelection campaign."[15]

In the nineteen articles about Iraq, the accusation that Bush's reelection and other domestic political concerns were behind both the timing of the invasion and the justifications offered for it by the administration surfaces eight more times, marking more than half the columns on the war. Ramos's denunciation of Bush's actions and the implication that they constitute a distortion of the democratic process stand out clearly against a backdrop of other reiterated themes, including Bush's loss of credibility, the failures of U.S. intelligence, the lack of a strategy to leave Iraq, and the essential error of committing to this war at this time. His perception of the influence of upcoming elections on a decision as momentous and far-reaching as going to war does not, however, prompt Ramos toward an analysis of the underlying political mechanisms that may be in play, and here we see an example of how his perspective on crucial and complicated issues in U.S. society frequently falls short. It is possible to identify any number of structural factors, such as campaign finance, the two-term presidency, or unlimited terms for congressional representatives, that distort and even corrupt the work done by the democratically elected U.S. government, but Ramos does not probe below the surface to examine them. This is in line with his view that a journalist's primary responsibility is to challenge those who hold power in society, and it results in a presentation of issues that is heavily weighted toward the personal and the anecdotal, and therefore suitable for popular consumption.

In conclusion, Jorge Ramos reads the North from the South through the eyes of an immigrant, and he sees the immigrant experience as continuing to be the most powerful force shaping U.S. society today and into the future. In the three books examined here and in many of his other writings, he presents a consistent, upbeat message about Hispanic immigrants: They come to the United States looking for work and they work hard; they contribute more to the economy than they receive from it; they are patriotic and are willing to defend the country; they maintain strong ties to their countries of origin and to the Spanish language; they endure discrimination based on racism and on an irrational fear of their growing numbers; and their presence creates an urgent need for an amnesty program and a workable immigration accord between the United States and Mexico. His view of the dominant U.S. culture is largely positive with regard to its internal economic and political structures, its defense of freedom as described in the Bill of Rights, and its historical diversity, although he perceives a need for a shift in moral values in the direction of those held by the majority of Hispanics. By working as a journalist in a variety of media, Ramos gives visibility to a perspective—that of the immigrant—which is not always widely represented and is, in fact, anathema to some powerful political interests and their constituencies. His contribution to the public discourse creates an alternative to the mainstream vision of the United States as a world power successfully engaged in exporting its model abroad, and therefore offering an opportunity and posing a threat to the others outside its borders. Ramos depicts a United States that has fallen away from some of its traditional core values and democratic principles, a nation in crisis because it has betrayed its better self. In a reversal on hegemonic anti-immigrant sentiments that credit the (Hispanic) other with the potential to destroy U.S. national integrity, he perceives that the saving of the nation lies with the Latino wave that has swept across its borders and made a new home in its "reconquered" territory.

NOTES

1. As noted in the biography section of Ramos's Web site, *Latino Leaders* magazine and *Time* magazine named Jorge Ramos to their list of the most influential Latinos in the United States in 2004 and 2005, respectively.

2. The Pew Research Center survey, entitled "Striking the Balance, Audience Interests, Business Pressures and Journalists' Values," was released on 30 March 1999. The data show a significant loss in public trust in journalism and the credibility of journalists since a similar survey was conducted in 1989.

3. Ramos relates that in his first job as a television newscaster, his use of Carlos Monsiváis and Elena Poniatowska as sources in a story on the Mexican character was going to be censored, and he resigned from the job over this (*No Borders* 57–58). There is a long history in Mexico of government control of the media through economic and political means. In a study of the Mexican press published in 1983, just when Jorge Ramos was starting his career, Petra Secanella describes the PRI's (Partido Revolucionario Institucional) widely recognized mechanisms of control of the press, which were powerful and effective for seventy years. These have included government control of supplies of newsprint, the media's reliance on official sources of information without engaging in independent investigation, the paying of subventions by the government to newspapers and to individual reporters, and the printing of articles written and paid for by government officials (10–11).

4. "los periodistas somos un balance del poder." "El sitio natural del periodismo es en la oposición, siempre cuestionando, balanceando el poder o luchando contra él." The translation in the body of the text is my own. Throughout this study, for works that have not been translated into English I have provided my own translations and I have included the Spanish original in a note.

5. This criticism of the U.S. press is the theme of a column entitled "Bush fuerte, prensa débil" (Strong Bush, Weak Press) published online 4 August 2003. *www.jorgeramos.com/articulos/articulos211.htm.*

6. Poniatowska and Fallaci are recognized as skilled interviewers and voices of opposition to the political status quo. They also practice an advocacy journalism in support

of marginalized social actors and groups. Fallaci's strong attacks on Islam later in her career make her a problematic role model for anyone espousing tolerance for diversity, but I find no evidence that Ramos endorses that part of the late journalist's work.

7.   "I also write because I am frustrated with television. After so many years of anchoring the news and not being allowed to give my own opinion, I have loads of things stuck in my throat" (Ramos, *No Borders* 3).

8.   The question of what it means for an intellectual to speak for less-privileged others has been a central concern of contemporary anthropologists and ethnographers. Writers of testimonial narratives, often journalists, have also entered this debate. Elena Poniatowska questioned her relationship with Josefina Bórquez, the "informant" behind her testimonial novel *Hasta no verte, Jesús mío* (Until I See You, My Jesus; published in English as *Here's to You, Jesusa!*) as early as the 1970s. In the 1980s and 1990s, ethnographers, especially, began to insist on problematizing and making visible their own role in the ethnographic process, beginning with feminist ethnographers working in third-world countries. Daphne Patai's work in Brazil is a good example, and her essay entitled "U.S. Academics and Third World Women: Is Ethical Research Possible?" in the volume that she coedited with Sherna Berger Gluck addresses the dilemma of speaking for others who lack their own direct access to sites of speaking and publishing. In mainstream journalism, this kind of self-awareness and self-doubt is, admittedly, less commonly seen, but these questions are part of contemporary thought and culture.

9.   In *The Other Face of America*, Ramos identifies an early public articulation of the concept of the "reconquest" of California and the American Southwest in a speech made in 1998 by José Angel Pescador, former consul general of Mexico in Los Angeles (45).

10. One of the weaknesses in Ramos's understanding of patterns of U.S. immigration is his apparent ignorance about the many ways in which earlier waves of immigrants (German, Irish, or Italian, for example) were severely excluded from and discriminated against by mainstream Anglo-American society. Many jobs, schools, and other opportunities were simply closed to the newest immigrant groups, which did not immediately and seamlessly assimilate, as Ramos believes.

11. The abundant theory of Latin American *testimonio* frequently contrasts the metonymic function of the testimonial subject to the metaphorical role of the subject of traditional Western autobiography. As Doris Sommer explains, metonymy is "a lateral move of identification-through-relationship" rather than the "identity-by-substitution" of metaphor (146).

12. In his essay "Toward a Theory of Literary Nonfiction," Eric Heyne discusses nonfiction literature as a mode of reading as much as a mode of writing, somewhat along the lines of Philippe Lejeune's assertion that autobiography is a mode of reading (30). Factual status, according to Heyne, is determined by the writer, while factual adequacy is judged by the readers of the text, who must use their own knowledge and competency to evaluate the accuracy and reliability of a nonfictional account.

13. Earlier in the chapter I mentioned the awards that Ramos has received for his journalism as evidence of his influential status. Another sign of one's influence is the degree to which one's work provokes a counterattack, and the existence of an anti-Ramos reaction can also be documented. One example of a virulent position against Ramos is expressed in numerous articles by Steve Sailer, published online on the VDARE.com Web site sponsored by the Lexington Research Institute and the Center for American Unity.

14. "La paz no le conviene por ahora al presidente de Estados Unidos, George W. Bush. Es con la guerra que está buscando su lugar en la historia, su reelección en el 2004 y,

también, fortalecer a Estados Unidos como única superpotencia ante la amenaza del terrorismo."

15. "El problema de Estados Unidos no es sólo por el clima en Iraq—pelear en el verano es prácticamente imposible—sino de calendarios políticos. Bush no quiere estar metido en una guerra a finales de este año o a principios del otro cuando tendrá que concentrarse en su campaña de reelección."

WORKS CITED

Heyne, Eric. "Toward a Theory of Literary Nonfiction." *Modern Fiction Studies* 33.3 (1987): 479–90.

Kovach, Bill, and Tom Rosenstiel. *The Elements of Journalism: What Newspeople Should Know and the Public Expect.* New York: Crown, 2001.

Lejeune, Philippe. *On Autobiography.* Trans. Katherine Leary. Minneapolis: University of Minnesota Press, 1989.

Morris, Stephen D. *Gringolandia: Mexican Identity and Perceptions of the United States.* Lanham, Md.: Rowman and Littlefield, 2005.

Patai, Daphne. "U.S. Academics and Third World Women: Is Ethical Research Possible?" *Women's Words: Feminist Practice of Oral History.* Ed. Sherna Berger Gluck and Daphne Patai. New York: Routledge, 1991. 137–53.

Ramos Avalos, Jorge. *A la caza del león.* Mexico: Grijalbo, 2001.

———. "Breve biografía de Jorge Ramos." Jorge Ramos Web site. *www.jorgeramos.com/biografia.htm.*

———. "Bush fuerte, prensa débil." Jorge Ramos Web site. 4 August 2003. *www.jorgeramos.com/articulos/articulos211.htm.*

———. "Las guerras que vienen." Jorge Ramos Web site. 23 December 2002. *www.jorgeramos.com/articulos/articulos179.htm.*

———. *The Latino Wave: How Hispanics Will Elect the Next American President.* Trans. Ezra E. Fitz. New York: HarperCollins, 2004.

———. *No Borders: A Journalist's Search for Home.* Trans. Patricia J. Duncan. New York: HarperCollins, 2002.

———. *The Other Face of America: Chronicles of the Immigrants Shaping Our Future.* Trans. Patricia J. Duncan. New York: HarperCollins, 2002.

———. "Sólo queremos que nos crean." Jorge Ramos Web site. 18 July 2005. *www.jorgeramos.com/articulos/articulos314.htm.*

———. "El terror después de la guerra," Jorge Ramos Web site. 10 March 2003. *www.jorgeramos.com/articulos/articulos190.htm.*

Secanella, Petra María. *El periodismo político en México.* Barcelona: Editorial Mitre, 1983.

Sommer, Doris. "No Secrets." *The Real Thing: Testimonial Discourse and Latin America.* Ed. Georg M. Gugelberger. Durham: Duke University Press, 1996. 130–57.

"Striking the Balance, Audience Interests, Business Pressures, and Journalists' Values." Pew Research Center for the People and the Press. 30 March 1999. *people-press.org/report/67/striking-the-balance-audience-interests-business-pressures-and-journalists-values.*

Contributors

Danny J. Anderson is Professor in the Department of Spanish and Portuguese and Associate Dean for the Interdisciplinary Programs and Area Studies Centers in the College of Liberal Arts and Sciences at the University of Kansas. He has published *Vicente Leñero: The Novelist as Critic* (New York: Peter Lang, 1989) and coedited with Jill Kuhnheim *Cultural Studies in the Curriculum: Teaching Latin America* (New York: Modern Language Association of America, 2003).

Hilda Chacón is Associate Professor of Spanish and Latin American Literature at Nazareth College in Rochester, New York, where she has directed the Women's Studies Program and the Emerson Language Lab. Her first career was as a journalist in her native Costa Rica during the 1980s. Since becoming an academic, she has published in a variety of scholarly forums on testimonial writings, the Internet, and polemic discourse. She is also a creative writer.

Robert Conn is Associate Professor in the Department of Romance Languages and Literatures at Wesleyan University. He is the author of *The Politics of Philology: Alfonso Reyes and the Invention of the Latin American Literary Tradition* (Lewisburg, Pa.: Bucknell University Press, 2002).

Ignacio Corona, Associate Professor in the Department of Spanish and Portuguese at Ohio State University, is the author of *Después de Tlatelolco: las narrativas políticas en México (1976–1990). Un estudio de sus estrategias retóricas y representacionales* (Mexico: Universidad de Guadalajara, 2001), and coeditor of *The Contemporary Mexican Chronicle: Theoretical Perspectives on the Liminal Genre* (Albany: SUNY Press, 2002); *The Meanings of Killing: Gender, Media, and the Representation of Violence on Mexico's Northern Border* (Tucson: University of Arizona Press, forthcoming); and *Post-national Musical Identities, Cultural Production, Distribution, and Consumption in a Globalized Scenario* (New York: Rowman and Littlefield, forthcoming).

Héctor Domínguez-Ruvalcaba is Associate Professor in the Department of Spanish and Portuguese at the University of Texas at Austin. He is the author of *La* *modernidad abyecta: formación de discurso homosexual en Latinoamérica* (Xalapa: Universidad Veracruzana, 2001) and *Modernity and the Nation in Mexican Representations of Masculinity: From Sensuality to Bloodshed* (New York: Palgrave, 2007).

Linda Egan is Associate Professor of Spanish at the University of California, Davis, and on the steering committee of the intercampus and international research group UC Mexicanistas. She is the author of *Carlos Monsiváis: Culture and Chronicle in Contemporary Mexico* (Tucson: University of Arizona Press, 2001) (*Carlos Monsiváis: cultura y crónica en el México contemporáneo* [Mexico: Fondo de Cultura Económica, 2004]) and *Diosas, demonios y debate: las armas metafísicas de Sor Juana*, (Salta, Arg.: Biblioteca de Textos Universitarios, 1997).

Oswaldo Estrada is Assistant Professor of Latin American Literature in the Department of Romance Languages at the University of North Carolina at Chapel Hill. His book *La imaginación novelesca: Bernal Díaz entre géneros y épocas* is forthcoming with Iberoamericana Vervuert, within the collection *Nueva Crítica Hispánica*.

Emily Hind is Assistant Professor of Spanish in the Department of Modern and Classical Languages at the University of Wyoming. She is the author of *Entrevistas con quince autoras mexicanas* (Madrid: Iberoamericana Vervuert, 2003). With coeditors Gabriela Cano and Patricia Vega, she has compiled *The Mexico City Reader* (Durham: Duke University Press, forthcoming).

Beth E. Jörgensen is Associate Professor of Spanish in the Modern Languages and Cultures Department at the University of Rochester. She is the author of *The Writing of Elena Poniatowska: Engaging Dialogues* (Austin: University of Texas Press, 1994). She coedited *The Contemporary Mexican Chronicle: Theoretical Perspectives on the Liminal Genre* (Albany: SUNY Press, 2002) with Ignacio Corona, and her revision of the E. Munguía translation of *The Underdogs* by Mariano Azuela was published by Random House in 2002.

Mary K. Long is Senior Instructor and Director of the International Spanish for the Professions major in the Department of Spanish and Portuguese at the University of Colorado, Boulder. She publishes in the areas of Mexican literature and culture of the twentieth and twenty-first centuries; cross-cultural communication and exchange between Latin America and the United States; and the effects of globalization on cultural identity. She is author of the "Nota introductoria" and, with editors Sergio González Rodríguez and Lligany Lomelí, compiled texts for the anthology *Salvador Novo: viajes y ensayos II: crónicas y periodismo* (Mexico: Fondo de Cultura Económica, 1999).

Salvador A. Oropesa is Professor of Spanish in the Department of Modern Languages at Kansas State University. His publications include *The Contemporáneos Group: Rewriting Mexico in the Thirties and Forties* (University of Texas Press at Austin, 2003), *La novelística de Antonio Muñoz Molina: sociedad civil y literatura lúdica* (Jaén: Universidad de Jaén, 1999), and *La obra de Ariel Dorfman: ficción y crítica* (Madrid: Pliegos, 1992).

Fernando Fabio Sánchez is Assistant Professor of Spanish in the Department of Foreign Languages and Literatures at Portland State University, where he is also part of the organizing committee of Cine-Lit, a biannual conference devoted to literature and film. He publishes on Latin American literature, culture, and film of the twentieth and twenty-first centuries, with an emphasis on Mexico. He also publishes poetry and fiction.

Maarten van Delden is Associate Professor of Spanish and Portuguese in the Department of Spanish and Portuguese at the University of Southern California. He is the author of *Carlos Fuentes, Mexico, and Modernity* (Nashville: Vanderbilt University Press, 1998), coauthor (with Yvon Grenier) of *Gunshots at the Fiesta: Literature and Politics in Latin America* (Nashville: Vanderbilt University Press, 2009), and coeditor (with Kristine Vanden Berghe) of *El laberinto de la solidaridad: cultura y politica en México, 1910–2000* (Amsterdam: Rodopi, 2002).

Index

Page numbers in italics refer to illustrations.